VIRGIL

VIRGIL

BY

T. R. GLOVER

SEVENTH EDITION

BARNES & NOBLE, Inc.
New York
METHUEN & CO. Ltd
London

First Published, 1904

Reprinted, 1969
by
Barnes & Noble, Inc., New York
and
Methuen & Co. Ltd, London

Printed in the United States of America

TO

DR JOHN WATSON

PROFESSOR OF PHILOSOPHY IN QUEEN'S UNIVERSITY, CANADA

How many a time, dear Watson, the snowy road we'd pace,
With the frozen lake behind us, and the North wind in our face ;
But the sun was bright above us in the blue Canadian sky,
As we walked and talked together of deep matters, you and I.

It was snow and air and sunshine ; and I look across the sea
To those days of glorious winter, and the life they meant to me ;
For my mind and soul caught something, as of sun and snow and air,
From the friend who walked beside me in those winters over there.

PREFACE TO THE FIRST EDITION

IT is generally recognized that at present there is a movement in education away from the Classics. The questions are being raised in the older English Universities, whether after all Greek is a necessary part of every branch of study, and whether it should remain a compulsory subject in every curriculum. In America and in the British Colonies a further stage has been reached. Tradition there has less power; Greek as a compulsory subject has been quite discarded, and Latin itself is in some places a more or less optional subject. The possibilities of danger to education generally which are involved in this attitude toward classical studies need no remark. Yet there is another aspect of the matter which deserves consideration, and here I may be allowed to speak from my own experience.

I found when I was Professor of Latin in a Canadian University a system of "options" in vogue, which permitted a man, if he so wished, to drop the Classics altogether at a very early stage. The higher study of Latin and Greek was, of course, as in England, a matter of free choice for the student who hoped for honours. But the second of the two pass classes in Latin, involving acquaintance with some half-dozen books, a little unseen translation, and a very little prose composition, *could* be avoided if a student so determined. Latin, in other words, had to compete with all sorts of subjects, and to stand on its own merits. A curious result followed. Not at all unfrequently a student, in spite of woeful preparation and a persistent inability to translate with accuracy or to compose without elementary blunders in syntax, would nevertheless realize something of the literary value of the poet or historian who was being read in class, and would persevere with an almost pathetic enthusiasm in a study in which he could hope for no distinction, but which he could and did enjoy. He realized, in fact, that the old Scottish term "Humanity" meant something.

What the presence of such men and women in a class meant to a teacher I need not say. When year after year a succession of such students made their appearance, one gained faith in the vitality of classical literature and in its power to maintain itself. Only it was plain that classical study had to be primarily the study of literature and of life—syntax, philology, composition, and so forth must be clearly means to an end, and of that end the class had never to lose sight. What the students may have gained from these courses they can best say ; that the experience was of immense value to the teacher I record with gratitude.

It is easy to see that the factors which have produced the present position of classical studies in Canada are at work in England, and, though the movement will be slower, it is not hard to predict that, unless steps are taken by those who believe in classical literature, the same results will follow here as in Canada. Opinions will differ as to what are the right steps to be taken. Personally I believe that none will be so effectual as the appeal to the threatened literature. This will mean that students must have their attention constantly directed to the human value of what they are reading, and further that the training of literary instinct must be more generally recognized as a main part of the teacher's work. Very often the teacher supposes that his class are a great deal nearer to him in taste and feeling for literature than they are; things are so obvious to him that he does not suppose it necessary to call attention to them, and as a result they are missed by the class.

In this book I have tried to apply to Virgil the method I suggest. During five years in Canada I had to lecture winter by winter on some three books of the *Aeneid* to a class of from forty to sixty students, and the following chapters are the indirect result. They have been written since my return to England. Scholars who know the literature of Virgil will recognize how much I owe to French scholars and critics—to M. Boissier, Sainte-Beuve, Patin, Girard and Martha, in particular. "The Gauls," Sainte-Beuve says, "early found their way to the Capitol." To my own countrymen I am also indebted, to Professor Tyrrell and Mr Mackail among the living, to Nettleship, Sellar, and Henry among the dead, and last but not least, to Virgil's great editor, Conington, whose work remains a monument of a great victory won long since for the cause of Liberalism in education.

When his work is at last done, and his book is going out into the world, a writer may be forgiven for wondering what will be its reception—particularly when he has tried once more to draw so well-known a figure. "This," the reader may say, "is not my idea of Virgil at all." No doubt he is right, and in more than his statement of fact. A great poet, expressing himself in great poetry, is not easily grasped in his entirety. For the great mind has the abundant suggestiveness of Nature and her work, and the critic, in proportion as he deepens his knowledge, has an increasing consciousness that he will not soon exhaust the meaning and suggestion of the great personality he studies. This picture of Virgil may not be the reader's, but it still may be a true one, and it has at least been drawn with growing affection for the poet. Goethe once expressed himself with some freedom upon Schlegel's criticisms of Euripides—the critic's point of view was wrong—"If a modern man like Schlegel must pick out faults in so great an ancient, he ought only to do it upon his knees." Whatever else may have been done aright or done wrong in this book, Goethe's word has not been forgotten.

T. R. G.

September 1904

PREFACE TO THE SECOND EDITION

FOR the new edition, the book has been carefully revised—indeed, twice, with a long interval between the revisions. It has not been re-written. Years bring new outlooks, and neither a book nor a picture can very well be made from two points of view. A man sees a thing, and expresses it as best he can there and then ; and, if later on he retouches it, memory and sometimes timidity confuse the impression.

I have added translations of (I think) all the passages of Virgil quoted—not always using the same words, I find, where the same passage came more than once. Readers of Virgil will guess the reason.

I should like to thank the reviewers in *The Times* and *The Athenæum* for criticisms which I have found of value and have used. Another reviewer elsewhere thought I might have added a chapter on Virgil in literature. I am glad to explain why I did not—by referring my readers at once to Domenico Comparetti's *Virgil in the Middle Ages*, in Mr E. F. M. Benecke's English translation, a delightful and most learned work which will appeal to every student of Virgil. Sir Archibald Geikie's *Love of Nature among the Romans*, a book full of Virgil, did not reach me till this volume was already in type.

In a lecture recently published Mr J. W. Mackail spoke with emphasis of what is to be gained from learning by heart the poetry of a great poet. There is something even in copying signal passages out for oneself. Virgil, as Mr R. A. Neil once playfully said to me, is not the author for a healthy boy ;—"perhaps more trivial airs may please thee better," as Humphry Moseley wrote when he published

Milton's poems in 1645. But it is only in boyhood that one has the opportunity, or perhaps the faculty, of learning much poetry by heart, and I would give a good deal now to have had my own mind charged from boyhood with Virgil and Wordsworth.

September 1912

PREFACE TO THE FIFTH EDITION

SINCE this book was first published, a great deal has been written upon the *Appendix Vergiliana*. How far is that collection of poems to be counted, in part or whole, genuine? How far is it to be used in reconstructing the life of the poet, and the story of his mind and its development? The answer to the second question evidently depends on the answer to the first.

The reader who wishes to pursue this line of inquiry will turn to the two little books of Franz Skutsch—*Aus Vergils Frühzeit* (Leipzig, 1901) and *Gallus und Vergil* (Leipzig, 1906). He will find an attractive essay in J. W. Mackail's *Lectures on Poetry* (1911), entitled *Virgil and Virgilianism*, which we heard given in Cambridge. Professor Edward Kennard Rand has a longer article, entitled *Young Virgil's Poetry*, which will be read with pleasure, in *Harvard Studies in Classical Philology*, volume xxx. (1919). Professor Tenney Frank has more recently published his *Vergil, a Biography* (New York, Henry Holt & Company, 1922). Professor Frank goes further than Dr Mackail or Professor Rand and tries to make a biography, about which I will say only so much, that, while I am always ready to speculate with guides so delightful as Dr Mackail and Professor Rand, and while my debt elsewhere to Professor Frank is considerable and of long standing, I cannot feel happy in the new life of the poet. When I go further and read Dr Norman Wentworth De Witt's *Virgil's Biographia Litteraria*, I fear I break into open revolt against them all and fall back on the orthodox canon of Virgil's writings and the great books of Sellar and Nettleship and Sainte Beuve.

So I leave my own book as it was. No doubt, as I suggested in 1912, if I were doing it again, the influence of my friends at Harvard and Johns Hopkins would be more traceable in my text; no doubt much else would be put differently. Which of us would study Virgil and write upon him, fresh from the same horrible experience of war which he knew, and not do it with a new intelligence and a new sympathy? But for the next few years I cannot hope for the leisure that would be needed, and I must content myself with referring my readers to the works of my friends, from whom one cannot even differ without profit.

Another book recently published to which I would wish to send my readers is the *Roman Poetry* of E. E. Sikes (Methuen & Co., 1923), a work which I have read twice, and each time with admiration.

In 1917 there was for some weeks a controversy in the *Times Literary Supplement* on the spelling of the poet's name. I did not take part in it, though my sympathies were all on the English side. Virgil may have spelled his name in Latin with an E; Homer assuredly did not use our spelling or our accent; the patriarch Jacob had somewhere in his name a terrible guttural, which I can do without—I prefer James, or Hamish; Alighieri may be a great Italian poet, but the familiar name is good enough for Englishmen. Virgil is written in our hearts, and I hope will stay there. Indeed I sometimes suspect that Vergil is part of a plot to kill the classics with the dead hand of information. Dr Tenney Frank should have refused to be bullied into that E. Those who love the poet call him Virgil.

QUEEN'S UNIVERSITY
KINGSTON, CANADA
July 1923

Don Quixote took it, and without speaking a word began to turn over the leaves. After a little while he returned it, saying :—

" In the little which I have seen I have found three things in this author worthy of reprehension. The first is some words which I have read in the prologue; another, that the language is Aragonese, for now and then he writes without articles ; and the third, which must stamp him for an ignoramus, is that he blunders and deviates from the truth in what is the important thing in the history, for here he says that the wife of Sancho Panza, my squire, was named Mari Gutierrez, and she is not so named, but Theresa Panza ; and he who errs in so considerable a point as this, there is much fear that he will err in all the rest of the history."

At this, cried Sancho :—" A pretty thing of a historian indeed ! "

Don Quixote, part ii. chapter 59

TABLE OF DATES

CONTENTS

xvii

CONTENTS

VIRGIL

CHAPTER I

THE AGE AND THE MAN

Οἴδαμεν γὰρ ὅτι πᾶσα ἡ κτίσις συστενάζει καὶ συνωδίνει.—St Paul.

IT is a commonplace that to understand a poet we need some knowledge of his time and place. His mind will take colour from his surroundings, by sympathy or antipathy. He will share at least some of the limitations of his age and generation, while, in common with his contemporaries, he belongs to a stage of moral and intellectual development in advance of his predecessors. At the same time it must be remembered that a great poet will generally also be in advance of his contemporaries in the fullness with which he realizes the life of his day, with its problems and its solutions of those problems; and he will represent in some measure, whether he means it or not, the standpoint of a later age.[1] He will have grasped all that his own age has to say, and he will feel more than other men the weak points in a position with which they are satisfied. Even if he does not consciously feel these weak points, they will often be brought out by his work. For while a great poet's work will rise to a region of feeling and insight where he has to handle things of eternal and universal significance, and where we forget that he is a poet of a certain time and place,—so truly does he present to us the permanent and common life of man,—yet even in such a region will his own age claim him, as he develops those aspects of truth which are wanting to the common thought of his day. A great

[1] "The artist," said Schiller, "it is true, is the son of his time; but pity for him, if he is its pupil, or even its favourite."

poet will, of course, not be what is called didactic, whatever
he may have to teach;—indeed, when he explains in prose
what he means, it is never quite the same thing. None
the less he will have something to say that is urgent
and significant, and this will have been suggested to him,
somehow, by the life around him—how we may not be able
to see very readily, for the processes of a poet's thought are
more mysterious than those of other men; but, somehow,
he will not be satisfied, his work will not please him, till
all is adjusted to the harmony which he feels must be the
mark of the right view of the universe.

Virgil is, of course, the great poet of the Augustan age,
according to the common account. M. Patin,[1] however,
suggests that neither Virgil's nor Horace's is the typical
poetry of the time, but that both represent a recoil from
the current fashion. Another French critic, M. Pierron,[2]
maintains that Virgil, if born fifty years earlier or later,
would still have been Virgil—a less perfect Virgil, but yet
Virgil—while Horace would not have been Horace at any
other time. "Horace," he continues, "if I may so say, is
the age of Augustus personified." Probably the poetry of
no great poet is ever, in the sense which M. Patin means,
"typical" of its age, for the poetry, or what passes for poetry,
of every age seems, like its prose, to be at best commonplace, or more probably bad. Yet Virgil and Horace must
after all be genuine representatives of their era, for their
contemporaries read and treasured their poetry, and left the
works of the rest to wrap the incense and the pepper of
which Horace speaks.[3] Is the poet, who touches the heart
of his time and his people, or the average poetaster, the
truer type of the age? Setting aside the poetasters, who
were many,[4] setting aside even names of greater note, such
as Tibullus and Ovid, are we to call Horace or Virgil the

---

[1] Patin, *Études sur la Poésie latine*, i. c. viii. ; cf. Tyrrell, *Latin Poetry*, p. 23 f.

[2] *La Littérature romaine*, 405-6. Compare the remark of Goethe cited by
Carlyle, *Essay on Diderot*: "Thus, as the most original, resolute and self-directing
of all the Moderns has written : 'Let a man be but born ten years sooner, or
ten years later, his whole aspect and performance shall be different.'"

[3] Cf. Horace, *Epp.* ii. 1, 267 ; Catullus, 95, 9 ; and Persius, 1, 43.

[4] Ovid, *ex Ponto*, iv. 16, enumerates some thirty contemporary poets.

poet of the period? Is Horace—Horace the prophet of common sense, who never transcended the sterling, but hardly inspiring, moralities of his most worthy father—is Horace really after all the interpreter of the life of the Augustan age? Is he fundamentally in sympathy enough with all men, or with any man, to tell his age all that is in its heart—its longing, its quest, and its despair? If Horace is not the poet we seek, is Virgil? Allowing at once that he sees beyond the men of his time, that he knows their spirit as they do not know it themselves, and that in many ways he is spiritually nearer to Marcus Aurelius than to Augustus, let us try to see him in relation to his age and to realize how he expresses the deepest mind of the Roman world around him.[1]

The "age of Augustus" is a phrase with which we are familiar, and it has a certain suggestion of splendour and promise, but more of this than we suppose may be due to Virgil himself. It is he who has taught us to associate greatness and prosperity with the name of Augustus, but, if we substitute for "Augustus" the name "Octavian," some of the grandeur and most of the hopefulness is lost. We find, in fact, that while Virgil bade his countrymen look forward for all that was happy to the age opening before them, he was himself the child of another and a darker age, and that his vision of a brighter day was at least as much prayer as prophecy. For the century which lay behind the inception of the *Aeneid* knew more of the works of Octavian than of Augustus. Augustus had indeed ended this century, and the system which he introduced into the Roman world was to save the world from its repetition. But it was one thing to prevent the recurrence of such a period of pain and of rapid decline, and quite another to undo the effects which survived from a hundred years of civil war. Let the Emperor have credit for all he did, but let us remember that if Virgil prophesied peace for that age

---

[1] " The Historian of a national Poetry," says Carlyle, " has to record the highest Aim of a nation in its successive directions and developments ; for by this the Poetry of the nation modulates itself ; this *is* the Poetry of the nation."—*Essay on Historic Survey of German Poetry*.

of Augustus, at the dawn of which he died, his life had been lived in times of confusion, of war, of treachery, and degeneration.

I

The Roman people had lost in some measure its early character. If war sometimes discovers the finer qualities of a nation, it also develops the worse and the darker. The long struggle with Hannibal displays in the most splendid way the stability and the manhood of Rome at her best,[1] but it profoundly affected the history of the Roman spirit. With it began the decline of Italian agriculture and the rise of the professional army, both attended with inevitable mischief. It was followed by the rapid extension of Roman power over the Mediterranean and the accentuation of the pride of the sword. Conquest brought wealth and the pride of wealth. Rich and conquering, Rome came into contact with the older and decaying civilizations of Greece and Asia, with peoples far advanced in moral and intellectual decadence. The old ideals of the Roman farmer-state were already shaken before the conquest of the East flooded Rome with the ideas and the luxury of Greece and of Asia. The old dignity gave place to the vulgarity of mind which sudden wealth produces when it is not accompanied by reflection. The Roman had never before conceived of the possibilities which life offered of enjoyment, and when they came he did not know how to use them, and plunged from one excess of self-gratification to another. This new appetite for unreserved indulgence was neither checked nor compensated by the simultaneous rise of Greek influence over Rome. It was a degenerate Greece that took her captor captive, and the arts she brought into rustic Latium were not as a rule those of Aeschylus and Phidias, nor were Plato and Aristotle the philosophers who made the first impression on Roman thought. A Polybius might meet a

---

[1] Two lines from a great passage of Claudian may be quoted here :
Nunquam succubuit damnis et territa nullo
vulnere post Cannas maior Trebiamque fremebat.—Cons. Stil. iii. 144.

Scipio on equal terms,[1] each to be the larger and broader-minded man for intercourse with the other, but too often the Greek teacher had neither ideas nor ideals. He retailed the dogmata of a doubtful philosophy, and led his pupil in the paths of a scarcely doubtful morality. The more gifted he was, the more dangerous a guide was he for one as much his inferior in intelligence as his superior in wealth.[2] The degeneration in Roman character, with the loss of the sense of responsibility and of the idea of self-restraint, becomes more and more marked with time. Whether the senate or the people at Rome had by the time of Tiberius Gracchus fallen furthest from the worth and dignity of the senate and people of an earlier time it would be hard to say. Oligarchy and opposition alike used the constitution according to the letter, regardless of the spirit, and not unnaturally came to disregard the letter itself. Open murder in the street, secret murder in the home, judicial murder in the court of law led up to avowed civil war, and the cynical practice, introduced by Sulla, of posting lists of victims who might be killed with impunity. Side by side with this went on the careless spoliation of the provinces, destined to produce evils from which the empire was never to recover. Rome had, moreover, quarrelled with Italy, and the Social war, fought out some twenty years before Virgil's birth, gained indeed the Roman citizenship for the Italians, but left them with a temper scarcely more friendly to senatorial government than before the war. The ultimate position of Transpadane Gaul, where the poet was born, was still doubtful.

Rome was after all repeating the experience of the Greek world, and with a somewhat similar result. Political life, with the opportunities it gave for the development of the political character and the political virtues, was gone, but room was left for the growth of other virtues less akin in the first instance to Greek or to Roman nature. Poetry and philosophy indicate the change coming over the world.

---

[1] Polybius himself tells the story of their friendship, and it well deserves reading. Polyb. xxxii. 9, 10.

[2] The career and the writings of Philodemus of Gadara are sufficient illustration.

The Tragedy of Euripides, the New Comedy of Menander, the idylls of Theocritus, the mimes of Herondas, and even the learned and didactic poetry of Aratus, show a shifting of the interest of mankind from the state to the individual, from high life to low life, from the city to the field. They show a certain contemplation of the virtues and feelings of people once overlooked, of humble people, shepherds, artisans, and slaves, which must be studied in conjunction with the new teaching of the philosophers. For the philosophers had left caring for the state, and were chiefly concerned in making life tolerable for individuals, who were now subjects rather than citizens. What was the temper best fitted for the subject of a great despot, of an Antiochus or a Philip? How should he face a world vaster than geographer had guessed, vaster in its awful unity than politician had ever dreamed, a world on which he could exercise no influence? How could he, for whom life had meant political activity, resign himself to sit with his hands tied? What virtues were needed for this new world to make human life still possible? A closer study of human nature was necessary for poet and philosopher alike, and this closer study brought to light many things which changed the whole aspect of life. The outlook was over a larger world, and its first great result was the discovery of the common humanity of man. *Homo sum ; humani nihil a me alienum puto*,[1] whether Terence said this spontaneously or took it from Menander, is a sentiment which is alien to the spirit of earlier Greece, and how much more to that of earlier Rome! The Aeneas of the *Aeneid* is unintelligible till we realize that between him and Homer's Achilles stands this new principle. And not only Aeneas, but, as we shall see later on, the gods of Olympus themselves have learnt the lesson.[2]

There is another result of the decline of state-life, which is not quite so conspicuous, but must not be overlooked. Philosophy, though not perhaps so early as it began to devote itself to the individual, turned an occasional glance

[1] "I am a man ; nothing human do I count alien to me."
[2] See generally Bernard Bosanquet, *History of Aesthetic*, ch. v.

to the great movements of the empires which rose from the ruins of Alexander's. The spectacle of mankind made one politically had been seen for a moment and lost again, but it had left an indelible impression on the minds of men. The incessant struggles of the successors of Alexander seem hard enough to link with any common idea, yet perhaps the idea is there, latent indeed and always further and further, it might seem, from realization, yet never forgotten. The world had been one. And when Polybius looked out upon the course of history he found the great idea again.[1] Other people might suppose if they liked, as long after him St Cyprian did,[2] that the kingdoms of this world rise and fall aimlessly by pure chance, but Polybius saw that it was otherwise. All things pointed one way, to the universal dominance of Rome, and when he looked at Rome he held that she was worthy. A deep-lying design, or at least some element of rationality, made all history intelligible and made it one, whose ever was the brain that conceived it. The philosophy of history had begun to be.[3] Probably Virgil never read Polybius, but that is immaterial, for great ideas are independent of books, and fructify in ways past tracing. At all events, we may say that the *Aeneid* presupposes this discovery of the common destiny of man as well as that of his common nature. A certain philosophy of history gives its unity to the poem, and marks it out from all poetry yet written.

"From every moral death," says Carlyle, "there is a new birth; in this wondrous course of his, man may indeed linger, but cannot retrograde or stand still." We see then

---

[1] Polybius opens his history by reference to the subjugation of almost the whole world by the single city of Rome in about fifty years, and asks what can be more valuable than to understand so unprecedented an event. At the beginning of the sixth book he returns to this problem, and endeavours to solve it in a discussion of the Roman character and constitution.

[2] Cyprian, *quod idola dei non sunt*, c. v. Cyprian is one of the less reflective of the fathers. For a nobler view, cf. p. 145.

[3] Diodorus Siculus, i. 1, on universal history: πάντας ἀνθρώπους, μετέχοντας μὲν τῆς πρὸς ἀλλήλους συγγενείας, τόποις δὲ καὶ χρόνοις διεστηκότας, ἐφιλοτιμήθησαν ὑπὸ μίαν καὶ τὴν αὐτὴν σύνταξιν ἀγαγεῖν, ὥσπερ τινὲς ὑπουργοὶ τῆς θείας προνοίας γενηθέντες . . . τὰς κοινὰς τῆς οἰκουμένης πράξεις, καθάπερ μιᾶς πόλεως, ἀναγράψαντες.

that amid the wreckage of old states and old systems man's unconquerable mind has risen, independent of state and system alike, to the possession of new truth. Yet it must be admitted that there is a difference between earlier and later philosophy, which is ominous for the time. The new lessons have not been learned in quite the old way. There is a growing suspicion of the mind and its powers, a mistrust of the intellect, which issues in the denial of the power of the mind to reach reality, in the rise of a sceptical tendency and of another, and a related, tendency to seek truth rather by intuition than by reflection. *Magnà illa ingenia cessere*,[1] if we may turn the phrase of Tacitus from history to philosophy, and men, mistrusting themselves and their contemporaries, are more content to accept and transmit *dogmata*, inherited from the great teachers of the past, than to ask questions and find answers for themselves. But when men forsake inquiry for opinion, when they once begin to deal in *dogmata*, in spite of the limitations of the *dogmatic* temper, the desire for intellectual safety prompts them to accept as many *dogmata* as possible, and eclecticism is born, and the same mind holds, or thinks it holds, the tenets of very different schools woven together in some strange reconciliation.[2] There is a growing desire to gather up the fragments that nothing may be lost, but with every gathering the fragments grow more fragmentary. Yet this breaking up of the results of thought is not all loss, for one might almost say that it is only so that they become available for mankind at large. Philosophy, if its gaze is not so clear, nor its note so certain, has at least a larger audience than before, and if, like the successors of Alexander, the successors of Plato and Aristotle are less and less great, nevertheless the general thinking of mankind is on a higher plane and on better lines than of old. Once more, we find this in the *Aeneid*. Aeneas has voyaged all round Greece, and he reaches Latium a philosopher.

Summing up, then, we may say that the poet of the first

---

[1] "The great intellects have ceased to be."

[2] "All eclectics," says Novalis, "are essentially and at bottom sceptics; the more comprehensive, the more sceptical."

century B.C. will have around him a society, more used to speculate, if not to speculate deeply, more open to receive truths of universal scope, more responsive to the gentler and tenderer emotions, in a word, more humane, than in any previous age.[1] While we have to remember that Virgil's earlier manhood fell in a period of war and bloodshed, when all the worst passions of human nature were given their fullest freedom, we must reflect that it was yet a period when the pain of suffering and seeing others suffer would be most keenly felt.

Still, though we speak of the decline of state-life[2] and its effects upon Greek thought, and recognize a similar process at work in the Roman world, we must not fail to notice that in Virgil's day the national life of Rome had not yet lost its zest and meaning. Doubtless there was already in many a mind that feeling of despair which everywhere comes from a sense of the hopelessness of personal activity on behalf of the state, and which, in the case of Rome, led later on to that general " indifference to the state, as if it did not belong to them," which Tacitus remarked as one of the leading characteristics of Romans under the Empire.[3] But still the sense of responsibility for the government and well-being of their country was a dominant feeling and motive in the minds of citizens. It was impossible to foresee the extinction of the republic. Even later on the elaborate pretence of "restoring the republic," which cloaked every fresh step taken by Augustus for the security and permanence of his system, is clear testimony to the vitality of republican and patriotic sentiment. Nor did this die till it became clear to every one that the empire belonged to no one but the Emperor, and that energy or enterprise on its behalf was a liberty which he might punish with death.[4]

[1] Cf. Lecky, *European Morals*, i. p. 227, on the influence exerted by Greece for gentleness and humanity.

[2] " The state," says Dr Edward Caird, " ceased to be an ethical organization of life, and became only the maintainer of outward order." *Greek Philosophy*, ii. pp. 40, 49, 154.

[3] Tacitus, *Hist.* i. 1. The "indifference" became far greater in the centuries that followed. Encouraged by the government, it was one of the strong factors in the fall of the ancient world.

[4] The story of Synesius and the barbarian invaders of the Cyrenaica may

In picturing to ourselves the Roman state which Virgil knew, we see it as a rule with the eyes of Cicero or Cato of Utica. To them, we know, it was painful to think of their country's present position. But we should remember that, while they were conscious of the decay of old ideals of citizenship, the Italians as a rule had only recently become citizens. To them the joys of citizenship and responsibility were new and real. Rome meant more to them than she had ever meant before. For centuries they had been subjects of Rome, now they were Romans ; they themselves were part of that great national life—they were Rome. When we turn to Virgil's own district of Italy, we find further that this position, so recently achieved by the other Italians, was still, during the earlier part of his life, a hope and a dream. Thus, side by side with the matured and even ageing philosophy of Greece, we find Virgil under the influence of a young and buoyant sense of national life.

For us who live under the British constitution, with its perplexing, if highly curious and interesting, medley of traditions and ideas, feudal, monarchical, aristocratic, romantic, and democratic, it is difficult to understand without explanation what may or may not be meant by loyalty to the state. To what are we loyal, and what do we mean by the state— which of all the elements blended in the constitution—the person of the monarch or the ideas of the race? To us this last is scarcely intelligible, but there are nations who have no difficulty about it.[1] For them, quite apart from sentiment and the claims of common blood and of a common land, certain ideas are associated with the thought of the people. This, or something like it, was true of the Romans. Greek and Jew were more conscious of race than of state :[2] the one had too strong a sense of the individual, while the other

illustrate this (about 404 A.D.). Cf. Synesius, *Epist.* 107. It is a pity that these delightful letters are not better known to classical students.

[1] Since this was first written, the swing of the pendulum is more clear, and perhaps for the moment we are more conscious of race than the facts of ethnology warrant. It is not so evident that we feel so strongly the highest ideas with which the history of our own people has been associated.

[2] I have to thank a friendly reviewer for the reminder that Athenian democracy is an exception here—that state in which πολίτης and πολιτεία come nearer together than anywhere else in antiquity or than in most lands of a more modern time.

tended to subordinate his state to his religion. With the
Roman race and state were one; he had certain clear
conceptions as to its claims upon himself, his own part and
responsibility in working out its history, and his own place
and lot in the outcome of such work no less. The charter
of the American colony, which proclaimed that he who
planted a tree should eat the fruits thereof, is an old Roman
notion that underlay the steady Roman antipathy to kings,
that inspired the Plebeians in their struggle against the
Patricians, that was the very essence of the Twelve Tables
and the law which grew from them. The Roman knew what
his state meant for himself and for every other Roman.
He had no speculative habit, but the root of the matter
was in him. Consequently he was full of the sense of the
state. It was the embodiment of the ideas of the race,
their expression of themselves.

But, unhappily, other ideals of life had made their
appearance, and with them had come disorder, self-seeking,
and the betrayal of the state. The sixty years of faction, of
wrong done recklessly or in cold blood to the idea of the
community, shocked every man who thought. Most of all
must they have been shocked who had newly come into
the enjoyment of what they saw being sacrificed to private
fancy and fury. Hence it is that Virgil's love of his country,
one of the great notes of all his poetry, gives such an
impression of depth and emotion; it is conscious love; it is
sympathy and anxiety.

II

Virgil was born at Andes near Mantua on October 15,[1]
in the year 70 B.C. The year is significant as that of the
consulship of Pompey and Crassus, when Sulla's constitution
was finally undone, and free scope was given to the powers
which worked for the destruction of the old republican
system. It is significant too that he was born in a country

---

[1] Suetonius, *vita Vergilii* (ed. Nettleship), 2 *Natus est Cn. Pompeio Magno M.
Licinio Crasso primum coss iduum Octobrium die in pago qui Andes dicitur et
abest a Mantua non procul*; Martial, xii. 68 *Octobres Maro consecravit Idus.*

race four cantons; herself, she is the cantons' head, and her strength is of Tuscan blood." [1]

When we turn from questions of ethnology to the poet's family history, we find an interesting, though short, account of his origin and upbringing. His father perhaps began life at Cremona; at all events he lived there, and perhaps he married there. Some said he was a potter; others, the hired servant of a petty official (*viator*) called Magius. A man of character and energy, he meant to get on in life and he succeeded. His industry won him his employer's daughter, by whom he had three sons. Of these, one, Silo, died in youth, another, Flaccus, in early manhood. Their father was not content with one occupation, but by keeping bees and by speculation in timber he made some money.[2] It is strange to think that Virgil owed his education to the turning of forest into lumber. It is clear that the father saw quality in his son and, with characteristic energy, determined to develop it to the utmost. Altogether, he made, as we shall see, a strong impression upon his son. One would like to know more of him.[3]

Meantime, it is a pleasant reflection that in the fourth *Georgic* Virgil is going back to boyhood, when he writes with so much humour and affection of the bees. Nor was his father's other business outside his interests. Mr Menzies in his *Forest Trees and Woodland Scenery*, cited and praised by Professor Sellar,[4] testifies to the general accuracy of Virgil's observation of woodcraft, maintaining that he must have watched keenly the details of the work which the foresters did around him, and adding that the art is indeed little advanced since the days of Virgil.

Yet there was one aspect of the lumberman's work in the forest, which may not greatly have moved himself, but

[1] *Aeneid* x. 198-203; Pliny, *N. H.* iii. 19 (23) *Mantua Tuscorum trans Padum sola reliqua.* Its importance as a fortress is medieval and modern—familiar to the student of nineteenth-century Italy.

[2] Suetonius *Vit. Verg.* 1, *egregieque substantiae silvis coemendis et apibus curandis auxisse reculam.* It should be remembered that, in the absence of sugar, honey was an article of more importance than it is to-day; *e.g.* Epictetus, *fr.* 11.

[3] All this is from Suetonius, *v. Vergilii,* 1. 2. 14.

[4] *Virgil* (2nd edition), p. 265.

which appealed to his poet son. The forest had to come
down ; the land on which it stood had been idle for years,
and man required it.[1] But while the axes swung and the
trees fell, the young poet, watching, saw the havoc made
of the birds' immemorial homes ; he saw the scattered nests,
he saw the frightened birds hovering in the air over the
spot where they were to build no more; and though he
hailed the cultivated field that was to be, he never forgot
the sorrow of the birds. The ploughman of Mossgiel farm
ploughed up the daisy and destroyed the nest of the field-
mouse, but he felt what he was doing, and made mouse
and daisy immortal. In later days Virgil lingered in his
story of the reclaiming of the land to pity the ruin of its
most ancient inhabitants. He too is

> Truly sorry man's dominion
> Has broken Nature's social union.

It is quite clear that Virgil was a "lover of trees."[2]

> Rura mihi et rigui placeant in vallibus amnes
> flumina amem silvasque inglorius [3] (*G.* ii. 485).

The wood with its crowded life and strange solitude
appealed to him, as we can see again and again in his
poetry. To take a striking instance, he sends his hero to
find his way to the other world by another route from that
of Odysseus. The Greek hero sailed there over the sea ;
the Trojan passed there through woods [4]—

> tenent media omnia silvae (*A.* vi. 131)—

[1] *Georgics* ii. 208 *Et nemora evertit multos ignava per annos,* | *antiquasque
domos avium cum stirpibus imis* | *eruit* ; *illae altum nidis petiere relictis.* Horace
also speaks of the reclaiming of forest lands, *incultae pacantur vomere silvae,*
Epp. i. 2. 45. Cf. Cowper, *Poplar Field,* "The blackbird has fled to another
retreat."

[2] Compare his glowing account of the use and beauty of the trees of the
forest in *G.* ii. 426-57, and the conclusion, *O fortunatos nimium agricolas!* On
the forests of Italy see Deecke, *Italy,* ch. xi. § 2, and the many immigrant trees
from America, Africa, and Australia, ch. viii.

[3] "Let me delight in the country and the streams that freshen the valleys—
let me love river and woodland with an unambitious love." (Conington.) The
whole passage deserves quotation.

[4] Strabo, v. 244, it is true, tells us that the region was surrounded by woods,
but the fact is one thing and the poetic use of it another.

and whether the wonderful line that describes the strange journey in the darkness,

ibant obscuri sola sub nocte per umbram

refer to this or a slightly later stage of his journey, Virgil couples it with the magnificent simile of the path through the forest by night—

Quale per incertam lunam sub luce maligna
est iter in silvis, ubi caelum condidit umbra
Iuppiter, et rebus nox abstulit atra colorem.[1]

With this love of trees we must link the poet's love of water—of river, stream and lake—no doubt likewise a love that went back to the island home of his boyhood.[2] Take his picture of the waters of Italy—

Fluminaque antiquos subterlabentia muros.
An mare, quod supra, memorem, quodque adluit infra?
anne lacus tantos? te, Lari maxume, teque,
fluctibus et fremitu adsurgens Benace marino [3] (G. ii. 157).

---

[1] *Aeneid* vi. 270-3. See Henry's comment, ad loc., in his *Aeneidea*. He says (p. 281): "The picture, as charming as the most charming of our author's always—when once rightly understood—charming pictures, cannot fail to recommend itself to every reader who, when travelling on a clear and fine dark night, has watched the spreading of the moonlight over the sky (LUCE MALIGNA) when, owing to the horizon being hid from him either by woods or high grounds, he was still doubtful whether the moon was actually above the horizon or not;" p. 285: "INCERTAM and MALIGNA are the very words of all others we would expect Virgil to have chosen to describe moonlight in a wood—INCERTAM expressing its uncertain, flickering appearance as seen through the branches of the trees . . . and MALIGNA expressing its scantiness."

[2] The name *Minciades*, applied to Virgil by Juvencus, *Minciadae dulcedo Maronis*, has more truth and feeling about it than the corresponding Μελησιγενὴς (of Homer), or "the bard of Avon."

[3] "The rivers that flow below ancient walls. Or shall I speak of the two seas that wash it above and below?—or of those mighty lakes—of thee, Larius the mighty, and thee, Benacus, rising with the waves and roar of the sea?" The reader will remember Tennyson's possession by these lines amid the scenery Virgil describes—

We past
From Como when the light was gray,
And in my head, for half the day,
    The rich Virgilian rustic measure
Of Lari Maxume, all the way,
Like ballad-burthen music, kept.

Or take the picture of the autumn rain-storm—

Ruit arduus aether
et pluvia ingenti sata laeta boumque labores
diluit; implentur fossae et cava flumina crescunt
cum sonitu, fervetque fretis spirantibus aequor [1] (*G.* i. 324).

We have one glimpse of Virgil's boyhood, which also serves to show us something of the country and its state. An epitaph is extant, which he is said to have written on a famous local brigand, an ex-gladiator, Ballista by name. It is a simple couplet, but it has a certain vivacity of expression, and it is perhaps not going too far to say that it shows the child as father of the man. From boyhood Virgil would seem to be on the side of order, on the side of industry and quietness. Perhaps, too, his grandfather was still a *viator*.

Monte sub hoc lapidum tegitur Ballista sepultus;
    nocte, die, tutum carpe, viator, iter.[2]

Another piece of verse, attributed to Virgil, which may belong to this part of his life, is a parody of Catullus' *phaselus ille.* It is turned to account for a mule-driver. It is a curious coincidence, if the poem is Virgil's, that both he and Milton should have begun by attempting humour upon carriers.[3] He is also said to have written, at the age of sixteen, a poem called the *Culex.*[4] This is well attested;

For Benacus (Garda) compare Catullus 31 (*O venusta Sirmio.*). It may perhaps be permissible to say that the line describing Benacus always brings Ontario before my mind, as I have seen it under a south-west gale. In many ways I think the scenery of the New World is nearer that of Virgil's Italy than most of what we see in Europe to-day, though I am afraid the old towns are wanting.

[1] "Down crashes the whole dome of the firmament, washing away before the mighty rain-deluge all those smiling crops, all for which the ox toiled so hard. The dykes are filled, the deep streams swell with a roar, and the sea glows again through every panting inlet" (Conington). Deecke, *Italy*, p. 80, says Italy belongs to the region of winter and autumn rains.

[2] Suet. *v. Verg.* 17. "Under this mount of stones Ballista lies, buried and hid; night and day, take thy way in safety, O traveller."

[3] The piece is *Catalepton* 10 (8). Catullus' poem must be dated shortly after his return from Bithynia in 56 B.C.

[4] "The traveller," says Baedeker, "is not recommended to spend the night at Mantua in summer, as the mosquitoes here are exceedingly troublesome."

and it was believed in early times that the poem was
that still extant under the name. Professor Nettleship
held dubiously that this might be true.[1] If Virgil wrote
it, we can only say that his later work is singularly
unlike it in rhythm and style and treatment generally,
but I believe the majority of critics are right in rejecting
the piece.

Virgil's early years were spent at Cremona, according to
Suetonius, and the eighth of the *Catalepton*. From there
his father sent him to study at Milan, and afterwards at
Rome. I do not know whether there was much continuity
in the story of a school in the Roman empire, but it is
interesting to notice that a century and a half after
Virgil the Milan school is the subject of a letter written
to Tacitus by Pliny. Two and a half centuries later
still St Augustine was engaged as a teacher of rhetoric
in Milan.[2]

Two at least of Virgil's teachers we know by name.
Parthenius taught him Greek, and Siro initiated him into
philosophy. The traces of their teaching abode with him
through life, but it is of more interest to study his emancipation from them, for it is characteristic. He was naturally
influenced by them at first, but he was still open to other
influences which corrected, and in time greatly modified, the
impression they made on him. It is the lot of most teachers
to be outgrown by their best pupils.

Parthenius is known to us by one surviving work, a handbook of love-tales (ἄθροισις τῶν ἐρωτικῶν παθημάτων), told in
brief (οἱονεὶ ὑπομνηματίων τρόπον), and dedicated to Virgil's
friend Cornelius Gallus, in the hope that he may find some
useful material among them for elegy writing. If we may
believe the statement attributed to a scholiast, the *Moretum*
is a translation by Virgil from the original Greek of Parthenius. Two questions are involved here; but whether
the extant *Moretum* is Virgil's or not, it is a delightful little
poem, and one would be glad to think that Virgil had a

---

[1] *Ancient Lives of Virgil*, p. 38. See Mr Mackail's most interesting lecture in
his *Lectures on Poetry* (1911).

[2] Pliny, *Epp.* iv. 13 ; Augustine, *Conf.* v. 13, 23.

teacher who could write anything so good.[1] The handbook
is an infinitely duller work.

It is quite possible to suppose with M. Pierron, that
Virgil, when he wrote the *Eclogues*, was "more familiar with
the poets of the Greek decadence than with those of *la belle
antiquité*," and that this was due to Parthenius, who would
probably lead his pupils where he most enjoyed going—to
Alexandria, in fact. The time came when Virgil sought
out other and greater Greek poets for himself. Yet he paid
Parthenius the same compliment as he did other poets,
better and less known, for Aulus Gellius tells us that the
source of Virgil's line.

Glauco et Panopeae et Inoo Melicertae (G. i. 437)

is one by Parthenius

Γλαύκῳ καὶ Νηρεῖ καὶ εἰναλίῳ Μελικέρτῃ.[2]

Many hard things have been said of Alexandrine poetry,
and not undeservedly, but Milton's countrymen can hardly
blame Virgil for his sensitiveness to the music and enchant-
ment of proper names, used as the Alexandrines used them.
His mind was, however, too Italian to yield altogether to the
Alexandrine manner, and the virile example of Lucretius

---

[1] See Teuffel, *Roman Literature*, § 230, and Schanz (1898) *Röm. Lit.* § 243,
on the *Moretum*. The poem has been happy in its translators, for Cowper did
it into English from Virgil's Latin.

[2] Gellius, *N. A.* xiii. 27; for Parthenius see Erwin Rohde, *Der Griechische
Roman*, pp. 113-7; Macrobius, *Sat.* v. 17, 18 *Parthenius quo grammatico in
Graecis Virgilius usus est* (but see van Jan's note). He was a favourite poet of
the Emperor Tiberius, who set up his statue along with Euphorion of Chalcis
and Rhianus (Suet. *Tib.* 70). Euphorion is referred to by Virgil (*E.* x. 50) as
imitated by Gallus, not, I think, by himself, as Pierron suggests (*Litt. Romaine*,
p. 387). Norden, *Neue Jahrbücher*, 1901, p. 267, says: "Die Bucolica sind
weniger im Stil Theokrits als der affectierten Manieristen Euphorion und
Gallus gehalten, und gehören daher zu den schwierigsten Gedichten in
lateinischer Sprache, die uns erhalten sind"; a very characteristic judgement
of this scholar, who has a great contempt for "aesthetic criticism." He continues: "Diese Manier überwindet er durch das Studium des Lucrez und
Ennius, des Homer und Apollonius, und setzt an die Stelle der *docta poematia*
grosse Werke in leichtverständlicher Sprache." The *Moretum* is a most vivid
picture of life, the servant (l. 32) might be drawn from the negress of
to-day, and the handmill (l. 19) is still used by the Italian poor; Deecke,
Italy, p. 194.

guarded his thought and style from its dangers, and gave him something of

> The graver grace, wherewith he crowned
> The wild and sweet Sicilian strain.[1]

Of Siro we know less than we do of Parthenius, but we are helped by having two little poems, attributed to Virgil and very probably genuine, of which he is the subject. The first of these dates from the moment when Virgil turned from his preliminary studies to begin that of philosophy. The poem is very short, but it is full of natural and spontaneous feeling.[2]

He bids an unregretted farewell to the rhetoricians, whom he had not found inspired, and to the grammarians—

scholasticorum natio madens pingui—

among whom he dares to include the great Varro,[3] and announces that he is setting sail for the haven of happiness,

---

[1] F. W. H. Myers, *Lugano*.

[2] For convenience the whole poem may be quoted—

> Ite hinc, inanes, ite, rhetorum ampullae,
> inflata †rhoso non Achaico verba, [†read *rore*]
> et vos, Selique Tarquitique Varroque,
> scholasticorum natio madens pingui,
> ite hinc, inanis cymbalon iuventutis.   5
> tuque, o mearum cura, Sexte, curarum
> vale, Sabine ; iam valete, formosi.
> nos ad beatos vela mittimus portus,
> magni petentes docta dicta Sironis,
> vitamque ab omni vindicabimus cura.   10
> ite hinc, Camenae, vos quoque ite salvete,
> dulces Camenae (nam fatebimur verum,
> dulces fuistis), et tamen meas chartas
> revisitote, sed pudenter et raro.

In line 7 there is a variant *morosi* ; the reading depends on whether we are to suppose that Virgil was addressing his fellow-students or his teachers. Line 3 is a restoration.

Norden (*Neue Jahrbücher für kl. Altertum*, 1901, p. 270, n. 3) accepts this poem as genuine, and characterizes it as beautiful. He makes the same point, that Virgil moved over to Stoicism. Nettleship (*Ancient Lives*, p. 38) says that "Virgil probably, if we may judge by the traces of antiquarian study in the *Aeneid*, learned in after years to form a very different opinion of Roman scholarship." Professor Nettleship, however, had a weakness for grammarians and antiquarians, as readers of his *Essays* know well.

[3] Perhaps he would have been less bold if he had known Varro, who certainly made Cicero nervous. See *ad Atticum*, xiii. 25, 3.

he is turning to the learned lore of Siro (*docta dicta Sironis*), and will thus rescue his life from all distracting care; the Italian Muses, the Camenae, dear as they have been to him, must henceforth leave him—no, they must visit him still, but only at comely intervals. He does not ask the grammarians and rhetoricians to revisit him; he had got from them all they had to give in quickening; hereafter their work is mere dead matter for him till it is touched by philosophy and the Muses. It was not every Roman poet who saw this so clearly. There is an air of "glad confident morning" about these lines, which is not that of Virgil's later and greater works—a suggestion of youth, and of hope, which gives the piece its truth. Later on he realized, by thought and pain, that not even the learned lore of Siro could rescue his life from all care.

Siro was an Epicurean, and it is surely not a strange coincidence that Virgil's philosophy in his earlier work is also Epicurean, though the fourth *Georgic* indicates already that he is perhaps not satisfied with the school. But probably an even stronger impulse than that of Siro was given to him in this direction by Lucretius, whose great work was in the hands of the Ciceros in the year 54 B.C.[1] Virgil, whether the parody of Catullus is genuine or not, had certainly been a student of his fellow country-man; and it is hardly overbold (in view of the great influence of Ennius on such men as Cicero and Lucretius) to suggest that Virgil's knowledge of Ennius dates from his youth, though perhaps he did not admire him so much then as later on in life. When then there appeared such a poem as that of Lucretius, great every way, in its grasp of principles, in its exposition of the philosophy to which Virgil had so joyfully looked forward, in its minute and sympathetic observation of nature, in its thoroughly stalwart Roman temper, and (not least perhaps in Virgil's eyes then or after-wards) in its brilliant handling of Latin metre, it is not surprising that Virgil was captured by it and remained its captive for many a year. It is characteristic, however, of

---

[1] Cicero, *ad Q. Fr.* ii. 9 (11) 4 *Lucretii poemata ut scribis ita sunt, multis luminibus ingenii, multae tamen artis.*

Virgil's genius that this loyalty did not interfere with other loyalties, and that philosophy is throughout subordinated to poetry. The combination of thought and art in Lucretius, which Cicero recognizes, may, as already suggested, have helped to save Virgil from subjection to Alexandrine methods in poetry. We may also remark that if Virgil was influenced by Lucretius, he also felt the influence of "the anti-Lucretius in Lucretius," as M. Patin very happily phrases it.[1]

He would thus return to Mantua with some part at least of his joyful prophecy fulfilled. He had escaped the pedants; he had entered under happy auspices on the study of philosophy; his interest in nature was deepened and quickened; and he had seen a wholly new field of serious art opened up before him. But he had not made his fortune. On the contrary, it is quite conceivable that practical people shook their heads over him. With all his philosophy and his rhetoric, he had not succeeded in his chosen vocation of a pleader. He had made one attempt in speaking at the bar, and then given it up altogether.[2] Once more we find that the poet

> Is weak; and, man and boy,
> Has been an idler in the land.

His poetical attempts were finding favour with people of importance; still the fact remained that he was twenty-seven years of age and not yet very sure of any noticeable success in life.

III

It may not be fanciful to suppose that perhaps the first public event of which Virgil took notice as a child or a boy

---

[1] Patin, _Études sur la Poésie Latine_, I. vii.

[2] We might find perhaps a hint of the forsaken profession in the speech of Aeneas to Dido (_A._ iv. 333), which suggests the lawyer a little. The rhetorical training for the profession may be similarly read in the speech of Turnus (_A._ xi. 377-444), where the rhetoric surely goes beyond what we should expect of the speaker. Drances is more intelligible. "It is a strange trade, I have often thought, that of advocacy," says Carlyle in writing of Jeffrey; of all trades perhaps farthest from poetry.

was the sedition of Catiline.[1]   There was some disturbance
at the time in Cisalpine Gaul,[2] and we can imagine the
anxiety felt through the country during the months at the
end of 63 and the beginning of 62, when it was yet uncertain
what Catiline would do. Would he get through into
Cisalpine Gaul—into Transalpine? Mantua may have been
well out of his way in fact, but this would hardly prevent
alarm.[3]

As he grew older Virgil would learn more of what Catiline's
rising had meant, and with other Italians he would learn to
hate Sulla and Sulla's men.[4] And then as the star of the
first Caesar rose, Virgil with all the Transpadanes would
watch with eager interest the career with which their own
destiny, their Roman citizenship, was involved.   In 49 Caesar
crossed the Rubicon and gave Transpadane Gaul the coveted
citizenship, and we may be sure that its inhabitants saw
without regret the fall of the Senatorial party with its Pisones
and Marcelli,[5] and five years later mourned the Dictator in
earnest. What Virgil thought of the murder may be read at
the end of the first *Georgic.*

The rise of Octavian was accompanied with pain to
Transpadane Gaul. Lands had been promised to the
veterans, and to fulfil the promise owners and occupiers were
turned out. Little was gained by this. The soldiers were
hard to satisfy, and made great disorder. The dispossessed
crowded to Rome to plead their case, but in vain ; Octavian

---

[1] Cf. *Aen.* viii. 668.

[2] Sallust, *Cat.* 42 *isdem fere temporibus in Gallia citeriore . . . motus erat.*

[3] See Sallust, *Cat.* 56 *Catilina per montis iter facere, modo ad urbem modo in Galliam vorsus castra movere.*

[4] He mentions Marius among the glories of Italy, *extulit haec Decios Marios magnosque Camillos, G.* ii. 169, but to Sulla he never alludes.

[5] Piso in 67 had been prosecuted by Caesar and the democrats for the murder of a Transpadane (Sall. *B. C.* 49), and Marcus Marcellus the consul in 51, after trying to get Caesar recalled from his province for enfranchising Novum Comum, scourged one of the new citizens and sent him to Caesar as a manifesto (Appian, *B. C.* ii. 26 ἔξηνε ῥάβδοις ἐφ' ὀτῳδή ; Cic. *ad Att.* v. 11. 2 *Marcellus foede de Comensi*). See Mommsen, *Roman History*, vol. iv. p. 546 n. and W. E. Heitland, *The Roman Republic* iii. § 1188. Caesar gave the *civitas* to Transpadane Gaul in 49, but it was not incorporated in Italy till after his death.

could not offend the army.[1] But the indignation of the
sufferers did not stop here; and the short rising of L.
Antonius followed. It was crushed at Perusia in 41, when
Octavian displayed great severity in the hour of victory.

Amongst the dispossessed was the family of Virgil.
Mantua had suffered from its nearness to Cremona, and
Virgil had to see a soldier take possession of his farm or his
father's—*barbarus has segetes*? His first care was to find a
refuge for his father, who must have been an elderly man,
and he found it in the little estate of his former teacher
Siro.

Villula, quae Sironis eras, et pauper agelle,
  verum illi domino tu quoque divitiae :
me tibi, et hos una mecum, quos semper amavi,
  siquid de patria tristius audiero,
commendo, in primisque patrem. Tu nunc eris illi
  Mantua quod fuerat, quodque Cremona prius.[2]

(*Catal.* 8 (10)).

One or two things should be considered here. First, we do
not know where this little villa was, nor what was Virgil's
position with regard to it. Siro must have been dead, if
the first two lines mean anything. Had he then left his
estate to Virgil, as a favourite pupil? In the second place,
this episode and this little peom should not be forgotten
when we read of Aeneas carrying Anchises from Troy. Of
all human relations in the *Aeneid* that of father and son is
dwelt on with most frequent and affectionate emphasis. Let
us take another illustration, the case of Iapis, the surgeon.
He was of all men beloved of Apollo; "to him Apollo

---

[1] Appian, *B.C.* v. 14 ἄλλο δὴ πλῆθος ἦν ἑτέρων πόλεων, αἳ ταῖς νενεμημέναις
γειτονεύουσαί τε [*Mantua vae miserae nimium vicina Cremonae*] καὶ πολλὰ πρὸς
τῶν στρατιωτῶν ἀδικούμεναι κατεβόων τοῦ Καίσαρος. ἀδικωτέρας εἶναι τὰς ἀποικίσεις
τῶν προγραφῶν· τὰς μὲν γὰρ ἐπὶ ἐχθροῖς, τὰς δὲ ἐπὶ μηδὲν ἀδικοῦσι γίγνεσθαι.
Suet. *Aug.* 13 *neque veteranorum neque possessorum gratiam tenuit.* Livy,
Epit. 125, 126.

[2] "Little farm, once Siro's, poor little field! but the wealth of him, when
he was thy lord; to thee I entrust myself, and these with me, whom I have
always loved, if tidings of ill come from my country—most of all my father
I entrust to thee. Thou must be to him now what once Mantua was, and
Cremona before."

himself offered his own arts, his own gifts—augury and
the lyre and swift arrows; but he, to prolong the days of his
father, given over to die, chose rather to know the virtues
of herbs and the craft of healing, to ply inglorious a silent
art."[1] Iapis rejected poetry for medicine; is it not that
Virgil learnt with sadness how little poetry avails to ease
pain, to give sight, to lengthen life? The father he loved—
in primisque patrem—was blind, partly or wholly. It is
a moving picture of the village home which we gain when
we realize that Virgil would have sacrificed his own supreme
gift, if, like Iapis, he could have given the blind father sight
and life.[2]

Suetonius passes rapidly over the episode of the planta-
tions, remarking that Virgil owed his escape from loss in
this distribution of lands to Pollio, Varus, and Gallus, and
that it was to celebrate them that he took to pastoral poetry.
Now Virgil does not give us any concise account of the
affair himself—one would hardly expect him to do so—and
it has been assumed that he was twice expelled, and that
after his restitution by Octavian he had to call in the help of
a friend nearer at hand to save him from the *barbarus*
in possession. It seems more probable that *Eclogue* ix,
instead of referring to a second assault and expulsion, is
really earlier in date than *Eclogue* i, and that the two poems
refer to different stages of one and the same story, the first
being set at the front of the book by way of special honour
to the ruler. In any case it appears that Virgil had already
been writing poetry of some sort, presumably Bucolic, as it
was on the favour which his poetry had won with Varus
and others that he relied for help in this time of trouble.
If not himself, others had supposed this influence would
secure him against dispossession. Yes, he says, so the story

---

[1] *Aeneid* xii. 393.

[2] Suet. *v. Verg.* 14. "Of all the forms of virtue," wrote Mr Lecky (*Eur.
Morals* i. 299), "filial affection is perhaps that which appears most rarely in
Roman history." As to the mother, who seems to have made a slighter
impression on the poet, it is conjectured that she married again, as Virgil left
most of his property to a half-brother. Incidentally, I do not believe that
Magia's name has anything to do with Virgil's medieval repute as a magician.
Rather, the popular mind could conceive of no other form of intellectual great-
ness. Plato, too, was made into a magician in the East.

went, but songs in time of war are helpless as pigeons
before the eagle—

> Audieras et fama fuit ; sed carmina tantum
> nostra valent, Lycida, tela inter Martia quantum
> Chaonias dicunt aquila veniente columbas (*E*. ix. 11).

Yet after all he underestimated the power of his poetry
for it led his great friends to intercede for him with Octavian
who after a personal interview in Rome guaranteed him
security for the future—a great concession, as we can see from
what Appian says. The story of the visit to Rome and the
interview is told in the first *Eclogue* in a curious and not very
happy allegory. And there the episode ends.

IV

We must now consider the poetry. His education
finished, and his one appearance made at the bar, Virgil, as
we saw, went back to Mantua, and began serious work upon
pastoral poetry. The mode was suggested by Theocritus,
whose influence is very clearly marked in passage after
passage of the poems. But, as we have seen, Virgil was not
a man of one allegiance, and other influences are to be found,
—as for instance that of Lucretius in *Eclogue* vi, which is nevertheless neither an imitation of Lucretius nor of Theocritus,
but, while enriched by both of them, an original work.
Critics have emphasized again and again Virgil's dependence
on Greek models, but here as everywhere else the sympathetic
reader will scarcely feel this. There may be imitation, but
the general effect is not that of imitative poetry. It is not
Theocritus, nor Lucretius, whom we are reading, but Virgil,
a poet and their peer. One is impressed with the justness of
Horace's characterization of these poems—

> Molle atque facetum
> Vergilio adnuerunt gaudentes rure Camenae (*S*. i. 10. 44);

the "exquisite playfulness and tenderness" [1] of Virgil leave

---

[1] This is Leslie Stephen's description of Cowper's temperament. Though
it was not intended as a translation of Horace's phrase, the parallel it
suggests may excuse the quotation. *Mollis* is used by Cicero to describe the
nature of his hot-tempered brother Quintus (*ad Att*. i. 17. 3); he means

the most vivid and delightful impression. "True humour," says Carlyle, "is sensibility in the most catholic and deepest sense,"[1] and Virgil has this mark of the great poet. It is a world that smiles to him—in spite of soldiers—and he smiles to the world. He goes hand in hand with Nature; and when he draws her, he does it as he sees her with his own eyes. Theocritus and Lucretius call his attention to this and that in Nature, but he consults herself before he quite believes them. His heart is open (*molle*) to the men and women around him too, and, if he has not yet sounded their deepest moods, he has still read them aright so far. Man and Nature are in harmony, and Virgil has already begun to make Silenus and Lucretius friends. He looks already to find truth in reconciliation.

The episode of the plantation of the veterans, like every real experience, left its mark upon the poet. Of course, from a worldly point of view, it made his fortune. It introduced him to Octavian, and thereafter he seems to have had little or no rough contact with the world in person. But this meant very little. The pain which he and his father had undergone had opened his mind. The sword had gone through his own soul also, and his own private trouble, soon healed as it was, became the symbol of universal suffering. He knew now. Perhaps it was not merely to compliment Cæsar that he set at the front of his book that *Eclogue* in which he tells of Cæsar's personal kindness to himself. Tityrus is restored to his beech-tree's shade and sings of his Amaryllis; the barbarian has restored to him his fields; but Meliboeus—what of him?

> Nos patriae fines et dulcia linquimus arva;
> nos patriam fugimus.[2]

sensibility. Quintilian may be consulted on *jacetum*, vi. 3. 19. Sainte-Beuve (on Medea, *Revue des Deux Mondes*, 1845): "Il est vrai qu'il n'y a pas seulement chez lui (Virgil) des traits de passion, on y trouve déjà de la *sensibilité*, qualité moins précise et plutôt moderne; mais pourtant on est trop empressé d'ordinaire à restreindre le génie ancien; en l'étudiant mieux et en l'approfondissant, on découvre qu'il avait deviné plus de choses que notre première prévention n'est portée à lui en accorder."

[1] *Essay on Richter* (1827).

[2] "We leave our country's borders and her sweet fields—we are exiles from our country."

Here in the forefront of his work is the picture of human sorrow, that sorrow which Virgil was to feel in ever-deepening intensity. It is a new element in his mind and heart, and it becomes the test by which he tries his philosophy and his poetry. As yet it has not shadowed the joy of life, but, as we shall see, it becomes more and more the background of all his thought—a part of his being. " Zeus," says Aeschylus, "made for man the road to Thought, and established ' Learn by suffering' to be an abiding Law." [1]

There is little episode in the remaining twenty years of Virgil's life. He became the friend of Maecenas and of Augustus, and they seem to have done all they could to make life easy for him.[2] It was probably not much that they could do.

> Sint Maecenates, non deerunt, Flacce, Marones [3]

said Martial, who was looking for a Maecenas. The sentiment has all the coarseness and want of inner truth that stamps so much of the poetry of Rome between Persius and Ausonius. Martial was wrong ; if any one man made Virgil, it was rather the *barbarus* than Maecenas, but all the king's horses and all the king's men, veterans and ministers, could never make a Virgil—least of all out of a Martial. Virgil owed something to Maecenas and Augustus, no doubt. The shepherd went to court, as Touchstone puts it, and learnt good manners—so they tell us. Myers, Sellar, and Sainte-Beuve all call attention to this, and doubtless Virgil did not mingle with men of affairs, with rulers and statesmen, without learning from them. Aeneas might not have been " the high and mighty prince" he is, if Virgil had not known Augustus ; he perhaps might not have had the grace and dignity of manner, nor the essentially states-

---

[1] Aesch. *Ag.* 176—

> τὸν φρονεῖν βροτοὺς ὁδώ-
> σαντα, τὸν πάθει μάθος
> θέντα κυρίως ἔχειν.

[2] Suet. *v. Verg.* 13 mentions 10,000,000 sesterces, and a house near Maecenas' gardens in Rome.

[3] Martial, viii. 56, " Let there be Maecenases, Flaccus, and Virgils will not be wanting."

manlike cast of mind, which Virgil obviously admired in Augustus.

But when one considers who and what manner of men made up the court, we begin to wonder whether Virgil after all had so much to learn from them, and we are hardly surprised that at last he shrank from Rome. Who were these men? In a most interesting essay on Horace, M. Goumy [1] enumerates some of them. They were not of the old aristocracy, in the main; they were new men, partisans and agents of Octavian (let us, for the moment, *not* say Augustus)—soldiers of fortune who had rallied to him as his opponents went down—Plancus *morbo proditor*; [2] Dellius *desultor bellorum civilium*; [3] Lollius [4] and Murena (by adoption, Varro) [5]—men who were enriched by the civil wars, by blood and confiscation. Horace addressed poems to these people, but even he, in spite of his curious pleasure in being the friend of the great, [6] found that in the long run he could have too much of Rome and the court. Virgil could hardly have met them without thinking of Siro's villa. Even Augustus must at times have shocked him. Suetonius tells us, for instance, that Augustus offered Virgil the estate of some exile, but Virgil "could not bear to accept it."— *non sustinuit accipere.* [7] One is tempted to try to picture the interview and to wonder how Virgil expressed himself,

---

[1] Goumy, *Les Latins*, pp. 224-38. No one who has read this book will fail to regret the early death of its author.

[2] Velleius Paterculus, ii. 83. 1. "Treachery was a disease with him."

[3] Messalla's designation of him, Sen. Rhet. *Suas.* i. 7. ("The circus-rider of the Civil Wars"—it means he always knew the exact moment when to 'ump to the next horse.)

[4] Vell. Pat. ii. 102; Pliny, *N.H.* ix. 35, 58, 118.

[5] See Verrall, *Studies in Horace*.

[6] Cf. *Satires*, ii. 1. 75 *tamen me | cum magnis vixisse invita fatebitur usque | invidia*; and even later in life he says the same, *Epp.* i. 17. 35 *principibus placuisse viris non ultima laus est*; and finally in his own literary epitaph he says it again, *Epp.* i. 20. 23 *me primis Urbis belli placuisse domique*. And yet he was no sycophant, and perhaps even a reluctant Caesarian. The boast of Horace is found again in a letter of Sir Walter Scott's given by Lockhart (ch. xxxix.): "To have lived respected and regarded by some of the best men in our age, is enough for an individual like me." I believe Horace may quite well have meant our Virgil in *Odes* iv. 12. The phrase (l. 15) *iuvenum nobilium cliens* as a description of Virgil would strike him much less curiously than it does the modern reader. [7] Suet. *v. Verg.* 12.

between conflicting feelings, for he would not wish to hurt his friend.

We have a picture of Virgil at court from the hand of a freedman of Maecenas, Melissus by name.[1] This man, though freeborn and entitled to freedom, had preferred to remain a slave to Maecenas. He was soon manumitted, and (says Suetonius) *Augusto etiam insinuatus est,* and became a librarian. At sixty years of age he began to compile books of funny stories (*Ineptiae*), and achieved no less than 150 volumes, beside writing some comedies. Melissus tells us that Virgil was "very slow of speech, and almost like an uneducated person," while his countenance was that of a rustic.[2] This is the hero as seen by the valet. Still, we must be grateful to him for a picture, which is most probably true, though we must interpret it for ourselves. Virgil's silence in the court of Augustus we can readily accept, but for the true explanation let us consult another poet. Browning in the *Epistle of Karshish* describes the air of the quickened Lazarus among friends and strangers, and the effect of

Heaven opened to a soul while yet on earth;

and substantially it is true of the poet.

He holds on firmly to some thread of life,
Which runs across some vast distracting orb
Of glory on either side that meagre thread, . . .
The spiritual life around the earthly life;
The law of that is known to him as this. . . .
So is the man perplext with impulses
Sudden to start off crosswise, not straight on,
Proclaiming what is right and wrong across,
And not along, this black thread through the blaze . . .

---

[1] Suet. *de Gramm.* 21. The books were probably not unlike those of English anecdotographers. Specimens may be found in Macrobius, *Saturnalia*, bk. ii, opening chapters. One of Macrobius' stories of Augustus I have heard told of Napoleon III. Pascal's "diseur de bons mots, mauvais caractère" may be remembered.

[2] Suet. *v. Verg.* 16 *in sermone tardissimum ac paene indocto similem fuisse Melissus tradit.* Ibid. 8 *facie rusticana.*

> Something, a word, a tick o' the blood within
> Admonishes ; then back he sinks at once
> To ashes that was very fire before . . .
> He merely looked with his large eyes on me.

The great poet spoke another language and thought other thoughts than these men of the court, and was probably never at home with them. He stumbled in his speech, and took refuge in silence, and then in flight from Rome, where there were other embarrassing incidents beside those of the court. For we are told that on one occasion, when his verses, probably the *Eclogues*, were being read in the theatre, he received from the people a demonstration usually reserved for Augustus.[1]

Yet we have glimpses of a circle which he found congenial. Horace more than once refers to him, and always in terms of warm affection ; while Virgil's feeling for Horace is shown by his introduction of him to Maecenas. It is difficult to see in the *Epodes* and earlier *Satires* anything very much akin to Virgil's genius ; but after all contrast is often a source of friendship, or at least of interest, and there was certainly a sturdy Italian manhood about Horace which may well have attracted Virgil. Of Varius we know little, but Horace classes him with Virgil among the " white souls," and Virgil made him his literary executor. Maecenas, the centre of the group, owes his immortality to his poet friends. With their aid and that of other writers, who have preserved memories of him, we can see him still—statesman, fop, husband, and friend, a man of affectations in dress and jewel, and precious beyond intelligibility in language ; who quarrelled a thousand times with his wife and had as many reconciliations, though without excessive faithfulness on either side ; who flaunted his dislike for the toga so far as to refuse to wear it even when acting as the Emperor's deputy ; who tormented his friends with his complaints

---

[1] Tacitus, *Dial.* 13 *populus qui auditis in theatro versibus Vergilii surrexit universus et forte praesentem spectantemque Vergilium veneratus est sic quasi Augustum.* Cf. Suet. *v. Verg.* 26 *Bucolica eo successu edidit ut in scaena quoque per cantores crebro pronuntiarentur.* Compare the triumph of *John Gilpin* in 1785, beyond the wish of the author.

about his health, gave them estates, listened to their poetry, and won their love; and who, finally, was a shrewd and moderate statesman, sparing the sword, never abusing his power, and guilty of no outrage but upon his mother-tongue.[1]

These and others were Virgil's intimates. It is easy to guess that it is to them that Suetonius refers when he speaks of Virgil reading his poems to others than Augustus, "but not often, and generally passages about which he was doubtful, with a view to criticism."[2] A poet who heard him read, Julius Montanus by name, "used to say that he would steal Virgil's voice and pronunciation and delivery, if he could, for verses would sound well when he read them which from any other lips were empty and dumb."[3]

We hear of these readings from Propertius, who seems to have been present at one or more of them, and gave his countrymen a hint of what to expect when the *Aeneid* should be published.[4] That Horace read some of his lyrical poems to his friends we learn from Ovid,[5] who heard him, though we can hardly imagine much intimacy between these two men. Virgil, however, Ovid neither heard nor met—*Vergilium vidi tantum* is the famous phrase.[6] Possibly Virgil's preference for living away from Rome was the cause; and in any case Ovid was only twenty-four years old when the great poet died.

Virgil fled from Rome to Naples, to the "sweet Parthenope," who cherished him "embowered in pursuits of inglorious peace."[7] There he lived and wrote the *Georgics*; there he was buried; and after death he became the great legendary hero or patron saint of the place for centuries.

---

[1] See Seneca, *Ep.* 114. 4-7; Macrobius, *Sat.* ii. 4. 12, and Horace, *passim.*
[2] Suet. *v. Verg.* 33.   [3] Ibid. 29.
[4] Prop. iii. 32, 59-66; cf. Suet. *v. Verg.* 30.
[5] Ovid, *Tristia,* iv. 10, 49. De la Ville de Mirmont, *Jeunesse d' Ovide,* 217, 218.
[6] Ibid. 51. This phrase is familiar to the English reader in Sir Walter Scott's account of his one meeting with Burns. *Life of Scott,* vol. i. p. 185.
[7] Conington's translation of the conclusion of *G.* iv. Heyne bracketed the four lines of biography, but they seem to be generally accepted. *Studiis florentem ignobilis oti* surely should be above suspicion. Tacitus alludes to this retreat as a happy contrast with the life of an orator—*malo securum et quietum Vergilii secessum,* says one of the persons in the *Dialogue on Orators* (13).

V

"I do not know whether the critics will agree with me," wrote Burns, who read Dryden's translation, "but the *Georgics* are to me by far the best of Virgil."[1] This was Dryden's own opinion. In scope and conception the *Georgics* are greatly in advance of the *Eclogues*. The poet has more range, more freedom, more depth of reflection and insight, and more music. He has added, critics tell us, Hesiod, Aratus, and Nicander to his sources, and perhaps others as well; but, as always in a great poet's work, our dominant impression is of a distinct and independent personality, an original mind.

For, as we read the *Georgics*, we grow more and more conscious that they are the outcome of experience, of impression and thought. Here and there we meet, it is true, reminiscences of Alexandrine literature, which we are sometimes glad to forget, as they disturb rather than help us. They are so far useful, however, that they show the hold which that literature had upon Virgil; and their relative unimportance in the *Georgics* as compared with the *Eclogues* reveals the progress of his emancipation. To one such passage we shall have to return. We may also, for the present, postpone all reference to Roman history, and, as far as possible, the consideration of the *Georgics* as a homage to Italy, and study the poem as a part of the history of the poet's mind.

The poet of the *Eclogues* had had his experience of danger and privation, but the great note of the *Eclogues* is after all happiness, a youthful happiness. Life—apart from military colonies and the disturbance they bring— is bright and sunny, with plenty of beech-tree shade when it is too sunny; and its main occupations are singing, while the goats graze, and making love to Amaryllis. Even in spite of his assertions, we hardly feel that the love-lorn shepherd is really inconsolable. But the *Georgics* show a different spirit. Here we find the grim realization that

---

[1] *Letter to Mrs. Dunlop*, May 4, 1788. So also judged Montaigne, *Essays* ii. 10 (Florio), Essay 67 (Cotton).

life involves a great deal more work than Menalcas and the rest had thought, hard work, and work all the year round; vigilance never to be remitted, and labour which it is ruin to relax. This Virgil brings out, in speaking of pulse—"spite of all patience in choosing, spite of all pains in examining, I have seen it degenerate all the same, except man applied himself (*vis humana*) year by year, to pick out the largest one by one. So is it, all earthly things are doomed to fall away and slip back and back, even as, if a boatman, who scarcely manages to force his boat up stream by rowing, relax his arms by chance, the headlong current whirls him away down the river" (*G.* i. 197-203). Over and over again the work has to be done, the vines must be dressed, a toil *cui nunquam exhausti satis est*; every year the ground has to be hoed "eternally" (*aeternum frangenda bidentibus*); round and round in a circle comes the husbandman's toil, as the year revolves upon itself (*G.* ii. 397-402).

Scilicet omnibus est labor impendendus—

the very rhythm tells its tale—work is to be paid into everything, and more than work, for *labor* is the toil that brings fatigue and exhaustion. And withal, "poor mortals that we are, our brightest days of life are first to fly; on creeps disease and the gloom of age, and suffering sweeps us off and the ruthless cruelty of death" (*G.* iii. 36). Even the bees—the Italians of the insect world—are not exempt from "the chances of *our* life" (*G.* iv. 251).

There are those who find pessimism in this unflinching picture of human life, but this is not just. The poet is doing his proper work in presenting to us faithfully one aspect of life which cannot be obscured. If he stopped there, and showed us only a monotony of merciless toil without any corresponding values, the charge of pessimism would be just. But the emphasis lies quite as much on the values—on the recompense of labour and on the consolations of Nature, the meaning of all which is only to be reached by a true apprehension of what they are required to do for us. They need their background, which is real experience of toil and pain.

The work of the farmer is heavy and unceasing. Earth is a hard mistress, but still she is the justest of all created beings—*iustissima tellus* (*G.* ii. 460)—and she makes no scruple about paying her wages promptly and in full, when the work required has been done for them—

> fundit humo facilem victum [1] (*G.* ii. 460).

Nature has appointed "laws and eternal ordinances" (*G.* i. 60), and it is the disciple of Lucretius who uses the words, knowing quite well what they mean. The tree will readily do what you tell it, if you take the right way of telling it (*G.* ii. 52). Virgil uses the same word of farm labour as he does of Rome's imperial work. Such phrases as *imperat arvis* (*G.* i. 99), *dura exerce imperia* (*G.* iii. 369), may be set side by side with the famous word of Anchises—

> tu regere imperio populos Romane memento [2] (*A.* vi. 851),

while the accompanying *pacis imponere morem* also suggests a comparison. The world of men and the world of nature are only to be ruled in one way—by obedience to the proper laws of their being.

It may not be fanciful, perhaps, to connect with this Virgil's practice of directing the farmer to watch the stars and to regulate his work by them; they mean as much to the farmer as to the sailor, he says. The Roman calendar had only recently emerged from incredible chaos, and it might easily have returned to it, but no college of pontiffs could reach the stellar system.[3] So long as the farmer, in Emerson's telling phrase, "hitched his wagon to a star," he was safe, he would reap the reward of his labour, and would have no cause to grumble at the universe.

But apart from such rewards as Earth gives him, the farmer has a reward within himself in the hardening of his fibre and the sharpening of his faculties. Using the form of an old story, the poet tells us that Jupiter chose

---

[1] "Earth, that gives all their due, pours out from her soil plenteous sustenance" (Conington).

[2] "Yours, Roman, be the lesson to govern the nations as their lord . . . to impose the settled rule of peace" (Conington).

[3] Suetonius, *Julius* 40, a very interesting chapter. See also p. 150.

that the culture of the land should not be easy ; by cares he meant to quicken mortal hearts. He himself gave the snake its poison, and bade the wolf raven, bade the sea toss, and put fire and wine out of reach, that experience by patient thought might hammer out the divers arts little by little. Thus came the arts—it was toil, unsparing toil, that won all the victories, and the pressure of want and grinding adversity—

labor omnia vicit
improbus et duris urgens in rebus egestas (*G.* i. 121-146). [1]

Look at the men whom this rough Italian farm-life has bred—those hard, and more than hard, frames they strip for the wrestling (*G.* ii. 531)—the Ligurian (a North Italian people, it should be noted) inured to hardship (*adsuetumque malo Ligurem, G.* ii. 168)—and the youth of Italy in general,

patiens operum exiguoque adsueta iuventus [2] (*G.* ii. 472).

Is it surprising that a people bred in this hard school to be masters of themselves are masters of the world, a people of Marii and Scipios (*G.* ii. 167-172, 532 f.)?

But man has other sources of happiness as well, and here, I think, the value of the *Georgics* is still unexhausted. The poet looks at Nature, and if he does not find, like Bernardin de St Pierre, some special profit or pleasure designed for mankind in every detail of creation, he at least finds a pleasure and a happiness in them all, which may or may not have been meant for him, but it is there. The trees, with all their beauties and their feelings too (*G.* ii. 82), plants and their ways, wild and cultivated (the lucerne, for example—"all Venetia is full of it," says Servius [3]), and birds and beasts and insects—he enjoys them all, thinks about

---

[1] " So Toil conquered the world, relentless Toil, and Want that grinds in adversity" (Conington). Compare a fine passage in Carlyle's essay entitled *Characteristics*, beginning "Nevertheless, doubt as we will, man is actually Here," and ending " Ever must Pain urge us to Labour ; and only in free Effort can any blessedness be imagined for us." Cf. Alleyne Ireland, *The Far Eastern Tropics,* pp. 8-10, on the growth of civilization in the temperate zone as distinct from the tropics.

[2] " A youth patient of toil and accustomed to scant fare."

[3] Servius on *G.* i. 215, *Huius plena Venetia est.*

them and smiles to them.   For all through the *Georgics*
runs the most delicate humour.   The farmer stamps out
the insect and the vermin as mere pests, but the poet
looks at things from their point of view, and the contrast
is for him full of pathos and humour.   The tiny mouse has
her mansions and her granaries, quite as significant to her
as his are to the farmer.   How can the poet of work find
in his heart anything but sympathy for the ant in her
anxiety about her old age (*G.* i. 181 f.)?   When he comes
to the bees, he enters so heartily and delightfully into their
concerns,—their care for their *parvos Quirites*, their loyalty
to their king, their true Italian passion for possession
(*amor habendi*), their Cyclopean energy, their laws and
constitution, their good looks, and those terrible commotions
that a handful of dust will quiet,—that one could almost
believe he had been a bee himself, but that bees on the
whole seem a little deficient in humour.   How much, in
short, is his conclusion, "we see in nature that is ours."

Turning to man's life Virgil finds it also full of charm
and happiness.   In passages that recall the humour and the
close description of Cowper's *Task*, he tells of the joys of
spring and autumn, of the genial winter (*genialis hiems*) in
general and the winter night in the cottage—

> I love thee, all unlovely as thou seem'st,
> And dreaded as thou art . . .
> I crown thee king of intimate delights,
> Fireside enjoyments, home-born happiness
> And all the comforts that the lowly roof
> Of undisturb'd Retirement, and the hours
> Of long uninterrupted evening, know (*Task*, bk. iv).

The sum of the whole matter is given in the great passage
which closes the second *Georgic*—*o fortunatos*—where the
poet sums up the joys of labour for the Earth and of her
rewards, of the settled low content, the sturdy character,
the yearly round with fresh pleasures in every season, and
all the happiness of honest married life and children.

There are signs in the *Georgics* of a change coming over
the poet's philosophy and his attitude toward Epicureanism.

This question must be reserved for treatment in another chapter. For the moment it is enough to say that he seems to be moving away from the position of Lucretius and Siro, and feeling his way toward another; and meanwhile though he congratulates the man who grasps the laws of Nature—

Felix qui potuit rerum cognoscere causas [1] (*G.* ii. 490),

he himself finds his happiness elsewhere—

Fortunatus et ille deos qui novit agrestes
Panaque Silvanumque senem Nymphasque sorores [2]
(ibid. 493);

happiness lying, that is, in the contemplation of Nature's beauty and the realization of the quieter joys possible to man.

He has made progress, too, in his delineation of passion. It is a considerable step from Amaryllis to Eurydice. There is too much that is Alexandrine in the closing episode of the fourth *Georgic*, but there is feeling in the lines—

Illa 'quis et me' inquit 'miseram et te perdidit, Orpheu,
quis tantus furor? en, iterum crudelia retro
fata vocant, conditque natantia lumina somnus.
Iamque vale; feror ingenti circumdata nocte
invalidasque tibi tendens, heu non tua, palmas' [3]

(*G.* iv. 494).

But Virgil was to do greater work than this, for the language of passion in the *Aeneid* is clearer, stronger, and more simple.

---

[1] "Happy the man who has gained a knowledge of the causes of things" (Conington). It is in such phrases as this—e.g. *sunt lacrimae rerum*—that Virgil is hardest to translate. He means, I think, by *rerum causas* the world and all the fabric of law on which it rests.

[2] "Blest is he also who has for his friends the gods of the countryside—Pan, and old Silvanus, and the sisterhood of Nymphs." Cf. Mr Warde Fowler's *Religious Experience of the Roman People*, lecture xviii, on religious feeling in the poems of Virgil, and especially pp. 406 ff. "Let us mark the word *novit*," he says of this passage.

[3] "She cried—'Oh! what madness, what monstrous madness has undone me, poor me, and thee too, my Orpheus? Look! again that cruel destiny is calling me back, and sleep is burying my swimming eyes. And now farewell. I am borne away, swathed in night's vast pall, and stretching towards thee powerless hands—thine own, alas! no longer'" (Conington). The English is less involved than the Latin.

Of course the *Georgics* secured Virgil's fame, even if it had not been secure before. Obscure people parodied occasional lines,[1] but the work was out of every one's reach but the author's. It touched Italy to the heart. It was the most Italian and the most poetic work ever done in Latin. If in some ways it clearly falls short of the *de Rerum Natura*, in concentration for instance, and in speculative grasp of principles, it has a wealth of poetry, which makes us forget its shortcomings, and which, with the *Aeneid* to support it, captured the reading world altogether from Lucretius.

The last ten years of his life Virgil devoted to the *Aeneid*. He lived, as we have seen, chiefly at Naples. In the year 19 B.C. he went to Greece, apparently meaning to give the *Aeneid* its finishing touches there.[2] At Athens he met Augustus, returning from the East, who persuaded the poet to return to Italy with him. Unfortunately they made a visit to the ruins of Megara[3] on a very hot day, and Virgil contracted some disorder.[4] The journey homeward made matters worse, and he was so ill on reaching Brundusium that he only lived a few days and died on September 21.

Suetonius tells us that before leaving Italy Virgil had charged his old poet-friend Varius to burn the *Aeneid* if anything happened to him, but that Varius had refused. In his last illness he wished to burn it himself, but no one would bring him his *scrinia*. Failing in this, he gave verbal instructions that Varius and Plotius Tucca—the two men whom Horace had grouped with him as "the whitest of souls"—were to take charge of his writings, but not to publish anything which he had not published himself. But he had reckoned without

---

[1] Suetonius *v. Verg.* 43. Some one called Numitorius wrote *Antibucolica*, of which Suetonius preserves three lines—*e.g. Tityre si toga calda tibi est, quo tegmine fagi?*—and some one else finished off *Nudus ara, sere nudus* (G. i. 299) *habebis frigora febrem.* Servius also on *E.* ii. 23 quotes the malicious punctuation of *Vergiliomastix.*

[2] Suet. *v. Verg.* 35 *Impositurus Aeneidi summam manum statuit in Graeciam et in Asiam secedere.*

[3] Five and twenty years before (45 B.C.) Servius Sulpicius had written the famous letter to Cicero (*ad Fam.* iv. 5), in which he spoke of the thoughts awakened in him by these very ruins.

[4] Horace, *Sat.* i. 5. 49, tells us of Virgil suffering from indigestion on their journey together from Rome to Brundusium with Maecenas. The satire is translated by Cowper (1759).

the Emperor, who knew too much of the *Aeneid* to allow it to be lost, and instructed Varius to give it to the world without addition. This Varius did, making only the slightest corrections. It must have been with emotion that he read after his friend's death two lines borrowed from himself and set in the very heart of the poem.[1]

Virgil had meant, it is said, to devote three more years to the revision of the *Aeneid*, and then give the rest of his life to philosophy.[2] If the reason for this be asked, is it not probable that he felt the unresolved problems of the *Aeneid*, and that, with the fuller knowledge of the cares of mankind, which he had gained with years, he longed still more for that haven of rest and happiness, which he had so long ago promised himself to find in philosophy,

tendebatque manus ripae ulterioris amore ?[3]

---

[1] Cf. Macr. *Sat.* vi. 1. 39. The lines of the *Aeneid* are vi. 621, and are modelled after Varius'

vendidit hic Latium populis agrosque Quiritum
eripuit : fixit leges pretio atque refixit.

[2] Suet. *v. Verg.* 35 *Triennioque continuo nihil amplius quam emendare ut reliqua vita tantum philosophiae vacaret.*

[3] *A.* vi. 314, "and stretched forth passionate hands to the farther shore" (Mackail).

CHAPTER II

LITERATURE.—1. LITERARY INFLUENCES

"There is through all art a filiation. If you see a great master, you will always find that he used what was good in his predecessors, and that it was this which made him great. Men like Raphael do not spring out of the ground. They took their root in the antique and in the best which had been done before them. Had they not used the advantages of their time there would be little to say about them."—GOETHE, *Conversations with Eckermann*, Jan. 4, 1827.

"Among the deadliest of poetical sins is imitation."—CARLYLE, *Essay on the State of German Literature.*

SOMEWHERE about the year 400 A.D. a great educational work was composed by the scholar Macrobius. He gathered up all that he considered best in the current criticism of Virgil, and, with some other cognate matter — literary, archaeological, and physiological re-miniscences — he constructed a long dialogue. The characters who take part in the conversation are some of the leading men in the pagan society of the time, with a few scholars and *savants*, and in particular Servius. The time is the festival of the Saturnalia, from which the book takes its name, and the scene is laid from day to day in the houses of Praetextatus, Flavian, and Symmachus, the chief political leaders of the pagan party. A large part of the dialogue is given up to the criticism of Virgil, but we might be over-estimating the seriousness of Roman society at the time if we believed that the guests enjoyed equally the whole of the discussion. The scholar Eustathius, for example, has spoken of Virgil's debt to Homer, and Avianius (the father of Symmachus) asks him to continue and enumerate *all* that Virgil has borrowed; "for what could be more delightful than to hear two supreme poets saying the same thing?" "Give me a copy of Virgil then," says Eustathius, "because as I go from passage to passage

I shall remember Homer's verses more easily." The book is duly fetched by a slave, and Avianius asks the learned scholar, who had hoped that a few passages would suffice, not to pick them here and there, but "to begin at the beginning and go steadily through the book."[1] This is duly done, and all the parallel passages are written out side by side by Macrobius. Perhaps it was hardly necessary for him to tell us in his preface that the conversation never actually took place, but that he groups his material as a dialogue that it may be more readily grasped and digested.

However, Macrobius hoped that this collection of parallel passages might be of use, and he followed it up by some criticism. Here Virgil excelled Homer; there the poets are equal, and there Homer is still pre-eminent. "Here Virgil is slighter (*gracilior*) than his model," for "remark Homer's swift movement without loss of weight" (*vide nimiam celeritatem salvo pondere*, v. 13. 2). Much of this work upon Virgil was inherited, and some of it may have come down from Virgil's own day, from Perellius Faustus who "collected Virgil's thefts," and Q. Octavius Avitus, who made "eight books of parallels containing the borrowed verses and their sources."[2] So early had this kind of criticism begun.

But Virgil did not merely borrow lines and phrases; he transferred whole episodes from Homer to the *Aeneid.* Let us hear Eustathius again, speaking to Symmachus and his friends. "And more, what of the whole of Virgil's work, modelled, as it were, from a sort of mirrored reflection of Homer's? For the storm is described with marvellous imitation—let any one who wishes compare the verses of them both[3]—and as Venus takes the place of Nausicaa,

---

[1] Macr. *Sat.* v. 3. 16; 4. 1. On the *Saturnalia* see Comparetti, *Vergil in the Middle Ages*, pp. 63 f.

[2] Suet. *v. Verg.* 44, 45. It is interesting that the same kind of unintelligent and anti-poetic criticism was early applied to Milton, who was supposed to have plagiarized from authors of Pisander's own eminence. See Masson, *Milton's Poetical Works*, vol. ii. § 4.

[3] I would recommend any one who accepts Eustathius' hint to go to Sainte-Beuve, *Étude sur Virgile*, pp. 209-16 (and the passages before and after, too), rather than to Eustathius himself, if he wishes to make a real comparison of the two poets.

daughter of Alcinous, Dido herself recalls the picture of King Alcinous presiding over his banquet. Scylla too and Charybdis and Circe are suitably touched on, and instead of the cattle of the Sun the Strophades islands are invented. Instead of the consultation of the dead we see Aeneas descend to them in the company of the priestess. Palinurus answers to Elpenor, the angry Dido to the angry Ajax, and the admonition of Anchises to the counsels of Tiresias. Then the battles of the *Iliad* and the description of the wounds (done with perfection of learning), the double enumeration of allies, the making of the arms, the variety of the funeral games, the treaty made between the kings and broken, the midnight reconnoitring, the embassy with a refusal from Diomedes (after Achilles' example), the lamentation over Pallas as over Patroclus, the altercation of Drances and Turnus drawn after that between Agamemnon and Achilles (for in both cases one thought of his own, the other of the public, good), the single conflict of Aeneas and Turnus as of Achilles and Hector, the reservation of captives to be slain at the burial"[1]—here I may anticipate Macrobius' *et reliqua*, and with him omit to supply my sentence with a verb. There is nothing here that is not quite obvious, and we may place beside this another example of Virgil's borrowing, which Macrobius mentions as "generally known," "the commonplace of schoolboys" (*pueris decantata*). For Virgil, he says, "transcribed the fall of Troy with his Sino and the wooden horse, and all the rest of the second book, from Pisander, nearly word for word." The English reader may not remember Pisander, but he "is eminent among Greek poets for his work, which begins with the marriage of Jupiter and Juno, and comprises in

---

[1] *Sat.* v. 2. 13-16. There is in Seneca, *Epistle* 108, 24 ff., an interesting passage on the different ways in which grammarian and philosopher would read the same passage of Virgil. The grammarian *deinde Ennianos colligit versus* (33), with a note on ancient usage ; and next *felicem deinde se putat, quod invenerit, unde visum sit Vergilio dicere* :

> quem super ingens
> porta tonat caeli :

Ennium hoc ait Homero subripuisse, Ennio Vergilium.

Seneca elsewhere speaks of having wasted time on the grammarians, *Ep.* 58, 5.

one continuous story the whole history of the world during
the intervening centuries down to Pisander's own age ; and
it makes one structure out of all the gulfs of time, and in it,
among other stories, the fall of Troy is narrated in this way,
and by a faithful translation Maro has devised for himself
his fall of the Ilian city." [1]

The case for the critics who enjoy the discovery of
parallel passages could hardly be put more tersely than
Macrobius has here stated it, but the allusion to Pisander
betrays the real value of criticism by parallel passages. For
Macrobius does not reject the popular account of Virgil's
debt to Pisander, but, for the time, disregards it as too well
known to need further discussion. If Virgil took the outline
of his story of Troy's fall from Pisander "nearly word for
word," and so many episodes, phrases, and verses from Homer
in the same way—if these statements are made in the same
breath, it would seem the natural conclusion that Virgil is
singularly little indebted to Homer. Let us take a somewhat similar instance of literary relations.

Shakespeare's debt to North's translation of Plutarch's
Lives is well known. Of *Julius Caesar* Archbishop. Trench
says, "it is scarcely an exaggeration to say that the whole
play is to be found in Plutarch. . . . Of the incident there is
almost nothing which he does not owe to Plutarch, even as
continually he owes the very wording to Sir Thomas North." [2]
He follows this out with a list of incidents taken from
Plutarch's *Lives* of Julius Caesar, of Brutus and of Antony.
From this last *Life* the play of *Antony and Cleopatra* was
drawn, and in one striking example Archbishop Trench
shows how Shakespeare uses at once the fact of Plutarch and

---

[1] *Sat.* v. 2. 4, 5. Shakespeare, Voltaire says, only turned into dialogue the
romance of *Claudius, Gertrude, and Hamlet*, written in full by Saxo Grammaticus,
"à qui gloire soit rendue."—*Appel à toutes les nations*, 1761 (*Œuvres*, xl. p. 263).
On Pisander and this passage, see A. Förstemann, *Aeneasmythus*, p. 6.

[2] Trench, *Plutarch : His Life, his Parallel Lives and His Morals*, 1874, pp.
66-74. Stapfer, *Shakespeare and Classical Antiquity* (Engl. tr.) p. 299, suggests
it might be shorter to say what Shakespeare had added or altered ; he has
followed Plutarch more closely and completely in *Antony and Cleopatra* than in
the other plays ; but in all "Shakespeare, who usually treated the sources of his
materials with but scant courtesy, showed the utmost deference and submission
towards Plutarch."

the words of North.[1] When the soldiers found Cleopatra dead, "one of them seeing her woman, Charmion, angrily said unto her: 'Is that well done, Charmion?' 'Very well,' said she again, 'and meet for a princess descended from the race of so many noble kings:' she said no more, but fell down dead hard by the bed." So Plutarch and North: and Shakespeare hardly alters it.

> *First Guard.*   What work is here! Charmian, is this well done?
>
> *Charmian.*   It is well done, and fitting for a princess Descended of so many royal kings.

On the other hand, while North and Plutarch tell how Antony unfolded the robe which Caesar wore when he was murdered, and how he "called the malefactors cruel and cursed murtherers," Shakespeare (as the necessities of drama required) made a speech for Antony, but what a speech! [2]

Here, then, we have illustrations in Shakespeare of verbal indebtedness and indebtedness for incident. How far are we to say Shakespeare is "influenced" by Plutarch, or "under the influence" of Plutarch? And in the same way, we may ask if we are after all much helped to a real judgement on Virgil by the information that he took such and such episodes, passages, lines or phrases from Homer or Pisander? Was his mind in the least degree influenced by Pisander? How far does Homer affect his mind?

A poet's work may show traces of the influence of a predecessor or a contemporary either in matter, or in style, or in spirit. Probably, so far as matter is concerned, a poet may borrow with the utmost freedom without impairing his independence or originality. Shakespeare seems never to have invented a plot.[3] Style, on the other hand, is so closely related to spirit, that if a poet go beyond a certain point in

---

[1] It has been remarked that Shakespeare follows North in his mistakes in translation.

[2] Heine, *Letzte Gedichte und Gedanken*, p. 230 "Wie Homer nicht allein die Ilias gemacht, hat auch Shakespeare nicht allein seine Tragödien geliefert—er gab nur den Geist, der die Vorarbeiten beseelte."

[3] Barrett Wendell, *The Seventeenth Century in English Literature*, p. 36, on Shakespeare's "somewhat sluggish avoidance of needless invention."

reproducing the style and manner of another, his claim to originality will be open to dispute.[1] For when we come to spirit, we are on safer ground, and the question is easier. If a poet is to be great at all, his spirit will be his own. Others may, and will, help to mould him, to train him in his business of seeing the world and of interpreting it to himself, as well as in the other part of his work, in his use of word and rhythm and colour, and the other means which he must employ to express his mind. Such and so much influence a multitude of masters may exercise over a poet's development, but if the influence of any of them goes beyond quickening, and becomes so great as to affect the independence of the poet's outlook on life, or even, we may probably add, of his habitual mode of expressing himself, then we may be sure at once that we are dealing with a mind of the second order.

I

Now let us look at Virgil's relation to Homer. That Virgil owes much of his matter to Homer we hardly need Macrobius to tell us. His hero he took directly from the *Iliad*, and many of his hero's adventures from the *Odyssey*, while the battle-pieces of his last six books he modelled as closely as he could after Homer's battles. He used the same metre and much the same scale of length, and he gave to his work as much as he could of the manner and movement of the Homeric poem. Yet it may be said that the epic of Quintus of Smyrna stands nearer to Homer in all this than does the *Aeneid*. Writing four centuries after Virgil, Quintus more studiously reproduces the matter and the form of Homer. But he so utterly subordinates himself to Homer that in the end he is infinitely further from Homer. For the one dominant characteristic of Homer is life, and that is a quality that cannot be learnt and cannot be copied, and it is this quality which Quintus entirely lacks, but which has made

---

[1] "The spirit and the manner of an author are terms that may, I think, be used conversely. The spirit gives birth to the manner, and the manner is an indication of the spirit." Cowper (on Homer and Pope), Southey's *Life of Cowper*, ii. p. 197.

the *Aeneid* the book of Western Europe for centuries. And what is true of Quintus is in measure true of Virgil—where in form and matter he reminds us most of Homer, there his work is generally least living; it has lost its power of appeal.

What then did Homer do for Virgil? He brought him into a world of men, where, like Odysseus, he might see the cities of many and learn their minds. He showed him the energies, the passions, and the infinite life of men and women in a larger air and on a grander and simpler scale than he could find it elsewhere, in art or in what people call real life. He showed him a broad, wide world, a world of battle and seafaring, of city and forest, where warrior, sailor, counsellor, fisherman, shepherd, all pursue their task with that keenness of interest, that calm in the face of danger and obstacle, and that fundamental content which a great poet can see, where a lesser finds only failure and despair, broken hopes and baffled endeavours. The minor poets—the people whom Goethe calls "the Lazaretto poets"—are overcome by the sense of man's failure, but Homer's note is different. In him, man triumphs over the world because he can and will look it full in the face and find in the human spirit something to overcome the world. There is probably no passage in Homer better fitted to illustrate this than Sarpedon's speech to Glaucus :—

"Friend of my soul, were it that, if we two were once escaped from this war, we should live for ever without old age or death, I would not fight myself among the foremost, nor would I send thee into the battle that gives men glory ; but, for fates of death stand over us, aye! ten thousand, which mortal man may not flee from nor escape, let us go on, and give glory to another or win it ourselves."[1]

Nor can Homer's language have been without its effect on Virgil's spirit. Here is a poet (Virgil lived long before Wolf, and we may for the present use the name " Homer," as Virgil did, without reference to the question of the single or divided origin of the Homeric poems)—a poet, who, to quote Matthew Arnold, " expressed himself like a man of adult reason," who

---

[1] *Iliad* xii. 322-8. The reader may be reminded of Matthew Arnold's discussion of this passage in his book (*On Translating Homer*).

"has actually an affinity with Voltaire in the unrivalled clearness and straightforwardness of his thinking ; in the way in which he keeps to one thought at a time, and puts that thought forth in its complete natural plainness."[1] Now Virgil's earlier interest in poetry had been directed to the writers of Alexandria, and it was probably comparatively late in life that he really found Homer. From the first his Roman sense and feeling had saved him from extreme Alexandrinism, and led him to leave Callimachus and Euphorion to Propertius and Gallus. The earnestness and passion of Lucretius helped him (if he needed help) to refuse that diction, which, though beloved of scholars, was neither earnest nor passionate. Then turning, a matured man, to the closer study of Homer, he found another language, " direct, simple, passionate, and noble."

To say that Virgil could not have written such a language himself, without Homer's example, would be absurd. Yet there can hardly be no significance in the fact that the Latin poet, who gave to Homer a closer and a more sympathetic study than any man of his day, is also the one among Latin poets who, in spite of all the differences and developments due to the growth of the world's mind in the centuries between, yet resembles Homer most closely in breadth of view, in keenness of interest, in manhood, in the sympathy with which he looks upon man and man's life, and in the simplicity, passion, and grandeur of his language.

But we cannot leave the matter here, for we have to recognize a great difference between the two poets. Virgil has the poet's eye for human life, but he does not see it with Homer's freshness. It is partly because Homer has done or watched the things about which he writes, while Virgil has read about them in books and pictured them with " the inner eye." Sainte-Beuve finds an excellent illustration of this detachment from the heroic age in the elaborate account of fire-lighting in the first *Aeneid*.[2] To Homer the operation is too obvious to need description ; for

---

[1] *On Translating Homer* (1896 edition), pp. 26, 27.
[2] *Étude sur Virgile*, p. 239 ; *Aen.* i. 174-6.

Virgil it was a little away from ordinary experience, far enough to quicken interest.

The most patent illustration, however, of the divergence between the Homeric and the Virgilian point of view is to be found in the descriptions of battle. On this point we may call a witness who, whatever his qualifications for literary criticism, at least understood war. Napoleon one day took the fancy to examine the second *Aeneid*, and he announced his conclusion peremptorily that in all that concerns the military operations it is absurd from one end to the other. Homer, he said, was a man who knew where he stood, who had made war; "the journal of Agamemnon could not be more exact as to distances and time, and in the life-like character of the military operations, than is the *Iliad*."[1] Virgil was "nothing but a regent of a college, who had never gone outside his doors, and did not know what an army was." It may be urged, on the other hand, that if Virgil had not made war he had some notions about it, for he alludes to modern operations which Homer's day did not know. He allows the Rutulians to assail Aeneas' camp with the formation known as the *testudo*,[2] and this without further remark. Quintus of Smyrna employs it too, but he makes it appear as a happy thought of the moment, the suggestion, of course, of Odysseus.[3] Virgil, again, in the eleventh book, sets Aeneas to attack Laurentum, and he tries to do it by a "turning movement."[4] Still, there can be little doubt that Napoleon is right. Virgil had not made

---

[1] See Sainte-Beuve, *Étude*, p. 238; Pierron, *La Lit. romaine*, p. 401. Cf. Paul-Louis Courier (writing from Barletta, March 8, 1805): "Do not think I am losing my time; I am studying here better than ever I did, from morning to night, after Homer's fashion, who had no books at all. He studied men; one sees them nowhere as one does here. Homer made war; do not doubt it. It was savage war. He was *aide-de-camp*, I dare say, to Agamemnon, or, very likely, his secretary. Nor would Thucydides either have had so true and so profound an understanding—that is not to be learnt in the schools. Compare, I beg of you, Sallust and Livy—the one talks pure gold (*parle d'or*), nobody could speak better; the other knows of what he talks. And who shall hinder me some day . . .? Why should I not make some pictures, in which might be found some air of that naïve truth which we find so charming in Xenophon? I am telling you my dreams."

[2] ix. 505 f. [3] *Posthomerica*, xi. 358.
[4] Boissier, *Nouvelles Promenades*, p. 340 (Engl. tr. p. 317).

war, and his pictures of it are drawn from what he had
read in books—and with a certain reluctance, even with
pain. His only experience of it brought home to him its
sufferings, not its exhilaration.

When Homer is busy with a battle, he is absorbed in it;
he thinks of it all the time and of nothing else; he feels the
exhilaration of it, the earnest satisfaction, the joy of action
and achievement; he deals every blow he describes, and
exults whenever the blow does its work. But Virgil draws
battle-scenes, not at all because he loves them, but because
he must draw them. He feels every blow that is dealt,
thinks of everything it involves, looks away from the battle
to untilled fields—

> squalent abductis rura colonis [1] (*G.* i. 507);

to funeral pyres and nameless graves—

> cetera confusaeque ingentem caedis acervum
> nec numero nec honore cremant [2] (*A.* xi. 207);

to lonely parents at their prayers—

> et nunc ille quidem spe multum captus inani
> fors et vota facit cumulatque altaria donis [3] (*A.* xi. 49).

The result of this is that Virgil falls far short of Homer in
expressing "the stern joy that warriors feel." If the war
spirit is to be depicted, Virgil's is hardly the way in which
it will be done. If we are to go through a battle in
earnest, whether in real life or in literature, we shall hardly
manage it if we take Virgil's spirit into it. It will cost us
too much. We need not perhaps deplore Virgil's failure to
give us the enthusiasm of war, as the world has heard at
least enough of the poetry of drum and trumpet.

[1] "The tiller is swept off and the land left to weeds" (Conington).

[2] "The rest, a vast heap of undistinguishable slaughter, they burn uncounted
and unhonoured" (Mackail). *Confusae* is the pathetic word here. All these
dead bodies were once individual breathing men, and now—. Compare the grim
effect of the adverb in Thucydides' account of what the Corcyreans did with the
murdered oligarchs (iv. 48. 4): καὶ αὐτοὺς οἱ Κερκυραῖοι, ἐπειδὴ ἡμέρα ἐγένετο,
φορμηδὸν (cross-wise, two over two) ἐπὶ ἁμάξας ἐπιβαλόντες ἀπήγαγον ἔξω τῆς
πόλεως.

[3] "And now he belike at this very moment in the deep delusion of empty hope
is making vows to Heaven, and piling the altars with gifts" (Conington).

But this difference between Homer and Virgil is but one phase of a deeper contrast in mind and outlook. For the same detachment from the immediate concern which we feel in Virgil's battle-scenes is to be felt more or less in all his work. He looks before and after, sees this and that, weighs things and ponders them, and when he comes to present either temper or action he is apt to be disconcerted by the multitude of his reflections. He looks at his object, but he looks beyond it, and there is something in his description which tells us he is dreaming. There is apt to be vagueness in his characters and halting in their actions.

The same criticism has to be made of Virgil's verse as contrasted with Homer's. With each his verse answers to the picture in his mind. Homer's verse Matthew Arnold pronounced to be direct, rapid, and simple, and at the same time noble and " in the grand style." Now Virgil's is also noble and in the grand style, but it is not always direct or simple. He perhaps felt this himself, for we are told that he said himself of his verses that he had to lick them into shape as a bear might its cubs. He would write a number of lines, then spend the rest of the day in polishing, reshaping, and reducing them.[1] The verses not unfrequently bear witness to this process, at once in their wealth of suggested meanings and in their bewildering constructions.[1] Virgil can write as simply and directly as any man—

nudus in ignota Palinure iacebis arena [2] (*A.* v. 871),

but, to take one of his most wonderful lines, what does he mean by his

sunt lacrimae rerum et mentem mortalia tangunt (*A.* i. 462)?

What does he not mean? It is quite easy to find *a* meaning for this line, but which is *the* meaning? Or are we to say that all the meanings are not merely to be found in the

---

[1] Suet. *v. Verg.* 22 *Cum Georgica scriberet traditur cotidie meditatos mane plurimos versus dictare solitus, ac per totum diem retractando ad paucissimos redigere, non absurde carmen se ursae more parere dicens et lambendo demum effingere.* So Gellius, *N. A.* xvii. 10.

[2] " Naked on an unknown shore, Palinurus, Thou must lie."

line, but were actually considered by Virgil? Professor Conington, at all events, who understood Virgil better than most commentators, says somewhere that with Virgil it is far less rash to suppose he realized any possible meaning for a line or a passage than that he did not. It is not at all that Virgil is obscure as Propertius and Lucan are in their several ways, for his obscurity is one that does not impress the reader at first. With those poets a little patience and a knowledge of mythology will often reveal the fact that the riddle is only a piece of vacuous pedantry or a half-finished epigram. But Virgil has his own Sibyl's habit—*obscuris vera involvens* [1] (vi. 100)—and his difficulty is due to excess rather than defect of meaning, to his seeing and trying to say several things at once.[2]

II

From Homer we pass to the Attic dramatists. Virgil tells us of his interest in them in a way that has embarrassed critics. *Agamemnonius scaenis agitatus Orestes* [3] (*A.* iv. 471) is a clear reference to Greek drama, and it is coupled with another to Euripides' play, the *Bacchae*. We need not now discuss the appropriateness of this allusion to the actual stage; it is enough that we have Virgil confessing to his tastes in literature, as he did when Silenus borrowed his song from Lucertius.

It is easy to find in Virgil suggestions taken from the Greek dramatists—phrases and thoughts.[4] Indeed, we can go further and rank the dramatists with Homer as his great

[1] "Robing her truth in darkness" (Conington).

[2] It is here that William Morris seems to me to fail as a translator of Virgil. His bent is toward narrative somewhat in the style of Chaucer (though much more mannered), and where Virgil is bewilderingly rich in suggestion, Morris is apt to be swift and simple.

[3] "Agamemnon's Orestes rushing over the stage" (Conington).

[4] For example, striking parallels have been remarked between the *Aeneid* and Sophocles' *Ajax*. Two may suffice—

Dido killed herself with Aeneas' sword, *non hos quaesitum munus in usus* (iv. 647), as Ajax fell upon Hector's sword, *Ajax* 661 τοῦτ' ἐδεξάμην παρ'Ἑκτορος δώρημα δυσμενεστάτου: and the famous lines, *disce puer virtutem ex me verumque laborem, fortunam ex aliis* (xii. 435), point to *Ajax* 550 ὦ παῖ, γένοιο πατρὸς εὐτυχέστερος, τὰ δ' ἄλλ' ὅμοιος.

authorities on that old world, the story of which Virgil made his theme. "It is perfectly clear," writes Dr Henry, "from the story of Polydorus with which Virgil begins, and from the story of Polyphemus with which he closes, the third book of his *Aeneid*—both of them told almost without a single variation in Euripides' own words—that Euripides was seldom absent from before Virgil's eyes while he was engaged in writing this part of his *Aeneid*." The narrative of Troy's fall has clear affinity with the *Troades* and *Hecuba*, in each of which are choral odes of deep feeling, beauty, and simplicity, telling from a captive woman's point of view the awful impressions of that night of surprise and bloodshed. Lastly, the story of Dido owes much in its conception to the *Hippolytus* and the *Medea*.

There is perhaps a closer bond of union between Virgil and Euripides than linked him to any other author.[1] Mr Murray emphasizes the sympathy of Euripides with the dumb and uninterpreted. The poet of the dispossessed, of the old Cilician, of weary ox and energetic bee, of the hard-worked labourer, and of all the obscure people, much-tried and much-bereaved, of whom we never long lose sight in the *Aeneid*—how could he help being drawn to "our Euripides the human"? But of all things the poets most resemble one another in their horror of war.[2] The one saw twenty years of the Peloponnesian war, the other saw the two great civil wars of Rome. Both had to witness bloodshed and brutality, the anguish of the victim, the coarsening of the soldier, ruin to city and country, the decline of ideals and the disappearance of the political virtues. Sensibility was natural to them both, and sore experience developed it; and with eyes opened by his own bitter lesson Virgil read Euripides for himself. In one way and another Euripides had long been a favourite with the Romans. From Ennius to Seneca they translated and imitated his plays. Lucretius took from him his Iphigenia, and found in him his own moral anticipated—

tantum religio potuit suadere malorum.[3]

[1] Euripides was also Milton's favourite among the Greek tragic poets. Cf. Courthope, *Hist. English Poetry*, iii. p. 448.

[2] Cf. W. Nestle, *Euripides der Dichter der Griechischen Aufklärung*, p. 309.

[3] "So much of evil could religion teach."

But Virgil found in him the story of his own life, his own thoughts and sorrows. Very different men they were, the one as markedly Greek as the other was Roman—one the citizen of the keenest-witted of all Greek cities, the other the child of an Italian farm—wide apart in outlook [1] and in philosophy, wider still in theology. But the two stand out together as the great exponents in the Greek and Latin world of sorrow and suffering in general, and the misery of war in particular. There is nothing in classical literature to match the *Troades* outside the *Aeneid*. If Euripides is " the most tragic " [2] of Greek poets, there is more tragedy in the *Aeneid* than in all the rest of the Latin literature we know.

To many readers the story of Dido is the chief interest of the *Aeneid*, and that story presupposes the Greek drama, and above all Euripides. Here, as in a tragedy, everything centres in the conflict of character and the coincident conflict of destiny. Our attention is directed to a man and woman, whose story unfolds itself in a simple and spontaneous way till it ends in betrayal, despair, and death. As we study it, we realize that this double conflict of destiny and character has a universal significance, that it goes beyond the actual history of Aeneas and Dido, beyond the story of Rome and Carthage, and that it represents the abiding riddle of our life. We see the unfolding of a woman's character; we see how what is best in her gives its opportunity to what is worst, her capacity for love leading her astray ; we see the triumph of her love become her ruin. Behind all this we see some dark, divine power forwarding a design, for which we find it hard to see an adequate reason, and yet for which the instinct and passion of a human creature are sacrificed, a life is crushed, and crushed by no strange or unseen agency of Fate, but by the act of one beloved. What does it mean ? What evil has she done ? What evil have the countless sufferers done, out

---

[1] Perhaps as great a contrast as any is that between Virgil's profound recognition of the significance of the State and that practical repudiation of State and statecraft and statesmen which recurs in the plays of Euripides and reminds the modern reader of Tolstoy and in a minor degree of Thoreau.

[2] Aristotle, *Poetics* 13, 6. "A master of emotional effect " is Professor Bywater's paraphrase.

of whose suffering, out of whose inexplicable suffering, has grown the world we know? What has Hecuba done that she should suffer as she does in the *Troades*? What is Phaedra's sin that Aphrodite should make a victim of her? Why is heaven so reckless of human sorrow, most careless of the keenest anguish?

Such questions are felt in Homer, but it is the dramatists who give them their fullest expression in Greek literature. And it is their presence in Virgil that explains or helps to explain the difference between his epic and Homer's. M. Patin, in emphasizing this influence of the Greek dramatists upon the genius of Virgil, adds a caution which we shall do well not to forget—they formed his genius indeed, but it was "with nature's aid." [1]

III

It is a matter of common knowledge that, beside the Greek dramatists, another notable school of Greek poets has had a share in shaping Virgil—the school of Alexandria. [2] They were learned people, too learned for human beings, but in one point they touched life, though remotely. In their pedantic way they were interested in love, and they told tales of passion. In particular, Apollonius of Rhodes had told of the love of Jason and Medea, and Virgil studied him closely. But here, as everywhere, he remained independent, still his own master. He will not be led into the side-paths of passion beloved of other Alexandrines, and he will use, but not follow, Apollonius of Rhodes.

M. de la Ville de Mirmont, in his very thorough if rather

[1] Patin, *Euripide*, vol. i. ch. xii. p. 395 " Virgile ne s'occupe pas laborieuse- ment de s'approprier par l'artifice de l'imitation telle pensée, telle image, tel vers du poëte grec. C'est son esprit qu'il lui dérobe, et en louànt chez lui ces traits d'une tristesse mélancolique que lui inspire le spectacle de la grandeur déchue, de l'esclavage, de l'exil—cette expression dont la vérité pénétrante n'est jamais altérée par la grâce, l'élégance, l'élévation du langage—il est juste de reporter une part de cet éloge aux modèles de la Grèce, qui, *avec la nature*, avaient formé son génie." I have italicized the words *avec la nature*.

[2] Goumy, *Les Latins*, p. 52; " L'avènement de l'alexandrinisme, cette puis- sance nouvelle, faite de deux éléments malsains, le pédantisme et le mysticisme, semble avoir brusquement desséché et tari la veine comique du génie grec."

long book on Virgil and Apollonius,[1] has made an elaborate comparison of these two poets, and his results are very instructive. Virgil has borrowed his episodes, not merely from Homer but also from the *Argonautica*, but he has borrowed with great caution. He rejects as unsuitable to his work, as "too peregrinate," the enormous learning of the Alexandrian poem, its obscure legends, its cosmogony and its remoter gods. He was no Propertius, and he knew that death is the inevitable offspring of pedantry in a work of art. It is a somewhat external judgement to say that he knew that Alexandrine erudition would be unpopular with the untutored Roman, as if he needed a monitor from without and did not know in himself that mere learning touches no spirit, and "makes no heart beat."[2] Yet the feeling of the unlearned Roman might not after all have been a bad criterion. Tertullian in a later day waved aside the philosopher, and made a bold appeal for his faith to the witness of the unsophisticated soul of man to God, the *testimonium animae naturaliter Christianae.*[3] Virgil similarly, we may say, looks past the pedants to the warm hearts, and even if he can please the pedants with his scrupulous care about ritual, he lives in virtue of Dido *exstinctam ferroque extrema secutam* and *ipsius umbra Creusae.*[4]

Sainte-Beuve, in his very suggestive lectures on the first book of the *Aeneid*, deals with another side of Virgil's relations with Apollonius.[5] He makes a text of the episode of Venus substituting Cupid for Ascanius. This is more or less modelled after a passage at the beginning of the third book of the *Argonautica.* There Hera and Athene visit Aphrodite to ask her aid in making Medea fall in love with Jason. They find her "sitting on a rounded chair, fronting the door; and both her white shoulders were clad with her hair, which she was combing with

---

[1] *Ap. de Rhodes et Virgile*, Paris, 1894. See especially pp. 15, 76, 245-7, 518, 732.

[2] Sainte-Beuve, *Étude sur Virgile*, p. 80.

[3] Tertullian, *Apologeticum*, 17, and *de Testimonio Animae.*

[4] "Dead—and the sword had done it sworst"; "the shade of Creusa herself" —passages cited with feeling by St Augustine, *Confessions*, i. 13, 21 and 22 (*Aen.* vi. 457, and ii. 727).   [5] *Étude sur Virgile*, p. 278.

a golden comb, and making ready to plait in long braids."
She rose to meet them and give them seats; sat down
"and with her hands bound up her locks uncombed; and
then with a smile bespoke them with winsome words"
(iii. 44-51). When they ask her to bid Eros inspire Medea
with love for Jason, she professes that she finds him hard
to rule; she has been quite angry with him and wanted
to break his arrows; "for he threatened me in rage that
if I did not keep my hands from him, while his spirit
was still under control, thereafter I should have but myself
to blame" (iii. 95-9). However, she agrees to approach
Eros, and she finds him dicing with Ganymede. She
promises him, if he will do what she asks, a golden ball
made by Adrasteia for Zeus, when Zeus was a child in the
cave of Ida, "and not from the hands of Hephaistos wilt
thou ever have a better toy" (iii. 135).

Now Virgil had read this whole passage, for he knew the
third book of the *Argonautica* well, and he used it, but all
this detail he entirely discarded. Venus in the *Aeneid*
calls Cupid to her aid against Dido, but she offers him no
bribe, for he is not the spoilt child of a sultan, but a young
god with a suggestion of the Roman about him—something
like the young Romans in the story, who attended the
senate's meetings but said never a word outside, as if
"Fortune, among her other bounties" (to quote Polybius),
"granted the Romans the privilege of being men of the
world from their cradles."[1] Yet it is not merely that
Cupid is a shrewd young Roman and Eros a child of the
Ptolemies. There lies behind this divergence something
more important. Virgil held a more serious view of poetry
than Apollonius. It is with him "a high and philosophic
thing tending to express the universal."[2] Nothing is trivial
to him if it is really relevant. He can find the universal,
for instance, in the fading flower a girl has picked—

virgineo demessum pollice florem (*A.* xi. 68);

but Apollonius' adornments, external and irrelevant, are a
betrayal of art. Apollonius introduces these things into his

---

[1] Polybius, iii. 20.   [2] Ar. *Poet.* 9. 3.

poem; he does not find them there. They are pictures, every one of them—and pretty pictures; Aphrodite combing her hair, Aphrodite breaking Eros' arrows, Eros playing with Ganymede at dice, Aphrodite giving Eros a ball—all of these are of the type which Alexandrian painters loved to paint,[1] but they have nothing to do with Jason and Medea. They are introduced to bribe the reader, as pictures are put into a child's reading-book. And they are trivial, in Ovid's style at best, and not very far from Lucian's *Dialogues of the Gods.* Irrelevant and trivial, a surrender of the true ideal of poetry, Alexandria loved them and Virgil refused them. What a poet rejects is as significant as what he chooses.[2]

IV

From the Greek poets, whom Virgil used, Macrobius turns to the Latin, and cites side by side the verses which Virgil borrowed, and the sources from which he took them. The two most important names are Ennius and Lucretius. To these we may add Catullus, and consider more generally how they contributed to Virgil. We may dismiss for the present Macrobius' method and try that of M. Patin.

" There is," he says, " for a literature a moment, slow to come and swift to pass, when the language, polished and made pliant by use, lends itself to the most vivid and most exact expression of conceptions, which have themselves been developed by the long labour of genius. It was thus with Latin literature, when from that branch, long since severed from the old Homeric trunk, which two centuries of culture had accustomed to the sky and soil of Latium, Virgil and Horace came to gather the fruits of poetry, mature at last. All that the epic poetry of Naevius and

---

[1] See Boissier, *Rome et Pompéi*, ch. vi. § 3 ; Mahaffy, *Greek Life and Thought*, p. 272.

[2] Cf. Wordsworth, Preface to *Lyrical Ballads*, 1800, " It is not, then, to be supposed that any one who holds that sublime notion of Poetry which I have attempted to convey, will break in upon the sanctity and truth of his pictures by transitory and accidental ornaments, and endeavour to excite admiration of himself by arts, the necessity of which must manifestly depend upon the assumed meanness of his subject." There can hardly be a better introduction to the study of poetry—or poetics—than to steep one's mind in this Preface.

of Ennius, the tragedy of Pacuvius and Attius, the comedy
of Plautus and Terence, the satire of Lucilius, the efforts
of poets of every class, had accumulated in the poetic
treasury of the Romans—well-defined terms, subtle shades
of meaning, natural analogies, graceful turns of expression,
happy phrasing, striking images, harmonious combinations
of words, that precision of form, that art in composition,
upon which the easy inspiration of Lucretius lighted by
happy chance, and which the skill and industry of Catullus
sought and found—all this, such was the fortune of their
birth, fell to Virgil and Horace to inherit, and entered
into the formation of their genius, very much as, at the
same time, the various powers of the republican constitution
gathered together into one single hand to form the absolute
authority of their imperial protector." [1]

This is admirably said. Two centuries had been spent
in the acquisition of ease, precision, and direction, and
Virgil gathered the fruits. It is immaterial how many lines
Virgil copied from Ennius, for Ennius' contribution to
him is not to be reckoned in that way. Ennius was the
first Roman who attacked Homer in earnest, who really
tried " to wrench his club from Hercules." [2] A man of action,
he carried his vigour into his poetry ; but the kingdom of
heaven is not always to be taken by force. Virgil himself
might have been glad to be the author of the line

> moribus antiquis stat res Romana virisque, [3]

but Ennius did not always write so well. Yet the spirit of the
line seems to pervade all he does—a certain strong Roman
quality, which he did not find in his Greek originals, which
sometimes fitted ill and uncomfortably with what he did
find there, but which is really, as Patin happily calls it,
a "prophecy of Virgil." [4] And to this we must add his
deliberate choice of his country as his theme.

There is a foolish story that Virgil, surprised with a copy

---

[1] Patin, *La Poésie latine*, i. p. 222.
[2] The phrase is Virgil's ; Suet. *v. Verg.* 46.
[3] Ennius, *Annales* xv. (Müller). "On ancient ways Rome's common weal
rests and on men."
[4] Patin, *La Poésie latine*, i. p. 164.

of Ennius in his hand, said he was looking for jewels in the dunghill of Ennius.[1] But, if we may judge Virgil by his *Aeneid*, he was more likely to class Ennius among the

> pii vates et Phoebo digna locuti [2] (*A*. vi. 662).

The poet who looked with pleasure on rustic songs in the Saturnian metre, *versibus incomptis* (*G*. ii. 386), must have recognized a real precursor of himself in this re-incarnated Homer, who thought the thoughts and told the deeds of Rome.

But it is when we reach his own century that we find the Latin poet to whom Virgil owes most. From Gellius onward critics have remarked his indebtedness to Lucretius, though Virgil, one may say, did not leave the critics to discover it, but announced the fact himself as plainly as the nature of his own subjects allowed. For instance, to take the first case, the sixth *Eclogue* pays homage to Lucretius. Silenus,

> Forehead and brow with the juice of a blood-red mulberry dyed (*E*. vi. 22, Bowen),

may seem remote enough from the austere poet of the *De Rerum Natura*, but he has hardly time to begin his song before it is clear where he learnt it. The rhythm of *namque canebat uti* is almost as explicit as the terminology of *magnum per inane coacta semina*, and together they bar the claim of Apollonius to be the original here, quite apart from the fact that his Orpheus gives the Argonauts not Epicurean but (properly enough) Orphic doctrine, with traces of Empedoclean teaching.[3]

The bard Iopas, who sings at Dido's feast as Demo-

---

[1] It is in the life attributed to Donatus.

[2] "Poets whose hearts were clean, and their songs worthy Phoebus' ear" (Conington).

[3] *Argon*. i. 496 f.—

> 'Ὡς γαῖα καὶ οὐρανὸς ἠδὲ θάλασσα,
> τὸ πρὶν ἐπ' ἀλλήλοισι μιῇ συναρηρότα μορφῇ,
> νείκεος ἐξ ὀλοοῖο διέκριθεν ἀμφὶς ἕκαστα.

See Dieterich, *Nekyia*, p. 101.

docus did at Alcinous', is another witness to Lucretius' power.

Hic canit errantem lunam solisque labores
unde hominum genus et pecudes, unde imber et ignes[1]
 (*A.* i. 742).

But the most famous of all the passages is that in the second *Georgic*, where Virgil speaks of the happiness of him who understands the principles underlying all nature, and by this knowledge has risen above all fears, above inexorable fate and the noise of greedy Acheron—

Felix qui potuit rerum cognoscere causas,
atque metus omnes et inexorabile fatum
subiecit pedibus strepitumque Acherontis avari (*G.* ii. 490).

This passage comes after the expression of Virgil's desire to be the poet of science (*G.* ii. 475-82); it is full of Lucretian phrases,[2] and it represents Lucretius' point of view.

Like Catullus,[3] Virgil read Lucretius with the close care of admiration and affection. His early longing for philosophy drew him to this great exponent of all nature. Virgil loved the country, and here was a man who looked on all the sights of field and shore with the eyes of genius, and gave a new meaning and a deeper value to all by subordinating all to great underlying principles—*causae rerum.*

Lucretius had also the simplicity of genius. If he is at times hard to understand, it is because his matter is itself difficult, sometimes too difficult for his verse or any verse. No poet could be more honest in his confession that he is seeking for charm of language, but what makes this quest unique is its entire subordination to the main purpose in hand.[4] No Roman poet is more absolutely true in his language, just as

---

[1] Sings of the moons that wander, of suns eclipsed and in pain,
Whence the beginning of man and of beast, of the fire and the rain.
(Bowen.)

[2] See Munro on Lucr. i. 78, 253; iii. 449. Cf. the beginning of the *Ciris*, which we are now told to attribute to Gallus. Cf. Skutsch *Aus Vergils Frühzeit*, and the delightful lecture of Professor Mackail on the Circle of Virgil, *Lectures on Poetry* (1911).

[3] See Munro on Lucr. iii. 57.

[4] Lucr. i. 143-5.

none is more single in his loyalty to truth in thought. He has nothing to say explicitly of his country and his people, but not Virgil himself is more profoundly Roman in solidity and integrity of thought and utterance. His verse is Latin in word, beat, movement, and there is much, for example, in Munro's suggestion that his avoidance of spondaic endings in his sixth book (though following the tradition of Ennius he had used them in the other five) is a sort of scornful criticism of the modish writing of poets around him, with whom the Alexandrine σπονδειάζων was the latest prettiness.[1] It was not Roman to be pretty. His master was Ennius, and he learnt of him a grander, a simpler, and a more severe speech. He is not so careful as Virgil to avoid monotony and roughness, but we shall not be far wrong in attributing to him some share in the creation of the Virgilian hexameter. If Catullus and his school gave it what M. Patin calls its precision, Lucretius contributed simplicity and dignity. Take as an example of "symphony austere" these lines—

> In caeloque deum sedes et templa locarunt,
> per caelum volvi quia nox et luna videtur,
> luna dies et nox et noctis signa severa
> noctivagaeque faces caeli flammaeque volantes,
> nubila sol imbres nix venti fulmina grando
> et rapidi fremitus et murmura magna minarum [2]
>
> (v. 1188-93).

Let these lines be tried by any test. The thought would be as sound in prose; the language is near enough to that used by men to suit Wordsworth's canon—long before Wordsworth framed that canon Bentley had magnificently quoted the line

> luna dies et nox et noctis signa severa

[1] Munro, Lucr. vol. ii. p. 14. Cf. Cicero, ad Att. vii. 2. 1 Ita belle nobis flavit ab Epiro lenissimus Onchesmites. Hunc σπονδειάζοντα si cui voles τῶν νεωτέρων pro tuo vendita; and Catullus, lxiv. 78-80, the three consecutive lines ending innuptarum, Minotauro, vexarentur.

[2] "And they placed in heaven the abodes and realms of the gods, because night and moon are seen to roll through heaven, moon day and night and night's austere constellations and night-wandering meteors of the sky and flying bodies of flame, clouds sun rains snow winds lightnings hail and rapid rumblings and loud threatful thunderclaps" (Munro).

as an example of the power of " common words " [1]—the sense is direct, the movement is rapid, and the passage has the note of grandeur.

Virgil might respond to the influence of Lucretius as he did to that of other poets, but he was no man's disciple. As he grew older he became dissatisfied with Lucretius' philosophy, and tried to reconcile it somehow with other aspects of truth, which he had himself realized. It became quite clear that this was not to be done, and Lucretius' Epicureanism had more and more to be modified. Virgil did not live to achieve the reconciliation which he felt to be necessary; and we find in him a man distracted with the spiritual necessity of holding opinions, which clearly conflict, but which are yet valid for him in virtue of undoubted elements of truth.

Οὔτοι συνέχθειν ἀλλὰ συμφιλεῖν ἔφυν [2]

might be a fair summary of his attitude to religious and philosophical thought. The temper is an entirely honest one; but while it is a necessary stage in development, it hardly seems a final or a happy position. The prolongation of this period of suspense developed in Virgil a certain indistinct habit of thought. Dissatisfied with obvious antitheses as superficial, but unable to penetrate them and discover some fundamental unity underlying them, he seems at times to confuse rather than to reconcile, and eventually everything he does is apt to be affected by the habit. The same unhealed division of mind shows itself in his verse, which rarely keeps for long the clear and unclouded directness of Lucretius. It reflects the poet himself, which is after all what a poet's verse should do; and it has its own grandeur, which is not that of Lucretius, but springs naturally from the poet's struggle, unsuccessful as it may be, to grasp the whole of things. It represents the last achievement of Roman poetry, for after Virgil no Roman poet rose to such heights of mind. His

---

[1] See Jebb, *Bentley*, p. 69.
[2] "'Tis not my nature to join in hating, but in loving." Sophocles' *Antigone* 523 (Jebb).

successors thought of little but style, and had no philosophy. Thus the last utterance of Roman poetry has the strong sad tone of Virgil's mind, that tone which led Tennyson to address the poet as

> Thou majestic in thy sadness at the doubtful doom of human kind.[1]

Lastly we come to Catullus. Virgil's interest in Catullus is proved by one of the most extraordinary examples of his habit of borrowing. In the world below Aeneas meets Dido's shade and addresses her—

> Invitus, regina, tuo de litore cessi[2] (*A.* vi. 460).

It is a bold, clear, good statement, but it suggests the most disconcerting of all possible parallels. For it is a reminiscence of the translation which Catullus made of Callimachus' *Coma Berenices*, where the severed lock, though already a constellation, professes to regret its departure from the queen's head—

> Invita, O regina, tuo de vertice cessi[3] (Catullus, lxvi. 39).

This is the very last thing of which we should wish to be reminded in the situation. Yet, though happily an extreme case, it is a typical instance of the habit, which Virgil shared with his contemporaries, of transferring good lines from the pages of others to his own.[4]

But after all it is quite accidental that Virgil finds in Catullus a line so readily to be converted to his own

---

[1] It has been suggested that too much emphasis has been laid on Virgil's sadness. The criticism is just, if it is not remembered that there are other elements in the poet's thought.

[2] "Against my will, O queen, I left thy shore."

[3] "Against my will, O queen, I left thy head."

[4] The reader will remember the episode of Johnson and Boswell leaving Inch Keith, when Johnson called for "a classical compliment to the island." "I happened luckily, in allusion to the beautiful Queen Mary, whose name is upon the fort, to think of what Virgil makes Aeneas say, on having left the country of his charming Dido.

'Invitus, regina, tuo de litore cessi.'

'Very well hit off!' said he" (*Tour to the Hebrides*, Aug. 18). Considering the origin of the line, one is tempted to say it is more in keeping here than in the sixth *Aeneid.*

purposes. His real debt to Catullus is profounder. I cannot do better here than to quote M. Patin once more.

"Catullus does not improvise [as Lucilius did]; on the contrary, he weighs words, he even counts them; he chooses, arranges, and plans; he has already in his composition and in his style those definite and precise forms, that fine and delicate touch, that tempered strength, which moderates itself, which of set purpose refrains, which cloaks itself under the graces of urbanity—

> urbani parcentis viribus atque
> extenuantis eas consulto—

in fact all those characteristics which are supposed to distinguish the poets of the following age." [1]

In other words, just as Tennyson affected the composition of English poetry, even apart from clear imitators of himself, by compelling a more self-conscious and more studied style, so Catullus abolished the school of Ennius—yes, and Lucretius too, before he had time to found a school, —and compelled all later poets to reflect more upon style and all its niceties and minutiae than had ever been the custom in Rome before. None of these—we may disregard for the moment those who really did not succeed in opening their mouths—meditated upon his style as Virgil did. Propertius, no doubt, thought of nothing very much apart from style, yet he cannot be said to have achieved any of Matthew Arnold's "notes" of the great poet. Virgil, however, spoke out and had something to say, and yet could choose, refine and concentrate his diction with more patience and more power than any poet of them all. And in this we may find the influence of Catullus. Yet his debt to Lucretius is greater, for the whole history of his mind is affected by his attitude toward Lucretius' philosophy.

Virgil, as we have seen, conformed to the contemporary practice in Rome and borrowed largely from his Greek and Latin predecessors, and often enough he transferred his material in a sufficiently external way. But yet, when

---

[1] Patin, *La Poésie latine*, i. p. 59; the quotation is from Horace, *Sat.* i. 10. 13.

every deduction is made for this, and when we have considered the real influence which his great precursors had upon his mind and upon his outlook on life, we realize the substantial truth of Goethe's saying that " To make an epoch in the world two conditions are notoriously essential—a good head and a great inheritance."[1] Supplement these with another condition, on which Goethe elsewhere lays great emphasis, and Virgil's endowment for his poetry is fairly stated. "We cannot deny," said Goethe of a contemporary poet, "that he has many brilliant qualities, but he is wanting in—*love*."[2]

[1] *Conversations with Eckermann*, May 2, 1824.
[2] Ibid. Dec. 25, 1825. He is generally supposed to have meant Heine. Cf. Arnold in his poem *Heine's Grave*.

CHAPTER III

LITERATURE—2. CONTEMPORARIES

> Not from a vain or shallow thought
> His awful Jove young Phidias brought ;
> Never from lips of cunning fell
> The thrilling Delphic oracle ;
> Out from the heart of nature rolled
> The burdens of the Bible old ;
> The litanies of nations came,
> Like the volcano's tongue of flame,
> Up from the burning core below—
> The canticles of love and woe.—EMERSON, *The Problem.*

ONE of the things that mark Virgil as different from the other poets of his day is the long and increasingly vigorous life of his poetic genius. Fate snuffed out some of his contemporaries in comparatively early manhood, but not, one thinks, before they had given mankind all, or nearly all, the light they had to give. Others survived their genius, and either became silent altogether or took refuge in imitating themselves. Horace avowed that poetry had been for him an affair of youth and poverty ; that, now he was older and more well-to-do, he did not care to write ; he preferred reading Homer and making excursions into popular philosophy ; somebody else, who, like the soldier of Lucullus, had "lost his purse," might write now.[1] It may have been that he felt, as he grew to have a deeper appreciation of the meaning and purpose of poetry, that he was not entirely fit for the work—though after all it is hard to see why a genuine Epicurean should ever wish to write poetry at all. But Virgil, on the other hand, shows a steady growth in insight and in power of expression. Poetry was not with him either an amusement or a trade. He wrote

[1] Horace, *Epp.* ii. 2. 26-40, and following (cf. *Epp.* i. 2. 1). Dean Wickham finds here " some irony and exaggeration, no doubt, but some substantial truth " (*Horace for English Readers*).

neither for popularity nor advancement, neither to please
others nor to amuse himself. Poetry was to him something
like the "burden" of a Hebrew prophet, a necessity. Thought
and feeling sought and compelled expression, not any expression, but their "inevitable" expression. This necessity
for the perfect utterance of his nature kept him beyond the
reach of the dangers of lesser artists. Indolence could
not rob the world of what was due to it from him, nor
impatience wring it from him before it was mature. In
him Art is "imitating Nature"; it has something of the
same inexhaustible vitality, the same necessity for self-
expression; it follows a somewhat similar method of evolution, relentlessly sacrificing the unfit to the fit, the fit to
the fittest, suffering nothing to go forth that has not life
in itself and that cannot transmit this life—in a word his
art is essentially quickening.[1]

Accordingly, as he began to feel himself nearer the com-
pletion of the *Georgics*, his mind ranged forward to his
next work. What was it to be? The limits, within which
he would seek a theme were narrower than we might
suppose, for it was the tradition so far of Latin poetry to
confine itself within the frontiers of Greek literature. The
early development of native Italian literature had been
slow—"the Romans had plenty of other things to do," says
M. Patin, "to make their constitution, to defend themselves,
to conquer the world. It was when they had achieved this
task, when they had subdued Italy, crushed Carthage, taken
possession of Greece, that they found poetry among their
spoils, so to say, along with the statues which Mummius
with such particular care, with such insensibility, gave
orders to pack. Transported, transplanted to Rome, poetry
flourished there under the influence of a luxury and a
leisure both quite new for the Romans. . . . Rome had
made a Roman province of Greece; by a sort of compensa-
tion, quite unexpected, Roman letters, Roman poetry became
provinces of the Greek imagination."[2]   Latin literature, one

---

[1] I am glad here to quote Macrobius (*Sat.* v. 1. 20): *Ignoscite nec nimium me
vocetis qui naturae rerum Vergilium comparavi.*

[2] *Études sur la Poésie latine*, i. p. 10.

might almost say, ceases to develop along its own lines. It is thoroughly Hellenized. At first it is rather that Greek ideas reappear in Latin phrase; and the progress of Latin literature is from handling these ideas awkwardly to handling them with ease. Of course this is not entirely true, for the greater minds were still Italian, and the literature they produced was, if written after Greek models, Italian in spirit. The Roman thought the thing out for himself, though he did it with more ease when he had a Greek at his elbow.

Bellipotentes sunt magi' quam sapientipotentes,

as Ennius said of the house of Aeacus.[1]

At first the Roman tried mere translation, and no doubt found some satisfaction in the task. Homer was hammered manfully and conscientiously into Latin hexameters.

Crudum manduces Priamum Priamique pisinnos

is a perfect translation of

Ὠμὸν βεβρώθοις Πρίαμον Πριάμοιό τε παῖδας,

except that, as is suggested by the scholiast who saved it from oblivion, it omits the feeling.[2] From Menander and Euripides the Roman poets turned to the Alexandrines, and the *cantores Euphorionis*[3] were the prevailing school in the latter days of the republic. Nothing was too formidable or portentous to find a translator. Even so great a poet as Catullus could hope to add to his fame by translating from Callimachus.

But, of course, the stronger writers as a rule would not translate or even be content with adaptation. It was rather that, after the careful study of the mind, the manner, and the phrase of a Greek author, they wrote something original and Latin, not without some very clear marks of its

---

[1] *ap.* Cic. *de Div.* ii. 56. 116. "Mighty in war are they rather than mighty in wisdom."

[2] *Labeo transtulit Iliada et Odysseam, verbum ex verbo, ridicule satis, quod verba potius quam sensum secutus sit. Eius est ille versus: crudum,* &c. Schol. ad Pers. i. 4. "Eat Priam raw and Priam's children."

[3] Cicero, *Tusc.* iii. 19. 45. "Singers of Euphorion" (Latin imitators of the poetry of Euphorion of Chalcis).

paternity. *Sit suo similis patri*[1] might almost be a canon of this literature. Yet the Latin poetry of the age of Julius, so much of it as survives, is in the main independent and individual, the natural expression of the Latin mind, if it be allowed that the Latin mind is thoroughly steeped in Greek literature and has, in most cases, taken at least suggestion, if not inspiration, from some Greek model. Thus Virgil's *Eclogues* are classed as imitations, in the first instance, of Theocritus, though they are, as we have seen, a great deal more. If his Italian scenery be, as critics say, confused with Sicilian and even with Arcadian, it is the Italian which leaves upon us the strongest impression. Poem by poem they are less Theocritean and more Roman and Italian. The Greek form fits the Latin spirit somewhat oddly to modern thinking, but it pleased the general Roman taste, even the cultured Roman taste. The *Georgics*, in like manner, owe suggestion to Hesiod—so Virgil says—

Ascraeumque cano Romana per oppida carmen[2] (*G.* ii. 176),

to Nicander and Aratus too; yet after all they owe but little to these Greek models, who have now little or no interest but for the fact that Virgil used them.

And now that the *Georgics* were accomplished, where was he to turn? to which of the Greeks? So far he had been indebted chiefly to Alexandria, perhaps because he was as yet more familiar with Alexandrine than with classical literature. There were, however, signs that he was by no means under the yoke of Alexandria. There is a sense of nationality about his writing, a directness of appeal to his own Italian people at large, and a genial frankness of utterance—foreign to the poets of the Museum and their Latin imitators, and promising something of even wider and deeper human interest than he had yet achieved. What would he do?

Setting aside didactic verse, we find that the enormous output of contemporary poetry may be roughly classified as dealing with mythology, the antiquities of Rome, history,

---

[1] "Let him be like his father."

[2] "The song of Ascra I sing through the towns of Rome."

personal experience, and national glory. Mythology came straight from Alexandria, entirely foreign, but fascinating and intimately connected with painting. The last days of the republic are marked by an astonishing outburst of anti-quarianism. History from Naevius and Ennius onward had been a favourite field for Roman poets. Catullus with his poems to Lesbia and his lampoons, Cicero with his auto-biographical epics, and Gallus, Propertius, Tibullus, and their school of erotic poetry, bear witness to the absorbing interest felt by the poets, if not always by their readers, in their own personal history. As for national consciousness, if Ennius had written histories in metre—

Olli respondit rex Albai Longai,[1]—

he had struck a nobler note in such utterances as his

Unus homo nobis cunctando restituit rem,[2]

or his

Moribus antiquis stat res Romana virisque.[3]

Virgil is, less than any of his contemporaries, an autobio-graphical poet.[4] Pressure was to be put upon him to deviate into a poetry of a personal character, though he was not much interested in it. But in the other four spheres of poetic activity mentioned he was keenly interested. He had given study and enthusiasm to them all, yet he was brought into bondage by none of them. It is instructive to inquire what his contemporaries were doing in these directions, and from the results of their attempts to deduce why Virgil would not go with them.

I

Mythology was one of the contributions of Alexandria to poetry, particularly mythology with an erotic tinge, but

---

[1] Müller, *Ennius Ann.* i. 66. "To him replied the King of Alba Longa."
[2] "One man by delaying gave us back the State."
[3] "On ancient ways rests Rome's common weal and on men."
[4] Four lines suffice him, lines full of character and charm—
>   *Illo Vergilium me tempore dulcis alebat*
>   *Parthenope studiis florentem ignobilis oti,*
>   *Carmina qui lusi pastorum audaxque iuventa*
>   *Tityre te patulae cecini sub tegmine fagi* (*G.* iv. 563-6).

scarcely, even on its erotic side, did it touch life. Still, mythological poetry received a warm welcome at Rome, and epics and elegies were written with the most Alexandrian tone and profusion. Propertius boasted to be the Roman Callimachus,[1] and wrote his elegies with unction, as we shall see, but the epics were too much even for his taste. Ponticus had written a *Thebaid*, which, Propertius protests "on his hopes of happiness," puts him next to Homer and even made Homer's primacy doubtful—*if only the fates would be kind*.[2] Yet he goes on to say that if Ponticus is ever in love he will be sorry he ever touched Thebes, and he will recognise Propertius' supremacy—

> tunc ego Romanis praeferar ingeniis.

In other words, Ponticus' *Thebaid*, like all the other *Memnonids* and *Thebaids* and *Argonautica*, might be never so meritorious, but it was dull—it had no vestige of human interest. Propertius did not seem to realize that one might have too much mythology even in an elegy.

Let us take an example of mythology in an elegy, a short poem which he wrote to Postumus, who goes eastward to fight the Parthians and leaves his wife Galla behind. Postumus will quaff the Araxes, and Galla will pine for good news. Postumus is happy in having a chaste wife —he is like another Ulysses with a faithful Penelope. At this point comes a sort of index to the *Odyssey*, a catalogue of Ulysses' adventures in twelve lines, so compact and complete that to count them on one's fingers is irresistible ;[3]

> Castra decem annorum et Ciconum manus, Ismara capta,
>   exustaeque tuae mox, Polypheme, genae,
> et Circae fraudes, lotosque herbaeque tenaces,
>   Scyllaque et alternas scissa Charybdis aquas,
> Lampeties Ithacis veribus mugisse iuvencos :

---

[1] iv. 9. 43 *inter Callimachi sat erit placuisse libellos* ; and v. 1. 64 *Umbria Romani patria Callimachi.* Yet his native town has forgotten him for Saint Francis.

[2] i. 7. 4 *Sint modo fata tuis mollia carminibus.*

[3] I hope no reader will complain, if I refuse to translate these foolish lines.

(This is a real masterpiece—how many of his readers will know who was Lampetie? The poet hastens to explain.)

> paverat hos Phoebo filia Lampetie:

(Yes, of course, if the reader had read his *Odyssey* with real care, he would not have needed this note in the text to tell him who Lampetie was. See the *Odyssey*, says Propertius, book xii. line 132—omitting to notice, however, that Homer does not identify Phoebus with Lampetie's father, the sun.)

> et thalamum Aeaeae flentis fugisse puellae

(This is an easy riddle—Circe, of course.)

> totque hiemis noctes totque natasse dies,
> nigrantesque domos animarum intrasse silentum,
> Sirenum surdo remige adisse lacus,

(We have left Homer's order of events here, but notice the fine allusiveness of *surdo remige*.)

> et veteres arcus leto renovasse procorum,
> errorisque sui sic statuisse modum.

"Oh! yes!" the poet remembers with a start, "Penelope, of course—Penelope's special fame is eclipsed by Galla."[1]

This is an easy example, for all the references are to a well-known book, but the genuine Alexandrine instinct was to make them to a book unknown if possible, as if the best poetry was that which could carry the largest and most irrelevant weight of dead matter—*Professorenpoesie*, in fact.[2] Virgil, however, was a poet interpreting life to the living, and he realized the wisdom of leaving the dead to bury their dead in cyclopaedias or poems as they preferred.

But there was another side to the mythology: another contemporary of Virgil's made his reputation by it. Ovid, like Propertius, was learned in all the wisdom of the Egyptians, but he did not take it seriously.[3] Gods and heroes lose in his hands that antique air which made them

---

[1] Propertius, iv. 11. 25-36.
[2] The word is taken from Wilamowitz-Moellendorff.
[3] See Boissier, *Rome et Pompéi*, ch. vi. § 4, p. 375 (Fr.); p. 405 (Engl. tr.).

venerable. He makes them into men, and men exactly like those among whom he lived. The heroines who write love-letters of such length and cleverness are really the contemporaries of Corinna, and have been in good society and learnt the etiquette of gallantry in the *Ars Amoris*. Ovid adds to his Alexandrian learning an air of humour which gives it quite a new complexion. In fact, as M. Boissier brings out, the mythology is no more to him than to the painters of Pompeii. Helbig has reckoned that, of nearly 2000 pictures found there, 1400 deal with subjects from the Greek mythology. Most of these subjects are love-stories— Danae, Io, Leda, Europa, Daphne, Aphrodite and Ares, coming over and over again—and they are not treated in any spirit of reverence or religion at all, rather with an air of mere sentimentalism, and occasionally of vulgarity. Jewelled heroines, old women selling little Cupids to young girls, Cupids dancing, gathering grapes, guiding teams of lions, bringing letters to Polyphemus from Galatea —it is to this that the mythology has come. Even before Virgil's day in so serious a poem as Catullus' *Ariadne*— a theme, by the way, treated in more than thirty Pompeian pictures—we have the pretty and the pictorial asserting itself—

> Non flavo retinens subtilem vertice mitram,
> non contecta levi velatum pectus amictu,
> non tereti strophio lactentis vincta papillas,
> omnia quae toto delapsa e corpore passim
> ipsius ante pedes fluctus salis alludebant [1] (lxiv. 63)

> Tum tremuli salis adversas procurrere in undas,
> mollia nudatae tollentem tegmina surae [2] (lxiv. 128).

[1] " Down dropp'd the fillet from her golden hair,
  Dropp'd the light vest that veil'd her bosom fair.
  The filmy cincture dropp'd, that strove to bind
  Her orbèd breasts, which would not be confined;
  And, as they fell around her feet of snow,
  The salt waves caught and flung them to and fro " (Sir Theodore Martin).
[2] " Anon she rush'd into the plashing sea,
  Her fair soft limbs unbaring to the knee." (Sir Theodore Martin).

Mythology, then, involved its votary in pedantry, or flippancy, or mere prettiness.

But Virgil had already made his experiments in Alexandrinism. "The frigid mythology," says Mr Myers, "with which the first *Georgic* opens is absolutely bad. It is bad as Callimachus is bad, and as every other imitation of Callimachus is bad too." Is Tethys trying to buy Augustus as a son-in-law with a dowry of all her waters? or does Augustus propose to be a new star [1] where a space is opening between Erigone and the Claws?—the Scorpion is drawing in his arms already. He surely will not prefer to be king of Tartarus in spite of Greek accounts of Elysium. What does all this mean? Does it mean anything? What would Lucretius say to it, coming from a pupil of his own? Virgil did not do it again. The meaning of the short clause at the opening of the second *Georgic* has been debated.

Non hic te carmine ficto,
atque per ambages et longa exorsa tenebo [2] (*G.* ii. 45-6)

Whom is he addressing? his reader? Does he mean that at some future day he will weave some romantic or mythical strain,—something long, involved, and Alexandrine,—as Conington half thinks the words (especially *hic*) may imply, or is it an apology for the unreality of the flattering exordium of the first book? [3]

At all events, when he reaches his third *Georgic*, he begins with a renunciation of Alexandria and its mythological themes which is clear enough. The episode of Aristaeus and Orpheus, at the end of the fourth, is indeed in the manner of that school, but it was not part of Virgil's original design, and in any case the story of the half-regained Eurydice redeems its setting. But the resolution of the poet not to go with any Callimachus, Cyrenian or Umbrian,

---

[1] The *reductio ad absurdum* of this is Claudian's account of how Theodosius, after a last address to his sons, shot up into heaven and left a path of light on the clouds (iii. *Cons. Hon.* 162-74)—a strange pagan end for a Christian emperor.

[2] "I will not detain thee here with mythic strains, or circuitous detail, or lengthy preambles" (Conington).

[3] Myers, *Essays Classical*, pp. 153-4.

is significant for the vigour with which he expresses it, and with which he adheres to it. "All the themes," he says, "which once could have laid the spell of poesy on idle minds (*vacuas mentes*, a very significant phrase), are, all of them, hackneyed now. Who knows not Eurystheus, hardest of masters, or the altars of Busiris, whom never tongue praised? Who has not told the tale of the lost boy Hylas, of Latona and her Delos, of Hippodamia and Pelops of the ivory shoulder, Pelops the driver of horses?" (*G.* iii. 3). Why does the poet reject such themes? Partly because the world had had far too many *Herakleids* and *Pelopids* and so forth already; and partly, and chiefly, because Virgil felt that these were really idle and empty themes; they did not touch life and they were irrelevant to his people.[1] Virgil's rejection of mythology and Ovid's application of it, coming as they did in the same generation, explain one another amply.

II

But if Virgil was right in refusing Greek mythology, Latin and Roman antiquities, it might be urged, stood on another footing. There was a general awakening of interest in these matters at the time.[2] Varro in the course of his long life set in order some forty-one books of *Antiquities*, according to St Augustine, twenty-five of which he gave to human subjects (six to men, six to places, six to chronology, and six to events (*rebus*), and one for an introduction), and sixteen to the gods. "Who," Augustine asks, " ever sought out these matters with more care than Marcus Varro? Who showed more learning in their discovery? Who pondered them with more attention, or grouped them with more acuteness, or wrote of them with more diligence or at greater length? Though he has not so agreeable a style, yet he is so full of information and ideas (*sententiis*), that in all those studies, which we call secular but they call liberal, he has as

---

[1] Cf. Patin, *La Poésie latine*, i. 209 : "Ces vieux sujets, sans rapport aucun avec les préoccupations de la pensée romaine."

[2] Norden, *Neue Jahrbücher für kl. Altertum*, 1901, has an interesting article on this movement, which he aptly calls Romanticism.

much instruction for the student of such matters as Cicero has delight for the student of words."[1]   But Varro was not alone in this.   Dionysius of Halicarnassus wrote his twenty books of *Roman Antiquities* in the reign of Augustus, and Livy his first decade dealing with the Roman kings and the early wars of the Republic.

The poets, too, began to look in this direction for inspiration. Propertius, after exhausting the poetic value of Cynthia, turned to Rome and her antiquities—

Sacra diesque canam, et cognomina prisca locorum [2] (v. 1. 69),

and he wrote one or two elegies dealing with the famous spots of the city, but he soon gave it up.   He was too clever for his matter.

Fictilibus crevere deis haec aurea templa [3] (v. 1. 5)

is a clever saying, but it hardly promises well for a really sympathetic treatment of the old days.   But there is a couplet in the poem which excels it and leaves no more to be said—

Optima nutricum nostris lupa Martia rebus,
qualia creverunt moenia lacte tuo [4] (v. 1. 55).

The task which Propertius gave up was undertaken by Ovid, who wrote twelve books of *Fasti*, dealing with old Roman customs and legends in the order of the calendar. Six alone have reached us, of which Mr Mackail remarks that "it cannot be said that Latin poetry would be much

---

[1] Augustine, *de Civitate Dei*, vi. 2 and 3.   In the chapters that follow the antiquary furnishes the saint with ammunition to be used against paganism.   He had a bad name already with pious pagans of the day, cf. Servius, *ad Aen*. xi. 787 *Varro ubique expugnator religionis*.   Varro was born in 116 and died in 28 B.C.   On Varro see Warde Fowler, *Social Life at Rome* (1908) pp. 335, 336 ; Varro, holding the Stoic doctrine of the *animus mundi*, co-ordinates it with the Græco-Roman religion of the State in his day—the chief gods represent the *partes mundi*, while the δαίμονες are used to rescue the Italian *lares, genii*, etc.

[2] " Of sacred rites and days will I sing, and of ancient names of places."

[3] " For gods of clay these golden temples rose."

[4] " Best of nurses for our State, O Wolf of Mars, what walls have grown from thy milk ! "

poorer" if they had been suppressed with the other six. The author of the *Heroidum Epistulae* was not of the genuine antiquary type, and however laboriously he might "dig the sacred usages out of the ancient annals,"[1] he did not really care for them. He wrote from his heart only when he was engaged on themes nearer himself and his day; let others play with antiquity, he preferred, he says, to be modern; his own age suited him exactly—

Prisca iuvent alios, ego me nunc denique natum
gratulor; haec aetas moribus apta meis (*A. A.* 3. 121).

Virgil too had felt the attraction of antiquity. Indeed at an earlier period of his life he had begun an epic dealing with the kings of Rome or of Alba, but he abandoned it. Apollo, he says, touched his ear and said that a shepherd's business was to feed sheep—

Cum canerem reges et proelia, Cynthius aurem
vellit et admonuit: pastorem, Tityre, pinguis
pascere oportet ovis, deductum dicere carmen[2] (*E.* vi. 3).

In plainer language, he did not like the subject. *Cum res Romanas incohasset, offensus materia ad Bucolica transiit,*[3] says Suetonius in his life of Virgil (§ 19). He probably felt himself unripe as yet for a great undertaking. But now he realized that the tales of Alba were after all as unimportant and as remote as the war of the Seven against Thebes. He wanted a larger theme, a subject of ecumenical significance, something involving a wider range of human

---

[1] *Sacra recognosces annalibus eruta priscis,* F. i. 7. "I have now," wrote Lord Macaulay, at the end of his Ovid, "gone through the whole of Ovid's works, and heartily tired I am of him and them. Yet he is a wonderfully clever man. But he has two insupportable faults. The one is that he will always be clever; and the other that he never knows when to have done. He is rather a rhetoric· n than a poet. There is little feeling in his poems. . . . He seems to have been a very good fellow . . . a flatterer and a coward; but kind and generous."

[2] "When I was venturing to sing of Kings and battles, the Cynthian god touched my ear, and appealed to my memory. 'It is a shepherd's part, Tityrus, that the sheep that he feeds should be fat, and the songs that he sings thin'" (Conington).

[3] "After beginning the history of Rome. he was displeased with his subject and turned to Bucolics."

sympathies, touching mankind at more points than a chronicle of village forays could possibly do. And he was right. In spite of the ease of Livy's style the reader wearies of the little wars and the long speeches in which the mythical chieftains of his first book indulge. So Virgil left the *Fasti* to Ovid, as he had left him the mythology.

III

But it might be suggested that, while undoubtedly Alba was very remote and dead, there were other periods of Roman history which were living, full of great men and great movements, capable surely of poetic treatment. Had not Ennius written of the Punic Wars? was not Varius writing of Julius and of Augustus? For the moment, let us reserve Varius and his epics, and ask why Virgil declined to write an historical poem. It brings us face to face with the other question, what is an epic? To discuss this with any fullness would take us too far away, but we can answer it in part by making clear the difference between an epic and an historical poem.

One of the chief differences is the want of unity which will not allow the metrical history to become a poem. The poet is shackled to the fact, to the conscientious narration of a series of details. Event follows event, and all must be chronicled, whether capable or not of being fused, of being related to the central conception, without which a poem is impossible. Incidents and episodes may come in thick succession, but they remain incidents and episodes, mere disconnected fragments. As a rule they refuse to become organic parts of one living whole ; they delay us rather than help us onward, they scatter rather than concentrate the thought.

Again, the functions of poetry and history are really distinct. " Poetry," says Aristotle, " is a more philosophical and a higher thing (σπουδαιότερον) than history; for poetry tends to express the universal, history the particular. By the universal I mean how a person of given character will on occasion speak or act, according to the law of probability or necessity. The particular is, for example, what Alcibiades did or suffered."[1] History is full of accidents, strange chances, and anomalies, while poetry has no more to do with these than art with the illustration of oddities in the natural world. Even the philosophical treatment of history, in spite of its effort to exclude the accidental and reach the universal, is scarcely a proper theme for poetry. The conflict of national characters, for example, though real enough in its way, or the conflict of great principles maintained by opposing peoples over a great space of time, can only be conceived by certain abstraction of thought, and can hardly be represented by any group of symbols which poetry would care to use.

Roman literature offers us two great examples of metrical history, of which one is absurd and the other tiresome. Silius Italicus wrote seventeen books of *Punica*, which he tried to embellish with what he supposed to be poetical ornament. Hannibal fights under Juno's blessing, because Dido had been a favourite of Juno. Anna, Dido's sister, appears to him on the eve of Cannae to tell him what to do (she had counselled her sister in the *Aeneid*), and begins by explaining to him at length why in distant ages she had left Carthage after Dido's death, and how she had become an Italian goddess. The wind, which the Romans found so disastrous during the battle, was sent by Aeolus, anxious once more to oblige Juno. Lucan discarded all such imbecilities in his *Pharsalia*, and tried to carry off his poem with masses of scientific information and academic declamation, though neither of these aids can hide the fact that his epic is broken-backed and,

Like a wounded snake, drags its slow length along.

We cannot tell whether Virgil had ever read Aristotle's *Poetics*, but he probably would not have needed Aristotle to advise him to avoid attempting an historical epic. His

---

[1] *Poetics*, 9. 3, 4, tr. Butcher, whose remarks in his larger edition, pp. 163, 183, should be studied. Thucydides, whose work was used as a source by the writer of the Ἀθηναίων Πολιτεία, but was little read in the fourth century B.C., might have suggested to Aristotle a higher conception of History.

friend Varius had given himself to this kind of work. Virgil always speaks of him with respect, and indeed made him one of his executors, but he must have felt that as a poet his friend was astray. Posterity seems to have agreed with him. Horace, like Virgil, refused to attempt anything of the kind, modestly saying that charming as it would be to tell how temple and tower went to the ground, how battles were fought on river and on shore, it was not for him.[1] Let us recognize once more the sanity of Virgil's genius and the sureness of his judgement.

IV

If historical poetry was to be avoided, the biographical epic was even less possible. To turn once more to Aristotle, "unity of plot does not, as some persons think, consist in the unity of the hero. For infinitely various are the incidents in one man's life, which cannot be reduced to unity; and so, too, there are many actions of one man out of which we cannot make one action. Hence the error, as it appears, of all poets who have composed a Herakleid, a Theseid, or other poems of the kind. They imagine that as Herakles was one man the story of Herakles must be also a unity. But Homer, as in all else he is of surpassing merit, here too—whether from art or natural genius — seems to have happily discerned the truth."[2]

This would be one objection to writing the deeds of Augustus in an epic, but there was another. While Augustus would have been, from Aristotle's point of view, quite as bad a subject as Herakles, from another he was even worse. For, if Virgil could have been content with historical truth and have been willing to sacrifice poetry, Augustus probably did not much wish for historical truth; he preferred, and no doubt meant to have, panegyric. Augustus must have known something of the lively admiration which Virgil had for him, but he can hardly have understood his poetic

---

[1] *Ep.* ii. 1. 250 f.
[2] *Poetics*, c. 8. 1-3 (tr. Butcher).

temper. He probably remarked that Virgil stood higher than Varius in general estimation, and concluded that if one of the friends could panegyrize him, the other, the greater of the two, would do it even better.

Indeed, Virgil seems to have given the suggestion some attention, and in the beginning of the third *Georgic*, after his rejection of mythology, he speaks of raising a temple in Caesar's honour, with pictures of the Nile and the cities of Asia, triumphal columns and trophies, and statues of the race of Assaracus—

Trosque parens et Troiae Cynthius auctor—

"for the meantime let us go back to the woods of the Dryads." So he went back to the Dryads, and his metaphorical temple was never built. Virgil has not given us, perhaps he did not give Augustus, his reasons for not fulfilling this promise, but it is possible that the considerations indicated above were among them, and, even if he had no reasons, his poetic instinct was monitor enough.[1]

So far we have considered the classes of subjects which Virgil rejected, and we now come to the theme he chose, which after all has its affinities with every one of these classes, and yet escapes most of their limitations. He needed a subject, which should have a unity of its own,

[1] Another view is advanced by Norden (*Neue Jahrbücher für kl. Altertum,* 1901, pp. 313-22). He quotes the passage I have taken from Aristotle, but dismisses the idea that Virgil was influenced in his change of plan by "aesthetic" reasons. (Norden elsewhere shows great contempt for "aesthetic criticism.") He urges that we must look for Virgil's reasons in the politics of the day. The civil wars were over, peace was restored to the world, and Augustus wished to emphasize the fact, as indeed he did in the Monumentum Ancyranum, in other monuments, and on coins. "It was under the influence of the great triumphs that Virgil had given the promise to celebrate the wars of Caesar : how could he have kept it in a time, which was the antithesis of the past age of terror, when the prince was actually inaugurating his programme of peace for it, by materially reducing the number of the legions?" Norden fortifies his position by reference to Horace's last ode (iv. 15 *Phoebus volentem*), in which he finds a clear interpretation of Virgil's motives side by side with the more obvious reference to the *Aeneid* (*Troiamque et Anchisen et almae Progeniem Veneris canemus*). I can only say that I have a fundamentally different idea of poetry—a higher idea, I think.

and a grandeur, one in which he might express his innermost thought upon what meant most to him, his thought upon his country and the life of man. Does Aeneas fulfil these requirements? The theme is hardly promising, a mass of obscure, straggling, and scattered stories, gathered accidentally around a Trojan of the second rank, who has no individuality, no renown, no legend in fact.

It is clear that a poem about Aeneas may be as dead as any *Thebaid*; it may be as petty as any legend of Alba, and as lacking in unity as the *Herakleid* which Aristotle condemned. But the *Aeneid* is one, it is "grand," it interests, it expresses the Roman people, and it rises from time to time to be the utterance of humanity. It absorbs as much of Greek mythology as the most exacting taste could demand; it is full of the ancient life and legends of Rome and Italy—so full as to make it the special study of antiquaries for centuries, and yet it is never borne down by its weight of learning; it touches and illumines the history of Rome from Rome's first origin in the decrees of Fate down to the achievement of the universal Roman peace under Augustus; it does more for Augustus than any panegyric ever did or could do for any monarch; and it has been the favourite poem of all Europe for eighteen centuries, expressing for the most living races of mankind more than any single work of one man all they have felt of love and sorrow.

The poem finds its unity in its central thought; it is the poem of the birth of a great people, of a great work done to found a great race, of a spirit and temper brought into the world which should in time enable that race to hold sway over the whole world and be to the whole world, with all its tribes and tongues, the pledge and the symbol of its union and its peace. It is not the story of the life and adventures of Aeneas—there were those who called it the *gesta populi Romani*,[1] a name which shows a fine sympathy with the poet's feeling, as if all the deeds of the Roman people sprang from and were summed up in the work of one man. It is

---

[1] So Servius, *ad Aen.* vi. 752. On this see Patin, *La Poésie latine*, i. 199; Myers, *Essays Classical*, p. 129.

the story of the planting in Italy of the seed from which came Rome—

Tantae molis erat Romanam condere gentem [1] (*A*. i. 33).

The poet looks down the history of his race from Aeneas, he looks back through it from Augustus, and he finds it one, one story telling of one spirit. It is one spirit, and the same spirit, that brought Aeneas from Troy to the Tiber; that carried the Roman kings through the early wars of Rome ; that sacrificed in Brutus a father's affection to love of country ; that took Decii and Scipios from victory to victory ; that put Carthage and Alexandria, with all they meant of cruelty and disorder, under the feet of Rome ; and that gave Augustus the world to pacify and to regenerate. Virgil finds still more in it. He finds here his philosophy of history, the unity of the story of mankind, the drama of the progress of man from war, disorder, and barbarism to peace and humanity. And he finds in this story of Aeneas a clue to the story of every man, the linking of divine decree with human suffering and service, something to explain waste of life and failure of hope by a broader view of heaven's purposes and earth's needs, a justification of the ways of God to men, not complete, only tentative, but yet an anodyne and an encouragement in an unintelligible world.[2]

---

[1] "So vast the effort it cost to build up the Roman nation " (Conington).

[2] It is curious and disappointing to find that so great a scholar as Wilamowitz - Moellendorff can write as he does of the *Aeneid* (*Reden u. Vorträge*[2], p. 266) : " Das Heldengedicht, an dem jetzt sein Ruhm, bei uns seine Unterschätzung hängt, ist ihm wohl wider bessere Einsicht durch Maecenas und Augustus abgenötigt worden." The fact is that, for whatever reason, the Germans do not enjoy the poetry of Virgil as the French do, and to be a sound critic of a poet it is necessary to enjoy him.

CHAPTER IV

LITERATURE.—3. THE MYTHS OF AENEAS [1]

" There is in genius that alchemy which converts all metals into gold."
CARLYLE, *Essay on Schiller.*

WHEN Virgil chose Aeneas as his theme his choice was not idly made. Aeneas played a part, not perhaps of the highest importance, but still not an insignificant one, in the war of Troy. Though he does not accomplish very much, nor waken any very keen interest, yet the *Iliad* seems to recognize in him a man of heroic nature and a man with a destiny. Consequently a poet who would treat of him again has the *Iliad* behind him, and stands as it were in the succession of Homer. His theme is at once Homeric, and epic. So much might perhaps be said of Sarpedon or of Teucer, but for Virgil these heroes would have lacked what he clearly desired in his theme — relevance to Rome. But with Aeneas the case was different, for, however it had happened, a mass of legend had grown up around him, which by degrees assumed some sort of consistency and at last became a more or less fixed tradition. Step by step it could be shown how Aeneas had made his way westward till he reached Latium, and though at one time it looked as if Sardinia might be a further stage in his westward journey, it was agreed that Latium was really his goal. Here he, or his son, or grandson,—Romus, Romulus, or some such person,—had founded Rome, or, if not Rome, Lavinium. At all events, if not Aeneas himself, some direct descendant of the hero had eventually founded Rome, and though chronologers might debate the number of intervening generations, there was an undoubted filiation between Rome

[1] The reader may consult the work of Albrecht Förstemann, *Zur Geschichte des Aeneasmythos*, Magdeburg, 1894.

and Troy. Thus in Aeneas Virgil had a theme, if not thoroughly Roman, still closely connected with Rome—a theme which in his hands might at last grow to be intensely national. At the same time, he would have indeed to make dry bones live; for though the story had been accepted by the Romans and even embodied in diplomatic documents, it was in no sense really popular, but was the creation of Greek scholars, evolved from a combination of discrepant local tales by a rationalizing and rather dull philology. Virgil made the story live, and so effectually that his reader is pursued by his influence even into the conscientious pages of Dionysius of Halicarnassus, and finds it hard to imagine what the story was before Virgil took it in hand. To strip from it all that he gave it is hard, but by doing so we may gain a clearer appreciation of Virgil's greatness, and for this it is worth while to read Dionysius, and to survey the confusing collection of fictions which he has preserved for us. Let us first see what Homer says of Aeneas, and then follow him through literature and legend down to Virgil's day.

I

Of the passages in the *Iliad* dealing with Aeneas the most important belong to the strata of the poem which critics pronounce to be late. Aeneas comes into conflict with Diomedes, with Idomeneus, and finally with Achilles. The last of these encounters is for our present purpose the most significant. It occurs in the twentieth book, with which it is only loosely connected, while with the story proper it has hardly any connexion at all. The real hero of the passage seems not to be Achilles so much as Aeneas himself, for whose glorification it is believed to have been inserted by the author, whoever he was. The situation is this. Achilles has been roused to fury by the death of Patroclus, and he starts from the Greek camp to find Hector (l. 75). The first enemy he meets is Aeneas, and here the story begins to waver. We are told that Apollo, in the form of one of Priam's sons, urged Aeneas to face Achilles (l. 79), but later on (l. 156 f.) Aeneas seems to be acting independently

However that may be, Achilles is strangely unlike himself. He had rushed into battle furious ; now he is sarcastic, and, meeting Aeneas, he stops and begins by sneering at his position in Troy :—

"Aeneas, why dost thou advance so far from out the crowd to stand here ? Doth thy spirit bid thee fight with me, because thou hopest to rule over the horse-curbing Trojans with the dignity of Priam ? But even if thou slay me, not therefore will Priam put his honour in thy hand ; there be his own sons, and he is sound of mind and dotes not yet " (xx ; 177-183).[1]

He goes on to remind him of a previous meeting when Aeneas had run away, and advises him to go back and "mingle with the multitude before evil befall thee, and encounter me not : the fool is wise too late." To this Aeneas replies :—

"Pelides, think not to frighten me with big words, like a child ; well skilled am I also to speak with jibe or with courteous phrase. We know each other's race, and each other's parents . . . I style myself the son of great-hearted Anchises, and my mother is Aphrodite. . . . But if thou wouldest know my generation, I will tell it thee, a generation known of many men ; first of my line was Dardanus, begotten of cloud-compelling Zeus ; and he builded Dardania, for holy Ilium was not yet builded in the plain, city of mortal men, but they dwelt in the skirts of many-fountained Ida. And Dardanus begat a son, Erichthonius the king, most opulent of men. [Here follows a further digression upon Erichthonius' miraculous horses.] . . . And Erichthonius begat Tros, king of the Trojans ; and to Tros were born three blameless sons, Ilus and Assaracus and Ganymedes. [Here follow the pedigrees of Priam and Aeneas ; Ilus, Laomedon, Priam ; and Assaracus, Capys, Anchises, Aeneas.] And now no more ; let us not prattle on, like children (l. 244) . . . come therefore (l. 258), let us speedily make trial of each other's force with the brazen spear.'

At the end of the previous book Achilles had held

---

[1] I quote from Purves' translation throughout.

converse with his horses, and when Xanthus "the twinkling-footed steed" had prophesied his death, he rejoined, "Xanthus, why nam'st thou death? It needed not. Full well I know myself that my fate is to die here, far from my father and from my mother; but yet I will not hold my hand until I have given the Trojans surfeit of war" (xix. 420-3). But now it would seem he has changed his mind, and "holds his hand" to hear "a generation known of many men"; and when Aeneas begins the battle by hurling his spear, Achilles "held his shield"—the very shield on which Hephaestus had wrought the wonderful pictures, it should be remembered—"away from him with his firm hand, *in fear*; for he thought that the long spear of great-hearted Aeneas would lightly pierce it through." Then he hurls his own spear with little effect. Hereupon Aeneas picks up a huge stone, and "then had Aeneas stricken him with the stone in his assault on helmet or on death-averting shield, and Pelides had come upon him and taken his life with the blade, had not Poseidon, shaker of the land, been quick to see." Poseidon, not usually a friend of Trojans, addresses Hera, as little their friend, and they both agree that Aeneas should be rescued. So Poseidon "lifted Aeneas from the ground and whirled him away; and many a line of men and many a line of horses did Aeneas pass over, as he bounded from the hand of the god; and he came to the verge of the tumultuous war," where Poseidon had a word for him.

So much for the fight of Achilles and Aeneas, but Poseidon's words to Hera deserve study. "Ah me, I am in pain," he says, "because of great-hearted Aeneas, who soon shall fall before Pelides, and go down to the house of death; foolish, who listened to the biddings of far-fatal Apollo; but he shall not deliver him from destruction. Ah, why should he stand thus in much sorrow, without a cause, himself guiltless, by the fault of others—he who ever renders acceptable gifts to the gods who hold wide heaven? Come, let us rescue him from the stroke of death, lest Cronides [Zeus] be angry should Achilles slay him; also it is his fate to come off safe, that the line of Dardanus perish not without seed, and vanish away; Dardanus, whom Cronides loved above all his children, who were born of himself and of mortal women : for Cronion [Zeus] loveth not the race of Priam any longer, but in days hereafter the might of Aeneas shall rule over the Trojans, he, and his children's children that shall come after him" (xx. 293-308).

We may dismiss the question as to whether Poseidon is quite clear about the scope of Fate, and do no more than remark the Virgilian character of *pietas* which the god gives to the hero. Two points stand prominently out in this speech and the passage to which it supplies the key. First, Aeneas belongs to the younger branch of the royal family, and there is jealousy between the two branches. We learn this even more explicitly in another passage (xiii. 460 f.), where Deiphobus "found Aeneas standing on the battle's verge; for he was ever wroth with divine Priam, because he honoured him not, though valiant among men"; a little later, Aeneas found the people following him to battle "as sheep follow the ram, when they come from the pasture to drink, and the shepherd's heart is proud, so did Aeneas' heart rejoice within him, when he saw the company of the people following" (xiii. 492-5). Second, the words of the god imply a tradition that the supremacy had actually passed from Priam's family to Aeneas' line, and this will bear examination.

It is quite clear that the encounter of Achilles and Aeneas is in itself entirely trivial, and that, moreover, it blocks the progress of the story. What is its explanation? It is generally pronounced to be a late insertion in the poem,[1] due to the desire of a Homerid poet to please some dynasty or great family of the Troad, who wished to connect themselves with the founders of Troy, and fixed upon Aeneas as

---

[1] See Ameis-Hentze, *Anhang zu Homers Ilias*, vol. ii. (1879-86), Introduction to book xx, for a conspectus of the views of critics; and also Leaf, *Companion to the Iliad*, Introduction, pp. 24, 25, and on the passages quoted. Sainte-Beuve, *Étude sur Virgile*, in his excellent chapter on Aeneas in Homer (iv), does not do justice to this theory. Mr Andrew Lang (*Homer and his Age*, p. 324) admits the passage to be an interpolation. Schwegler, *Römische Geschichte*, i. 279-99, may also be consulted with advantage.

their ancestor,[1] just as the great families of the Ionian cities traced their descent from Neleus of Pylos, or Codrus, king of Athens.[2] This explanation seems satisfactory, and we find it corroborated by one or two local traditions of the Troad. Dionysius (i. 47) says that, when Aeneas sailed for the west, he left Ascanius, his eldest son, behind, and Ascanius ruled over a people in the district known as Dascylitis, where lake Ascania is, but afterwards with Hector's son, Scamandrius, he moved back to Troy. This may have been a local story, or perhaps some grammarian's attempt at history.[3] However, Strabo (607-8) tells us definitely that at Scepsis in the Troad the tradition was clear.[4] Old Scepsis was higher up on Ida, but Scamandrius, Hector's son, and Ascanius, Aeneas' son, brought the people down to the Scepsis known to history, where both their families were "kings"[5] for a long time. But this story, Strabo continues, does not agree with the popular accounts to the effect that Aeneas was spared on account of his quarrel with Priam (*Il.* xiii. 460, cited above) and went westward; while Homer himself agrees neither with the one nor the other, "for he shows that Aeneas remained in Troy, and received the sovereignty, and left the succession to his children's children, the family of Priam being extinguished; 'for Cronion loveth not the race of

---

[1] Keller remarks how well the poet knew the ground and the old folk-tales of the region (*Landessagen*), and concludes that the whole lay (*Lied*) comes from an old legend, and is designed for the glory of Aeneas, as ancestor of a house established on Mount Ida for centuries after the fall of Troy.

[2] See e.g. Hdt. i. 147; Strabo, c. 633.

[3] *See* Dion. H. i. 53 for a mass of grammarians' efforts at once to keep Aeneas in the Troad and to send him to Italy—were there two heroes called Aeneas, or did the genuine one first go to Italy and then return?

[4] Strabo was a man of real discernment, as can be seen in his chapters on Scepsis, "a place so called either for some other reason or from its being a conspicuous place (περίσκεπτον), if it is right to find in Greek words the etymology of old-time barbarian names" (607). His criticism of the stories of Aeneas, in view of Homer's actual words, is beyond most of the ancient authorities. The account of the connexion of Aristotle's library with Scepsis, with which he continues his record of the place, is most interesting and important. Dionysius (i. 53) denies that Aeneas' ruling over the Trojans implies his ruling in the Troad; "was it not possible for him still to rule over the Trojans, whom he took with him, even if they had a city elsewhere?" Dionysius finds it easy to be orthodox.

[5] The name, of course, rather implies a special hereditary priesthood than royalty in any modern sense.

Priam any longer, but in days hereafter the might of Aeneas shall rule over the Trojans, he and his children's children that shall come after him' (*Il.* xx. 306, as cited) . . . Still less does he agree with those who say Aeneas wandered as far as Italy and make him end his life there.   There are some, however, who write, 'The race of Aeneas shall reign over *all*, and his children's children,' meaning the Romans."[1] This was of course a mere violation of the text, which is confirmed by a closely similar prophecy in the Homeric hymn to Aphrodite, spoken by the goddess herself to Anchises.[2]

The introduction, then, of Aeneas' fight with Achilles and his rescue by Poseidon is explained by the existence of this dynasty or sacred family in the Troad with its tradition of descent from Aeneas.   And in the same way we may explain the somewhat similar, though less feeble, story of his fight with Diomedes and his rescue by Aphrodite and

---

[1] It may be well to put side by side the two versions of the passage from the *Iliad*—

Νῦν δὲ δὴ Αἰνείαο βίη Τρώεσσιν ἀνάξει,
καὶ παίδων παῖδες, τοί κεν μετόπισθε γένωνται (Homer).
Νῦν δὲ δὴ Αἰνείαο γένος πάντεσσιν ἀνάξει
καὶ παίδων παῖδες   (*Anon. ap. Strab.*).

It will be noticed that Virgil's rendering is nearer the latter—

Hic domus Aeneae cunctis dominabitur oris
et nati natorum et qui nascentur ab illis (*Aen.* iii. 97).

Servius says Homer took the words from Orpheus, as Orpheus had taken them from the oracle of Apollo.   Long after Virgil, Quintus of Smyrna used the old Homeric prophecy again—

Τὸν γὰρ θέσφατόν ἐστι θεῶν ἐρικύδεϊ βουλῇ
Θύμβριν ἐπ' εὐρυρέεθρον ἀπὸ Ξάνθοιο μολόντα
τευξέμεν ἱερὸν ἄστυ καὶ ἐσσομένοισιν ἀγητὸν
ἀνθρώποις, αὐτὸν δὲ πολυσπερέεσσι βροτοῖσι
κοιρανέειν· ἐκ τοῦ δὲ γένος μετόπισθεν ἀνάξειν
ἄχρις ἐπ' ἀντολίην τε καὶ ἀκαμάτου δύσιν ἠοῦς.
                                        Posthomerica, xiii. 336.

[2] *H. Aphr.* 197 (with note of Allen and Sikes)—

Σοὶ δ' ἔσται φίλος υἱός, ὃς ἐν Τρώεσσιν ἀνάξει,
καὶ παῖδες παίδεσσι διαμπερὲς ἐκγεγάονται.

Hesiod, *Theogony* 1008, records the birth of Aeneas, the child of Cythereia and Anchises, but makes no prophecy about him.   He then adds that Circe bore to Odysseus sons named Agrios and Latinos who dwelt far in a recess among the islands and ruled over all the Etruscans.   It is open to any one to question the authenticity and the date of these latter lines.

Apollo, which we find in book v. But in the meantime
we have discovered, with some assistance from Strabo, that
Homer (if we may use the name again as the Greeks used it)
knew nothing of Aeneas' adventures in any western region,
near or far, but thought of him as continuing the race of
Dardanus in Dardanus' own land, which, in spite of Virgil,[1]
was not Italy but the Troad. So far only does Homer stand
with Virgil, that, hymning a patron's ancestor, he makes that
ancestor a great warrior, great enough to face Achilles and
Diomedes, and dear enough to the gods, at once for his piety
and his descent, to be rescued by miracle and reserved to
fight again, "when Achilles dies and finds his fate" (*Il.* xx.
337), and to found a line of kings.[2]

II

The problem now rises as to how, in the face of the words
of Homer and of the traditions of the Troad, the story grew
which brought Aeneas to Italy and to Rome. The growth
of the story it is comparatively easy to trace, but why it
should have grown at all is not so clear. No doubt the
natural passion most men feel for pedigrees of their own
and of other people plays a great part here, and so does the
Greek habit of off-hand etymologizing. The connexion of
Aeneas with Aphrodite is also an important factor, though
the origin of this requires some explanation.

First, let us see how Aeneas left Troy. Various accounts
of this are quoted by Dionysius. Menecrates of Xanthus,
for example, began his tale with Achilles' burial, and went
on to narrate that Aeneas, from hatred of Priam and Paris,
betrayed the city to the Achaeans. This version was hardly
likely to be productive in literature, and it will suffice to

---

[1] *Aen.* iii. 163 *Est locus, Hesperiam Graii cognomine dicunt* . . .
　　　167 *Hae nobis propriae sedes, hinc Dardanus ortus.*

[2] A scholiast on *Il.* xx. 307 tells us that Acusilaus of Argos (a logographer
of the sixth century, B.C.) discovered the real reason of the Trojan war in
Aphrodite's ambition for her son. She set the whole war on foot simply and
solely to transfer the sovereignty from the house of Priam to that of Aeneas—a
very suggestive interpretation, which may be illustrated at large from the history
of Greek cities and their tyrants and factions — ἕκητι Συλοσῶντος εὐρυχωρία
(Strabo, c. 638).

say merely that Servius believed Virgil knew of it, that Dares adopted it, and that Gower used it in his *Confessio Amantis.*[1] The next story is more famous and more fruitful. "Sophocles, the tragic poet," says Dionysius "in his drama of *Laocoon* has represented Aeneas on the eve of the city's capture as repairing to Ida, for so he was bidden by his father Anchises, in remembrance of the charge of Aphrodite; while in view of what had just befallen the family of Laocoon, he conjectured the approaching destruction of the city. His iambics, spoken by a messenger, are as follows :—' And now Aeneas, son of the goddess, is at the gates; on his shoulders he bears his father, the matter dripping on his robe of byssos from his back, burnt by the thunderbolt; and round about are all the company of his servants; and with him follows a multitude, beyond what thou thinkest, of Phrygians who desire to be of this colony.' "[2] This is perhaps the only known reference to Aeneas in Greek tragedy. Xenophon adds a little more information. "Aeneas saved the gods of his father and of his mother (τοὺς πατρῴους καὶ μητρῴους[3] θεούς), and saved his father too, and won thereby a name for piety, so that the enemy granted to him alone of all whom they conquered in Troy immunity from being pillaged."[4]

But neither of these accounts satisfies Dionysius of Halicarnassus,[5] and he gives us "the most reliable story" as told by Hellanicus in his *Troica*—an explicit narrative of

---

[1] See Chassang, *Histoire du Roman,* p. 364. Servius, *ad Aen.* i. 242, 647. Antenor more commonly is credited with this betrayal. Cf. Strabo c. 608.

[2] Dion. H. *Ant. Rom.* i. 48. Soph. *Frag.* 344 (Nauck). There are some slight variations in reading.

For κεραυνίου νώτου, cf. *h. Aphr.* 287-9—

    Εἰ δέ κεν ἐξείπῃς καὶ ἐπεύξεαι ἄφρονι θυμῷ

    ἐν φιλότητι μιγῆναι ἐϋστεφάνῳ Κυθερείῃ,

    Ζεύς σε χολωσάμενος βαλέει ψολόεντι κεραυνῷ—

and *Aeneid* ii. 647—

    Iam pridem invisus divis et inutilis annos

    demoror, ex quo me divom pater atque hominum rex

    fulminis adflavit ventis et contigit igni.

[3] Who were these?   [4] Xen. *de Venatione,* 1. 15.

[5] "Ce bon Denys d'Halicarnasse," Boissier calls him, and the phrase is in itself a suggestive criticism.

how Aeneas managed to hold the Acropolis; and how when great numbers of Trojans had found their way to him, he successfully evacuated it and fell back on Mount Ida, resolved to wait there till the Greeks sailed for home; and how, when the Greeks, instead, prepared to attack him, he made a treaty with them binding himself to leave the Troad; and how accordingly, after building a fleet, he crossed to the promontory of Pallene in Europe.[1]   So began the wanderings of Aeneas; and he was to wander far, and to found many cities, and to die and be buried in many places, before ever he reached Latium.

To begin at the beginning, Dionysius quotes "Cephalon of Gergithes"[2] to the effect that Aeneas died in Thrace, and that one of his four sons, Romus by name, went to Italy and founded Rome. Cephalon was "an ancient and reputable writer," he says, but Athenaeus informs us that the real author of Cephalon's *Troica* was Hegesianax of Alexandria in the Troad, a contemporary of Flamininus.[3] That a Greek writer of so late a day should tell a story so different from the orthodox tradition is very significant. By and by, we find that Aeneas got as far as Arcadia, and lived at Orchomenus or "the Island, so called, though in the heart of the country, because it is surrounded by marshes and river," and there apparently he died after founding Capyae (named after his ancestor Capys)—or else he went to Hesperia and became the father of Romulus.[4]   In fact, his tomb was to be found in so many places, that Dionysius is afraid it may disconcert students, "as it is impossible that the same man should be buried in more than one place. But let them reflect," he goes on, "that this difficulty is common to many heroes, especially those who have had remarkable fortunes and lived lives of wandering; and let them learn that while one place only receives the actual body, memorials have been raised in many places from

---

[1] Dion. H. i. 46, 47.
[2] "The Gergithes who were left behind as a remnant of the ancient Teucrians," Hdt. v. 122.
[3] Dion. H. i. 49. 72 ; Athen. ix. 49, p. 393 ; Schwegler, *Röm. Gesch.* i. 303.
[4] Dion. H. i. 49.

goodwill for kindness rendered, especially if any of the hero's race have survived, or because the hero founded the particular city, or stayed there a long time and was a benefactor." And in this way he explains the graves of Aeneas in Ilium, Bebrycia, Phrygia, Pallene, Arcadia, and Sicily and "many other places," where after death "he was honoured with mounds and much building of tombs."[1]

We have, however, still better evidence of the course of his wanderings than his various tombs, for as the son of Aphrodite he built temples to his mother wherever he went. We learn from Dionysius that he founded temples to Aphrodite at Pallene, Cythera, Zacynthus, Buthrotum, and other places, while at Leucas and Actium, and on the river Elymus in Sicily, the temples bore his own name coupled with his mother's—being dedicated to Aphrodite Aineias. Moreover, his journey is commemorated by a town Aineia on Pallene, by Capyae in Arcadia, by the " race-course of Aphrodite and Aeneas " (with wooden images of themselves) on Zacynthus, by a hêrôon of Aeneas in Ambracia (with a small archaic image), by the brazen cauldrons "with very archaic inscriptions" which he set up at Dodona, by the harbour of Anchises and a hill called Troia at Buthrotum, by the harbour of Aphrodite on the Iapygian promontory where he first landed in Italy, and by his foundations of Aegesta and Elymus in Sicily.[2] All this Dionysius tells us,[3] and other writers add the island of Aenaria off Cumae,[4] the hill Anchisia with a tomb of Anchises at Mantinea,[5] and the towns Aphrodisias and Elis in Arcadia.[6]

It is, as Dionysius remarks, quite clear that a man cannot die and be buried in more than one place, but we shall

---

[1] Dion. H. i. 54. Jupiter himself had at least one grave in Crete.

[2] Thucydides (vi. 2) says, "After the capture of Troy, some Trojans who had escaped from the Achaeans came in ships to Sicily ; they settled near the Sicanians, and both took the name Elymi. The Elymi had two cities, Eryx and Egesta." Dionysius (i. 52) expands this with a wonderful story of a Trojan Elymus, born in Sicily the child of refugees, who returned to Troy and, after the Trojan war, co-operated with Aeneas in Sicily.

[3] Dion. H. i. 49-53.   [4] Pliny, *N.H.* iii. 12, § 82.

[5] Pausanias, viii. 12. 8.

[6] Pausanias, iii. 22. 11 ; viii. 12. 8. See Schwegler, *Röm. Gesch.* i. 300 ff.

not now be inclined to explain Aeneas' multitude of tombs as his historian does. All Dionysius' archaeological evidence, his very archaic wooden statues and his very archaic inscriptions, prove nothing. The world was full of such things. Agamemnon's staff[1] and the disc of Lycurgus[2] were to be seen, and even the remainder of the lump of clay out of which Prometheus made the first man.[3] The difficulty of being sure of St Edmund's bones, all of whose adventures fall within what we may call modern history, should make us very sceptical of Dionysius' pronouncements on relics from before the day of Homer. But we may use the evidence he quotes to establish a different thesis.

Dr Farnell, in his interesting account of the worship of Aphrodite,[4] suggests that the story of the wanderings of Aeneas is the legendary record of the diffusion of a cult of Aphrodite over the Mediterranean. Aeneas in Homer is unlike the other heroes; he is a mysterious figure with a future in reserve; and this suggests that it was from the goddess that the name Αἰνείας passed directly to a clan of worshippers,[5] and that, to explain their name and position, the sacred hero Aeneas was imagined, as such ancestors often were. As to the meaning of the name, it has been variously derived from αἴνη or αἶνος, i.e. " the glorious," and from αἰνέω, i.e. " the consenting "[6]; and again from Αἴνη, the name of the goddess of Ecbatana to whose temple Polybius alludes.[7]

The cult of Aphrodite Aeneas then, we should suppose, spread from the Troad to the various places which Dionysius and the others mention. There were other cults of Aphrodite widely diffused, and with some of these it would blend. For

---

[1] Pausanias, ix. 40. 11. It was honoured with daily sacrifices at Chaeronea.

[2] Plutarch, *Lyc.* 1, says it was used as evidence by Aristotle.

[3] Pausanias, x. 4. 4, near the Phocian Panopeis. The remnants consisted of stones as large as a wagon-load, and smelt very like human flesh.

[4] *Cults of the Greek States*, vol. ii. c. xxi. pp. 638 ff.

[5] We have seen that Strabo calls them kings—a name which may well imply priesthood, as at Athens and Rome.

[6] See Schwegler, *Röm. Gesch.* i. 302, n. 16.

[7] See Farnell, *op. cit.* p. 640 ; Polybius, x. 27. She is also called Anaitis.

instance, Eryx [1] had a Carthaginian cult, to judge from its similarities with that at Carthage ; and near Eryx, our authorities tell us, there were temples associated with the name Aeneas. At Cythera, too, was a shrine of great age and sanctity. " It was the Phoenicians," says Herodotus,[2] "who founded the temple in Cythera, coming from the land of Syria." Aphrodite is already Cythereia in Homer,[3] while Hesiod [4] says that it was from Cythera that she passed to Cyprus. All or most of the shrines of Aphrodite are on the sea-coast, and it is generally held that they tell a tale of Phoenician occupation.

To explain the name of the priestly tribe the eponymous hero Aeneas was invented, and he had the good fortune to play a considerable part in Homer's poetry. Anchises answers closely to such legendary figures as Adonis and Cinyras, but, thanks to the author of the Homeric hymn to Aphrodite, he has a clearly marked and individual character of his own. His son, in like manner, gained from the *Iliad* a renown far beyond that of eponymous heroes in general. One might say that he, like Achilles,[5] had gained everything by the obscuration of his divinity in his human nature. He became a figure in literature. Thereafter, when the Greeks met the name Aeneas, masculine or feminine, they thought of Homer first, just as the name Falstaff to an Englishman must invariably suggest one man of the name, whom we have learnt to know in a particular author. But what could be the connexion between Aeneas and (for instance) Leucas ? We have seen how Dionysius settles our difficulties. Aeneas obviously visited all these places, and when he had come so far, to cross the Adriatic was easy. Italy was near, it had no legends of its own, and it had shrines of Aphrodite.

It has been supposed that Stesichorus first sent Aeneas to Italy, but this is merely an inference from the pictures of the *Tabula Iliaca*. This monument represents in a series

---

[1] See Farnell's references on p. 742, n. 83, and Boissier, *Country of Horace and Virgil*, 2. § 4. The identification of Dido with this goddess as worshipped in Carthage has been suggested as the original explanation of Aeneas' connexion with her.

[2] Herodotus, i. 105.   [3] *Odyssey*, 18. 193.   [4] Hesiod, *Theogony*, 191.

[5] Achilles was a sea-god, lord of the Euxine, till he was ousted by St Phocas.

of pictures the scenes of the Trojan war, and it indicates in the spaces between them the sources from which they were taken,—the *Iliad* for instance, the *Aethiopis* of Arctinus, and lastly, the *Iliupersis* of Stesichorus. The last picture represents Aeneas, holding the hand of Ascanius, Anchises carrying the sacred things, and the trumpeter Misenus behind them, as they embark, and it bears the inscription Αἰνήας σὺν τοῖς ἰδίοις ἀπαίρων εἰς τὴν Ἑσπερίαν.[1] As Latin sources are not mentioned, it has been supposed that this last picture must come from Stesichorus—a Greek poet of Himera, in Sicily, who is supposed to belong to the seventh century B.C. But the table is Roman and is generally supposed to date from the early empire, so that one feels a reasonableness in the view of M. Hild, that this particular picture and those near it may have been influenced by Virgil as much as by Stesichorus.[2] Or, if Welcker's view, cited by Schwegler, is right, and the table dates from the age of Julius, the tale of Aeneas coming to Italy could obviously not be entirely ignored in a work designed for educational use in Rome.

Whatever we conclude about Stesichorus, we have seen that in Thucydides' day the Trojan foundation of one or two Sicilian towns, belonging to the " Elymi," was generally allowed.[3] This was of course earlier than the time when the Greeks began to think of finding a heroic origin for Rome. The temple of Aphrodite Aineias at Elymus would fix the Trojan tradition and connect it permanently with the name of Aeneas. When he was once in Sicily, and had founded one temple, it was easy to let him found another, the more famous one on Eryx. Different opinions have been hazarded as to the real founders of this great temple. One would naturally suppose it to be Phoenician, and even if a pre-Phoenician worship of a nature goddess on the summit of the mountain is to be conceded, still a strong Phoenician element has to be recognized in the cult as known to history. Boissier quotes M. Salinas, a distinguished archaeo-

[1] See Schwegler, *Röm. Gesch.* i. 298-9.
[2] Hild, *La Légende d'Énée avant Virgile*, cited by Boissier, *Nouvelles Promenades*, p. 134 (tr. *Country of Horace and Virgil*, p. 126). Förstemann, *Aeneasmythus*, p. 9.
[3] Thuc. vi. 2.

logist of Palermo, for the fact that the great substructions of the plateau, works so vast that the ancients attributed them to Daedalus, and that in more modern times they have been described by the hardly more enlightening term "Cyclopean," bear letters cut upon them, and that these letters are Phoenician.[1] Boissier's statement, that the foundation of the temple was made by the Carthaginians, seems a little loose, for the rise of Carthage only followed the decline of Tyre before the Assyrians in the eighth and seventh centuries B.C. Phoenician influence was widespread in the Mediterranean long before that period, though it does not necessarily follow that they were in possession of Eryx at a very early date, and the view is held that they came to Sicily after the Greeks.[2] In any case the great name of Venus Erycina was enough to bring Aeneas to Eryx, even if he had been further away than Elymus.

We have now reached the longest and most difficult step which Aeneas had to take—from Sicily to Latium—even if he made two steps of it by pausing at Cumae. Müller (cited by Schwegler[3]) sets forth Aeneas' connexion with Cumae thus. The Aeneadae of the Troad became the subject of the prophecies of the Sibyl of Gergithes, who lost her identity in the more famous Sibyl of Erythrae; when the Italian Cumae was founded, in part by Aeolians from Cyme, near neighbours of the Teucrian Gergithes, Cumae in turn became the seat of a Sibyl, and the Sibylline oracles foretelling the destiny of Aeneas' house came with the Sibyl to Italy, and with them came Aeneas. This is most ingenious, but unhappily the oracles of Sibyls seem, as a rule, when they indicate anything at all definite, to have been composed after the event, and accordingly we may rank the Sibyl's contribution to our story, with Virgil's

---

[1] Boissier, *Nouvelles Promenades*, p. 236—a very interesting section on this Venus, her influence on the maritime world, and her worship, and on the Madonna di Trapani, whose church exactly at the foot of Eryx has inherited some of the honours of the pagan shrine. Salinas, *Le mura fenicie di Erice*, in *Notizie degli scavi*, April, 1883.

[2] See Beloch, *Griechische Geschichte*, i. 186. Thucydides vi. 2, 6, is the great authority for the priority of the Phoenicians.

[3] Schwegler, *Röm. Gesch.* i. 312-5.

own, as a recognition of a pre-existing tradition rather than as a source whence such a tradition sprang.

III

Every city must have some founder, and the Greeks who first became familiar with Rome began, after their habit, to look for some suitable hero who should have founded the city. Aristotle is quoted as the authority for the existence of a story to the effect that some Achaeans, blown out of their course on their voyage from Troy, reached Latium, and, overtaken by winter, waited there for the spring, but some captive Trojan women, less anxious than they to reach Greece, burnt their ships.[1] Another story, told by Xenagoras, was that Romus, a son of Ulysses and Circe, founded Rome, while his brothers Antias and Ardeas founded Antium and Ardea.[2] Cape Misenum, it should be remembered, took its name from Misenus, who was at first one of Ulysses' men and was afterwards turned over to Aeneas.[3] As to Rome and her founder, all sorts of variants are quoted by Plutarch,[4] and the interpolator of Servius.[5] Dionysius cites Hellanicus and the chronicle of the Argive priestesses (if this has any value whatever independently of Hellanicus) for Aeneas' foundation of Rome.[6] But the story only began to have a real significance in the time of Pyrrhus' war with Rome. It was then convenient that Rome should not have been founded by a Greek, and in Aeneas the Romans could have an ancestor traditionally hostile to Pyrrhus' ancestor Achilles.[7] A generation later, at the end of the first Punic war, the Acarnanians needed help against the Aetolians, and solicited the aid of Rome on the ground that, alone among the

[1] Aristotle, *ap.* Dion. H. i. 72. Plutarch, *Rom. Quaest.* 6. See Schwegler, *R. G.* i. 4.

[2] Dion. H. i. 72.

[3] Strabo, c. 26; *Aen.* vi. 162 f.   [4] Plutarch, *Romulus*, 2.

[5] *ad Aen.* i. 273.

[6] Dion. H. i. 72, in conjunction with Odysseus, of all people.

[7] Pausanias, i. 12. 1 μνήμη τὸν Πύρρον τῆς ἁλώσεως εἰσῆλθε τῆς Ἰλίου, καί οἱ κατὰ ταὐτὰ ἤλπιζε χωρήσειν πολεμοῦντι· στρατεύσειν γὰρ ἐπὶ Τρώων ἀποίκους Ἀχιλλέως ὢν ἀπόγονος.

Greeks, their ancestors had *not* joined in the campaign against Troy.[1] It was probably the first time that a Greek state had ever made such a boast, and it implies a belief at least in Greece that Rome had accepted her Trojan origin. From this date onwards the fact is allowed and even emphasized by diplomacy and literature.

It was not perhaps in harmony with the old and native legends of Rome's foundation, and by what process it came to be accepted it is hard for a modern to understand. Timaeus could, no doubt, satisfy himself easily enough that the Penates of Lavinium were of Trojan clay, and the heralds' staffs of brass and iron Trojan too. Similar stories were adopted by other towns in Latium and in Italy. Tusculum and Praeneste were founded by Telegonus; Lanuvium by Diomedes; Ardea by a son of Circe or of Danae; Politorium by Priam's son Polites[2]; the Salentini were planted by Idomeneus; Petelia by Philoctetes[3]; Argyripa by Diomedes.[4]

It is useless to ask the reason of such tales, though we may hazard the guess that they were more familiar to the readers of Greek books upon antiquities than to those who knew the legends of their own countryside alone. Where the tales were really taken in hand, they were well managed by the Greek scholars in Italy. Variants were dropped where they could not be harmonized, and chronology was carefully adapted to fit both the local and the foreign tales. It was, for example, a recognized fact (no doubt owing something to the same school of Greek redactors) that Rome had had seven kings only.[5] Consequently Rome could not

---

[1] Justin, xxviii. 1. 6; 2. 2; cf. Dion. H. i. 51.

[2] See Schwegler, *Röm. Gesch.* i. 310, for all these places. Tusculum, Propert. ii. 32. 4; Dion. H. iv. 45, &c. Praeneste, Horace, *Odes.* iii. 29. 8; Ovid, *Fasti*, iii. 92; Virgil (*A.* vii. 678) and the Praenestines, however, said Caeculus, and there were also other stories. Lanuvium, Appian, *B. C.* ii. 20. Ardea, Dion. H. i. 72. Politorium, cf. Servius on *Aen.* v. 564 *nomen avi referens Priamus, tua cara, Polite, | progenies, auctura Italos.* Sulmo by Solymus, Ovid, *Fasti*, iv. 70-82.

[3] Virg. *Aen.* iii. 400.   [4] *Aen.* xi. 243-8.

[5] The work of Ettore Pais seems to me to have shaken the orthodox tradition as to the Roman kings (especially Servius Tullius), though this is not to say that all his theories are fully established.

have been founded more than seven generations before the year at which the lists of consuls began. By a happy coincidence with Athenian history this year was 510 or 511, and reckoning roughly the usual three generations to a century (some authorities, however, preferring forty years to a generation), the historiographer reached the date 753 or 754. But Troy fell, by current reckoning, based e.g. on the date of Lycurgus (776) and his distance from his ancestor Herakles, some three hundred years earlier, and thus Aeneas could leave plenty of room for Romulus. Hence Aeneas did not found Rome, but Lavinium,[1] which may or may not have been (as some critics suppose) a kind of federal foundation in Latium, and therefore without a local legend of a founder. This explanation does not seem to account for Praeneste, Ardea, and the other places, though Schwegler and Boissier accept it.[2]

It now only remained for some ingenious person to collect and harmonize the tales of Aeneas' wanderings, and this was gradually done. Fabius Pictor adopted the story. Naevius, who served in the first Punic war, and wrote its history in Saturnian verse, was the first poet to touch the tale. He is supposed to have traced the feud of Rome and Carthage back to Aeneas and Dido,[3] telling of Troy's burning, of the escape of Aeneas and Anchises, the voyage, and the visit to Dido.[4] Ennius in his turn touched the tale, and made Ilia the daughter of Aeneas, and Romulus his grandson, a proceeding which, as we have seen, needed correction.[5] By this time the fiction was common property. Philip V of Macedon had to recognize in a treaty with Ilium the town's hereditary connexion with Rome.[6] Flamininus, the great phil-Hellen, described his countrymen as Aeneadae.[7] Later on the fashion set in at Rome of finding ancestors among the Trojans. Julius Caesar,

---

[1] The Lavinium story was helped by the coincidence that a neighbouring spot bore the name Troia—proof positive.

[2] Schwegler, *Röm. Gesch.* i. 316 f. ; Boissier, *Nouv. prom.* p. 145.

[3] Timaeus, cited by Dion. H. i. 74, said Carthage and Rome were founded contemporaneously.

[4] Schwegler, *Röm. Gesch.* i. 85.   [5] Preller, *Röm. Mythologie*, ii. 311, n. 1.

[6] Livy, xxix. 12.   [7] Plutarch, *Flamininus*, 12.

in his famous speech at the funeral of his aunt, the widow of Marius, laid claim to descent from Iulus, the son of Aeneas.[1] This of course settled the question of Aeneas' son, for so far, as we have seen, it had been uncertain whether Ascanius came to Italy or not. And indeed an Italian son of Aeneas by Lavinia is a competitor for the honour of being the Emperor's ancestor.[2] But many Romans beside Caesar claimed Trojan blood, and to some of these families Virgil gave credentials, while Varro (rather earlier) wrote a book on the whole subject—*de familiis Troianis.*[3]

Among Virgil's contemporaries several, whose works survive, touched the story of Aeneas. Livy, for instance, begins his history with it, and even he leaves it shadowy and unsubstantial.[4] Tibullus has left us a long address supposed to be delivered by a Sibyl to Aeneas, in which his future wanderings and arrival are told, but if Tibullus had never written in another vein this poem would never have made his name immortal.[5] Horace and Propertius were both faintly interested in the ancient history of Rome, but Propertius never found very much inspiration in any theme but Cynthia, and Horace was no more an archaeologist than Omar Khayyam.

> They say the Lion and the Lizard keep
> The Courts where Jamshýd gloried and drank deep:
> And Bahrám that great Hunter—the Wild Ass
> Stamps o'er his Head, but cannot break his Sleep.

What is this but a more poetical variant of

> Ire tamen restat Numa quo devenit et Ancus?

Thus, when Virgil took the theme in hand, he found it a fairly complete and coherent tradition, but still, in spite of his predecessors, imbued with the prosaic flavour of the

---

[1] Suetonius, *Julius*, 6. Norden (*Neue Jahrbücher für kl. Altertum*, 1901, p. 258) cites Babelon (*Monnaies de la Rép. Rom.* ii. p. 9 ff.) for the fact that the head of Venus appears on coins of the Julii about the period 154-134 B.C.

[2] See Norden (*Neue Jahrbücher für kl. Altertum*, 1901, pp. 276-9) for a discussion of the whole matter.

[3] Servius, *ad Aen.* v. 704. Atticus did the same sort of genealogical work, Nepos, 18. 2.

[4] Livy, i. 1-2.   [5] Tibullus, ii. 5. 19-65.

Greek chronographers; and how prosaic and tiresome a Greek
writer could be, no one knows who has not made excursions
into Greek chronologies. The treatment of Naevius and
Ennius was not that which Virgil would care to give to his
story. No great poet would wish, in his happier moments,
to be an annalist. If Virgil then was to make anything of
the story of Aeneas, he must redeem it for himself. Homer
no doubt, might help him in battle pieces, but he had no
Homer to give him his Italians. Evander, Remulus, Turnus
are his own creations, even if legend had known them of old.
The voyage of Aeneas might be made easier by reminiscences
of the *Odyssey*, and the episode of Dido by the *Hippolytus*
and the *Argonautica*.

But the substantial originality of Virgil is not diminished,
even if we concede that he borrowed as much as the most
hostile critic would wish to assert. No great poem was ever
made entirely of borrowed material, and that the *Aeneid* is
a great poem is beyond dispute. Its subject had so far
inspired no great poetry whatever, and it is only under the
touch of Virgil that we realize that it had any poetic
possibilities in it. He found it a Greek antiquary's tale—
to call it a fancy might imply too much imagination—he
wrought it into life, and he left it a nation's epic, filled
through and through with the national Roman spirit, and
so instinct with human feeling that for generations men, to
whom Rome was not what she was to Virgil, found in the
Aeneid the word for every experience of human life. Conversely, the poverty and the dryness of the story before
Virgil, when we compare it with the wonderful epic, bring
home to us in a new way the genius of the Roman poet.

CHAPTER V

THE LAND AND THE NATION.—1. ITALY

Open my heart and you will see
Graved inside of it, "Italy,"
Such lovers old are I and she:
So it always was, so shall ever be.—BROWNING.

AMONG the most original and significant features of
the poetry of Virgil is its conscious appeal to a nation,
as we understand the word "nation" to-day, to a
people of one blood living within well-defined but broad
limits, a people with various traditions all fusing in one
common tradition.   It is the poetry of a nation and a country,
for the poet will not think of them apart; and it is not the
least of his greatness that he has linked them thus closely,
and made people and land as a unity so distinct from the
rest of the world.

It was a new thing in literature.   The Homeric poems are
of course addressed to all the Greeks, and all Greeks saw
in them a common inheritance, but the underlying idea is
quite other than that of Virgil's Italy.   Greeks lived here
and there in Europe, Asia, and Africa, under every form of
government, divided into many independent and often
antagonistic communities, conscious indeed of their being of
one blood, but resolved never to submit, if possible, to being
under one government.   Greek sold Greek to the barbarian
as uniformly then as in a later age one Christian people in
Eastern Europe has betrayed another Christian people to
the Moslem.   The conception of one Greece and a common
citizenship of all Greeks was as impossible from Greek ways
of thinking, even in the days of Aristotle, as it was geographically incapable of being realized.   If one may use an
illustration from Aristophanes with a slight extension of its
suggestion, the anxiety felt by Strepsiades, on his first

inspection of a map, to have Sparta removed as far as possible from Athens, would seem to have been shared by almost every Greek state with reference to its neighbours, unless there were some strong probability of those neighbours being subdued and annexed.

ὡς ἐγγὺς ἡμῶν· τοῦτο πάνυ φροντίζετε,
ταύτην ἀφ᾽ ἡμῶν ἀπαγαγεῖν πόρρω πάνυ [1] (*Clouds* 215).

"How near to us!" Such an exclamation never led to national unity.

Later Greek literature offers us no such ideal.[2] The plays of the great Athenian dramatists were primarily for Athens, and though they might be read and were read abroad,[3] they would waken little more consciousness of common nationality than the best American literature may in England. The literature of Alexandria was still less national, produced as it was under a dynasty which steadily became less and less Greek, and by scholars who grew more and more unconscious of the possibility of an appeal to any audience not as learned or as city-less as themselves. That Greek literature was throughout so independent of national or political interests, few will count to be an unmixed loss to mankind. For the moment, however, this aspect of it may be emphasized to raise into greater prominence the novelty of Virgil's conception.

Virgil, then, gave for the first time its literary expression to the triumph of a nation, politically, racially, and geographically one, over the clan and over the city-state. Like all great conceptions, this was the fruit of long years, of centuries of maturing. It was, we might say, foreshadowed by the blind Appius Claudius, when he counselled the Senate to make no peace with Pyrrhus so long as he was on Italian soil. The old man must not be supposed to have divined the far distant union of all Italians in a common citizen-

---

[1] "How parlous close it is! Let this be your sole study—to shift it leagues away from us" (Starkie).

[2] Isocrates may be cited, but his views of national unity are hardly Virgil's.

[3] Cf. Plutarch, *Nicias* 29, the popularity of Euripides in Sicily, attested by the famous story of the Athenian captives in 413 B.C.

ship, yet from this assertion by Appius Claudius of the unity of Italy Virgil's conception is lineally descended. It was some feeling of this kind that kept so much of Italy loyal to Rome throughout the Hannibalic war.[1] The expansion of Rome over the Mediterranean served to heighten this sense of Rome and Italy being one. Roman and Italian served together in the same army, and the Roman merchant and the Italian did business together in a hundred cities of the East under the common security of the Roman name. Just as to-day the signficance of the British flag is best learned abroad, we may believe that the opening of the old world of the East and the new world of Spain and Gaul to Italian commerce helped forward the detrition of old clan distinctions and made Marsian and Apulian conscious that they were both Italian in blood and Roman in fact, if not yet in the letter of the law. The Social War was essentially, like the American Civil War, a war for unity. The day of tribal independence was gone, and the Italian fought for Italy, and for a united Italy, against the Roman, who fought for a divided Italy. The significant new name given to Corfinium, the federal capital, is evidence enough. Italica was to be the capital of Italy, and we may say that the conception embodied in this renaming of Corfinium carried the day. Corfinium was a failure, but Italica was triumphant. After one year of war the Romans accepted Italica—*not* Corfinium—and peace came as soon as Rome became the new Italica. The name was dropped and forgotten, but the great idea lived, and when Caesar in 49 extended the Roman citizenship to Transpadane Gaul, he gave to it its full and complete realization. Though the incorporation of Cisalpine Gaul was not actually achieved for some years, still Italy was at last admittedly one in idea, one people, and one country from the Alps to the straits of Messina ; and with her unity came her poet. This great achievement of Caesar's was one of the links that bound the poet to his house. There is thus a significance in the poet's language when he describes the battle of Actium. It is not the victory of Rome so much as

[1] Cf. Horace, *Odes*, iii. 6. 33-44.

of Italy. Italy has her place in senate and people; they are Italian gods who bless Caesar's cause, and the troops he leads are Italians—

Hinc Augustus agens Italos in proelia Caesar
cum patribus populoque penatibus et magnis dis
(viii. 678).[1]

For the sake of clearness we may group what Virgil has to say of Italy under the headings of the country, the inhabitants, and the Trojan invasion.

I

Virgil did for Italy in some degree what Scott did for Scotland. He called the attention of his people for all future time to the beauty of the land, and linked the scenery with its history in language that could not be forgotten, while in emphasizing the unity of the Italian people he did a great deal more than Scott did or needed to do.

This interest in scenery and in nature was a comparatively new thing in the world, and we may say that it was one of the fruits of literature. An unlettered people is seldom much affected by scenery ; to feel the charm and the sublimity of a natural scene implies more reflection than they can readily achieve. And again, a people keenly absorbed in political or commercial life is apt to be interested in man to the exclusion of nature. This explains the inattention of Homer to landscape, as compared with later Greek writers and with Virgil.[2]

---

[1] "On this side is Augustus Caesar leading the Italians to conflict, with the senate and the people and the home-gods and their mighty brethren" (Conington). We may compare Horace, *Odes*, iii. 5. 9-12, where the combination of Roman and Italian names is highly significant. He is speaking of the soldiers who surrendered after Crassus' defeat at Carrhae, 53 B.C.—

Sub rege Medo Marsus et Apulus,
anciliorum et nominis et togae
oblitus aeternaeque Vestae,
incolumi Iove et urbe Roma.

[2] One might almost say that Homer is more interested in sea than land—

At a later day than Homer's we find Socrates startled and surprised by the aspect of a country spot, a mile or two from Athens, and when Phaedrus, who has brought him there, exclaims that he talks as if he were a complete stranger to the region, he admits it. He is, he says, fond of instruction, and "country places and trees will not teach him anything." [1]

But a change was coming over the world, for we find Aristotle writing on natural history (περὶ ζῴων) and his pupil Theophrastus on botany. Socrates had been amazed at the grass, as if he had seen it for the first time. Aristotle, on the other hand, was an acute and careful student of nature, and his powers of observation, according to Huxley, were, if not of the highest class, at least very good. [2]

With the decay of political life, as we have seen, men turned their minds to matters which they had ignored in the days of the city state, and they found ever increasing interest where of old they had suspected none. And Nature, they found, repaid their study, and the poets, while still thinking first of man, began to look at her. To go no further, we find abundant evidence of a certain interest in her in the poetry of Theocritus and Meleager. The fashion was set, and everybody began to draw flowers and trees and so forth—not necessarily from nature, but from Theocritus perhaps—and from the Greeks the mode passed to Rome. How popular it was, may be seen in Horace's lofty contempt for these second-hand artists. It was for their groves and streams that he coined one of his most famous phrases—the

a thoroughly Greek habit of mind ; while Virgil, an Italian, is of the opinion expressed by Lucretius—

> Suave mari magno turbantibus aequora ventis
> e terra . . . spectare (ii. 1).

But he gives a memorable line to the fisherman on the sea (*G.* i. 142).

[1] *Phaedrus*, 230 C, D. The sentiment has been surprisingly echoed in our own day. "When Wordsworth tells us," writes Viscount Morley, in the introduction to his edition of Wordsworth, "that 'one impulse from a vernal wood may teach you more of man, of moral evil and of good, than all the sages can,' such a proposition cannot seriously be taken as more than a half-playful sally for the benefit of some too bookish friend. No impulse from a vernal wood can teach us anything at all of moral evil and of good."

[2] Huxley, *Science and Culture*, Lect. viii.

"purple patch."[1]   Horace himself does not altogether disregard Nature—

domus Albuneae resonantis
et praeceps Anio ac Tiburni lucus et uda
mobilibus pomaria rivis [2] (*C.* i. 7. 11)—

but he cannot be accused of wasting time upon her. He was a friend, but a lukewarm friend,[3] of the country in spite of *O rus divinum.* The country, in fact, was a refuge from tiresome people who worried him in Rome.

But to turn from Nature to scenery, we find, until the invasion of Rome by Greek literature, little trace of interest in history or travel.

Vixere fortes ante Agamemnona, [4]

but the very names of their battlefields perished with their own, unsung. It was Greek literature that first quickened Rome; and when the Roman waked to the charm and interest of legend and history, it was to the stories of the great Greek past that he turned ; and they, with the art and architecture of Greece, wooed him abroad. Italy was a land of prose, but Greece of poetry, of heroism, and romance. The great towns and scenes of Greece drew pilgrims in increasing numbers, and some of them went home with deepened experience and larger sympathies. When Tullia died, Servius Sulpicius wrote to Cicero reflections which had been called forth within him by the ruins of Megara.[5]

---

[1] Horace, *A. P.* 15 *purpureus, late qui splendeat, unus et alter | adsuitur pannus, cum lucus et ara Dianae | et properantis aquae per amoenos ambitus agros, | aut flumen Rhenum aut pluvius describitur arcus.*

[2]   " Bright Albunea echoing from her cell.
        O headlong Anio ! O Tiburnian groves,
        And orchards saturate with shifting streams." (Conington).

[3] Boissier, *Nouvelles Promenades Archéologiques*, i. § 2 " Horace fut longtemps un ami assez tiède de la campagne."

[4] Horace, *Odes* iv. 9, 25 :
        " Before Atrides men were brave :
        But ah ! oblivion, dark and long,
        Has lock'd them in a tearless grave,
        For lack of consecrating song " (Conington).

[5] Cicero, *Fam.* iv. 5.

In the last years of the Republic and the early years of the Empire there was a great deal of foreign travel for pleasure. If Catullus went on business to the province that repaid him so ill, he chose his homeward route to please himself. Horace talks of men who travelled to sunny Rhodes, to Corinth on its isthmus, Delphi and Tempe, but, like a good Epicurean, he wonders why they should go so far.

Caelum non animum mutant qui trans mare currunt

is his conclusion to a letter to a friend who travelled in Asia Minor.[1] What they seek may be found nearer home— the quiet scene, comfort and content. But not everybody would accept such a doctrine, denying as it virtually did any real value to experience. Something was to be gained by seeing the islands "where burning Sappho loved and sung." Horace was wrong.

It is here that Virgil comes into our story. He would agree with the traveller. It is something to stand on the site of Troy as Caesar did after Pharsalia, to wander along the Simois and think of Homer and of Hector and Achilles.[2] But there is another land beside Greece full of charm, romance, and poetry. Why look for such things only in the mythical, the distant, the unknown? Are there no stories of great deeds and great inspirations but in Colchis, no rivers of charm and suggestion but Hermus and Ganges, mythical and half-unknown, no beauty in earth's gifts unless they come from Arabia and the fabulous Panchaia? Or is it not truer that Italy herself is no land of prose, but is full of every charm, every appeal to imagination and sympathy, which Greece can boast? Look, he cries in the second *Georgic*, look at our own land, consider her fields and crops and herds, think of her streams and of her lakes—are these lacking in poetry, in beauty, in appeal? Think of her people and their inglorious heroism—

---

[1] *Epp.* i. 11.
   " We come to this; when o'er the world we range,
      'Tis but our climate, not our mind we change" (Conington.)
[2] Lucan, *Pharsalia*, ix. 961.

the hardy race, schooled to bear evil, the patient builders of the little towns on the hill-tops—look at what they have done, look at their conquest of Nature, look at the fights they have fought for home and country, look at their victory over themselves—

Salve magna parens frugum, Saturnia tellus,
magna virum! (*G.* ii. 173).[1]

What Virgil did once in the *Georgics* he does again in the *Aeneid.* The scene is still Italy, but by the time the poet lays down his pen it is a new Italy, full of poetic associations, every region rich with heroic legend told in great language, itself moving and stimulating.

[1] "Hail to thee, land o Saturn, mighty mother of noble fruits and noble men" (Conington). I have resisted, but succumb to, the temptation of quoting here Ausonius' greatest poem, the *Mosella*. With much inferior matter intermingled, he really does represent the spirit of Virgil again after four centuries of external imitation. He studies a river of his native land (I use the term broadly), and finds it as full of inspiration and suggestion as Virgil found Italian waters. He goes indeed beyond Virgil in his study of Nature, e.g. his picture of the river-bottom—

> *Sic demersa procul durante per intima visu*
> *cernimus, arcanique patet penetrale profundi,*
> *cum vada lene meant liquidarum et lapsus aquarum*
> *prodit caerulea dispersas luce figuras :*
> *quod sulcata levi crispatur arena meatu,*
> *inclinata tremunt viridi quod gramina fundo ;*
> *usque sub ingenuis agitatae fontibus herbae*
> *vibrantes patiuntur aquas, lucetque latetque*
> *calculus, et viridem distinguit glarea muscum . . .*
> *intentos tamen usque oculos errore fatigant*
> *interludentes, examina lubrica, pisces (Mosella,* 59 ff.).

Does he need to tell us *ast ego . . . Naturae mirabor opus* (l. 51) ? Later on he quotes our passage of the *Georgics* for his own land—

> *Salve magne parens frugumque virumque Mosella !*
> *te clari proceres, te bello exercita pubes,*
> *aemula te Latiae decorat facundia linguae.*
> *Quin etiam mores et laetum fronte serena*
> *ingenium Natura tuis concessit alumnis.*
> *Nec sola antiquos ostentat Roma Catones,*
> *aut unus tantum iusti spectator et aequi*
> *pollet Aristides veteresque illustrat Athenas* (Ibid. 381).

That the form of this is Virgilian is clear, but the spirit also is the same, and the inspiration comes from the same source—*vincit amor patriae.*

Even before Aeneas reaches Italy we have evidence of
the new interest in scenery—

iam medio apparet fluctu nemorosa Zacynthos [1] (iii. 270).

This is no mere imitation of Homer's ὑλήεσσα Ζάκυνθος
(*Od.* 9. 24). It is the imagined sight of the island rising
from the sea and slowly showing more and more of its
forests as the ships come nearer. But we are told that Virgil
made slips in his pictures of the islands and other places
on the voyage. Myconos is not lofty, though Aeneas tells
Dido that it is (iii. 76). Mr W. G. Clark doubts whether
Virgil knew at first hand any of the scenery through
which Aeneas sailed till he reached Italy, and there seem
to be difficulties not only in the Aegaean but on the west
coast of Greece.[2] Still, the interest in scenery is clear
enough, if some of the scenes are confused; and, after all,
these places are only passed on the way to the promised
land. At last it is sighted, and here at least, one feels,
Virgil was recalling a homeward voyage of his own and
his first home-thoughts from abroad. He had himself seen
at daybreak the dim line of land along the horizon. At all
events he draws the low-lying shore of the Brindisi coast
exactly as it looks from the sea.

Iamque rubescebat stellis Aurora fugatis,
cum procul obscuros collis humilemque videmus
Italiam, Italiam primus conclamat Achates,
Italiam laeto socii clamore salutant [3] (iii. 521).

But now, save for the storm that drove the fleet to
Carthage and the lamentable delay there, Virgil is done with
foreign seas, and Aeneas coasts up the western shore of Italy,
and point by point the headlands rise, and receive the

---

[1] "Now from mid sea rises Zacynthos with its woods."
[2] W. G. Clark, *Peloponnesus*, pp. 20, 21, cited by Conington on *Aen.* iii. 76.
Compare the question of the temple, *Aen.* iii. 275-80, where Actium and Leucas
are in some confusion.
[3] "And now the stars were fled away and Dawn was reddening, when afar we see
the dim hills and low line of Italy;—'Italy!' Achates was the first to cry;
'Italy!' my comrades salute her with a glad shout."

names they bear in history, Palinurus, Caieta, Misenum.[1] Virgil could do little for Corcyra; it had its legend and he could only recall it; but, while he found the tale of Palinurus, for example, ready to his hand, a mere archaeological fancy, based on a sailor's story, he made the legend for all time. The cape Palinurus would always thereafter recall the story of the lost pilot and his chief's lament, lines among the most unforgettable ever written by Virgil for their simplicity and pathos—

O nimium caelo et pelago confise sereno
nudus in ignota Palinure iacebis arena [2] (v. 870).

The meeting of Aeneas and his pilot in Hades no doubt was suggested by the similar meeting of Odysseus and Elpenor in the *Odyssey*, but in its development we can see the method of Virgil. Elpenor has no abiding name or home in the Greek world[3]; Palinurus wakes memories of Italy, and makes a new and splendid tradition—

aeternumque locus Palinuri nomen habebit [4] (vi. 381).

The story is localized, it becomes Italian, and Italy is enriched by one more poetic association.

Similarly Virgil takes a pleasure in gathering up the old legends of Italy. The modern expert in folklore would find fault with him for his occasional addition of a slight Greek colouring to them. On the other hand, the great editor Heyne (Carlyle's Heyne) found an element of " the rough and rustic " in them, which survived even the "elegance of Virgil." Such stories as those of Camilla, the little girl sent flying

---

[1] For Palinurus and Misenus see Dion. H. *Ant Rom.* i. 83. Preller, *Röm. Myth.*[3] ii. 316, " A mariner's tale, such as were common in the Mediterranean, a personification of the favourable wind, πάλιν οὖρος, which is turned into a steersman." Capes of the name are found near Cyrene and near Ephesus. (See chapter iv.)

[2] " Ah, too trustful in calm skies and seas, thou shalt lie, O Palinurus, naked on an alien sand " (Mackail).

[3] For the real value of the episode of Elpenor the reader should consult Miss Stawell's chapter on " The House of Death " in her brilliant book, *Homer and the Iliad.*

[4] " For evermore shall the place keep Palinurus' name " (Mackail).

across the swoln stream lashed to her father's spear,[1] of Caeculus, the child of a spark of fire,[2] of Cacus breathing flame,[3] of the famous white sow with thirty porkers,[4] and of the twins nursed by the wolf, were told in Italy long before Virgil's day, the genuine heritage of the countryside. Simple old tales they were, loved by the people; and the poet of the Italian people loved them too, and was glad to weave them into the great epic.

In the same spirit he placed in Italy the entrance by which Aeneas made his way into the lower world. Odysseus had gone sailing over the sea, no man knew where, to find a way; but Virgil, true to Italy and to Italy's legends, reasserts the old popular story. Lucretius had refuted it a generation before with elaborate etymological and scientific explanations and parallels—

ianua ne forte his Orci regionibus esse
credatur, post hinc animas Acheruntis in oras
ducere forte deos manes inferne reamur [5] (Lucr. vi. 763).

Virgil had read the passage, for he borrows a striking phrase from it,[6] and we may remember his Epicureanism of the first *Georgic*. Had he been cross-questioned, he must have confessed to sharing the belief of Lucretius, but here is one striking difference between the two poets. Lucretius will pursue truth into prose ; Virgil, on the other hand, will avail himself of legend, though, as here, it may be scientifically demonstrated to be untrue, if by use of it he may develop some higher and poetic truth. And, whether we allegorize it or not, there is suggestion in the idea that to

---

A. xi. 562 *sonuere undae, rapidum super amnem | infelix fugit in iacu. stridente Camilla.* Her figure, says Conington, "is a bright relief to the tedium o the Virgilian battle."

[2] Servius, *ad A*. vii. 681.   [3] *A.* viii. 251.

[4] Varro, *R. R*. ii. 4. 18, says bronze images of the sow and the pigs are to be seen at Lavinium, *et corpus matris ab sacerdotibus, quod in salsura fuerit, demonstratur.* Virgil disposed of it differently, *A.* viii. 81-5. Dion. H. *Ant. Rom.* i. 56, 57, also has the tale.

[5] " That the gate of Orcus be not haply believed to exist in such spots ; and next we imagine that the manes gods from below do haply draw souls down from them to the borders of Acheron " (Munro).

[6] *Remigium alarum, Aen.* vi. 19 ; *remigi pennarum,* Lucr. vi. 743.

reach the other world we have not far to go over the sea, that the entrance is at our feet, here in Italy.

This contrast may be traced still further. Lucretius' poem abounds in close and brilliant observation of nature, and with the instinct of the man of science he links together what he sees, and makes one thing illustrate another, as he expounds some general principle to cover all the cases. His observations were uniformly made in Italy; their subjects are familiar sights of the countryside and also of the seaside. Virgil is not so spontaneous an observer, but he too observes with care and precision, looking, as a rule, in accordance with his instincts, landward. But the great difference is here. Lucretius obviously delights in observation because it leads him to the apprehension and confirmation of the principles of nature. Virgil watches nature, because it is nature, and because it is also Italian nature, and every fresh discovery makes Italy dearer to him—

> Contented if he might enjoy
> The things which others understand.

The charm of Italy does not depend on legends. It is the country itself, its beauty, the simple natural features, that Virgil gives back to his reader. Macrobius contrasts Virgil's "catalogue" with Homer's. Homer begins with Boeotia, "not for any special merit of Boeotia, but he chooses a celebrated promontory to start from," and then in a systematic way works through the geography of Greece. Virgil unhappily forgets geography and tangles Clusium, Populonia, and Pisa, then flies back to Caere and other places near Rome, and off again to Liguria and Mantua.[1] We can perhaps forgive him. His interest is in the places, and their people. He speaks of what most charmed and interested him in the places when he saw them; of "steep Praeneste and the fields of Juno of Gabii, cool Anio, and the Hernican rocks dewy with streams" (vii. 682)—and if we could not draw a map from his account of Italy, we know

---

[1] Macrobius, *Sat.* v. 15. Similarly in the review of Roman heroes in bk. vi, it has been remarked that Virgil has not thought it his duty to deal with them in chronological order.

the country, we have seen it with a poet's eyes. We see the
olive-groves of Mutusca (vii. 711), "the Massic lands glad
with wine" (vii. 725), and Abella city looking down from
amid her apple orchards (vii. 740).[1] We pass from stream
to lake, from "the shallows of Volturnus river" (vii. 728) to
"Mincius, child of Benacus, draped in grey reeds" (x. 205)[2];
from the strange Lake Amsanctus among its woods [3](vii. 563)
to Fucinus of the glassy waters [4] (vii. 759); from where "the
ploughshare goes up and down on the Rutulian hills and
the ridge of Circe" (vii. 798) to "where the marsh of Satura
lies black, and cold Ufens seeks his way along the valley-
bottoms and sinks into the sea" (vii. 801). Descriptions like
these could not fail to touch the hearts of those who loved
their country, and open the eyes of those who had never
known their native land.

Virgil was perhaps not so keen an observer of the life of
Nature as Lucretius, but he loved her as much, perhaps even
more, and here as elsewhere love is more potent than
intellect to find truth. In the *Aeneid* he is of course more
specially concerned with man, and we learn more of Nature
from the *Eclogues* and *Georgics*. Yet there is the same
character running through all his work. A German critic [5]
emphasizes that in the *Eclogues* the flowers and plants are
not mere aesthetic additions to the pictures, but belong to

[1] It is here that a dash of poetry comes into Varro's scientific and patriotic
explanation of why Italy is a more cultivated land than any in the world.
He speaks of zones, climates, &c., and then he asks, *non arboribus consita
Italia ut tota pomarium videatur? Re Rust.* i. 2. 6. The old Cilician pirate of
the *Georgics* will occur to the reader, and how in old age he took to growing
flowers on a patch of waste land under Oebalia's towers (*G.* iv. 125). Lecky
(*European Morals*, i. 265) finds a strange anticipation of Cowper's thought that
"God made the country, and man made the town" (*Task*, i. 749) in Varro,
R. R. iii. 1. 4—*Divina natura dedit agros; ars humana aedificavit urbes.*

[2] One may recall here the pleasant phrase of Juvencus, not the meanest of
Virgil's lovers and imitators, when he speaks of his master—*Minciadae dulcedo
Maronis, Praef.* ii. 9.

[3] Lago Amsanto still exhales its sulphuretted hydrogen (Deecke, *Italy*, p. 72),
but its woods are gone.

[4] See Deecke, p. 107, on Fucinus. In 1875, by means of a tunnel, 36,000
acres of arable land were reclaimed from the lake, and the hold of malaria
upon the region reduced.

[5] E. Glaser, *Publius Virgilius Maro als Naturdichter und Theist* (Gütersloh,
1880), pp. 20-1

them, and are an essential and inseparable part of them. The poet is intimately concerned with all that lives and moves. It is all Italian. How full the *Georgics* are of Italian nature needs no mention here. In like manner Virgil uses by preference the trees, the birds, and beasts of Italy for his similes in the *Aeneid*. His fancy for the musical names of Greek poetry may lead him to call his cranes "Strymonian" (x. 265), and to picture his swans in the "Asian fen" (vii. 701), but we may be sure that it was in no Asian fen that he learnt the swan's note, but "among the vocal pools on the fish-filled river of Padusa" (a mouth of the Po, xi. 456). And note that the swans are compared to Italian troops singing their king as they go—

With measured pace they march along,
And make their monarch's deeds their song ;
Like snow-white swans in liquid air,
When homeward from their food they fare,
And far and wide melodious notes
Come rippling from their slender throats,
While the broad stream and Asia's fen
Reverberate to the sound again.
Sure none had thought that countless crowd
   A mail-clad company ;
It rather seemed a dusky cloud
Of migrant fowl, that, hoarse and loud
   Press landward from the sea (vii. 698-705, Conington).[1]

When Virgil describes the thronging of the dead to the bank of Acheron, he uses Bacchylides' simile of the wind driving the fallen leaves,[2] though he introduces a characteristic touch of his own, *autumni frigore primo*.[3] To this he adds "birds that swarm landward from the deep gulf, when the chill of the year routs them overseas and drives them to sunny lands" (vi. 310). He must have watched them on the Adriatic shore of Italy.

---

[1] Warde Fowler, *A Year with the Birds* (2nd ed.), p. 153, says this swan is the *Cycnus musicus*, or "whooper." In Northern Europe it is the bird associated with the charming swan-princesses of fairy tale.

[2] Bacchylides, v. 63 ἔνθα δυστάνων βροτῶν | ψυχὰς ἐδάη παρὰ Κωκυτοῦ ῥεέθροις, | οἶά τε φύλλ' ἄνεμος | Ἴδας ἀνὰ μηλοβότους | πρῶνος ἀργηστὰς δονεῖ.

[3] "At the first cold of Autumn."

One very interesting question rises in connexion with Virgil's birds. In the third *Eclogue* (68) he speaks of the stock-dove nesting—

Namque notavi
Ipse locum, aeriae quo congessere palumbes.[1]

In the *Georgics* he pictures the rook (*corvus*) returning to its brood at the approach of rain.[2] But to-day it is doubtful if the stock-dove breeds at all in Italy, and the rook does so only in the sub-Alpine region. The swan, once familiar in the region of Mantua,[3] is now rarely to be seen, while the stork with the other birds passes over Italy for northern latitudes. How are we to explain this? Are we to say that Virgil is a bad observer, or can we save his credit?[4] It seems in fact that the explanation lies in a change in the Italian country and climate.[5] The great forests are gone, and with them the cooler air, which the breeding bird seeks; and the swamps and marshes of the swans and storks have been dried up by drainage and by the clearing of the forests. Ufens, Conington says, has no longer to look for a way, for one has been dug for him.

But one inhabitant of the marshes is still to be found where he was in Virgil's days. The wild boar, to which he compares Mezentius, is still there—

> Long fostered in Laurentum's fen
> 'Mid reeds and marish ground (*A.* x. 709).

It was there that Pliny hunted him, notebook (*pugillares*) in hand; and there he is hunted to-day, probably as he was then, but without notebooks.[6]

---

[1] "For I have marked the place, where the doves have built high in air."

[2] *G.* i. 414 *Progeniem parvam dulcesque revisere nidos.*

[3] *G.* ii. 198—

> *Et qualem infelix amisit Mantua campum*
> *pascentem niveos herboso flumine cycnos.*

[4] The reader may recall the terrible efforts made to keep the lark from the window in *L'Allegro.*

[5] Warde Fowler, op. cit. pp. 143, 148, 153. Similar observations of change in the climate are being made in North America to-day. Cf. Deecke, *Italy*, p. 185, on the forests of Italy, of which he gives a somewhat melancholy account.

[6] Cf. Boissier, *Country of Horace and Virgil* (tr.), pp. 304-6, and Pliny, *Epp.* i. 6.

II

From the country we pass to the people.[1] There are readers to whom the second half of the *Aeneid* seems to be remote, if not rather dull; the poet seems to have fallen from the heights he reached in the earlier books. But this is hardly Virgil's view. As an Italian, it would seem to him that now was the moment when his poem touched the heart most nearly, when it told—

> quibus Itala iam tum
> floruerit terra alma viris (vii. 643)—

how even then (*iam tum*) the dear motherland flowered with heroes. The metaphor is a fine one. Flowers are the natural outcome of right seed in right soil.

On the other hand, there are those to whom Virgil seems to have lost his opportunity. What might he not have told of old Italian wont and use, if only he had been willing to sink the poem in the dictionary? Virgil is quite sensible of the picturesque aspect of his subject,[2] but it is as a poet rather than as an antiquary. Latin scholars of a later day loved to think of him as one of themselves, but it was an injustice to him. Thus while he tells us of the dress and arms of this ancient tribe and that, the charge which Carlyle brought against Scott, that he drew his men from the jerkin inward, does not lie against Virgil. He is more interested in the character of the people than their clothing. It is on this that he spends most care. He is a philosophic student of history, and he is tracing for us the emergence of the higher life of Italy from barbarism. He watches throughout the process the continuance of the strong and worthy qualities

---

[1] *Pandite nunc Helicona deae* (*A.* vii. 641). Virgil's invocation may be compared with Spenser's, when he comes to his Chronicle of Briton Kings (*F. Q.* ii. x.)—
    "Who now shall give unto me words and sound
    Equal unto this haughty enterprise?" &c.

[2] See Bernard Bosanquet, *Hist. of Aesthetic*, p. 92, on Virgil's praise of Italy, in which he finds blended affection for the scenery, historical sentiment, the sentiment of national duty, "heightened by appreciation of the picturesqueness in life and manners, produced by the relations of Rome with all quarters of the known world."

that underlay the barbarism, and he shows their independence
of it. Remulus Numanus is a survival of the old days and
the old ways, but every manly attribute he boasts for his
people survives in Evander and Pallas, not a whit lessened,
though refined. We shall understand the whole scope and
purpose of the *Aeneid* more truly, if we realize that the work
of Aeneas, like that of every man who has helped mankind
forward, has been heralded by many another working in the
same direction and with a similar inspiration. The rise of
Italy is the theme of the whole book and of its parts—

Romanam condere gentem.

There is occasional vagueness in Virgil's account of early
Italy, but it is possible to collect a tolerably consistent story
from what he says. Let us begin with Evander on Italian
history (viii. 314 f.). "In these woodlands dwelt fauns and
nymphs sprung of the soil, and a tribe of men born of
stocks and hard oak, who had neither law nor grace of
life; they never learnt to yoke the ox, nor to garner their
stores, nor to husband what they got; but the boughs
nurtured them and the hard living of the hunter." (It
is very characteristic of the good Italian to regard the men
as barbarians who

haud componere opes norant aut parcere parto.[1]

Thrift was the first virtue of civilization.) Saturn brought
civilization into Italy, and after him came others, not all
of his mind. Last, Evander himself, like Saturn an exile,
"driven from his native land and voyaging to the ends of
the seas, all-powerful Fortune and inevitable Destiny set
on these shores." Progress has not had an uninterrupted
course, and there are plenty of barbarians yet, though the
people are not content with them. Mezentius has been

---

[1] Cf. Horace's account of the country mouse, who is a thorough Italian
peasant, *asper et attentus quaesitis* (*S.* ii. 6. 82). The mouse, however, is as
hospitable as Evander himself, to do him justice. We may again compare
Spenser (*F. Q.* ii. x. 7) on the early inhabitants of Albion who "by hunting and
by spoiling liveden," though in the case of our own land the Trojan "Brutus
anciently deriv'd, From roiall stocke of old Assaracs line" abolished the savage
foe. Italy's story, as we shall see, was different.

expelled from Etruria, and Turnus has to face a hostile party among his people. These men still represent brutality and violence, qualities not incompatible in the case of Mezentius with a certain chivalry and deep affection.

Remulus pictures a midway stage between the earliest barbarism and the new civilization. He is of the school and family of Turnus, and on the whole prefers the barbarism. Still, he emphasizes some of the real virtues of the Italian. "A hardy breed," he says, "we carry our new-born sons to the streams, and harden them in the cruel cold of the waters. Our boys spend wakeful nights in hunting and tire out the woodland; their sport is to rein the steed and level shafts with the bow. Our youth, schooled to labour and trained to want, subdues the soil with the mattock and shakes the city walls with battle. All our life bears the mark of iron; to prick the steer's flank we turn our spear. Old age, which dulls the force of all else, weakens not our strength of spirit nor abates our vigour. White hairs bear the helmet, and it is ever our delight to bring home fresh spoil and live by plunder" (ix. 603-13).[1]

Some of this was not new.

Patiens operum parvoque adsueta iuventus

was a phrase Virgil had used in the *Georgics*,[2] when he was praising country life.

O fortunatos nimium sua si bona norint
agricolas[3] (*G.* ii. 458),

he cries; and this character is part of their blessedness; but, where Remulus adds his *vivere rapto*, Virgil prefers to emphasize *sacra deum sanctique patres*.

Now if we turn once more to Evander, we shall find this latter combination in his little town of Pallanteum. He himself and his son Pallas fall short in no degree of the

---

[1] Cf. *Hymn to Demetrius Poliorcetes* Αἰτωλικὸν γὰρ ἁρπάσαι τὰ τῶν πέλας.
[2] *Georg.* ii. 472, but for *parvo* he there has *exiguo*. See ch. i. § v. p. 36.
[3] "O happy, beyond human happiness, had they but a sense of their blessings, the husbandmen." (Conington).

manhood of Turnus, but it is significant that when first we see them they are engaged in sacrifice to Hercules. They represent in the heroic age all the virtues of Roman and Italian at the best period of their history—simplicity, dignity, hardness, faith, courage, and piety. And these men are the allies of Aeneas. When he welcomes Aeneas to his house, Evander bids him enter in a sentence which probably sums up his own philosophy of life and perhaps the poet's, a sentence which has not lost its charm and its value—Fénelon, we are told, could never read it without tears—

> aude, hospes, contemnere opes et te quoque dignum
> finge deo, rebusque veni non asper egenis [1] (viii. 364).

III

To such an Italy the Trojans came. If it is to them the land of promise, they are no less promised to Italy. They are to deliver the Etruscans from the rule of Mezentius—a symbolic action. They are to bring to Italy all that is signified to a Trojan by Troy, all that Evander found wanting in the old life of the country—*mos* and *cultus*—

> pacisque imponere morem.

They are to bring the gods to Italy; indeed, they find some of their own gods waiting them; Cybele is already an effective power in the Tiber.

M. Boissier even held that the *Aeneid* is a religious epic, and that the chief purpose of Aeneas is this introduction of the gods into Latium. But Virgil at least links with this another idea, which elsewhere seems to overshadow it. Take these lines—

> Multa quoque et bello passus, dum conderet urbem
> inferretque deos Latio—genus unde Latinum
> Albanique patres atque altae moenia Romae [2] (*A.* i. 5)

---

[1] "Dare thou, my guest, to despise riches; mould thyself to like dignity of godhead, and come not harsh to our poverty" (Mackail). *Quoque*, because Evander is referring to the visit of Hercules to that house.

[2] "Much too he suffered in war, ere he might found a city and bring his gods into Latium; from whom is the Latin race, the fathers of Alba, and the walls of lofty Rome."

with the line a little below, in which he sums up his theme again—

Tantae molis erat Romanam condere gentem [1] (i. 33).

Virgil had not been an Epicurean for nothing. The gods whom Aeneas was bringing to Rome the poet might now recognize as symbols of divinity, but he could scarcely attach such superlative importance to these particular symbols. At any rate for the reader their significance is rather slight.[2] Aeneas carefully brought them from Troy, but it is clear that they derive their importance from Rome, and that Rome does not owe her importance to them.

The foundation of Rome—of the Roman race—is the centre of the whole story, but Rome is to be no Trojan town nor her people Trojans. She is to be rather the summing up of all that is excellent in Italy. The Trojan element reaffirms the ideals of the Italian race; all it does is to add the slight touch that changes nothing while it alters everything.

This is brought out by the speech in which Juno makes her submission to Fate, and by Jupiter's reply.[3] By a certain looseness in regard to the letter, Conington has given a heightened expression to the spirit, and the passages may be quoted in his rendering. Juno concludes—

> Vouchsafe me yet one act of grace
> For Latium's sake, your sire's own race:
> No ordinance of fate withstands
> The boon a nation's pride demands.
> When treaty, aye, and love's blest rite
> The warring hosts in peace unite,
> Respect the ancient stock, nor make
> The Latin tribes their style forsake,
> Nor Troy's nor Teucer's surname take,
> Nor garb nor language let them change

---

[1] "So mighty a task it was to found the race of Rome."
[2] In *A.* iii. 147 they come in a dream to Aeneas and bid him seek Italy, promising fame and empire to him and to his race.
[3] *A.* xii. 791-840.

For foreign speech and vesture strange,
　　But still abide the same :
Let Latium prosper as she will,
Their thrones let Alban monarchs fill ;
Let Rome be glorious on the earth,
The centre of Italian worth ;
But fallen Troy be fallen still
　　The nation and the name.

Jupiter replies—

Ausonia shall abide the same
Unchanged in customs, speech, and name
The sons of Troy, unseen though felt
In fusion with the mass shall melt :
Myself will give them rites, and all
Still by the name of Latins call.
The blended race that thence shall rise
　　Of mixed Ausonian blood
Shall soar alike o'er earth and skies
　　So pious, just, and good.

The Italy of Aeneas is not externally like the Italy of Augustus. The golden Capitol of Augustus has replaced the brakes and bushes of Evander's day, but the god, the unknown god, who haunted the place in the Arcadian times haunts it still, and now he is known as the Roman Jupiter. The race is still the same. Italians they were when Aeneas came, and after a thousand years the strength of Rome is still the Italians. Nor is this all, for with the blood the character still prevails. The Italians are still

patiens operum parvoque adsueta iuventus,

and the words of Evander are still the key-note of that character which brought the world under the sway of Italy.

CHAPTER VI

THE LAND AND THE NATION.—2. ROME

Gloriosa dicta sunt de te, civitas Dei.

"WHAT is it," asks M. Patin, "that makes the story of Aeneas establishing himself in Italy into a Roman epic? It is the eminently national character of the legend used by the poet; it is also something more closely concerned with his art—I mean the perspectives continually opened down the history of Rome, which, seen thus from the heart of the fable, as it were from a distance, becomes what it never yet had been with Virgil's predecessors—poetic, epic."

In the preceding chapter we discussed Virgil's feeling for Italy, and it remains to consider what he has to say of the city which made the land one, and what of its race of soldiers and citizens. It will hardly be needful to repeat that Virgil will look deeper than many other patriots and poets for the grounds and meaning of Rome's greatness. He will probably not be so ready as some of his fellow citizens, *varicosi centuriones*, to find the cause and the justification of Rome's rule in her strong arm. That theory he leaves for Remulus Numanus, the Rob Roy of Latium.

> The good old rule, the ancient plan,
> That they should take, who have the power,
> And they should keep who can,

has its parallel in

> semperque recentis
> comportare iuvat praedas et vivere rapto [1] (ix. 612).

It was not merely the theory of Remulus; it was also the idea underlying Sulla's constitution—the divine right of

---

[1] " Ever fresh booty it is our delight to gather and to live by plunder.'

126

the senate to misgovern and to plunder as long as there
was a decent equality of opportunities. This theory was
hardly likely to commend itself to Virgil the philosopher
any more than to Virgil the farmer—*barbarus has segetes?*
It had brought endless misery upon mankind, and it had
ruined the old Republic. It offended the patriot, who
thought of his country as larger than any *pomoerium* could
encircle. It repelled the thinker, who had caught the spirit
of the gentler philosophy of later Greece. It shocked the
poet.

> Felix qui potuit rerum cognoscere caussas.[1]

So Virgil wrote of Nature and her laws, and we may be
sure he would apply the same language to the history
of man. Why did Rome conquer the world? Or, to
put it otherwise, what end does Rome's dominion of
the world serve? What is Rome's moral title to rule?
Questions which not every one asked, but questions on the
answers to which a poet felt everything depended.

But there are other things which come into a poet's
view—the life of man with its endless variety of form and
spirit, all the ways in which human nature seeks to express
itself, all the things which shallower reflection would call
external, but which the poet loves as the outcome of
something within—garb, phrase, and usage,—ambitions and
achievements, failures, too,—through which, through all of
which, he sees the marvellous mind of man, hoping, striving,
failing, but, generation by generation, gaining ground, never
giving up the forward struggle.

> Πολλὰ τὰ δεινὰ κοὐδὲν ἀνθρώπου δεινότερον πέλει.[2]

And of all the wonderful endowments of man, the most
amazing, Virgil would agree with Sophocles, and the most
godlike are " speech and wind-swift thought and all the
moods that mould a state "

> καὶ φθέγμα καὶ ἀνεμόεν φρόνημα καὶ ἀστυνόμους ὀργάς.[3]

---

[1] " Happy he who could learn the laws on which the world rests."
[2] " Many are the wondrous things, and nought than man more wondrous."
Sophocles, *Antigone*, 332.   [3] Ibid. 354.

Thus history, and particularly the history of his own race, is to the poet no empty tale, but a long self-manifestation of the human spirit, of the utmost interest and pathos; and to make it his own, to interpret it to himself, and to bring it home to others, is the necessity laid upon him.

Nor was it only the past that Virgil found so full of meaning; he was no mere antiquary, and the past would have been nothing to him if the present had had no interest. The Empire as he saw it, and the City which was the Empire's heart, touched him and held him. Rome, the world's mistress, Rome, the centre of all the history of his people, was the Rome he walked the streets of,—the Rome he fled from to Naples,—the Rome his heart could never forget. All these links that bound him to Rome are to be found in the *Aeneid*, and we shall not understand Virgil and his poem until we begin to feel with him something of what he felt for Rome.

I

In the first *Eclogue* Virgil has recorded his first impression of Rome. Tityrus tells Meliboeus that he had imagined Rome a sort of bigger Mantua, but still like Mantua, as a big dog is like a puppy, but that he had found it something quite different—something distinct in the nature of things. It was not so much the size as the splendour and the beauty of Rome that impressed him. He later on emphasizes this explicitly; Rome is the most beautiful thing in the world—

scilicet et rerum facta est pulcherrima Roma [1] (*G.* ii. 534).

This judgement is also Plutarch's, who quite independently pronounces Rome "the most beautiful of all the works of man." [2] Virgil gently laughs at the splendid portals of the houses and the swarms of clients, who gape at the doorposts inlaid with tortoise-shell, the gold embroidery and the bronzes of Corinth (*G.* ii. 461); but, though he can

---

[1] "Yes and Rome has become the most beautiful thing in the world."
[2] *De fortuna Romanorum* 316 E τῶν ἀνθρωπίνων ἔργων τὸ κάλλιστον.

dispense with them, they have not escaped him, they have made their appeal to the quick eyes of the poet.[1]

Not much attention has been called to it, but it is certainly remarkable what a charm the great city had for this poet of country life. He had been caught by the spell of the "rivers gliding under the ancient walls" of Italy, and of such little towns as Abella on its hill-top among the orchards; but the power of a great city is different, and does not always appeal to the mind that Abella will fascinate. Yet it is hard to think he was not moved himself, when we read of the effect of the sight of Carthage on Aeneas—the towers, the great stones in the walls, the temples, the theatre; yes, but also the harbour, the life and movement of the streets, and the *noise* of a great city—

Miratur portas strepitumque et strata viarum [2] (i. 422).

Where Juvenal and Horace draw pictures, vivid and realistic, of the streets of Rome and the discouraging details

---

[1] *Faciles oculi*, *A.* viii. 310. A poet is the best interpreter of a poet, and even if it seems a shade irrelevant, the reader may be reminded of Browning's conception of a poet at large in the streets of a town. The whole poem should be studied.

> He walked and tapped the pavement with his cane,
> Scenting the world, looking it full in face . . .
> He stood and watched the cobbler at his trade,
> The man who slices lemons into drink . . .
> He took such cognizance of men and things,
> If any beat a horse, you felt he saw ;
> If any cursed a woman, he took note ;
> Yet stared at nobody.   (*How it strikes a Contemporary.*)

Horace confesses to a weakness for loafing and looking round the streets (*Sat.* i. 6, 111), but for all his looking, I think he saw less than Virgil.

[2] " He marvels at the gates and the noise and the paved ways." *Strata viarum* : note here what Strabo says of Rome, c. 235 οὗτοι (the Romans) προὐνόησαν μάλιστα ὧν ὠλιγώρησαν ἐκεῖνοι (the Greeks), στρώσεως ὁδῶν καὶ ὑδάτων εἰσαγωγῆς καὶ ὑπονόμων τῶν δυναμένων ἐκκλύζειν τὰ λύματα τῆς πόλεως εἰς τὸν Τίβεριν. ἔστρωσαν δὲ καὶ τὰς κατὰ τὴν χώραν ὁδούς . . . the ancients (c. 236) neglected the beauty of Rome πρὸς ἄλλοις μείζοσι καὶ ἀναγκαιοτέροις ὄντες, but later, and especially in these days of Augustus, the city has been filled full of ἀναθημάτων πολλῶν καὶ καλῶν. Cf. also Wordsworth's description of London, *Prelude*, bk. vii—

> The quick dance
> Of colours, lights, and forms ; the deafening din ;
> The comers and the goers face to face.

9

which a poet would meet there, the greater poet looks through the dust and the detail, and feels that

Earth has not anything to show more fair.

If the *Georgics* are, as Dean Merivale phrased it, "the Glorification of Labour," the poet recognizes work in the great city too, and hails it. He compares the busy hum of men with the labour of the bees, and it is the poet of the fourth *Georgic* who does so, sympathetic alike with the industry of bees and men.

It is curious, too, that twice he gives us pictures of the sack of a great city, with something of that feeling of pain for the waste of humanity which he shows in telling of such a death as that of Galaesus.[1] The fall of Troy, told by Aeneas to Dido, may naturally call for sympathy—

urbs antiqua ruit multos dominata per annos [2] (ii. 363).

But in the other case it is Carthage herself, and the poet is haunted by the pathos of the scene, the horror of the irrational flames and the wreck they make of homes and temples, places where human memories are clustered most—

non aliter quam si immissis ruat hostibus omnis
Karthago aut antiqua Tyros, flammaeque furentes
culmina perque hominum volvuntur perque deorum [3]
(iv. 669-71).

Nor was the river on which Rome stood without its charm for the poet.[4] He makes the river-god at once the

---

[1] *Iustissimus unus qui fuit* (vii. 535); *foedatique ora Galaesi* (vii. 575).

[2] "The ancient city falls, after her long years of empire."

[3] "Even as though all Carthage or ancient Tyre went down, as the foe poured in, and the flames rolled furious over the roofs of house and temple." It may be noted that there were great historic sieges of both Tyre and Carthage. Kingsley, in *Hereward the Wake*, touches on the psychological effect of the flames blazing in daylight over a building with associations; and the spectacle of a hospital burning in the sunshine of a Canadian Christmas remains in the writer's mind.

[4] *Fluvio Tiberinus amoeno* (vii. 30-viii. 31); *caelo gratissimus amnis* (viii. 64). *Amoenus* is, as Professor Sellar remarks, a strong and emphatic word, "lovely."

friend and benefactor of Rome's great ancestor (viii. 31).
He recalls with interest its ancient name—

amisit verum vetus Albula nomen [1] (viii. 332).

But his most important picture of the river is that of Aeneas'
first entrance. The story of Aeneas' coming was an old one,
and a century before Virgil's day a Roman writer, Fabius
Maximus, had looked at the Tiber and its mouth, and given
his own feelings to Aeneas—"he was not at all pleased to
have come to a country so very bare and shingly." [2] "This
vigorous phrase," says M. Boissier, "represents to admiration
the aspect of the country as we see it to-day," but he goes
on to point out that in Virgil's day it was otherwise.
Pliny the Elder, in an interesting chapter on the river,
says "it will admit even great ships coming from the
Italian sea, a most peaceful trafficker in everything that
the whole world produces; and, one river as it is, it has
almost more villas than all the rivers in all the lands,
planted and beautiful, upon its banks." [3]

Aeneas reached the Tiber's mouth at dawn. [4] "And now
the sea reddened with shafts of light, and high in heaven
yellow Dawn shone in her rosy car; when the winds fell, and
every breath sank suddenly, and the oar-blades toil through
the heavy ocean-floor. And on this Aeneas descries from
the sea a mighty forest. Midway in it the pleasant Tiber
stream breaks to sea in swirling eddies, laden with yellow
sand. [5] Around and above fowl many in sort, that haunt

[1] "It has lost the true name of old, Albula."
[2] Interpolated in Servius, *ad Aen.* i. 3, *Fabius Maximus annalium primo: tum Aeneas aegre patiebatur in eum devenisse agrum, macerrimum litorosissimumque.*
[3] Boissier, *Horace et Virgile*, p. 266 (Fr.); p. 248 (Engl. tr.); Pliny, *N. H.* iii. 5 (9).
[4] W. Warde Fowler, *Social Life at Rome*, p. 2. "Virgil showed himself a true artist in bringing his hero up the Tiber. . . . He saw that by the river alone he could land him exactly where he could be shown by his friendly host, almost at a glance, every essential feature of the site, every spot most hallowed by antiquity in the minds of his readers."
[5] Elsewhere Virgil alludes to the Tiber's habit of wearing away its banks, viii. 63 *stringentem ripas*. Servius tells us there that it was to this the river owed its ancient name Rumon, *quasi ripas ruminans et exedens*. It is possible that Rome was named from the river, though at best this is a guess. Deecke,

his banks and the channel of his flood, solaced heaven with song and flew about the forest" (vii. 25-34, Mackail).

Turning now to the "sights" of Rome, we find that Virgil manages to bring some of them already into prominence in Evander's town. Here is the cave of Cacus, and Evander tells its legend. Here is the Carmental gate, the grove which in later days Romulus made his asylum, the Lupercal, the wood of Argiletum, the Tarpeian rock, the Capitol, "golden now, of old rough with bush and thicket," yet even then the abode of a great god, whom the Arcadian settlers take to be Jove himself. Aeneas and the king pass on and see "the cattle lowing all about the Roman forum and down the gay Carinae."[1]

It was not idly that Virgil gave time and thought to these memorials of the oldest Rome. The sympathy with the primitive and simple life of the old days, expressed in the thought which he gives to Evander—

aude, hospes, contemnere opes, et te quoque dignum finge deo, rebusque veni non asper egenis [2] (viii. 364)—

was deeply rooted in his nature. He was the child of the country—bred simply by rustic parents, in a land of woods and standing waters. He at least had no contempt for the old and poor Rome ; the Capitol was for him as much the seat of Juppiter Capitolinus in the days of bush and forest as in the new and golden splendours of his own day. He has no such feeling as lurks in the epigram of Propertius—

For gods of clay these golden temples rose.[3]

More of reverence dwells in the greater poet. And quite apart from his sympathy for the plain life of the old days, these relics helped him to realize the men who made Rome, till he knew them as Livy did not.

Italy, p. 86, says the Tiber has a yellowish-brown appearance in spring—the season of Aeneas' coming, according to Virgil's indications. On p. 93 he gives some extraordinary figures as to the solid matter carried by the river.

[1] Cf. Propertius, v. I, 3 *atque ubi Navali stant sacra Palatia Phoebo | Evandri profugae concubuere boves.*

[2] "Dare thou, my guest, to despise riches; mould thyself to like dignity of godhead, and come not harsh to our poverty" (Mackail).

[3] Prop. v. I. 5 *fictilibus crevere deis haec aurea templa.*

II

Virgil looks upon Roman history as one from first to last. From the oldest days to the latest there has been a continuity of usage and religion, a succession of patriots and heroes, one and the same spirit animating every great Roman in his turn, and filling with meaning those rites which he learnt from his father and taught to his son. Aeneas is nobly forgetful of the ways of Homeric Troy, and observes faithfully the religious usages of historic Rome. At his first sacrifice on Italian soil he veiled his head, as bidden by the seer Helenus.[1] There is a legend, quoted by Servius and by Plutarch, that he did this to avoid seeing the face of Diomedes; but the custom was no doubt Roman before the Romans ever heard of Diomedes or Aeneas—

hac casti maneant in religione nepotes[2] (*A*. iii. 409),

says Helenus, a clear indication. De la Ville de Mirmont calls attention to the further fact that in the *Aeneid* magic and unlawful rites are left to the enemies of Rome.[3] Dido uses magic, and Amata practises Bacchic orgies; for Aeneas and his followers the dignified and ancient ritual of Rome suffices.

The most elaborate account given by Virgil of ritual and service concerns the sacrifice to Hercules at the Ara Maxima. This sacrifice, however, was offered with Greek usages, but it was of immemorial antiquity, and it was still in Virgil's day a yearly event. Mommsen dissevers Hercules the Latin god of gardens from the Greek Herakles, but Dionysius of Halicarnassus[4] and Livy,[5] like Virgil, connect the feast with Herakles' slaying of Cacus, the brigand who stole his cattle—the cattle he himself had taken from Geryon. Dionysius indeed says that that is the "more mythical" story, and he follows it up with a more surprising if "truer account," one of those attempts which M. Chassang

---

[1] *A*. iii. 404, 545; Plutarch, *Quaest. Rom.* 10.

[2] "Let the piety of generations to come abide in this observance" (Conington).

[3] *Ap. de Rhodes et Virgile*, p. 149 f.

[4] Dion. H. *Ant. Rom.* i. 39-42.   [5] Livy, i. 7.

happily characterizes as "the torturing of mythology to the detriment of poetry, without profit to history."[1] Some explanation had to be given of the foreign ritual. Livy says it was the only foreign ceremony adopted by Romulus, and suggests that he had a prophetic sympathy for a deified hero. Virgil lets it date, foreign as it is, from the earliest town on the destined site of Rome, and he eliminates some of the features that appear in Livy. Hercules is a deliverer, and no mention is made of his being *cibo vinoque gravatus*.[2] Evander is very careful to make it clear to Aeneas that the sacrifice is not a mere novelty lightly adopted, as new religions were adopted at a later day in Rome.[3] "No idle superstition," he says, "that knows not the gods of old, hath ordered these our solemn rites, this customary feast, this altar of august sanctity; saved from bitter perils, O Trojan guest, do we worship, and most due are the rites we inaugurate" (viii. 185, Mackail). The proper, traditional priestly families of Potitii and Pinarii wait upon the altar, already and for ever the *Ara Maxima*. The sacrifice is followed by a sacred dance of the Salii and a hymn in honour of the hero. In the general revival of ancient ceremonies under Augustus, the sacrifice, which does not seem to have fallen into disuse, would not lose importance, and Virgil by this account of it links the generations together.

It is curious that, while Virgil emphasizes more than once the poverty of Evander, he should give so much splendour to Latinus, whose palace has the most Roman and patriotic air. "His house, vast and reverend, crowned the city, upreared on an hundred columns, once the palace of Laurentian Picus, amid awful groves of ancestral sanctity. Here it was held of good omen that the kings should receive the sceptre and have their fasces first raised before them; this temple was their senate-house; this their

---

[1] Chassang, *Histoire du Roman*, p. 74.

[2] "Heavy with food and wine." Virgil would have leant to Balaustion's version of *Alcestis*—even against Euripides.

[3] Tacitus, *Ann.* xv. 44 *quo cuncta undique atrocia aut pudenda confluunt celebranturque*. The historian is explaining how it was that the Christian religion came to Rome.

sacred banqueting-hall; here, when a ram was slain, the elders were wont to sit down at long tables. Further, there stood a-row in the entry images of the forefathers of old in ancient cedar,[1] Italus, and father Sabinus, planter of the vine, still holding in show the curved pruning-hook, and ancient Saturn, and the likeness of Janus with two faces, and the rest of the kings from the beginning, and they who had suffered wounds of war in fighting for their country. Moreover, there hung much armour on the sacred doors, captive chariots and curved axes, helmet-crests and massy gateway-bars, lances and shields, and beaks torn from war-ships. He too sat there, with the augur-staff of Quirinus, girt in short augural gown, and carrying on his left arm the sacred shield (*ancile*), Picus tamer of horses; he whom Circe his spouse, blind with passion, smote with her golden rod and turned by her poisons into a bird of dappled wing" (vii. 170-91). "This edifice," says Conington in his note on the passage, "combines the temple and the senate-house. Virgil has also employed it as a sort of museum of Roman antiquities."[2] The ceremonies of entering on office, the gathering of the senate, the archaic statues of the king's ancestors, the trophies on the walls (most glorious ana-chronism of all, the *erepta rostra carinis*), the *lituus*, the *trabea*, the *ancile*—all these things were full of suggestion to the Roman reader, and reminded him of all that was noble and triumphant in the national history. They might also remind him a little of a palace and a temple on the Palatine, where another and a greater ruler was gathering up the nation's traditions in himself, amidst surroundings as crowded with revivals of old memories.

Take again the description of the ancient usage of Latium in proclaiming war—"a custom kept sacred by the Alban cities and kept to this day by Rome, mistress of the world, when they stir the War-God to enter battle;

---

[1] The reader will remember how many ξόανα mark the track of Aeneas through the pages of Dionysius of Halicarnassus.

[2] Robertson Smith, *Religion of the Semites*, p. 147, on sanctuaries as "public parks and public halls," and their use for the accumulation of treasure. The antiquarian interest of Latinus' building is due to the spirit of Virgil's age.

whether it be against the Getae they purpose to carry tearful war,[1] or against the Hyrcanians, or the Arabs, or to reach to India and track the Morning-Star to its home and reclaim the standards from the Parthians" (vii. 601-6). Here the last achievement of Roman power, the recovery of the standards lost by Crassus at Carrhae, is brought into connexion with the remotest antiquity of Rome—could the continuity of the nation's life find more striking expression? For, while we may doubt, and Virgil might agree with us in doubting, the existence of King Latinus, a religious or semi-religious practice of this kind is a genuine survival and tells a tale, much as the strange ceremonies employed at the opening of Parliament—ceremonies the origin of which no man perhaps knows certainly—speak of seven hundred years of English history, of the slow winning of freedom and democracy, and of the continuity of the race through it all. Nor should we forget that Virgil, in speaking of the opening of the twin gates of War, reminds his readers that they had been shut, when at last Rome had come within sight of her goal of universal peace under Augustus.

And more, through all the years which have seen these customs live Rome has never ceased to be *felix prole virum*[2] (*A*. vi. 784). With a fine daring Virgil takes a picture from Lucretius—the mother of the gods in procession; but it is not as a type of Nature that he uses her, but as a parable of Rome, mother of heroes. And then, as if to match the Phrygian procession following the goddess, Virgil lets us see these heroes—Romulus, the founder; Numa, like so many of the Romans rising from small estate to glory,

> Curibus parvis et paupere terra
> missus in imperium magnum[3] (vi. 811);

Brutus, the liberator, unhappy in having to choose between his sons and his country, but a Roman in his choice; Camillus; the Scipios; Fabius Maximus the Delayer, saviour

---

[1] Notice how the adjective *lacrimabile* escapes Virgil even here.
[2] "Happy in her warrior brood."
[3] "Sent from his homely Cures and a land of poverty into a mighty empire. '

of the commonwealth; Caesar, Pompey, and Augustus. No age has failed to produce its own brood of heroes, every variety of man doing all kinds of service, but all in the same spirit and all for the same city.

The shield of Achilles in the *Iliad* is, like the *Iliad* itself, a picture of life, of human activity, Greek no doubt, but hardly Greek in any exclusive or self-conscious way. But the shield of Aeneas serves a different purpose. Its pictures are not ornament; they are to be prophecy, inspiration, history. The matter of this shield answers in like manner to the poem—both tell of Rome, of Roman life and Roman men—

res Italas Romanorumque triumphos (viii. 626).

Here we have more colour and action than in the other passage with its silent procession of the unborn. We see the mother-wolf with the Roman twins, proper founders for their race, *impavidi*; the rape of the Sabine women and the peace they made between husbands and parents; Porsenna, baffled and angered by the boldness of a Cocles and a Cloelia; the Capitol saved by Manlius and the geese; the punishment of Catiline among the dead; Cato on the throne of Rhadamanthus; and finally the last great battle of Rome against the East at Actium, the marshalling of Augustus and his Italians against Antony and his motley barbarian hordes, of the gods of Rome and Italy against dog-faced Anubis and the monsters of the East, and the victory of right over wrong, of the Roman over the Oriental spirit. These are the pictures upon the shield—pictures of joy and hope—

rerumque ignarus imagine gaudet (viii. 730).

Critics have objected to the line, which ends the passage, as being something more like an epigram than one would expect of Virgil, yet, if we have caught the spirit of the poet, we can see how alien the suggestion of an epigram really is. The hero, bearing the shield pictured with the destinies of his race, symbolizes what he is in sober earnest. The pictures he carries are emblems of the destinies which he also carries—his race and its future are really as well as symbolically laid upon him, as he goes

attollens humero famamque et fata nepotum [1] (viii. 731).

The poet, says Mr Myers, one of his most sympathetic critics, "was summing up in those lines like bars of gold the hero-roll of the Eternal City, conferring with every word an immortality, and, like his own Aeneas, bearing on his shoulders the fortune and the fame of Rome." [2]

But there is more than a continuity of ritual and a recurrence of heroism. Through all these centuries there runs a continuity of character clearly to be traced.

In his interesting study of Aeolus in Homer and in Virgil Sainte-Beuve remarks the wide difference between the Homeric god, "a good enough fellow, a genuine patriarch among his family, given over on his island to enjoyment, to mirth and good cheer," and the Virgilian Aeolus, "this subaltern of a god, sombre, uninquisitive, a little bored upon his rock." "The rude Roman discipline," he continues, "has passed over the brow of Virgil's Aeolus; he is one of those chiefs who, as was said of Burrus, could have grown old in the obscure honours of some legion. There is in him something of the centurion, or the military tribune, ennobled, deified." [3]

"Il y a en lui du centurion." It is exactly this that marks the great difference between Greek and Roman character, between the men and gods of Homer and the men and gods of Virgil. Greek history abounds in men who leave upon the mind a vivid impression of character, good or bad, but individual; while in Roman history we instinctively think first of the state, and find as a rule only a very much modified individuality in the citizens. The Greek's gift of looking the world and nature, as it were, between the eyes

---

[1] "He joys in the portraiture of the story he knows not, as he lifts upon his shoulder the fame and the fates of his children."

[2] *Essays Classical*, p. 143.

[3] *Étude sur Virgile*, p. 204 ; De la Ville de Mirmont's objection that the "centurion" is very ready to forget his military allegiance under the blandishments of Juno may be dismissed. Fimbria and Galba could give us plenty of parallels.

for himself contributed at once to the political impotence and the intellectual and artistic sovereignty of his race. The Roman had less imagination; he was more content to take orders from a magistrate or an officer and to carry them out without any special reference to first principles. He is above all things *par negotio neque supra* [1]—a type of character, no doubt eminently useful, but not supremely interesting.

This national character asserts itself in the *Aeneid.* Aeolus is something of a centurion. When Juno bribes him with a wife, she thinks of lawful Roman wedlock—

connubio iungam stabili propriamque dicabo [2] (*A.* i. 73).

" Elle sera comme une matrone romaine, une *materfamilias* du bon temps," for Pronuba Juno promises offspring too. When Jupiter rises from his golden throne the gods escort him home as if he were a Roman magistrate—

caelicolae medium quem ad limina ducunt (*A.* x. 117). [3]

The council of Jupiter is not like that of Zeus. " Zeus," says Homer " bade Themis call the gods to assembly from the head of deeply-delled Olympus; and she went hither and thither, and bade them come to the house of Zeus. No river was not there, save only Ocean, no nymph of the pleasant groves, or the river fountains, or the meadow leas; they came to the house of cloud-compelling Zeus " (*Iliad,* xx. 4-10; Purves). In fact the Homeric gods gather in a general assembly, much like the Homeric soldiers in the second *Iliad.* Virgil only admits the great gods; he does not let them drink before deliberating, and he makes them sit, grave as senators of the better sort in the senate-house. [4]

[1] " Equal to his task and not above it."
[2] " I will unite her to thee in lasting wedlock, and consecrate her thine own " (Conington).
[3] " The heavenly people surround and escort him to the doorway." Cf. Ovid, *Epp. ex Ponto,* vi. 4. 41 *inde domum repetes toto comitante senatu,* cited by Conington.
[4] See Boissier, *La Religion romaine,* i. 254. The Roman dignity of the Virgilian Jupiter may be brought out by a few lines from Ovid, *Met.* ii. 847 :

sceptri gravitate relicta
ille pater rectorque deum, cui dexta trisulcis

The same Roman character marks Aeneas' men, and indeed in such a degree as to impair to some extent the vigour of the poem. Not one of them has any clearly individual character, any "physiognomy," to use Sainte-Beuve's word for it. Achates of course is *fidus* ; he carries Aeneas' bow, and is always ready and at hand ; he is the first to sight Italy and to hail it; but we do not know him. Gyas and Serestus are each of them *fortis*. Gyas, it is true, on one occasion forgets himself (*oblitus decoris sui*—what a rebuke is in the phrase !) and throws his steersman overboard, but such outbreaks of individuality are rare. Ilioneus twice makes diplomatic speeches, grave, to the point, and dignified, as became a Roman ambassador, but he does not let himself go. The reason for all this can hardly be accident. The poet looks at these men much as a Roman general would have, and he conceives that Aeneas did the same. Watchful of their general interests, careful, kindly, Aeneas will not concern himself too closely with them as individuals, he thinks of them as a body. If Aeolus is a centurion, Aeneas is an *imperator*. He says "to this man, Go, and he goeth; and to another, Come, and he cometh"; and when the brave Serestus has loyally done what he is told to do, there is no more to be said about him. We might have preferred that realization of the last and least individual upon the scene, which we have in Homer, and above all in Shakespeare; but yet, if we had been given it by the poet, it might after all have made the general picture less Roman. The Roman Empire was made by men of little individual "physiognomy," if men of a wonderfully uniform practical capacity ; by "average men," but men of an unexampled high average, every one of them gifted by nature with the instinct to rule and to be ruled. *Fessi rerum* they work on undaunted.[1] Hence Aeneas' men—quiet, patient, reliable, Roman as they are—are hardly so interesting as his enemies.

> *ignibus armata est, qui nutu concutit orbem,*
> *induitur faciem tauri mixtusque iuvencis*
> *mugit et in teneris formosus obambulat herbis.*

A later Greek poet, Nonnus, seizes this occasion to make Zeus say δείδια μυθοτόκον πλέον Ἑλλάδα (*Dionysiaca*, i. 385).

[1] *A.* i. 178.

III

Virgil, in Aeneas and his men, shows us what he holds to be the ideal Roman temper. These are the people whom he sends to Latium to fuse with Latin and Italian, to conquer and to rule the world, and it is on this destiny of theirs that the epic turns.[1] He has discarded the mock-epic motive he played with in the first *Georgic*—

Laomedonteae luimus periuria Troiae [2] (*G.* i. 502).

It is true that as a sort of after-thought (a tribute to the legends of Troy) he credits Juno with some resentment born of slighted beauty—*spretae iniuria formae*; but he draws her on a large scale, as a nobler Livy might have drawn Hannibal. Juno means empire. She too has something of the Roman in her, for, whatever her original motive, she plays a great game for a great stake, involving world-wide issues. Fate has decreed that one people shall rule the world; she prefers another, and she tries conclusions with Fate. Aeneas as the instrument of Fate suffers. Hence Dr Henry was less awake than he thought when, "just as he went to sleep and began

---

[1] In a tract, which is by no means as good as its title, Plutarch discusses the Roman Empire (*De Fortuna Romanorum*). He recognizes its greatness, and calls Rome, in language curiously anticipatory of Claudian, πᾶσιν ἀνθρώποις ἑστίαν ἱεράν, ὡς ἀληθῶς, καὶ ὀνησιδώραν, καὶ πεῖσμα μόνιμον καὶ στοιχεῖον ἀίδιον, ὑποφερομένοις τοῖς πράγμασιν ἀγκυρηβόλιον σάλου καὶ πλάνης (316 F)—his metaphors, he says, are borrowed from Democritus. Just as the elements were at war till the κόσμος united them, so Rome united the world, and he raises the question: Does she owe more to 'Αρετή or to Τύχη? He thinks she owes much to both, but his tract falls away into a discussion of the services Chance has rendered Rome, e.g. the co-operation of Romulus' wolf, and Manlius' geese, and the occasional quarrels or pre-occupations of Rome's enemies. The reader is disappointed to find so very little recognition that Rome owed her greatness to character. Schlemm calls the tract "a mere rhetorical exercise," and one would like to believe him for Plutarch's credit. Dr Oakesmith (*Religion of Plutarch*, p. 83), however, following Wyttenbach, includes Providence as well as Chance under Τύχη, and finds little in the tract that clashes with Plutarch's established opinions. See also Gréard, *La morale de Plutarque*, p. 35; he holds it to have been designed for a Roman audience.

[2] "We have atoned the perjuries of Laomedon and his Troy." It is interesting to note this passage as an unconscious hint of the *Aeneid* to come, as it is to study the list of subjects which Milton sketched out for his eventual theme.

to forget himself," he parodied Conington in the graceful line,

Juno's vixen and not fell.[1]

It is rather on *quo numine laeso* that the stress falls—on Juno's divine will and purpose as crossing and thwarting the order of things decreed by Fate.

For Fate has decreed that Aeneas shall found

populum late regem belloque superbum [2] (*A.* i. 21).

This is a profoundly true and forcible description of the Roman people.   If Cineas found the Senate an "assembly of kings," outside its doors he might have found a sovereign people, sovereign as no other ancient people ever was.   The world knew *Alexander rex, Ptolemaeus rex*, but here was *populus rex*.[3]   That very want of physiognomy, which marked the individual Roman character, gave force and power to the national character.   The private citizen was content, was glad, to be fused in the *populus Romanus*. Roman generals might lose battles, Roman governors might govern ill, and Roman judges might sell justice; yet the nation never failed to carry a war through to victory; the nation ruled the world better than it had ever been ruled before; the nation formed a body of laws which shaped the character of European institutions and differentiated, once and for all, Western from Oriental ideas of law, justice, and government.

For this people Fate "appoints neither period nor boundary of empire, but dominion without end "—

his ego nec metas rerum nec tempora pono,
imperium sine fine dedi [4] (*A.* i. 278).

Fate, Jupiter continues, ordains them to be

Romanos rerum dominos gentemque togatam [5] (*A.* i. 282).

---

[1] *Aeneidea*, i. p. 56.

[2] "A nation, monarch of broad realms and glorious in war" (Conington).

[3] Cf. Cic. *pro Plancio*, 4. 11 *huius principis populi et omnium gentium domini atque victoris.*

[4] "To them I set neither limit of time nor space; empire without end I have given them."

[5] "Romans, lords of the world, the race of the toga."

This is an addition to what we have heard. The sovereignty of the world is to belong to the collective Roman people (*rerum dominos*), but the people is one whose distinctive mark is the garb of peace.[1] A nation of citizens, unarmed, is to govern the world in peace, and the very object of its rule is peace. For, Jupiter adds, the day shall come when, under Augustus' sway, "the iron ages shall soften and lay war aside; the gates of war shall be shut," and the war-fury shall be shackled, a helpless prisoner.

If Jupiter's prediction is not enough, we have the crowning word which Anchises speaks in the lower world on the duty and destiny of Rome—

Excudent alii spirantia mollius aera
(credo equidem), vivos ducent de marmore vultus,
orabunt causas melius, caelique meatus
describent radio et surgentia sidera dicent:
tu regere imperio populos, Romane, memento
(hae tibi erunt artes) pacisque imponere morem,
parcere subjectis et debellare superbos [2] (*A.* vi. 847-853).

---

[1] "Not merely," says Henry, on *gentem togatam*, "the Romans, whose national dress is the toga, commanding the world; but the Romans *in their garb of peace, the 'toga,'* i.e. in their civilian character—a nation of citizens—commanding the world." Conington, however, finds "no need to seek a point in any antithesis between *arma* and *toga.*"

[2]   Others will mould their bronzes to breathe with a tenderer grace,
        Draw, I doubt not, from marble a vivid life to the face,
        Plead at the bar more deftly, with sapient wands of the wise,
        Trace heaven's courses and changes, predict us stars to arise.
        Thine, O Roman, remember to rule over every race !
        These be thine arts, thy glories, the ways of peace to proclaim,
        Mercy to show to the fallen, the proud with battle to tame. (Bowen.)

Cf. the statement of Augustus on the Monument of Ancyra (3), *Victor omnibus civibus superstitibus peperci. Externas gentes, quibus tuto ignosci potuit, conservare quam excidere malui.* Also Horace, *Carmen Seculare* (B.C. 17, two years after Virgil's death), l. 50, *Clarus Anchisae Venerisque sanguis . . . bellante prior, iacentem lenis in hostem.* We may contrast the account of Persia, which Aeschylus ironically put into the mouth of a Persian, on the eve of the arrival of news of Salamis (*Persae*, 101 f.)—

θεόθεν γὰρ κατὰ μοῖρ' ἐκράτησεν τὸ παλαιόν, ἐπέσκηψε δὲ Πέρσαις
πολέμους πυργοδαίκτους
διέπειν ἱππιοχάρμας τε κλόνους, πόλεών τ' ἀναστάσεις.

The last clause explains why the Persian Empire failed to leave any such impression as Rome's—there was no *pacis imponere morem.*

Pacis imponere morem, says Virgil, and the best commentary which can be quoted on the phrase is a passage of Claudian, written four centuries later—

Rome, Rome alone has found the spell to charm
The tribes that bowed beneath her conquering arm,
Has given one name to the whole human race,
And clasped and sheltered them in fond embrace;
Mother, not mistress, called her foe her son,
And by soft ties made distant countries one.
This to her peaceful sceptre all men owe,
That through the nations, wheresoe'er we go,
Strangers, we find a fatherland; our home
We change at will. We count it sport to roam
To distant Thule, or with sails unfurled
Seek the most drear recesses of the world;
That we may tread Rhone's or Orontes' shore
That we are all one nation evermore.[1]

Claudian's tone is not exactly the same as Virgil's, but his thought is inspired by Virgil's thought. He sees very much the same empire that Virgil saw, but he sees it after four hundred years of the rule of that Roman spirit which Virgil portrays in the *Aeneid.* His story is the fulfilment of Virgil's prophecy, and his central thought is the

Claudian, *Cons. Stil.* iii. 150. The rendering is Dr Hodgkin's—

Haec est in gremium victos quae sola recepit
humanumque genus communi nomine fovit
matris non dominae ritu: civesque vocavit
quos domuit, nexuque pio longinqua revinxit.
Huius pacificis debemus moribus omnes,
quod veluti patriis regionibus utitur hospes,
quod sedem mutare licet, quod cernere Thulen
lusus et horrendos quondam penetrare recessus,
quod bibimus passim Rhodanum potamus Orontem,
quod cuncti gens una sumus. Nec terminus unquam
Romanae dicionis erit. Nam cetera regna
luxuries vitiis odiisque superbia vertit.

It is also interesting to find the same sort of thought in Epictetus, who probably like all the Greeks ignored Virgil and Latin literature :—ὁρᾶτε γὰρ ὅτι εἰρήνην μεγάλην ὁ Καῖσαρ ἡμῖν δοκεῖ παρέχειν, ὅτι οὐκ εἰσὶν οὐκέτι πόλεμοι, οὐδὲ μάχαι, οὐδὲ λῃστήρια μεγάλα, οὐδὲ πειρατικά· ἀλλ' ἔξεστι πάσῃ ὥρᾳ ὁδεύειν, πλεῖν ἀπὸ ἀνατολῶν ἐπὶ δυσμάς (*D.* III. xiii.).

same. His *pacifici mores* represents very closely Virgil's *pacis imponere morem*. The intervening ages had not been so golden as Virgil had hoped, at least not so glittering, but they were a period of the diffusion of the old world's gains and of a deepening and quickening of the human spirit. If the fabric of the Roman state did not wear so well as Virgil had predicted, the mind of mankind had caught the mood and temper of the poet, and had learnt to find in a teaching which he never knew the satisfaction of the yearnings which he had uttered for ever in his poetry. The spiritual development of the Western world under the Empire is quite in consonance with Virgil's prophecy and with his own feelings. The connexion between this spiritual growth and the pacific rule of Rome is brought out and emphasized by Claudian's contemporary, Prudentius, who sees still deeper into the significance of Rome.[1]

Rome's purpose was not mere conquest. Augustus was not the only great conqueror of his day. Virgil shows us Antony

victor ab Aurorae populis et litore rubro [2] (*A.* viii. 686),

---

[1] Prudentius, *contra Symmachum*, ii. 586 ff. :

> Discordes linguis populos et dissona cultu
> regna volens sociare Deus, subiungier uni
> imperio, quidquid tractabile moribus esset,
> concordique iugo retinacula mollia ferre
> constituit, quo corda hominum coniuncta teneret
> relligionis amor : nec enim fit copula Christo
> digna nisi implicitas societ mens unica gentes . . .
> Miscebat Bellona furens mortalia cuncta
> armabatque feras in vulnera mutua dextras.
> Hanc frenaturus rabiem Deus undique gentes
> inclinare caput docuit sub legibus isdem
> Romanosque omnes fieri . . .
> Ius fecit commune pares et nomine eodem
> nexuit et domitos fraterna in vincla redegit . . .
> Hoc actum est tantis successibus atque triumphis
> Romani imperii ; Christo iam tunc venienti,
> crede, parata via est, quam dudum publica nostrae
> pacis amicitia struxit moderamine Romae . . .
> Iam mundus te, Christe, capit, quem congrege nexu
> pax et Roma tenent.

[2] " Conqueror from the races of the East and the Red Sea."

but Antony has abandoned the ideals of Rome. Self-indulgence and indifference to his country's claim have denationalized him, and he comes to battle with Cleopatra at his side and under the tutelage of dog-headed Anubis and the portentous gods of the East. Against him are "the fathers and the people, the Penates and the Great Gods," and the world passes from his grasp to one who will rule it with more loyalty to the ideas and to the spirit of his race.[1]

Sainte-Beuve, in comparing the *Argonautica* of Apollonius with the *Aeneid*, allows it every claim it can lay to learning, elegance, and ingenuity, but, he concludes, it was the epic of no nation—"il ne fit battre aucun cœur." There, in that word, lies the supremacy of the *Aeneid*. It is a poem which appealed to a great people and to every citizen, and which still, though that people has ceased to be, "makes the heart beat."[2]

[1] The battle of Actium, *A.* viii. 675-713.

[2] I am glad to find a similar view held by Mr Warde Fowler. See his *Religious Experience of the Roman People* (1911) pp. 409, 410. He finds the mission of Rome in the world recurrent, like the subject of a fugue, through the whole poem. "There are drawbacks," he owns—e.g. the intervention of the gods after the Homeric manner, and "the seeming want of warm human blood in the hero" —"but he who keeps the great theme ever in mind, watching for it as he reads, as one watches for the new entry of a great fugue-subject, will never fail to see in the *Aeneid* one of the noblest efforts of human art—to understand what makes it the world's second great epic."

CHAPTER VII

THE LAND AND THE NATION.—3. AUGUSTUS

Nam genus humanum, defessum vi colere aevom,
ex inimicitiis languebat ; quo magis ipsum
sponte sua cecidit sub leges artaque iura.—LUCRETIUS, v. 1145.

" For myself," Goethe continued, " I have always been a royalist."
ECKERMANN, *Conversations with Goethe*, Feb. 25, 1824.

PROBABLY there is nothing that startles the modern reader of Horace and Virgil so much as the deification of the Emperor Augustus. To us he hardly seems a poetical, still less a divine, figure.[1] A shrewd and successful adventurer, without ideas of his own, he lived by assimilating the ideas of his uncle and adoptive father, while he cautiously discarded, either from inability to grasp them or from a feeling that they would militate against his success, some of those conceptions and thoughts of Julius which most appeal to us to-day. He is essentially the " middleman " who comes in the train of genius to break up, to distribute, and to utilize those gains, which genius can indicate but cannot gather either for itself or for the world. Like other political and intellectual middlemen, he was eminently successful in life, and owed his success at once to his practical adroitness and his intellectual inferiority. He stood near enough to Julius to understand his political plans, while he stood nearer than Julius did to the people he had to rule, nearer in the limitation of his outlook, in his slighter power of handling ideas, and in the resulting ability to follow the workings of the average Italian mind. Genius is apt to see too far, and range too high, and look reality too clearly in the face, to sympathize with the pedestrian limitations of its neighbours;

[1] A friendly critic has held that this paragraph looks too like a final judgement, but it was definitely intended to represent one side of the case ; the other side, it was hoped, was presented strongly enough in the rest of the chapter.

and Julius met his death through his mistake in supposing
that the men about him were as much moved as he by the
logic of realities and as little satisfied with the surfaces of
things.[1] Augustus, on the other hand, had a clearer notion
of the ways of the common man and a more kindly feeling for
his prejudices. He was intensely practical, he had a wonderful faculty for learning from the mistakes of others and for
avoiding the repetition of his own, but he hardly seems to us
the man to quicken a poet's imagination. Dexterity,
calculation, coolness are excellent qualities for a business
man, but they hardly suggest inspiration.

Yet Virgil and Horace write of Augustus with an enthusiasm which, if not entirely real, is in the main genuine
enough. When the utterances of both are weighed, it will
be found perhaps that Horace has said more and meant less
than Virgil. It is Horace who speaks of Augustus as a
possible incarnation of Mercury or some other god,[2] who
pictures him attaining godhead (*caelum*) by the methods of
Bacchus, Pollux, and Hercules, and "reclining among them
to drink the nectar with purple lips ";[3] who goes further still
and proclaims that he shall be a god while yet he lives.[4]
But the poet of the odes to Lalage and Lydia may fairly
ask not to be taken too seriously, and we find that in the
more prosaic affairs of life Horace held aloof from the
Emperor; he refused to become his private secretary, declined to write an epic for him, and abstained from asking
favours, till the Emperor wrote and accused him of despising
his friendship, and asked if the poet were afraid posterity
would count it against him to have been the intimate of
Augustus.[5]

But Horace is not alone in speaking of Augustus as a god.
Does not Tityrus say

deus nobis haec otia fecit?[6] (*E.* i. 6).

[1] See Suetonius, *Julius* cc. 76, 77, for evidence on this point.
[2] *Odes*, i. 2. 41.   [3] *Odes*, iii. 3. 9-12 *purpureo bibit ore nectar.*
[4] *Odes*, iii. 5. 2 *praesens divus habebitur Augustus.*
[5] The letters are extant in the short life of Horace by Suetonius, and well
deserve attention.
[6] "It was a god that gave us this peace."

Is there not at the beginning of the first *Georgic* an elaborate discussion of the Emperor's godhead ? Is not the *Aeneid* full of Augustus? For Virgil poetry is a higher, a more serious, thing—σπουδαιότερον—than for Horace. What then does he mean by this repeated adoration of the ruler ? How should a man of peace glorify the author of proscription and confiscation ? How should the pupil of Siro and Lucretius make a god of this man, who was assuredly no Epicurus? How should the poet of Dido and Evander and Pallas find a place in such a company for a figure so essentially prosaic ?

To answer these questions we must understand the relations of the poet and the Emperor. The base suggestion which makes of Virgil a sort of glorified Martial, and finds the explanation of everything in a farm near Mantua and a house at Naples, may be at once dismissed. Great poetry does not spring from such motives. Nor can we say at once that Virgil was influenced merely by friendly or patriotic considerations. He was indebted to Augustus, he was his friend, and he admired him as a statesman ; and in view of all that Augustus was to the poet personally, and of all that he had done for their country, we cannot blame Virgil either for his friendship or his admiration. To connect his great work with such a friend's name would surely be a venial offence, if an offence at all. But Virgil has done more than this, for, whether it appear to us legitimate or not, he has tried to bring Augustus into vital relation with the whole of the *Aeneid,* and to make the whole poem turn, or at least seem to turn, upon the destiny of Augustus. Is it a triumph of the friend over the poet? That is a dangerous and doubtful suggestion to make about a great poet, as it involves misconception of a poet's habits of mind. The poet will generally be found to think first of truth and poetry, and, where these are concerned, to have a singular faculty of clear vision. Whatever his relations with philosophy, whatever the coincidence or difference of philosophic and poetic truth, the poet will always agree with the philosopher that " it is the best course, and indeed necessary, at least where truth is at stake, to sacrifice even what is near and dear to us ; for, where both are dear to us, it is a sacred duty to prefer truth."[1] Is there then any poetic truth in Virgil's presentment of Augustus?

It will perhaps be simplest to try to obtain some clear idea of what Augustus did and was; and then to study the impression he made upon the poet; and, thus prepared, to consider how the poet embodies his impression in his poetry.

I

" Ce trop habile homme, par peur des poignards, n'organisa que le viager, et ne consacra que le mensonge."

In this striking and epigrammatic form M. Goumy has summed up a great deal of criticism upon the imperial system which Augustus devised and handed down to his successor.[2] To attempt to reconcile such a judgement with "poetic truth" may seem like propounding a paradox, particularly when it must be owned at the outset that M. Goumy in his way is right. But we have to distinguish between what Augustus did and what he wished the Roman world to think What he did was to carry into effect the ideas of Julius; but he wished his fellow countrymen to suppose that he was doing the opposite.

Now the very essence of the ideas of Julius was the recognition of the actual. It is hardly fanciful to take his correction of the Calendar as typical of all he did in the reorganization of the government at large. "When he turned to set the republic in order," says Suetonius, "he put the Calendar right, which had been brought, by the recklessness of the pontifices in intercalation, to such confusion, that the harvest festival was not in summer, nor the vintage in

---

[1] Aristotle, *Ethics*, i. 4. 6, p. 1096 a : βέλτιον εἶναι καὶ δεῖν ἐπὶ σωτηρίᾳ γε τῆς ἀληθείας καὶ τὰ οἰκεῖα ἀναιρεῖν, ἄλλως τε καὶ φιλοσόφους ὄντας· ἄμφοιν γὰρ ὄντοιν φίλοιν ὅσιον προτιμᾶν τὴν ἀλήθειαν.

[2] M. Henri Rochefort in the days of the Dreyfus troubles put the same thought in a maxim of wider range :—" Every one knows, and the Ministers best of all, that to govern is to lie (*gouverner c'est mentir*)." See F. C. Conybeare, *The Dreyfus Case*, p. 156. It is a brilliant phrase and many people, in ancient times and modern, have believed it—practical politicians and their critics—yes, and thinkers like Euripides and Tolstoi have said it in bitterness of heart. It deserves study.

autumn. He adjusted the year to the course of the sun."[1]
There at least Julius was in touch with the ultimate fact.
It is clear throughout everything he does that his intention
is to grasp the real state of the case, and then, in full view
of everything material, to plan real provision for real need.
This is the statesman's temper. It is recognizable in Julius
from the beginning; he of all men took the truest measure
of Pompey from the first. But it was in Gaul that he had
his first chance of exercising and developing his faculty.
There he had a great country to deal with, large problems
to face, and freedom in working them out. When he found
himself master of the Roman world, he worked on in the
same way. What were the real facts, the real requirements?[2]

The first and most clamant need of the Roman world was
government. The Roman constitution had not been con-
trived for the inclusion of a subject empire. As province
after province was added, one expedient and another were
devised to meet each case as it came; but wise and good as
many of these expedients might be, there was an air of
makeshift about the whole. By Caesar's day it was plain
that the sovereign people would not take the thought and
trouble necessary for the working of these expedients, while
the upper classes looked upon the provinces chiefly as sources
of private revenue for senatorial governors and for the
leaders of the financial world, and hence as mere counters
in the game of politics.

In short, there was no serious government any longer,
nothing but improvisation. There was no continuity of
policy for the province; there were no general principles
of policy for the empire. The empire was not looked at
as a whole; it was not studied with intelligence; even
considered as a collection of estates it was badly managed.
Yet it made itself felt in Rome, and now and then men
recognized that the peculiar problems it presented required
special and intelligent treatment. For instance, in 67 B.C.

---

[1] Suetonius, *Julius*, 40. May we quote Virgil in a new connexion: *Solem
quis dicere falsum audeat (G.* i. 463)?

[2] Compare Carlyle, *French Revolution* vol. iii. bk. 3, ch. 1 : " Whatsoever man
or men can best interpret the inward tendencies it [the Movement] has, and give
them voice and activity, will obtain the lead of it."

piracy had reached such dimensions, that it was seen to be an imperial question, not to be managed by partial operations in the various provinces. It was clear that the thing needed was a central and comprehensive plan, steadily directed and controlled by an organizing mind, which must be in possession of all the facts to be faced, and able to set in motion forces adequate for the work to be done. The Gabinian law gave Pompey a free hand on the tacit condition that he actually did the work. This was, in fact, a direct denial of the whole scheme of senatorial and popular rule. The " talk of the dictatorship " current in Rome during Caesar's absence in Gaul proves that people recognized the want of government in the city itself and in the world at large.

The first task of Caesar, therefore, was to govern. Government means responsibility, and Caesar undertook this himself. The whole executive of the empire became directly or indirectly responsible to himself, and he took care to be served by capable and reliable men. They were not always people of good family—he appointed a eunuch, the son of a freedman of his own, to be over three legions in Alexandria, and some of his slaves he set over the mint and the public revenue department. The old families of Rome grumbled ; but Caesar meant work to be done, and picked men who would do it, irrespective of old traditions—*spreto patrio more*.[1]

He realized further that the old division of the world into Rome and the subject empire had become, by the substitution of himself for senate and people as the ruling power, even more obsolete than it had virtually been for some long while before. His introduction of Gauls into the senate was the expression of this belief. The angry verses quoted round the town show what the Romans thought of this—

> Caesar led the Gauls in triumph; to the Senate-house he led ;
> And the Gauls took off their trousers, wore the laticlave instead.[2]

---

[1] Suetonius, *Julius*, 76.

[2] Suetonius, *Julius*, 80 *Gallos Caesar in triumphum ducit, idem in curiam, Galli bracas deposuerunt, latum clavum sumpserunt.*

The remark, which Suetonius tells us Caesar made, though a tactical blunder, was nevertheless a profound truth, and the basal truth of the whole imperial system. "The republic," he said, "was nothing—it was a mere phrase without form or substance."[1] For this *nothing* Caesar substituted an intensely real *something*, which corresponded with every reality in the empire—the control of a single intelligence, which should make itself felt uniformly and everywhere in steady and intelligent government.

Julius, we might perhaps say, was murdered for what he said[2] rather than for what he did. Augustus realized the one mistake of his uncle and did not repeat it, but what Julius had done before him he did again. He regained the personal control of the entire government, and established throughout the world at large that real *something* which Julius had seen to be demanded by the empire. Only in Rome, because the Romans had a traditional preference for the *nothing*, he gave it them in words. Whenever by change or development of plan he got a firmer grasp of everything and made the reality of his government more real, he repeated in a more noticeable tone his phrase about "the restoration of the republic."[3] He took care also to emphasize the time-limits set to his tenure of offices, which he intended all the same to keep as long as he lived and to hand on to his successor. This is what M. Goumy means by "organizing the temporary and consecrating falsehood." Augustus, it is said, on his death-bed asked his friends whether they thought he had played the farce of life well enough.[4] Viewed from this standpoint, his life was in measure a farce, but it was far from being this in reality.

Augustus had maintained his power by the methods with which he won it. When the world was divided between

---

[1] Suetonius, *Julius* 77 *Nihil esse rempublicam, appellationem modo sine corpore ac specie.* It is of course possible that Caesar had more tact than to say so.

[2] Or what people said he said—a rather different thing, though often enough a manufactured anecdote hits off a situation more accurately than a true one might.

[3] On one such occasion he doubled the pay of his guards.

[4] Suet. *Aug.* 99, *ecquid iis videretur mimum vitae commode transegisse.*

himself and Antony, he had captured the general goodwill by genuine service of mankind. He had crushed piracy on the sea and brigandage in Italy; he had given quiet to all the West; he had enabled industry and business to regain their ordinary activity—the fall in the rate of interest was the sign of this; by sense and firmness, combined with clemency, he had gained the confidence of serious people; and in negotiation and war he had maintained the credit of Rome with the foreigner. In every one of these details his success stood in vivid contrast to the failure of Antony. When he died, public talk in Rome owned that "no resource had been left for the distracted country but the rule of one man; under his rule the frontiers had been pushed forward to the Ocean or to distinct rivers; the provinces, the armies, and the fleets of the empire had been brought into communication with one another; justice had been dispensed at home; consideration had been shown to the allies; and the city itself had been sumptuously adorned." [1]

All this is true work, and has to be weighed against the lies of statecraft with which the Emperor kept the senate quiet. We may go further still, and say that if, as most people admit upon a broad view of it, the genius of Rome was "to govern the nations, to crush disorder, to spare the subject, and to set up and maintain the wont and use of peace," Augustus was a genuine embodiment of this genius, and, whatever his defects of mind and character, he had, on the soberest estimate, fulfilled the destiny of his people, and given recognition and satisfaction to the instincts and demands of the whole Mediterranean—in other words, that his work was an honest endeavour to give expression to the truth of the world around him.

II

Virgil first came into contact with Augustus, or Octavian as he was then called, in connexion with the confiscation

---

[1] Tacitus, *Annals*, i. 9. The hostile criticisms quoted by Tacitus in the following chapter are personal, and do not touch the record of his real political services.

of his farm. That famous interview he describes—not very clearly, nor, even, very happily—in the first *Eclogue.* He had seen Rome, the city without peer, and he had seen the young Caesar—

> hic illum vidi iuvenem (42)—

who had in the most bucolic terms encouraged him to go on with his farm life, and incidentally to make music with his pipe—

> ludere quae vellem calamo permisit agresti [1]—

and who will, in consequence, be to him a god, whose face he can never forget.

> O Meliboee deus nobis haec otia fecit
> namque erit ille mihi semper deus [2] (6).

Disentangling Virgil and his pipe from Tityrus and his cattle, we find that Augustus restored his farm to the poet, and made it possible for him to live the life of " inglorious quiet" (*G.* iv. 564) which his genius required. In process of time their relations became closer, and Virgil received from him various gifts of land and house property, though he refused, as we have seen, to accept an exile's confiscated estate. Eventually a warm friendship bound them to each other. Augustus, from his peculiar position and the temper it bred, was a somewhat dangerous and even uncomfortable friend to have. He did not, we learn, make friends easily, but he kept them when he made them, and was willing to tolerate their vices and foibles "in moderation." [3] It should be remarked to the credit of Augustus, that of all who shared his friendship, two of the most successful in retaining it without loss of dignity or independence were men of humble origin, one indeed

[1] " He set me free to play as I pleased upon my rustic pipe."

[2] "O Meliboeus it was a god who gave us this peace—for a god he shall ever be to me."

[3] Suet. *Aug.* 66, *sed vitia quoque et delicta, dumtaxat modica, perpessus,* an interesting chapter on the Emperor's friendships. Cf. Horace, *Sat.* ii. 1. 20 *cui male si palpere recalcitrat.*

a perfect man of the world, the other a shy and silent student—the poets Horace and Virgil.

The intimacy rested on character and poetry, and it is pleasant to note the interest which Emperor and poet took in each other's work. Virgil, we learn, on one occasion read the whole of the *Georgics* to Augustus, spreading the work over four days, and handing the manuscript to Maecenas when his voice grew weary.[1] In the *Aeneid*, as was natural, the Emperor was keenly interested, and in the course of the Cantabrian war he wrote to the poet from Spain letters full of playful entreaties and equally playful menaces to wring from him "either a first draft of the poem, or at any rate some part of it."[2]

Whether the letter of Virgil, which Macrobius has preserved, was written in answer to these letters of Augustus from Spain it is impossible to say certainly, but it may very well have been. He begins, "I am receiving frequent letters from you"; and, lower down he continues, "As to my Aeneas, if I really had him in a state worthy of your ears, I would gladly send him; but the subject I have taken in hand is so vast, that I feel it was madness to attack so big a work, particularly when I have, as you know, to devote other and more important study to that work."[3] However, at a later date, Virgil read the second,

---

[1] Suet. *v. Verg.* 27 *Georgica reverso post Actiacam victoriam Augusto atque Atellae reficiendarum faucium causa commoranti per continuum quadriduum legit, suscipiente Maecenate legendi vicem, quotiens interpellaretur ipse vocis offensione. Pronuntiabat autem cum suavitate tum lenociniis miris.* Nettleship, *Ancient Lives*, p. 52, calls attention to the fact that the date given here by Suetonius is "merely a general expression."

[2] Suet. *op. cit.* 31 *efflagitabat ut sibi "de Aeneide" ut ipsius verba sunt vel prima carminis ὑπογραφή vel quodlibet colon mitteretur.*

[3] Macr. *Sat.* i. 24. 11 *Ipsius enim Maronis epistula, qua compellat Augustum, ita incipit " Ego vero frequentes a te litteras accipio" et infra " de Aenea quidem meo, si mehercle iam dignum auribus haberem tuis, libenter mitterem, sed tanta* [v. l. *tantum*] *incohata res est ut paene vitio mentis tantum opus ingressus mihi videar, cum praesertim, ut scis, alia quoque studia ad id opus multoque potiora impertiar."* It is suggested that *ad id opus* may mean "beside that work."

Tacitus (*Dial.* 13) seems to imply that the letters of Augustus to Virgil were extant: *neque apud divum Augustum gratia caruit . . . testes Augusti epistolae.* Seneca the elder may be referring to Virgil's letters, when he says (*Controv.* iii. praef.* 8), *Ciceronem eloquentia sua in carminibus destituit, Vergilium illa felicitas ingenii in oratione soluta reliquit.*

fourth, and sixth books of the *Aeneid* to Augustus and Octavia. Suetonius records that, when the poet came to the famous passage *Tu Marcellus eris*, Octavia fainted.[1]

Finally, it was when travelling with Augustus that Virgil contracted, on a visit to the ruins of Megara, the illness of which he died.

It has long been remarked how congenial Virgil found the political changes of Augustus. It was partly because neither hereditary nor personal ties bound him to the old order which Augustus had ended; and partly that the real gains, which the rule of Augustus meant for the world and for Italy, appealed to the poet. The silence of the forum, which Cicero had found intolerable under Julius, meant nothing to the native of Cisalpine Gaul. "How many were left who had known the republic?" asks Tacitus, when he is explaining the peacefulness of the later period of Augustus' reign.[2] He refers to Romans. But the republic was little or nothing to Italians, excepting individuals who sought their fortune at Rome. For Cicero nearly the whole of life was bound up with republican constitution and usage; but even he, popular as he was with the Italians, could wake in them no enthusiasm for a government which had meant to them oppression of every kind. The Senate and people of Rome had treated Italy with contempt and injustice; they had refused the franchise, and, when it was wrung from them by force of arms, they had in great measure neutralized it by political chicane. The traditions of Sulla were all associated with that senatorial rule which he had laboured to make secure, and they made it the more unpopular; nor had the careers of "Sulla's men," of Pompey and of Catiline, done anything to abate the ill-will which still attached itself to the name of Sulla.

Virgil was no doubt familiar from childhood with the story of the political aspirations of his fellow-countrymen, of Sulla and the Senate, and all his national feeling would direct his sympathies away from the fallen republic to the great house which had made Italy one. It must be

---

[1] *V. Verg.* 32. Marcellus was her son who had died young.
[2] *Annals*, i. 3. 7.

remembered, too, that Virgil neither had, nor, apparently, wished to have, any experience of political life—hardly any of active life of whatever kind. For all his interest in Roman history, he had little or no sympathy for republican institutions, for the spectacle of a great people governing itself. The old Roman commonwealth, praised by Polybius and sighed for by Cicero, was a thing foreign to his mind. His own people had been governed for centuries; they had not governed themselves; they had had no share in the inner movement of Roman political life; they had been ruled from without. Consequently the republic, lying quite outside Virgil's experience, touched his imagination but little or not at all.

And, again, Virgil's whole nature was on the side of peace. His ideal was a quiet life unruffled by the storms of political disorder, and, still more, unassailed by the fiercer storms of civil war; and for a century republican government had meant incessant strife, bloodshed, war, and confiscations—the utter unsettlement of life—

> tot bella per orbem,
> tam multas scelerum facies, non ullus aratro
> dignus honos, squalent abductis arva colonis [1] (G. i. 505).

It was not until the republican party was finally driven out of Italy that the land began to recover itself; nor, until it was crushed throughout the world, that wars ceased and the temple of Janus was closed. In a word, the victory of Augustus meant the restoration of the proper and normal life of man.

> Augustus Caesar, divi genus, aurea condet
> secula qui rursus Latio regnata per arva
> Saturno quondam [2] (vi. 792).

---

[1] "So many wars throughout the world, so many forms of sin ; none of the honour that is its due is left to the plough ; the husbandman is marched away and the fields lie dirty."

[2] "Augustus Caesar, true child of a god, who shall establish again for Latium a golden age in that very region where Saturn once reigned" (Conington). The original *aurea secula* were under Saturn's rule, according to Evander (*Aen.* viii. 324).

This return of the golden age carried with it the restoration of all that was venerable and worthy in the past. Augustus restored or rebuilt the ancient temples, beside building new ones. " The number, dignity, and allowances of the priests he increased, particularly those of the Vestal virgins," says Suetonius ; " some too of the ancient ceremonies, which had gradually fallen into disuse, he reinstituted, as for example the *Augurium Salutis*, the flaminate of Jupiter, the Lupercal festival [we may add the Arval Brothers]. . . Honour next to that of the immortal gods he paid to the memory of the generals who had found the Roman people's empire small and made it great." [1] Everything that an Emperor could do he did by statute and example to encourage morality and family life. It must be owned that his laws compelling marriage were not very successful, but his severity in dealing with his luckless daughter Julia is evidence that he was in earnest in his resolve that marriage should be respected. [2] Just as he tried to purge the popular pantheon of alien unauthorized gods, such as Apis, [3] he purged the Senate of its more unworthy members—no doubt, including among them some of the Gauls whom Julius had made senators—and he took care to restore to that body its ancient decorum and splendour, but not its old power. Even the dress of his fellow citizens did not escape the Emperor's eye, and in after years he could and did quote, "with indignation and in a loud voice," a great line of Virgil to support his zeal for the toga. [4]

This religious reformation was bound to be superficial [5] ; it was certainly a piece of studied policy like the more elaborate pretence of " restoring the republic " by permitting the election of magistrates with republican titles. In the

---

[1] Suet. *Aug.* 29-31.

[2] See Boissier, *L'Opposition sous les Césars*, pp. 133 ff., who shrewdly remarks that the Emperor's cold-blooded method of marrying and remarrying her, without reference to her own wishes, to men whom he forced to divorce wives really loved, was hardly calculated to "make a Lucretia of Julia." For the laws, cf. Suet. *Aug.* 34.

[3] Suet. *Aug.* 93. The Emperor frowned on Judaism, too, among Romans.

[4] Suet. *Aug.* 40 *Romanos rerum dominos gentemque togatam.*

[5] There was, however, a real revival of religion, which began at this time, but it did not develop along the lines laid down by the Emperor.

long run the one was found to be scarcely more genuine or real than the other. But, for the moment, this great idea of restoration appealed to the imagination of serious people. It was supported by the poet Horace, who wrote a number of Odes to show that he too would be as happy as the Emperor himself to see other people married and pious.[1]

Virgil, too, was interested and took his share in the work, though the solemn utterances of Horace about violet-beds and pier-building, about the restoration of temples and the *lex de maritandis ordinibus*, hardly came into his conception of poetry. Still, he was attracted, and probably more really attracted than Horace, by this aspect of the Emperor's work, inasmuch as he was of all the poets of Rome the most interested and intelligent student of Roman and Italian antiquities. The old garb and phrase, the old use and ritual, appealed to him as a poet. They were not to him, as to the antiquary, mere curiosities of history, but relics which made a forgotten day live again, symbols that expressed the real grandeur of an ancient people, with whom he and his day might still feel a spiritual kinship. If to Augustus this restoration of the past was a political device—and perhaps even to him it was more—for Virgil it had a deeper import, and his regard for the Emperor, as his personal friend and as the giver of peace to his country, was deepened by the thought that in him the present was being re-linked to the past in a hundred ways, all full of poetic significance and suggestion.

We may go further and recognize in Virgil a certain admiration for the personal character of Augustus—an admiration which the historians do not make it very easy for us to share, but which should at least be considered

---

[1] Horace in a short ode informs us of his conversion from "insane philosophy." But Faunus and Jupiter acting in concert to convert the Epicurean poet, the one holding up the falling branch and the other thundering from a blue sky, are more delightful than convincing. *Odes* ii. 17, 27 ; and i. 34. There was rather more than a strain of superstition in Augustus, and as little of it in Horace as in any-body. The odes, in which he takes the high imperial line of virtue and reformation, are very curious. It is hard to imagine anyone taking them very seriously who knew Horace at all well, and it is impossible to suppose them to be banter. Perhaps Augustus thought they would do for his public.

along with their judgements upon the Emperor. It is part of the poet's character to "count nothing human as alien," and it not infrequently happens that the man of reflection finds a peculiar interest in the man of action, of capacity, of achievement—in the man who *does* things.[1] In a world of scattered minds, of minds wasted by diffusion of effort, there is something magnetic in the man who will set before him one definite goal, who will steadily resist, even to the point of seeming insensible to them, the temptations offered by pleasure or by pain to lead him aside, and who at last achieves his goal in virtue of this singleness of aim. Augustus was a man of this type. The famous interview with Cleopatra is the standard illustration of his inflexibility; but his whole life is one long repression of instinct and impulse, and not merely of his own, for he demanded as much of those around him—as his daughter and as Tiberius could testify. A hard, cold man, neither friendship nor hostility could distract him from policy. He could be reconciled to Plancus; he could sacrifice his sister Octavia to Antony. But to his great purpose of ruling and regenerating the Roman Empire he was inexorably faithful. How far self-interest and patriotism conflict or conspire in shaping the purposes of a great ruler, especially of a ruler who has to fight his way to power, it is difficult to estimate in any case. Probably the mere love of personal power, which a vulgar mind feels, is in the case of greater men lifted into a higher region, and becomes a love of achievement, of construction; and the man who is really fitted to use power enjoys it, not so much for possessing it, as for the opportunity it gives him to accomplish something of broad reference, which could not be done, or could not be done so well, by another. Hence in a character like Augustus—or even Sulla—what in a smaller man we should have to regard as merely selfish has in reality a nobler element. The personal motive is subordinated to

---

[1] Cf. Prof. Dowden, *Shakespeare, His Mind and Art*, ch. vi. p. 281: "Shakespeare's admiration of the great men of action is immense, because he himself was primarily not a man of action." There is of course a school of critics who hold the opposite view—that Shakespeare preferred Richard II. to Henry V. See also Froude's *Carlyle's Life in London*, 19 February 1838, vol. i. p. 138.

wider and more really generous considerations, and, while we have to own that the character is still unlovely, we have to admit a certain nobility. Thus in the case of Augustus, Virgil looks to the higher quality of the man, to his real patriotism, to his political wisdom, to his love of peace, and never forgets that, whatever the superficial or even the essential weakness and inadequacy of the Emperor's nature, he had in truth sought and achieved peace and regeneration for his country and the Empire.[1]

Virgil finds the colour and movement of human life and the unfolding of human character more moving than the play of political principles. When he contemplates Roman history, he is attracted more by the heroes than by the great forward movement of political thought implied in the growth and progress of the Roman republic. The temper and qualities, which he admires in the hero, are rather those necessary to any stable human society than those required for the self-governing state. Even if he speaks of *populum late regem*, it is rather of Rome's government of the conquered that he thinks than of the republican constitution. A well-known simile in the first book will illustrate his mind.[2]

As in a great assembly,[3] when Discord leaps at a word
Suddenly forth, and ignoble crowds with fury are stirred,
Firebrands fly, stones volley, the weapons furnished of wrath,—
If peradventure among them a Man stand forth in the path
Loyal and grave, long honoured for faithful service of years,
Seeing his face they are silent, and wait with listening ears :
He with his counsel calms their souls, assuages their ire.

(*A.* i. 148-53, Bowen.)

This is not a sympathetic picture of Democracy, though it is fairly true for the last century of the republic ; and, when

---

[1] Cf. J. R. Green, *Stray Studies*, p. 283 ; and Pierron, *La Lit. rom.* p. 399.
So Georgii in a Programm (Stuttgart, 1880), cited by Norden, *Neue Jahrbücher für das kl. Altertum*, vol. vii. p. 250 : "Augustus wird von Vergil nur verherr-licht, sofern er die römischen Dinge aus kläglicher Verwirrung gerettet, den Weltfrieden begründet und das römische Volk zu seinem Berufe zurückgeführt hat."
[2] Cf. Sainte-Beuve, *Études sur Virgile*, pp. 229-32.
[3] The word is *populo*, and it is significant.

we set beside it the hopeless scene where Latinus consults his people (*A*. xi), and the sketch of the typical democratic leader Drances, *largus opum, lingua melior, seditione potens* [1] (xi. 336-41), a man with some doubtful places in his pedigree, it can hardly be maintained that Virgil's admiration for the old Roman character included any regard for the old government. It is the *vir pietate gravis ac meritis* whom he prefers—the hero. Poets as a rule are not politicians, and, as they grow old, they often lapse into preferring freedom to be "sober-suited." The author of our only "revolutionary epic" became a Tory prime minister and an earl.[2]

Virgil then found in Augustus a friend, a saviour of his country, and a heroic character. Each of these considerations may help us to realize that, however much exaggerated we may think it, his praise of the Emperor is at least the outcome of honest feeling, and is so far legitimate. It remains now to review his references to Augustus in his poety, direct and indirect.

III

Quite early in the *Aeneid*, in fact in the first utterance of Jupiter, we find the prophecy of Augustus' reign (i. 257). Whether the *Julius* (288) of Jupiter's speech is Augustus, as many editors think, or Julius the Dictator, as Dr Henry maintains, the immediate allusion to the closing of the temple of Janus clearly refers to Augustus. Venus may be

---

[1] "Lavish of his wealth, a master with his tongue, powerful in the arts of faction."

[2] See Dowden on Shakespeare's attitude to Democracy (*Shakespeare, His Mind and Art*, ch. vi. § 3, pp. 319 ff.): "It was only after such an immense achievement as that of 1789, such a proof of power as the French Revolution afforded, that moral dignity, the spirit of self-control and self-denial, the heroic devotion of masses of men to ideas and not merely interests, could begin to manifest themselves." See Wordsworth, *Prelude*, bk. ix. 354-389, on his discussions with Beaupuy in 1793, with the spectacle before their eyes of

a people from the depth
Of shameful imbecility uprisen,
Fresh as the morning star. Elate we looked
Upon their virtues ; saw, in rudest men,
Self-sacrifice the firmest ; &c.

reassured; for in spite of the hate of Juno, the storms of Aeolus, and the violence of Turnus, Destiny will have its way; Rome shall go forth conquering, until under Augustus, her last conquest complete, she sheathes the sword. The reign of Augustus is thus the crown and culmination of Roman history, and the two heroes,—Aeneas, sent to Latium to found the race, and Augustus, born to regenerate the race and complete its work,—are brought together from the very beginning of the poem. Nor are they ever long separated.

When Aeneas descends to the other world the same revelation is made to himself. He sees the long line of his descendants, and chief among them the often-promised Augustus—

> Restorer of the age of gold
> In lands where Saturn ruled of old :
> O'er Ind and Garamant extreme
>   Shall stretch his boundless reign.
> Look to that land which lies afar
> Beyond the path of sun or star,
> Where Atlas on his shoulder rears
> The burden of the incumbent spheres.
> Egypt e'en now and Caspia hear
> The muttered voice of many a seer,
> And Nile's seven mouths, disturbed with fear,
>   Their coming conqueror know :
> Alcides in his savage chase
> Ne'er travelled o'er so wide a space,
> What though the brass-hoofed deer he killed,
> And Erymanthus forest stilled,
> And Lerna's depth with terror thrilled
>   At twanging of his bow :
> Nor stretched his conquering march so far
> Who drove his ivy-harnessed car
> From Nysa's lofty height, and broke
> The tiger's spirit 'neath his yoke.
> And shrink we in this glorious hour
> From bidding worth assert her power,

Or can our craven hearts recoil
From settling on Ausonian soil?

(vi. 792-807, Conington.)

Whatever effect this may have had on Aeneas,—and it is
not clear that in the rest of the poem the thought of
Augustus recurs so much to him as Anchises here hoped
it might,—the passage must have appealed to the Emperor.
It set him before mankind at once as the vindicator of
Roman majesty throughout the whole world—for even
the allusion to Indians was not without an actual historical
inspiration—and as the restorer of the golden age.

The last fifty lines of the eighth book contain an even
more elaborate account of the battle of Actium and of
the triumph of Augustus over Antony and Cleopatra, of
his temple-building and of the embassies of the nations,
all pictured on the shield of Aeneas. Nettleship conjectures
that the passage may have been rescued from the epic
on Augustus, which Virgil was asked to write, and for
which he may have designed this brilliant series of pictures.
At all events we forget Aeneas for the moment in the
glories of his descendant.

These are the great passages which celebrate the Emperor,
but we meet allusions to him again and again. Here it
is the festival of Actium, here the game of Troy, now the
closing of the Temple of Janus, again the Parthian surrender
of Crassus' standards, once more the Palatine temple of
Apollo, and the death of Marcellus. Even so small a
matter as the Trojan ancestry of the Emperor's maternal
grandfather is not overlooked, though nothing is said of
the Octavii—

Atys, genus unde Atii duxere Latini [1] (v. 568).

Further detail will not be needed. The poem could hardly
carry more of this direct kind of allusion to the Emperor.
There is more of it than the modern reader—the non-Latin
reader—cares to remember. Yet there are critics who go
further still in looking for Augustus in the poem.

[1] " Atys, from whom are descended the Latin Atii."

It is sometimes said that Aeneas is drawn from the Emperor. Dunlop, cited by Sainte-Beuve, carries the parallel into detail.[1] Aeneas has a remarkable filial piety for Anchises, as Augustus for Julius;[2] he is compared to Apollo, as Augustus loved to be;[3] the descent of the one into hell answers to the other's initiation into the mysteries; the war against Turnus, Latinus, and Amata, reproduces that against Antony, his brother Lucius, and Fulvia; and Dido is Cleopatra herself. Turnus is Antony, says Dunlop; Achates is Agrippa; Lavinia, Livia; the orator Drances ("oh! ici je me révolte") would be Cicero.[4] "Non, non, encore une fois non, me crie de toutes ses forces ma conscience poétique," cries Sainte-Beuve, and every one with any poetic conscience at all will agree with him.

But is there then no connexion between the characters of Augustus and Aeneas? An illustration (if one is needed) from English literature may help us to a right point of view. Browning was beset with questions by people who wished to know if his poem *The Lost Leader* referred to Wordsworth —*was* Wordsworth the Lost Leader? In 1875 he wrote to one of these correspondents the following explanation: "I *did* in my hasty youth presume to use the great and venerated personality of Wordsworth as a sort of painter's model; one from which this or the other particular feature may be selected and turned to account; had I intended more, above all, such a boldness as portraying the entire man, I should not have talked about 'handfuls of silver and bits of ribbon.' These never influenced the change of politics in the great poet. . . . But just as in the tapestry on my wall I can recognize figures which have *struck out* a fancy, on occasion, that though truly enough thus derived, yet

[1] Sainte-Beuve, *Étude sur Virgile*, p. 63. Merivale, *Hist. of Romans under Empire*, vol. v. ch. xli. pp. 107-8, traces a somewhat similar series of parallels, though he owns that "the opinion that Augustus himself is specially represented by Aeneas cannot be admitted without great reservation"—e.g. Aeneas' omens and tears and betrayal of Dido should be deducted.

[2] Cf. Monument of Ancyra, § 2 *qui parentem meum interfecerunt, eos in exilium expuli iudiciis legitimis ultus eorum facinus.*

[3] See Patin, *La Poésie latine*, i. p. 64; cf. Suetonius, *Augustus* 70.

[4] I gather from Conington's edition that Dunlop is not alone here.

would be preposterous as a copy, so, though I dare not deny
the original of my little poem, I altogether refuse to have
it considered as the 'very effigies' of such a moral and
intellectual superiority."[1]

These words of Browning may fairly be applied to the
case of Aeneas and Augustus. Virgil was "turning to
account" many features which he admired in the character
of the Emperor, and the Emperor was "a sort of painter's
model," though we must not forget that after all the ideal
figure, in which Virgil has embodied so many borrowed
features, stands, as his ancestor, in a closer relation to the
model than the Lost Leader did to Wordsworth. If we go
beyond this we shall find it difficult to explain what advantage the *Aeneid* has over a mere historical poem. A
creaking allegory, with a figure drawn from life in the very
middle of it, is not likely to have been Virgil's idea of an
epic. The poet draws the largest and most heroic figure he
can conceive, and even if in some of its traits it resembles
Augustus, it is more truly an ideal for the Emperor to
follow than a portrait of what he actually is.

A somewhat similar reply may be made to the critics who,
without adopting the theory of Dunlop in all its wooden-
ness, speak nevertheless as if the main purpose, or one of
the main purposes, of the *Aeneid* was to serve as a sort of
political pamphlet, "a vindication of monarchy," to quote
Dean Merivale.[2] Olympus and Troy are monarchical; all
the demi-gods and heroes have been kings. "Hence the
Romans may submit without dishonour to the sceptre" of
Augustus, who "has recovered the kingdom of his ancestors,"
and whose "legitimate right may be traced to his illustrious
ancestors"; for by the extinction of the house of Ilus, "all
its rights and honours, its hopes and aspirations, have
reverted to the offspring of the cadet Assaracus." A French
critic, who is generally sounder, takes the same line—"Qui
dit monarchie, dit légitimité. Virgile allait offrir, dans
l'*Énéide*, les parchemins attestant la légitimité de la maison

---

[1] The Cambridge edition of Browning, p. 164 (Houghton, Mifflin & Co.,
Boston and New York).

[2] Merivale, *op. cit.*, pp. 104-5, from whom I gather the phrases which follow.

Julienne." [1] We may forgive M. Goumy for his epigram,
but both he and Dean Merivale seem here to have left poetry
for prose of the most commonplace level. To begin,
Augustus was not king, and aimed at avoiding any appearance of monarchy; and though Virgil, as we have seen, had
no regrets for the old days of the republic, he understood
and shared Roman feeling too deeply to flaunt a thoroughly
un-Roman ideal. Aeneas is a king, but Augustus stands in
the line of Brutus, of Fabius Cunctator, of Scipio, a hero and
a saviour. Of course the *Aeneid* is full of personal rule—so
is the *Iliad*, which it professes to follow—but personal rule
is with Virgil a means and not an end. He has given us
again and again Augustus' title to rule—his fulfilment of
Rome's destiny and his embodiment of the great ideas of
the race. Aeneas' claim to Trojan loyalty is not his descent
so much as his nature. Descent as a title to sovereignty
was German and Oriental, and not Roman till Diocletian's
era.[2] There is a vindication of Augustus, and a great one,
running through the *Aeneid*; but to suggest that this appeal
to ancestry and the monarchical Olympus is Virgil's
conception of a defence of his hero is to mistake the values
of things fundamentally, and to misrepresent the poet—and
perhaps the Emperor, and certainly the Roman people, who
were not to be won by such flimsy pleading. And, what is
more important, if such a presentment of monarchy was
politically futile, it was even more to be condemned from the
point of view of poetry. Poets, it is true, have written to
support all sorts of things—even to defend capital punishment.[3] But Virgil, as we have seen, had deliberately
rejected the project of writing an epic about Augustus, and
he would probably have felt that to inculcate "royalist" or

[1] Goumy, *Les Latins*, p. 200. One feels M. Goumy must have been thinking
of the Comte de Chambord and his cousins. Indeed English scholars have not
always been exempt from the charge of thinking about France and her revolutions
when they supposed they were writing ancient history.

[2] The "divine right of kings" has a Levitical ancestry, and owes a good deal
to the fact that it could be used against the papal theory that all kings derived
their power from the pope. See Trevelyan, *England under the Stuarts*, p. 105.

[3] Whether the political value of such poetry has been more or less trifling than
its poetical value, may be questioned. Did Horace do more to promote marriage
or Wordsworth to delay the Reform Bill?

"legitimist" opinions in the course of the work he had chosen would have been to go back to an idea which he had rejected as unpoetical. Virgil put too serious a value on poetry to care to spend his genius on a matter so essentially trivial and external.

Closely connected with this subject is another question. What was the attitude of Virgil to the deification of Augustus? In the first *Eclogue* he announces that Octavian "will ever be a god for him," and that in his honour many a lamb shall stain the altar with its blood. In the beginning of the first *Georgic* he again speaks of Augustus' deity with much disquisition on the various spheres in which he may hereafter exercise his divine power. What does it all mean?[1]

Far too much stress may be laid on these passages. In the first place, the *Eclogue* is after all largely symbolic throughout. Virgil was not Tityrus, or at most he was only partially Tityrus; and, however appropriate or inappropriate the proposal to make a god of Octavian may have been in the mouth of a herd and a freedman, there is so much in the rest of the poem which is manifestly absurd, if applied directly to Virgil, that it is wiser not to take this passage as the indication of any feeling of Virgil's other than gratitude. He was an Epicurean still, and even if gratitude made him write frigid poetry, it could not rob him of his sanity. As to the passage in the first *Georgic*,[2] it should be compared with the rendering which Catullus made of the *Coma Berenices*. The elaborate enumeration of the realms of heaven, hell, and the sea, with all the accompanying mythological ornament, is a mere piece of Alexandrinism, and means absolutely nothing. Virgil had before him the precedent of Lucretius invoking in Venus a heavenly power in whom he did not believe, and the Epicureanism, which he expresses later on in the book, once more shows that he did not and could not believe in Augustus' godhead. In fact the passage is an experiment,

---

[1] On deification see Plutarch's *Life of Romulus* 28—a striking sentence at the end of the discussion shows how philosophic minds could find it natural and reasonable.

[2] See Sellar, *Virgil*, ch. iii. p. 217.

which Virgil was content perhaps to have made, but which he never repeated. Thereafter, when he praised Augustus, it was for his real services to mankind, and his praise is sincere and not unworthy of our respect.

Once in the *Aeneid* Virgil alludes to the deification of a Caesar, but whether it is Julius or Augustus is disputed (i. 286-90). He also compares Augustus to Bacchus and to Hercules, both semi-divine conquerors who attained heaven by services to mankind,[1] but he does not picture him, as Horace does, "drinking nectar with purple mouth" in their company. The worship of the Emperor was no doubt already prominent though not so much emphasized by the government as it was a generation or two later. It was Greek and Asiatic rather than Roman, more fitted for the Ptolemies than the Julii. If Virgil could have been questioned on his views on the matter, he might probably have leant rather to some such doctrine as Cicero sets forth in his *Dream of Scipio*—the future rewarding and glorification in a higher and more divine region of all who have served their country. Indeed, if we can draw any safe inference from the vision granted to Aeneas in Hades, Augustus stands on essentially the same footing, and is subjected to the same conditions, as the other patriots there revealed — within and not without the cycle of recurrent life. But as a rule Augustus' glories are of this world, and the poet looks more to his power to benefit mankind by his human activity than to any shadowy apotheosis.

To sum up; Virgil was drawn to Augustus by personal affection, by admiration for his character, and by belief in

---

[1] Julian the apostate flattered himself that he was of the order of Dionysos and Herakles. I do not now go so far as Vollert in construing this as a claim laid to actual deity. The whole question of the deification of a living emperor, or the incarnation in Julian or Augustus of some divine being, is bound up, I now see, with the Daemon theory, as set forth by Plutarch and Apuleius. In view of the current belief in daemons, scarcely distinguishable from men's souls except that the latter for the moment are possessed of bodies, it is quite easy to see how even a reasonable man could believe an emperor to be an incarnation of something divine. I may perhaps be allowed to refer the reader to *The Conflict of Religions in the Early Roman Empire*, where daemons are discussed at some length.

his power and his will to save Italy and the Empire. In his earlier works he used expressions and methods, untrue and unpoetical, which he subsequently discarded. If the introduction of Augustus into the *Aeneid* must be conceded to be a failure to achieve the highest poetic truth, it was at least prompted by honest motives, and the attention of the reader is uniformly called to the really valid and sound features of the Emperor's work and character.

CHAPTER VIII

INTERPRETATION OF LIFE.—1. DIDO

Strong and fierce in the heart, Dear,
  With—more than a will—what seems a power
To pounce on my prey, love outbroke here
  In flame devouring and to devour.
Such love has laboured its best and worst
To win me a lover ; yet, last as first,
I have not quickened his pulse one beat,
Fixed a moment's fancy, bitter or sweet :
Yet the strong fierce heart's love's labour's due,
Utterly lost, was—you !—BROWNING.

OVID tells us that no part of the *Aeneid* was so popular as the episode of Dido.[1] Though he makes this statement in self-defence we may well believe him in view of the abiding attraction of the story. Macrobius says that for centuries painters, sculptors, and workers in embroidery had turned to Dido, as if it were the only subject in which beauty was to be found, while the very actors had never ceased to tell her sorrows in dance and song.[2] Augustine himself confesses that he wept to read of Dido and "how she slew herself for love," and he links her story with *ipsius umbra Creusae*.[3] And to-day there are still those who maintain that "what touch of human interest the *Aeneid* can claim it gains from the romance of Dido."[4] That Dido has ruined the character of Aeneas with nine-tenths of his readers is the admission of one of Virgil's most sympathetic critics, who proceeds to ask the pertinent question whether the poet failed to see what his readers have seen, and why, if he saw it, he used the story as he did.[5] Some

[1] Ovid, *Tristia*, ii. 533.
[2] Macrobius, *Sat.* v. 17. 5-6 *tanquam unico argumento decoris.*
[3] Augustine, *Conf.* i. 13. 21.
[4] Bernard Bosanquet, *History of Aesthetic*, p. 88.
[5] J. R. Green, *Stray Studies* : the essay on Aeneas is one of the best treat-

explanation is necessary if we are to understand the *Aeneid* as a whole.

I

We need not here discuss at length the possibility of Dido being another name for the goddess known in other lands as Ashtoreth, Semiramis, and Aphrodite, though this identification would give us an attractive explanation of the original connexion of the names of Dido and Aeneas. It is enough at present to refer to the lost *Punic War* of the old Roman poet Naevius, a work "as delightful as Myro's sculpture."[1] It had appealed to Ennius, it charmed Cicero, and Virgil borrowed from it. So at least Macrobius tells us. "In the beginning of the *Aeneid* a tempest is described; Venus complains to Jove of the perils of her son, and is assured of the prosperity of his future. This whole passage is taken from Naevius—from the first book of the *Punic War*."[2] It is generally conjectured that the poem went on to tell of the meeting of Dido and Aeneas and of the queen's unhappy love.

If this be so, we have no longer to explain how Virgil came to introduce Carthage and Dido into his story, for they were in the story already. The question is rather why he retained the episode, for it was not unchallenged. Tertullian, the most brilliant of early Christian writers, was a Carthaginian, and three times over he alludes to Dido having preferred the pyre to marriage.[3] Macrobius says that everybody (*universitas*) knew the tale to be false; it was well known that Dido laid hands on herself to save her fair name—though, he adds, every one prefers the version of Virgil. The interpolator of Servius adds something more disconcerting still. He quotes Varro to

ments of the character I have seen. I quote his pages from the first edition, 1876. Cf. also Warde Fowler, *Religious Experience of the Roman People* (1911) p. 416. "If for us the character of Aeneas suffers by his desertion of Dido, that is simply because the poet, seized with intense pity for the injured queen, seems for once, like his own hero, to have forgotton his mission in the poem."

[1] Cicero, *Brutus*, 19. 75 *bellum Punicum quasi Myronis opus delectat.*
[2] Macrobius, *Saturnalia*, vi. 2. 31.
[3] *Apology* 50 ; *ad martyras* 4 ; *ad Natt.* i. 18.

the effect that it was Anna, and not Dido, who immolated herself for love of Aeneas.[1] And in the generation after Virgil, Velleius Paterculus wrote that "sixty-five years before Rome was founded, the Tyrian Elissa, whom some people call Dido, founded Carthage."[2] Thus here as elsewhere Virgil had considerable freedom of choice as to the turn he might prefer to give to the legend.

If the conjecture as to Naevius be right, the tale of Dido and Aeneas formed in his poem a background to the Punic war. But with Virgil it is the other way; the historical is the background of the legendary. He finds legend and history already linked, and he accepts them in their existing connexion, but he brings them into far closer contact. Dido and Aeneas formed a mere episode in the poem of Naevius. The Punic war is no episode at all in the *Aeneid*, and yet it underlies the whole narrative of the meeting and parting of the founder of Rome and the foundress of Carthage. We are not explicitly told of it, but we feel again and again, tingling and burning through our tale of love and hate, memories of the conflict of the two nations. If the *Aeneid* was to be the epic of the Roman people, as the Romans recognized it to be, that great struggle could not be forgotten. From the very beginning, and before the beginning, Carthage was the enemy of Rome, and the simple *Annals* of Naevius gave Virgil his opportunity for a more splendid and imaginative treatment of that rivalry, on the issue to which had turned the destiny of his people.

For it is in virtue of the imaginative element that the old fable rises into poetry. Without it, however quaint it

---

[1] Heinze, *Virgils epische Technik*, p. 113, n. 1, suggests that it may be merely a conjecture of Varro's to reconcile the discrepant stories of Dido.

[2] Macr. *Sat.* v. 16. 6; Servius, *ad Aen.* iv. 682; Vell. Pat. i. 6. The cool phrase *quam quidam Dido autumant* may explain the remarkable judgement of Velleius, who coupled Virgil with Rabirius, the author of a historical poem on the downfall of Antony. Ovid, *ex Ponto* iv. 16, 5, calls him *magni Rabirius oris*; and Quintilian x. i. 90 classes him with Pedo as *non indigni cognitione, si vacet* —a discouraging qualification. It is thought that some 67 hexameters on the Egyptian war, found in a papyrus roll at Herculaneum, may belong to the epic of Rabirius—they are the work of "a moderately gifted poet." Schanz, *Röm. Lit.* § 316.

might be, it would be foolish, an impertinence in a serious work. But the poet transforms his hero and heroine into representatives, each embodying and expressing the genius of a race. The Punic wars are now no longer the result of hatred accidentally produced, but the inevitable outcome of the clash of two national tempers. Historically, Rome and Carthage fought for Sicily and the command of the sea—a struggle of greed with greed, some might say, but that is an inadequate way of judging history. Rather it is that the nations, seeking the realization and fulfilment of the life within them, came into conflict inevitably,[1] and brought into it so many armies and fleets, no doubt, but also ideas and principles. Providence, we have heard, is on the side of the biggest battalions, and perhaps it is true ; for the biggest battalions naturally gravitate to the side of the larger ideals. In the Punic wars these were unquestionably on the Roman side. Two great types of national thinking are in conflict—the Oriental and the Western character meet, and bring with them all that they imply, ideals of state and government, of citizenship, of law and thought. And when Virgil draws us Aeneas and Dido he gives us back this identical conflict.

But beside the main issue there enter into every great struggle other issues, which complicate it and make decision difficult, and men from right motives take the wrong side. It is this confusion of issues that lies at the heart of all Tragedy,—the conflict of good with good, the division of the spirit against itself.[2] Put the question as directly as man can, the answer will never be a plain Yes or No. But if the case is brought before us, not on the large and more nearly abstract scale, where nations are involved, but on a smaller stage, where the representatives of the ideas in conflict are individual men and women ; if the principles they maintain are entangled in all the reactions of personality upon personality, and we have to hold firmly to the thread,

[1] This adverb is open to criticism, but I think the conflict of Rome and Carthage, in view of the position of things in the Mediterranean and the commercial theories of the age, was inevitable.

[2] See Mr A. C. Bradley on Hegel's theory of Tragedy, in his *Oxford Lectures on Poetry*, an essay to which I owe a great deal.

which study of the final issue alone can give us, and to disregard for the while every appeal of sympathy and instinct, the task of judgement is immeasurably more difficult.

For us to-day the issue between Carthage and Rome is so far away as to be relatively simple. If the poet chose to present it to us in a purely symbolic form, we might decide it easily, but we might not be greatly interested in it. If Dido and Aeneas were merely figures in an allegory, probably no one would ever have wept over Dido

extinctam ferroque extrema secutam. [1]

"Abstract Ideas," says Carlyle, "however they may put on fleshly garments, are a class of character whom we cannot sympathize with or delight in." [2] We must have flesh and blood if we are to be moved as well as interested. Let hero and heroine represent types of national character, but they must still be individual, personal, human. Then the poet will touch us indeed, for in the persons of two creatures of our own nature he will let us see the same sort of warfare as too often occupies ourselves to this day, dividing brother from brother, and wrenching the same heart asunder, as love and duty pull different ways. If there is anything gained by using more technical language, the poet must show us the universal in the particular.

Virgil took his theme from Naevius, if we are right in following conjecture. But in all probability his treatment of it was very different, for he had other models beside the old annalist. He had before him the tragic poets of the great age of Greece, and the Alexandrines, his own earlier allegiance,—in particular Euripides and Apollonius, both of whom it is clear that he studied with care and affection. Greek tragedy had delighted to show the conflict of character with character, and from the first had depicted with sympathy the play of passion and principle upon feminine nature. But when we come to Euripides we find that a great many of his plays deal with woman primarily, and only secondarily with man. Hecuba, Andromache, and Alcestis

---

[1] See p. 56, n. 4.   [2] *Essay on Werner.*

are pictures of woman as wife and mother, but the poet did not stop there. In Phaedra an altogether new note in poetry is struck, for one of the main motives of the *Hippolytus* is the struggle of the heroine to resist passion. Love has been added to the domain of poetry, never to be lost again. Euripides was essentially a pioneer ; and those who followed him into this region were many, especially when, by the Macedonian conquest of the world, the thoughts of men were turned from the state to the individual.

The love-tale in one form or other is one of the main constituents of Alexandrine poetry, sometimes overlaid with masses of irrelevant learning and cleverness, sometimes, though less often, clear of all irrelevance, strong, direct, and true, as in Theocritus' Simaetha.[1] From Euripides and the Alexandrines the love motive found its way into Latin poetry, and in Virgil's day it had perhaps more vogue than ever before or after in the history of Latin literature.

Parthenius, for example, the teacher of Virgil, made a handbook of love-tales for another pupil, Gallus ; and however little or much influence Parthenius may have had on Virgil, Virgil was closely connected with Gallus and read his poetry, if indeed the two young poets had not for a while a sort of literary partnership.[2] He also steeped himself in Catullus, whose story of Ariadne deserted by Theseus, and whose *Attis* he must have read with care. Ovid's *Letters of the Heroines* published perhaps a few years after Virgil's death, are an indication of the taste of the period before and after their appearance, a proof of the absorbing interest in pictures of passion.

Virgil was too closely in touch with the great literature of the past and with the life of his time not to feel the attraction of this particular study of human nature. It was essentially cognate to his peculiar gift of tenderness and sympathy, and we can almost trace the growth of his interest

---

[1] Erwin Rohde in his book, *Der griechische Roman*, has given a comprehensive and minute survey of the Alexandrine literature concerned with love. See Part i.

[2] See the interesting essay of Mr J. W. Mackail on the Virgilian circle in his *Lectures on Poetry*.

in it. But perhaps nowhere can the sanity of Virgil's genius be more clearly remarked than here. Nothing will seduce him from the universal. The peculiar, the exaggerated, the pathological case alike repel him. The unbalanced and abnormal mind shocks and disgusts him, and he will not waste his mind upon it. He may use it at times as a foil, but no words are needed to show his entire acceptance of the words of Catullus at the end of the *Attis*—

> Procul a mea tuos sit furor omnis, era, domo;
> alios age incitatos, alios age rabidos.[1]

Every line he writes is a tacit protest.

The lovers in the *Eclogues* are delightful and amiable young men, but we hardly think that they are really very much in love. When we come to the story of Orpheus we are tempted to believe that we have a more serious record of human experience, and yet a closer study of metre and language raises a doubt, which it is hard to lay. All is so stately, so musical, so picturesque. Take the very central words of the story, Eurydice's farewell—

> Illa "quis et me" inquit "miseram et te perdidit, Orpheu,
> quis tantus furor? en iterum crudelia retro
> fata vocant, conditque natantia lumina somnus.
> Iamque vale: feror ingenti circumdata nocte
> invalidasque tibi tendens, heu non tua, palmas"[2]

$$(G. \text{ iv. } 494).$$

The passage is beautiful, but does not its structure suggest meditation rather than emotion, painting rather than experience? The first sentence with its double *quis* and its *tantus*; the third with its rare and sleepy rhythm, far more effectively used elsewhere to describe in the third person sleep overcoming Palinurus;[3] are they not a little studied? But the last sentence is surely conclusive. Five thoughts clustering about one verb, and above all the parenthesis *heu non tua*, speak only too clearly of the distance between

---

[1] "Far from my house by all thy madness, goddess; others drive thou head-long, other drive in frenzy."

[2] For translation see p. 38.

[3] *A.* v. 856 *cunctantique natantia lumina solvit.*

utterance and realization. Emotion does not express itself in periods so involved, least of all in the moment of suffering.

> Do you see this? Look on her, look, her lips,
> Look there, look there!

So cries the dying Lear. There is a moving simplicity in those lines of quiet despair which Catullus wrote at his brother's grave, in such passages as the address of Mezentius to his horse[1] and his dying request to Aeneas,[2] which speaks straight from the heart to the heart. The sentences are short, direct, and rapid; they do not suggest skill; but they throb with feeling and truth.

In short, the story of Orpheus and Eurydice is not a genuine transcript of passion, nor an imaginative present-ment of it.[3] It is more like a masque of the Triumph of Music. Its nearest analogue is the *Ariadne* of Catullus, which also is somewhat disconnectedly set in the middle of another poem. But when we reach Dido we come into touch with the most serious mind of the poet. Here is real passion, drawn with all the power and truth that the poet could put into his work.

II

One preliminary question has to be asked before we begin to study the tragedy of Dido, for here, as in the *Hippolytus*, we have a prologue, but a more difficult one. Whatever we make of Aphrodite in the play of Euripides, whether we suppose the poet to be directing a covert and ingenious attack on the Olympian gods,[4] or hold that he is figuring "a force of Nature or a Spirit working in the

---

[1] *A.* x. 861 *Rhaebe, diu, res si qua diu mortalibus ulla est,* | *viximus.*

[2] *A.* x. 900-6.

[3] After eight or ten years I let the passage stand as I wrote it, but while I do so, I should like to suggest that what my words might seem to deny is also true—that with the art there is still feeling in the passage of the fourth *Georgic.* None the less the fourth *Aeneid* stands on a far higher plane of truth to feeling.

[4] "Serait-il téméraire de prétendre qu'Euripide, qui, tout en usant, comme poëte, des croyances de sa patrie et de son temps, ne s'interdisait pas de témoigner qu'elles répugnaient à sa raison, a voulu, lorsqu'il les a ainsi présentées aux regards dans toute leur nudité, protester indirectement contre elles?" Patin, *Euripide,* i. p. 44.

world," [1] a fact real enough, however hateful—whatever our conclusion about her, the language and the purpose of the goddess are alike clear. She announces her intention to punish Hippolytus for his neglect of her, and to use Phaedra as her instrument. She quite well realizes that this will mean Phaedra's undoing, but she does not care. [2]

> Seeing he hath offended, I this day
> Shall smite Hippolytus . . .
> And she, not in dishonour, yet shall die.
> I would not rate this woman's pain so high
> As not to pay mine haters in full fee
> That vengeance that shall make all well with me.

Virgil's prologue, if the word may be used, is in two parts. We have in the first book the interview of Venus and Cupid, and the later dialogue of Venus and Juno in the fourth book.

As a result of Juno's storm, Aeneas has been driven ashore close to the town, which of all places was to be most hostile to him and his race. His mother in alarm intercedes with Jupiter, and Mercury is sent to soften the hearts of the Carthaginians—especially the queen's—towards the newcomers. [3] Accordingly when Dido and Aeneas meet, it is in perfect amity and courtesy. But Venus is not yet at ease. She does not like the double-tongued Tyrians; and the thought comes to her again and again that her son is in the very stronghold of the foe, and practically at the mercy of Juno. She resolves to storm the enemy's citadel, and to detach Dido from the schemes and influence of her patron-goddess by making her fall in love with Aeneas. Then, at least, Dido will do him no harm, and he will come away safely. Dido's fame or feelings she does not consider. She is only afraid

---

[1] Mr Murray in notes to his translation, which I quote in the text.

[2]
  Ἃ δ' εἰς ἔμ' ἡμάρτηκε, τιμωρήσομαι
  Ἱππόλυτον ἐν τῇδ' ἡμέρᾳ· (21)
  ἡ δ' εὐκλεὴς μέν, ἀλλ' ὅμως ἀπόλλυται,
  Φαίδρα· τὸ γὰρ τῆσδ' οὐ προτιμήσω κακὸν
  τὸ μὴ οὐ παρασχεῖν τοὺς ἐμοὺς ἐχθροὺς ἐμοὶ
  δίκην τοσαύτην ὥστ' ἐμοὶ καλῶς ἔχειν (47·50).

[3] A. i. 297.

of treachery, and, once secure against that, she thinks no
more of Dido than Aphrodite does of Phaedra in the
Hippolytus. Whether she means that the passion, which
she intends to wake, should culminate as it does, or remain
concealed, as Phaedra would have kept hers, Venus does
not say, nor, very probably, does she greatly care.[1]

When we next overhear the discussions of the gods
things have advanced materially.[2] Venus has successfully
out-manœuvred Juno, and Juno has realized it and is now
concerned to make the most of the present position. She
scornfully congratulates Venus on trapping Dido—she
understands the motive perfectly—but how long is the
struggle between them to continue? why not end it by
marrying their favourites? Venus instantly sees the design
—if Aeneas cannot be destroyed by storm at sea or by
Tyrian ashore, he can be kept an unconscious prisoner
at Carthage, and Rome will not be founded. Accordingly
she answers Juno in the most conciliatory way. Who
would wish to engage in a quarrel with the queen of
Jove? She herself is not quite sure, she hints, whether
destiny will permit the fusion of Trojans and Tyrians in
one city—but Jove's wife should be able to learn this
from Jove. Juno, in reply, undertakes to do all that is
needed. She will manage the union of Dido and Aeneas,
and, if Venus agrees, it shall be marriage. Venus says
no more. She only laughs, for she knows the intentions
of destiny better than Juno does, and she sees that her
enemy's new move will be ineffectual. There will be no
marriage, nothing but a temporary union, to be ended
in due time. Rome is secure and Juno is outwitted.

This then is the "prologue." The whole question of the
part and place of the gods in the *Aeneid* must for the present
be reserved. But it should be noted that here, as in the
Hippolytus, the intervention of Venus effects nothing that
could not have occurred independently of it. "It is to the
heart of man that the dramatic struggle is transported; the
actors are our faculties themselves; the subject of the piece
is that inward war of sensibility and reason, old as our

---

[1] *A.* i. 657-694.   [2] *A.* iv. 90, f.

nature, and as eternal." So writes M. Patin of the dramas of Euripides,[1] and it is true of Virgil's tragedy.

*Ην οὐμὸς υἱὸς κάλλος ἐκπρεπέστατος,
ὁ σὸς δ᾽ ἰδών νιν νοῦς ἐποιήθη Κύπρις,*

said Hecuba to Helen.[2] Could not Venus say the same, and say it justly, to Dido? If Aeneas was not beautiful as Paris was, he had his appeal to Dido's heart, and that heart, confronted by that appeal, was Venus enough. In fact, the parallel with the *Hippolytus* holds, and we may for the purposes of our present study disregard the action of the gods, without deciding at once whether or not they are after all mere epic machinery. Here, as throughout the *Aeneid*, they really contribute little but their names to forces already at work.

III

In studying this tragedy of Aeneas and Dido, the first thing to be done is to realize Virgil's conception of the central figure, and this is of course Dido. She is at once a woman and a queen, a woman in the large and ample sense, in instinct, feeling, and sympathy, and a queen in her ideas and her achievements.

Dido is a woman. Calypso in Homer is a goddess. Medea in Apollonius is a girl, even if a magician and a princess.[3] Catullus' Ariadne is little more than a child. Dido has been a wife and is a widow.

She has a woman's eye for the stature and the carriage of the hero [4]—

quem sese ore ferens, quam forti pectore et armis (*A.* iv. 11).

---

[1] *Eschyle*, p. 47.
[2] *Troades*, 987—
   " My son was passing beautiful, beyond
   His peers; and thine own heart, that saw and conned
   His face, became a spirit enchanting thee " (Murray).
[3] On Medea, see Girard, *Études sur la poésie grecque*, p. 331, who calls attention to the startling contrasts in her character as presented by Apollonius; Sainte-Beuve, *De la Médée d'Ap.* in *Rev. des deux Mondes*, 1845, vol. xi.
[4] " What a face and carriage! what strength of breast and shoulders " (Conington). For the appeal of physical beauty a parallel may be quoted in the case of Euryalus—*gratior et pulchro veniens in corpore virtus* (*A.* v. 344).

For Aeneas, we are told, is like a god in countenance and shoulders,

> os humerosque deo similis (*A.* i. 589).

When Charon takes Aeneas into his craft, the size of the hero is emphasized in contrast to the craziness of the boat (*A.* vi. 413). But more striking is an allusion in the tenth book. It is a battle-scene. Aeneas pursues a foe, who stumbles in his flight. One moment of consciousness is left him, and he realizes a great shadow falling across him, and instantly he dies by the hand of Aeneas.[1]

Perhaps in this connexion it may be permissible to find a feminine trait in Dido's pleasure in the gifts which Aeneas brings her—the mantle of gold embroidery, the veil, the beaded necklace, and the circlet of gold,

Dido has imagination. She can understand this great, tall, and rather melancholy hero better than many of his readers have done.

> My story being done,
> She gave me for my pains a world of sighs:
> She lov'd me for the dangers I had pass'd.

To this Dido was helped by her own story.

> Non ignara mali miseris succurrere disco [2] (*A.* i. 630).

For, in many particulars, the experience of both has been the same. She has left a lost husband, as he a lost wife, in a native land never to be seen again. She has been "tossed by the fates," and the wars of Africa,

> terra triumphis
> dives (*A.* iv. 37),

---

[1] *Quem congressus agit campo, lapsumque superstans*
immolat, ingentique umbra tegit (*A.* x. 540).

The *Times* reviewer (16 December 1904) suggests that this is letting "literary instinct take the bit in its teeth," adding that "such over-subtle interpretation as this is to be deprecated with any great artist." He may very well be right, but I leave the passage and quote the criticism—not the only one which I have found of value to me in the review—and suggest that the reader decides the point for himself.

[2] "Full well I know evil and learn to succour the unhappy."

have taught her what the long Trojan war meant. She too has sought a city. She has ruled, and she knows instinctively the ruler of men.

She loves children. If she takes Ascanius to her heart, taken by his likeness to his father—

> genitoris imagine capta (*A.* iv. 84),

it is hardly too much to say that the child helped to win her for the father. The elaborate substitution of Cupid is really needless. Even before the god in disguise begins his work we are told that she is moved alike by the child and by the gifts—

> pariter puero donisque movetur (*A.* i. 714).

She watches the boy with eyes and heart open, and takes him to her bosom—

> Haec oculis, haec pectore toto
> haeret et interdum gremio fovet (*A.* i. 717).

But she is herself childless, and she feels it. When she learns of the Trojan preparations to sail, and challenges Aeneas with them, before his coldness wakes her rage, the last cry from her heart is that of the childless woman. Had she only a little Aeneas to play in her hall, to recall his look! Aeneas has a child, she has none.[1]

> Saltem siqua mihi de te suscepta fuisset
> ante fugam suboles, si quis mihi parvulus aula
> luderet Aeneas, qui te tamen ore referret
> non equidem omnino capta ac deserta viderer[2] (*A.* iv. 327).

She is childless and a widow—and what a story she has to remember! It is the marring of her life. In the back-

---

[1] Queen Elizabeth is reported to have exclaimed, on hearing of the birth of the child, afterwards James I : " The Queen of Scots is the mother of a fair son, and I am a barren stock." The diminutive *parvulus* should be remarked. It is, I think, the only one in Virgil's works—the only deliberate diminutive, in which the form has its force ; and it is very significant.

[2] " Had I but borne any offspring of you before your flight, were there but some tiny Aeneas to play in my hall, and remind me of you, though but in look, I should not then feel utterly captive and forlorn " (Conington).

ground of all her thoughts is the murder of her husband, Sychaeus, by Pygmalion, her brother. Heedless of her love in his greed of power and gold, he made his sister a widow. This may have been the legend, but the poet divined what it meant to a sensitive being—the crushing of natural instincts; a wound dealt to the spirit, where it would be most felt; the killing of human love. Virgil's methods are not Hawthorne's, or he might have analysed the effects of such a blow upon character and nature, in the disordering of the natural courses of feeling, the accentuation of tendencies to extravagance and hysteria, the pathological susceptibility to be overcome by passion and emotion. These features of her disposition are not set out and catalogued, but they are there, and they make themselves felt in the progress of the story.

Dido is a queen, and a great queen. Without going into the ancient history of the word, the Romans of Virgil's day had learnt in Egypt the meaning of *regina*.[1] It has been suggested that Dido has been drawn from Cleopatra, but this is absurd, though Virgil may well have borrowed suggestion. He is not writing a historical epic, and he looks beyond the actual. Still, Cleopatra had revealed one side of feminine nature to the Romans, which, in spite of Clytaemnestra, antiquity had not known. Medea in Euripides is an injured and angry wife; Deianira is injured and forgiving. In Phaedra the queen, a queen-consort at most, is sunk in the woman. Ariadne is a forsaken girl. But Dido is a queen and always a queen. Her greatness and her fall hang together. The key-note is to be caught throughout—

> dux femina facti [2] (*A.* i. 364).

Her magnificence is a queen's—

> urbem quam statuo vestra est [3] (*A.* i. 573).

The dowry she brings to Aeneas is a people, an empire;

---

[1] *A.* viii. 696 *regina in mediis patrio vocat agmina sistro* ; Horace, *Odes,* i. 37.

[2] The Englishman in Elizabeth's reign saw the meaning of this phrase.

[3] "The city I found—is yours."

the sneer may be Juno's, the generous act is Dido's.[1] And when she dies, she dies a queen and the founder of a nation;[2] and in Hades itself she retains her queenly dignity.[3]

IV

One of the most obviously impossible things to explain is why any two people fall in love with each other; and even if in the case of Dido and Aeneas we refer to the plotting of rival goddesses we are not much enlightened. Dido's love began in sympathy for one whose lot had been so like her own. It was helped forward by her fondness for his child. His story, we are told and we can well believe it, was not without its effect; and in the imperceptible way in which these things happen the queen fell in love with her guest.

From the first we can see it will go ill with her. Despite their splendour and charm, those gifts, which Aeneas has brought from the ships, are not all of happy omen. The robe of stiff gold embroidery and the veil had been Leda's once, and then Helen's—

Ornatus Argivae Helenae, quos illa Mycenis
Pergama cum peteret inconcessosque hymenaeos
extulerat[4] (*A.* i. 650).

Their story was not a good one. They came from a family of bad women.[5] They had already seen broken wedlock and all the ruin and suffering it brought. The later gift of the sword was scarcely happier.[6]

[1] *A.* iv. 101—

> Communem hunc ergo populum paribusque regamus
> auspiciis ; liceat Phrygio servire marito
> dotalisque tuae Tyrios permittere dextrae.

[2] *A.* iv. 653—

> Vixi et quem dederat cursum fortuna peregi,
> et nunc magna mei sub terras ibit imago :
> urbem praeclaram statui, mea moenia vidi.

[3] *A.* vi. 450-474.

[4] " Adornments of Argive Helen, which she carried away from Mycenae, when she went to Troy and to her unblest bridal."

[5] Cf. Dr. Verrall's note on Agamemnon's address to Clytaemnestra (Helen's sister) beginning Λήδας γένεθλον, Aesch. *Ag.* 914.

[6] *A.* iv. 647. The still surviving superstition on giving knives may be compared—" knives," we are told, " cut love."

Dido's love, moreover, has from the first the promise
of misery in itself. It is too fierce and passionate, over-
mastering her like the madness of Attis. She can know
no rest, for the new passion is battling with an old pre-
possession.

She complains to her sister Anna that she is haunted
by dreams. Dr Henry suggests that they are visions of her
husband Sychaeus, in view of Anna's pointed allusion to the
Manes of the dead.[1] It will be remembered that dreams of
Sychaeus had influenced her before in her flight from Tyre.[2]

She has bad dreams, and yet—who is this strange guest?
What a man he is! What a countenance he has and what
a frame! No doubt, a child of gods. And what a life he
has lived! All this hints at passion, and the hint is
immediately confirmed by her reference to her long-fixed
resolve never again to marry. But for that, she "might
have yielded to this one reproach. Anna—for I will own
the truth—since the fate of Sychaeus, my hapless husband,
he and he alone has touched my heart, and shaken my
resolve till it totters. I recognize the traces of the flame
I knew of old." The truth is out, and she realizes that
there has been a weakening in her purpose. And here
the poet is true to experience, for she instantly fortifies
her wavering resolution with a curse, an appeal to her
honour (*pudor*), and an invocation of her old love—and
bursts into tears.

It is now that Anna comes into the story. The sister
of the heroine is a familiar figure in Greek tragedy.
Ismene, in the play of Sophocles, takes a lower and less
reflective view of duty than Antigone, and is quite unable
to grasp what it is that moves her sister to action. So
here Anna represents a more commonplace type of mind.
She is shrewd enough. Probably long before Dido got
so far as *Anna fatebor enim* Anna had summed up the
situation, and by the time the curse and the tears ended
the speech she knew quite well what her own line would
be. Anna is a woman of the common-sense school, not
at all of an imaginative habit. To prove this, it is only

[1] Henry, *Aeneidea*, ii. p. 558, on *A.* iv. 9.   [2] *A.* i. 353.

necessary to anticipate by a little the moment when Dido
ha* resolved to kill herself. Of such an outcome Anna
never dreams for an instant—

nec tantos mente furores
concipit aut graviora timet quam morte Sychaei (iv. 501).

" I think," wrote Fox, " the coarsest thing in the whole
book (not, indeed, in point of indecency, but in want of
sentiment) is verse 502. *She thought she would take it as
she did the last time* is surely vulgar and coarse to the last
degree." [1] Dr Henry warmly apostrophizes " Mr Fox " in
an almost Montanist outburst upon second marriages in
general, and ardently repels the suggestion that Virgil is
coarse or deficient in sentiment. But whether Fox imagined
or not that the view which he condemned as coarse was
Virgil's own, the criticism is entirely just, if it is directed
upon Anna. It is Anna's view, and it is " coarse " and
" wanting in sentiment." But it is hardly more so than her
first speech to Dido on the subject of her new passion.
It is a most significant utterance. Why, she asks, should
Dido forgo the pleasures of husband and children? She
has remained unmarried so far out of loyalty to Sychaeus.

Id cinerem aut manes credis curare sepultos ? [2] (iv. 34).

Sychaeus, like Frederick Prince of Wales in the old
rhyme—

Was alive and is dead ;
There's no more to be said.

Anna asks herself why Dido has never married again, and
the only reason of which she can conceive—the only reason
that could weigh with herself—is that she had not so far
wished to do it. But if she wishes to now, why should she
not ? Iarbas and the Africans—she might well (shall we
say ?) mislike them for their complexion; but Aeneas is a
hero of another colour ; and if Dido cares to marry him—

placitone etiam pugnabis amori ? [3] (iv. 38).

---

[1] Letter to Wakefield, in Russell's *Memoirs of Fox*, vol. iv. p. 426, cited by
Henry *ad loc.*
[2] " Think you that ashes and a ghost in a grave heed this ? "
[3] " Will you contend even with a love that is to your liking ? "

Anna is a Cyrenaic in her philosophy, and inclination is her guide in life. She proceeds to fortify her advice by a number of political considerations—

nec venit in mentem quorum consederis arvis ? [1] (iv. 39).

Gaetulians, Numidians, Barcaeans and Tyrians are all threatening Dido, and only to be overcome by the aid of Aeneas. But the real reason is still transparent.

Tu lacrimis evicta meis,

says Dido later on, when she has realized her mistake.[2]

τί σεμνομυθεῖς; οὐ λόγων εὐσχημόνων
δεῖ σ᾽, ἀλλὰ τἀνδρός.

So says her nurse to Phaedra in the play of Euripides,[3] and Anna's feeling is no other.

Dido, we have seen, is a woman of some character and greatness, but her forte is action rather than reflection. Hers after all has been an "unexamined life," and, in her hour of need, she has nothing adequate on which to fall back. She surrenders at once, and gives up her ideal for her inclination. Virgil marks this definitely enough. Dido had invoked on herself the most awful curse—

ante, pudor, quam te violo aut tua iura resolvo [4] (iv. 27)—

and now Anna's words have achieved exactly what Dido in her excitement had deprecated.

His dictis incensum animum flammavit amore
spemque dedit dubiae menti solvitque pudorem [5] (iv. 54).

It is easy to underestimate and to overestimate this comment of Virgil's by giving little or much emphasis to *pudor*. Conington [6] and Mackail both render it *honour*,

---

[1] "Nor do you think upon whose lands you have settled?"

[2] "Overcome by my tears," iv. 548.

[3] *Hippolytus*, 490. "Why speak so proudly? 'Tis not fair words thou needest, but—the man !"

[4] "Ere I do thee wrong, my woman's honour, or break thy laws."

[5] "By these words she added fresh fuel to the fire of love, gave confidence to her wavering mind, and loosed the ties of woman's honour" (Conington).

[6] In the prose rendering. In the verse translation he makes it "woman's shame."

but of honour there are various conceptions. Different minds will form different judgements upon a widow, who owns to herself that a new love has taken possession of her, and who resolves to win the man she loves. A certain school, not altogether free from the charge of prudishness, will at once condemn her. But the serious student will rarely begin by taking the unkindest view. *Pudor* is something easier to feel than to define. It is a peculiar and unexplained sensitiveness, which Anna, as we have seen, could not understand—loyalty to an ideal, and an ideal with which reason has less to do than instinct. Many readers will accordingly think little of it, as Anna did. But in spite of argument Dido's conscience is still on the side of this instinct of hers ; and though she decides to follow inclination, slightly cloaked by reason, her heart condemns her all the time. *Se iudice nemo nocens absolvitur* said Juvenal, a phrase much used by moralists of later days.[1] It would be unfair to Dido to suppose that she has yet lost what the world would call *pudor*, as she lost it later on. But the end is the outcome of the beginning. To resolve to win the love of Aeneas is no wrong thought or action, but to attempt it against her conscience is the first step toward shame.

Dido has made the great refusal, and at once she and her sister betake themselves to the temples, There is something startling in Virgil's abrupt combination of these ideas.

> His dictis . . . solvitque pudorem.
> Principio delubra adeunt pacemque per aras
> exquirunt (*A*. iv. 53-56).

"In the true spirit of tragic irony," writes Professor Nettleship, "Virgil represents Dido and her sister as sacrificing to win the favour of heaven, from which she has just invoked a curse on her faithlessness; and to what gods does she sacrifice ? To Ceres, Apollo, and Lyaeus, the gods presiding over the foundation of cities and the giving of laws, when she is forgetting her duty as a queen ; to

---

[1] "No guilty person is ever acquitted by himself." Juvenal, xiii. 3 ; cited by Macr. *Comm. Somn. Scip.* i. 10. 12.

Juno the goddess of marriage, when she is forgetting her faith to her husband." [1]

> Heu vatum ignarae mentes ! quid vota furentem,
> quid delubra iuvant ? (iv. 65).[2]

This is Virgil's comment on Dido's sacrifices—one of those utterances in which he seems to speak his innermost mind about gods and sacred things. What help is there in shrine or sacrifice for one resolved to do what seems wrong ? Dido's prayers and offerings are superstition, an indication of a mental flaw in her, which is more emphasized by and by.

Her courting of Aeneas proceeds. She leads him with her through Carthage ; she displays to him the treasures of Sidon ; he is seeking a city, and she shows him a city built and finished, to be his for the asking ; she begins to speak and stops—will he not see that she is offering him the city he seeks, offering him herself the queen of it ? He does not see. Then evening by evening, again and again, she recurs to the story of Troy. But he does not understand, and they part, he to sleep, she to return to the couch on which he had lain in the banqueting-room, to see and hear him once more in imagination. She takes Ascanius to her heart to find her way to his father's. So the days pass.

The surrender of one ideal begins to affect her general sense of duty. She neglects Carthage. In the first book Virgil gives a picture of her activity before this fatal passion began. The Tyrians are hot at work—

> instant ardentes Tyrii—

raising huge walls, digging harbours, laying foundations for the theatre, hewing columns from the rock, busy as bees (i. 423 f.). As Venus says, Dido is the moving spirit of it all—

> dux femina facti—

---

[1] *Essays in Latin Lit.* i. p. 127.

[2] " Alas ! for the blind hearts of seers ! What help have vows, what help have shrines for the madness of love ? " Contrast with the passage in Apollonius, where the crow laughs at the prophet who has forgotten that two is company and three none, *Argon.* iii. 931.

and we see her pressing on the work, her kingdom that is to be—

instans operi regnisque futuris (i. 504).

But now the towers she had begun cease to rise; no more is there practice in arms; no heed is given to harbour or bastion, the work hangs suspended, "frowning and giant towers, grim engines mounting the sky."[1] The crane with its long arm idly reaching to heaven is a poor augury for the ultimate value of Anna's political considerations.

At this point comes the episode of Juno and Venus. The plan, which Juno unfolds, is fulfilled to the letter. The hunting-party takes place; it is interrupted by the storm. In the excitement and confusion, which follow, Dido speaks her mind. *Pronuba Juno* it may be who contrives the match; but when Aeneas later on says

nec coniugis unquam
praetendi taedas aut haec in foedera veni [2] (iv. 338),

it is well to remember that, whether or not the words sound harsh and heartless, they are true, and Dido knows that they are true.[3]

If Carthage was neglected before, it is still more neglected now. Rumour denounces both Aeneas and Dido as

regnorum immemores turpique cupidine captos (iv. 194).

For her pains the poet elaborately describes Rumour as a fiend,[4] but she is only saying what heaven will have to

---

[1]
Non coeptae adsurgunt turres; non arma iuventus
exercet, portusve aut propugnacula bello
tuta parant: pendent opera interrupta minaeque
murorum ingentes aequataque machina caelo (*A.* iv. 86).

[2] "Nor did I ever hold out the marriage torch or enter thus into alliance" (Mackail).

[3] I am glad to find this view supported by M. Girard, *Études sur la poésie grecque*, p. 348: "Il donne à Junon, qui préside à l'union d'Énée et de Didon, le nom respecté de *Pronuba* . . précisément au moment où elle assure le succès d'une surprise de l'amour et emprunte le rôle de Vénus. Cette confusion volontaire qu'il fait dans un passage capital ne trompe ni Didon elle-même, malgré ses efforts pour s'abuser, ni surtout Enée, qui ne sait que trop nettement la valeur d'un tel engagement." Sainte-Beuve has some good criticism in his essay on the Medea of Apollonius (*Rev. des deux Mondes*, 1845, vol. xi. p. 889).

[4] *Monstrum horrendum, dea foeda, malum quo non velocius ullum* (*A.* iv.

say very soon. Indeed, the Omnipotent Jupiter himself, when his attention is called to it, recognizes that the fiend spoke truth. He looks at Carthage and he sees that the lovers have indeed forgotten their better fame—

> oblitos famae melioris amantes (iv. 221).

So much for Anna's advice. *Solvit pudorem.* Dido turned her back on her ideal for inclination, and found that inclination demanded more and more, and, at last, the sacrifice of everything she honoured in herself. She has been taken further than she meant to go.

V

Omne malum aut timore aut pudore natura perfudit,[1] wrote a great Carthaginian. Tertullian's saying might well be illustrated from this story of the foundress of his city. Dido has achieved the gratification of her inclination, but it has hardly contributed to her happiness. All seems well, and she is afraid because it does so seem—

> omnia tuta timens (iv. 298)—

and she cannot find rest. She is watching Aeneas all the time. She knows the story of his seven years' quest; she knows the long direction of his mind to Italy; can she be sure of his remaining with her? All seems safe and assured—yet she has presentiments of pain—

> hunc ego si potui tantum sperare dolorem[2] (iv. 419).

She knows everything that the Trojans are doing. The first suggestion of movement among them reaches her instantly (iv. 296). This uneasiness of mind is seen in her whole conduct. She is, as Aeneas puts it to himself, a *regina furens* (iv. 283). All the disorder of her mind is asserting itself now that the control of duty is thrown off.

Nor is Aeneas happier. So complete a change of life and purpose could not be made without many a return

---

[1] " Nature has steeped every evil thing either in fear or shame."
[2] " If I have been able to foresee this mighty grief."

of thought to past years. When the strain of watching Dido's moods is relaxed, the old and more real mind asserts itself. He thinks of the Troy left behind ; perhaps of the wife taken from him on the last night of Troy ; of that Italy which so many oracles and prophecies had bidden him seek ; and of all the years of voyaging. He thinks of his father, the Anchises of the second and third books, long partner of his quest, bound up, while life lasted, in the hopes of a great future for his race in the new land ; and when he sleeps, he sees his father's face troubled (*turbida*, iv. 353)—no longer his "solace in every care and chance"—

> omnis curae casusque levamen (iii. 709),

but an object of fear—he cannot look him in the eyes (*terret*, iv. 353). He thinks of his son, of the wrong he does the child who also had shared the wanderings, and for whom the bright future overseas must mean more (iv. 354, 355). And all this makes the frantic passion of the queen less and less tolerable. Yet she too has a hold upon him ; he feels for her (iv. 332, 395).

The turning-point is reached when Mercury appears to Aeneas, and, faithful to the instructions of Jupiter, asks him the questions he has been asking himself—

> " He, he, the Sire, enthroned on high,
> Whose nod strikes awe through earth and sky,
> He sends me down, and bids me bear
> His mandate through the bounding air.
> What make you here? what cherished scheme
> Tempts you in Libyan land to dream?
> If zeal no more your soul inflame
> To labour for your own fair fame,
> Let young Ascanius claim your care :
> Regard the promise of your heir,
> To whom, by warranty of fate
> The Italian crown, the Roman state,
> Of right are owing." Hermes said,
> And e'en in speaking passed and fled.[1]

[1] *A.* iv. 268-76, Conington.

Heaven's "mandate" takes, as it frequently does, the form of a question, the articulate expression of what the mind has been shaping to itself. To such questions the answer is always ready. *Heu quid agat ?* What is he to do ? Aeneas has not been told to leave Carthage. If Jupiter uttered his wish in one word, *naviget*, it was to Mercury, and Mercury did not repeat it. Aeneas will sail. On that he is clear enough, but how is he to do it ? How is he to broach it to the queen, who is even now only on the border-line of sanity—*reginam furentem ?* This task he postpones, and Dido does it for him.

The successive utterances of Dido from this point to the end are not to be translated, and here a bare summary must suffice. She at once charges Aeneas with the intention of leaving her. Her love goes for nothing. It is winter ;[1] he is not even homeward bound ; he seeks an unknown shore—and yet he leaves her. By everything that can move him, by everything she has been to him, she pleads for his pity. Her neighbours hate her on his account. Her good name has been sacrificed for him—

> te propter eundem
> extinctus pudor.

His going means death to her. If only she had a child to recall his face, a *parvulus Aeneas*, she would not be so utterly lost.[2]

Aeneas replies, and his answer is for the student one of some difficulty through its alternations of feeling and coldness. He admits what Dido has done for him, yet his phrase jars upon the ear ; he will never forget her—

> nec me meminisse pigebit Elissae.

"But to come to the matter in hand "—

> pro re pauca loquar—

he had not thought of stealing from her land, though he had never meant to stay there. Then in a strong outburst of truth

[1] We might almost have divined this from the beautiful song of Iopas, *A.* i. 7 44 f.　　　　[2] iv. 305-30.

he tells her that, if fate allowed him to choose his life to please himself, first and foremost would he set the city of Troy, all that was left of his people—a new Troy should rise. But he is compelled by the gods to seek Italy. Let her think what Carthage has been to her, a new town as it is and on an unknown shore, and she would wonder no more at his seeking a strange land. He tells her of his dreams of his father, of his thoughts of his son, of his vision of Mercury. Let her not set herself and him on fire with words of passion. He has no choice.

Italiam non sponte sequor.[1]

The response of Dido is a wild outbreak of fury, in marked contrast to the delicacy and kindliness of her welcome of Aeneas in the first book, but after all nothing new or strange in her much-wronged and disordered heart. It has not shown itself markedly till now, but we realize at last that there is some touch of the Oriental in Dido, and we recognize that we have had hints of it before. Venus felt it—

quippe domum timet ambiguam [2] (i. 661),

but we have better evidence in the tale which Ilioneus tells. He had been attacked by the Carthaginians on the shore, and his ships were in danger of being burnt; shipwrecked mariners, they were forbidden "the hospitality of the sand" (i. 522-41). In the graciousness of Dido's reply; we do not notice that she admits her own responsibility for this outrage on humanity—

Res dura et regni novitas me talia cogunt
moliri et late fines custode tueri [3] (i. 562).

The savage element in her nature lies dormant during the early part of Aeneas' stay, but we have seen signs of its waking, and now it is not only awake but entirely master of her.

Her eyes roll in fury, and she speaks in taunt and curse.

---

[1] iv. 331-61.   [2] " She fears the two-faced generation."
[3] " It is the stress of danger and the infancy of my kingdom that make me put this policy in motion and protect my frontiers with a guard all about." We may recall how Venus put a cloud about Aeneas on his way to the city (*A*. i. 411).

Goddess-born! not he! he is not even human! Have her
tears cost him a sigh? Look at his hard, cold eyes—have
they wept? Has he pitied her? She had pitied him, a
shipwrecked beggar on her shore. So the gods send him
to Italy! And here Dido shows that, for all her superstition, a hedonist is apt to be Epicurean. She has appealed
to Juno and Jupiter, but now—

> Scilicet is superis labor est, ea cura quietos
> sollicitat (iv. 379).[1]

Let him go, if he likes, and hunt a kingdom through the
waves—and be wrecked—if there is such a thing as divine
justice and if it has so much power—

> siquid pia numina possunt.[2]

She will have vengeance.[3]

She flings herself away, and leaves him "hesitating and
fearing and thinking of a thousand things to say."[4] He can
do nothing but push on his preparations, openly now.

Dido's mood changes as she watches from her palace, and
she sends Anna to entreat, but not now for the *coniugium*
of her former hopes, not for the abandonment of his quest
of Latium—with a dash of bitterness she calls it "beautiful Latium"; she only asks time, empty time, a breathing-
space to give her madness rest and room, till fortune teach
her grief submission. But Aeneas will be entangled no
more. His tears flow as he listens to Anna, but they flow
in vain, his mind is unshaken—

> mens immota manet[5] (*A*. iv. 449).

Despair achieves Dido's descent into insanity. She sees
awful sights, and tells no one, not even her sister. The
screech of the owl becomes an omen. All her Oriental

---

[1] "Aye, of course, that is the employment of the powers above, those the
cares that break their rest" (Conington).
[2] Does Virgil mean to recall Aeneas' words, i. 603? [3] *A*. iv. 362-87.
[4] *A*. iv. 390 *linquens multa metu cunctantem et multa parantem dicere*.
[5] I am glad to think that Dr Henry holds the *lacrimae volvuntur inanes* to
refer to Aeneas, though Conington dissents.

superstition is quickened, and her bad dreams become more frequent and terrifying. In her sleep

> Aeneas with unpitying face
> Still hounds her in a nightly chase;
> And still companionless she seems
> To tread the wilderness of dreams,
> And vainly still her Tyrians seek
> Through desert regions, ah, how bleak![1]

She resolves to kill herself, and with the cunning of madness deceives her sister into making the preparations she requires by talking of magic. Anna's unemotional sanity fails, naturally enough, to divine her sister's feelings in the least. It will, she expects, be no worse than when Sychaeus was killed.[2]

All is made ready, as Dido bids, and in the silence of night her trouble wakes again. What is left open to her? To trust herself to Aeneas and go with him? Trust human gratitude, the gratitude of the race of Laomedon? Better to die, since she has not kept faith with Sychaeus.[3]

Meanwhile all is ready on the Trojan fleet. Aeneas, resolved upon departure, is asleep on the poop of his ship, when Mercury again appears—this time in a dream—and tells him how things stand. Dido is resolved to die, but before she dies she will have vengeance; by morning the harbour will be a scene of flame and wreckage. Let him be up and going. " A thing of moods and fancies is woman."[4] And with these words the god is gone. Aeneas leaps up, calls his men and cuts his cable; his fleet is off and away; and for him the story of Dido is ended—save for surmise and pain.[5]

With the first gleam of dawn Dido is at her outlook and sees the harbour empty, and in her uncontrolled outburst of rage she shows how well founded was the warning of

---

[1] Virgil is thought to have had in mind some lines of Ennius: *Annals*, i. fragm. xxxii. *ita sola | postilla, germana soror, errare videbar | tardaque vestigare et quaerere te neque posse | corde capessere*; &c. *ap.* Cicero, *de div.* i. 20. 40.
[2] *A.* iv. 450-503.   [3] *A.* iv. 521-53.
[4] *Varium et mutabile semper femina, A.* iv. 569.   [5] *A.* v. 5-7.

the dream. She begins with a scream of fury at his escape
—can they not overtake him? Out with their oars and
firebrands, down to the water with the ships! Then the
queen in her asserts itself; her practical genius is aghast
at her madness—

Quid loquor? aut ubi sum? quae mentem insania mutat?

> O! that way madness lies; let me shun that;
> No more of that.

"Poor Dido!" she says in quieter strain, "now dost thou
feel thy wickedness? That had graced thee *then*, when
thou gavest away thy sceptre."[1] But the very thought of
what she had given to Aeneas wakes madness once more,
and her momentary self-control is gone ; she falls a-cursing,
unpacks her heart with words. Murder is her thought—
could she not have murdered him—his men—Ascanius—or,
better, have killed the boy, and, like Thyestes, given him
to his father to eat? Suppose there had been a battle?
There might have been danger? What danger, when she
meant to die, would die? She pauses, and a change comes
over her mood. When she speaks, it is in a quieter tone,
and she utters the last great curse, the curse that embroils
Roman and Carthaginian for ever.

> Eye of the world, majestic Sun,
> Who see'st whate'er on earth is done,
> Thou, Juno, too, interpreter
> And witness of this heart's wild stir,
> And Hecate, tremendous power,
> In cross-ways howled at midnight hour,
> Avenging fiends, and gods of death
> Who breathe in dying Dido's breath,

---

[1] Surely Henry and Mackail are right in taking the *facta impia* to be Dido's
own. Henry cites Euripides, *Medea*, 796 ἡμάρτανον τόθ', ἡνίκ' ἐξελίμπανον
δόμους πατρῴους, and *Hippolytus*, 1072 τότε στενάζειν καὶ προγινώσκειν ἐχρῆν, ὅτ'
εἰς πατρῴαν ἄλοχον ὑβρίζειν ἔτλης, and for the *tangunt* the most dramatic line
of the *Hippolytus* (310). Is the cause of Phaedra's sorrow, asks the nurse, her
stepson ?
'Ιππόλυτον ; ΦΑΙ. οἴμοι. ΤΡ. θιγγάνει σέθεν τόδε ;
These plays were very carefully studied by Virgil, and their evidence confirms
the interpretation, if confirmation is needed.

Stoop your great powers to ills that plead
To heaven, and my petition heed.
If needs must be that wretch abhorred
    Attain the port and float to land ;
If such the will of heaven's high lord,
    And so the fated order stand ;
615 Scourged by a savage enemy,
    An exile from his son's embrace,
So let him sue for aid, and see
    His people slain before his face ;
Nor, when to humbling peace at length
    He stoops, be his or life or land,
But let him fall in manhood's strength
    And lie unburied on the sand.
This last of prayers to heaven I pour,
This last I pray, and pray no more.
And, Tyrians, you through time to come
    His seed with deathless hatred chase :
Be that your gift to Dido's tomb :
    No love, no league, 'twixt race and race.
Rise from my ashes, scourge of crime,
    Born to pursue the Dardan horde,
To-day, to-morrow, through all time,
    Oft as our hands can wield the sword :
Fight shore with shore, fight sea with sea,
Fight all that are or e'er shall be ![1]

The preparations she had ordered have been made; all is
ready and she is ready. "Fluttered and fierce in her awful
purpose, with bloodshot restless gaze, and spots on her
quivering cheeks burning through the pallor of approaching
death, she bursts into the inner courts of the house and
mounts in madness the high funeral pyre." On it lay the
bed—

              lectumque iugalem
        quo perii (*A.* iv. 496)—

---

[1] *A.* iv. 607-27, Conington, but with an alteration or two. The reader will
remember the anecdote that Charles I., drawing for a *sors Vergiliana*, lit on the
lines 615 f.—*at bello audacis populi vexatus et armis*, &c.

the dress of Aeneas, an image of him,[1] and his sword, begged of him as a keepsake, but for no such use as now it finds. She drew it from its sheath, and pressed her bosom to the bed.

> "Sweet relics of a time of love,
>   When fate and heaven were kind,
> Receive my life-blood, and remove
>   These torments of the mind.
> My life is lived, and I have played
>   The part that fortune gave,
> And now I pass, a queenly shade,
>   Majestic to the grave.
> A glorious city I have built,
>   Have seen my walls ascend,
> Chastised for blood of husband spilt,
>   A brother, yet no friend.
> Blest lot! yet lacked one blessing more,
> That Troy had never touched my shore."
> Then, as she kissed the darling bed,
> "To die! and unrevenged!" she said,
> "Yet let me die: thus, thus I go
> Rejoicing to the shades below.
> Let the false Dardan feel the blaze
> That burns me pouring on his gaze,
> And bear along, to cheer his way,
> The funeral presage of to-day."[2]

These are the last words of Dido. We need not linger to listen to Anna's lament, or to watch the slow death-struggle with its strange ending, suggested by the story of Death and Alcestis.[3] The story is told. St Augustine wept over Dido *quia se occidit ob amorem*;[4] she killed

---

[1] This to deceive Anna, perhaps. The use of an image in magic is familiar. Cf. Theocritus, ii. 28, and Virg. *E.* 8. 80.

[2] *A.* iv. 651-62. Conington's version. There are weaknesses in this translation, but in what translation of the passage are there not? I am more and more conscious of my own inability to render Virgil.

[3] The cutting of the lock of hair, done by Death in the case of Alcestis (Eurip. *Alc.* 74), is managed in Dido's by Iris, *A.* iv. 704.

[4] *Conf.* i. 13. 20.

herself for love, and let us end with that. Love for Aeneas after all has mastered her madness, and her hatred, and it is the dominant note in her death.

VI

Whereupon all the friendly moralists
Drew this conclusion: chirped, each beard to each:
"Manifold are thy shapings, Providence!
Many a hopeless matter gods arrange.
What we expected never came to pass:
What we did not expect gods brought to bear;
So have things gone, this whole experience through!"

Thus Browning and Euripides tell us that the Chorus of the play will not pluck out for us the heart of the poet's mystery, but that if it is to be done we must do it for ourselves. Virgil seems to be of their opinion; at any rate he gives us no Chorus and very little comment. What does he mean?

We have the story of an entanglement, which results in the woman's death, while the man apparently escapes scot-free. Dido is drawn with such truth and interest by the poet, that she has enlisted the sympathies of all readers. Of whatever mistakes she is guilty, whatever the flaws of her character, she is a great woman. There is nothing incredible in her story—it happens every day—and our sympathies go with her, right or wrong. Our sympathies—but our judgement? If the view here put forward has been true to Virgil's mind, we shall have to own that our judgement must reluctantly be given against her—but in the same spirit as it is given against Oedipus or King Lear. Like the ideal tragic hero of Aristotle, she falls from a height of greatness, and "the disaster that wrecks her life may be traced not to deliberate wickedness, but to some great error or frailty."[1] Her ruin is due to a failure of will. Accident throws Aeneas in her way, he becomes

---

[1] Aristot. *Poet.* xiii. 3; Butcher's essays, pp. 311 ff.

to her a temptation, and she sacrifices her sense of right to her inclination.

So much perhaps may be agreed, but we have to deal with the part of Aeneas in the tragedy. There is a declension from ideals in his case also, which may be judged from various standpoints with very different conclusions. It is quite clear that he goes wrong in two ways, first, by staying in Carthage when his duty was to push on to Italy; and then by agreeing to the proposals made by Dido in her weakness. To-day readers will lay more stress on the second of these points, but at the time, when the *Aeneid* was written, probably the former would seem the more serious.

We must remember that at that period marriage and love were terms which did not suggest each other. The connexion between them to-day seems so natural and inevitable that it is hard to realize the ancient point of view. We are taught to admire Penelope for refusing the suitors, but it is not suggested that we should feel the least surprise at the relations of Odysseus with Circe and Calypso. Outside the plays of Euripides—the "woman-hater"—it is hard to recall in ancient literature a case of love between man and woman parallel to that of Hector and Andromache. The Roman feeling is sufficiently revealed by the difficulty felt by Catullus in expressing his love for Lesbia. He wishes to describe a love pure of all selfish elements, and he says that he loved her, not as man would love a mistress, but as a father would his sons and sons-in-law.[1] This extraordinary comparison indicates plainly enough the distance between the ancient and modern attitude. Hence faithfulness in a husband and chastity in a man were neither expected nor particularly admired. No one thought less of Julius because of his relations with Cleopatra, except in so far as he was under her influence.[2] Roman opinion would not condemn Aeneas for a lapse—if lapse

---

[1] Catullus, 72. 3, 4 *Dilexi* (contrast the verb with *amare*) *tum te non tantum ut vulgus amicam, sed pater ut gnatos diligit et generos.*

[2] Cf. the letter of Antony, Suet. *Aug.* 69 : and the story of Titus and Berenice, Suet. *Titus*, 7.

it were[1]—far less conspicuous than those of his great descendant.

And yet the same story comes differently from Suetonius and from Virgil. What is quite unnoticed in the commonplace prose of the one makes the most painful impression when it comes in the poem of the other. Whether the poet felt as his readers feel to-day may be questioned.[2] He would perhaps not have been so much shocked at such an episode in the life of a contemporary, but it is almost inconceivable that he did not see how it would jar in the setting of his poetry. But whatever he thought or felt, he has at least made clear to his readers the real significance of such action. The character of Aeneas, as conceived by Virgil, is a background against which such conduct is seen for what it is—it becomes something very like sin. It is the reader, not Aeneas, who realizes this. And in his portrayal of Dido, too, the poet broke fresh ground.

> Nec me meminisse pigebit Elissae,

says Aeneas (iv. 335), and Dido's reply is to kill herself with his sword. Can a thing be right, or even only slightly wrong, which makes such a painful contrast with the ideal of manhood and which costs so much to woman?

We are told often enough that literature has nothing to do with morality. In a sense this is true. The poet and the artist are concerned with reality, and have no business to preach; but if their work is true, it has inevitably, like all life, morality implied in itself. It may be true that no one has abstained from evil because of the story of Dido and Aeneas, but it is probably as true,

---

[1] I should have thought it needless to explain that the words "if lapse it were" were designed to represent Roman opinion, not my own; but, as a reviewer in a journal of repute has mistaken the meaning intended, it is perhaps as well to be explicit.

[2] But cf. Suet. *v. Verg.* 10 *Vulgatum est consuesse eum cum Plotia Hieria. Sed Asconius Pedianus adfirmat ipsam postea narrare solitam invitatum quidem a Vario ad communionem sui, verum pertinacissime recusasse.*

or truer, that the faithful telling of it by Virgil has contributed to the development of the moral sense of mankind.

But Virgil, so far as his words go, lays more stress on the wrong done by Aeneas to Rome, upon the failure in patriotism. In the books that follow there is little suggestion that Aeneas thought of Dido again after their meeting in the lower world.[1] Of course, it might be urged that the vision of Dido beyond the grave, restored to Sychaeus and at peace, has in it some hint of what in a tragedy we might call reconciliation, but this might be carrying things further than Virgil really went. And again it might be replied that, if the poet does not record, neither should he record, all that goes on in his hero's mind, and that memories of Dido would be irrelevant in the Italian campaign. Still Dido is left behind, and Rome is the first concern of hero and poet; and we ask, are they right as to the supreme importance of Rome? Is it true that Rome is also the first thought of the gods? Can Rome be a supreme moral issue? Is it not an external thing, essentially?

We have to allow something for the necessity which epic tradition laid upon the poet of representing an inward call or monition as an immediate instruction from an external deity. Virgil himself gives us a hint of another psychology—

Dine hunc ardorem mentibus addunt,
Euryale, an sua cuique deus fit dira cupido?[2] (*A.* ix. 184).

But in general he must stick to the old and rather clumsy way of Epic. With this in mind we shall better understand what is meant by the reiterated emphasis on the fact, that the quest of Rome is laid upon Aeneas

[1] It may partly be due to the irregular way in which Virgil worked here and there at his poem as he pleased. Suet. *v. Verg.* 23 *Aeneida prosa prius oratione formatam digestamque in xii libros particulatim componere instituit, prout liberet quidque et nihil in ordinem arripiens.*

[2] "Is it the gods, Euryalus, that make men's hearts glow thus? or does each one's ungoverned yearning become his god?" (Conington).

from without. He tells us that it is under compulsion he leaves Carthage—

Italiam non sponte sequor.

It is the bidding of the divine voice—of many divine voices. There is, however, many readers will urge, in the anguish of Dido a voice as divine as any brought by Mercury to Aeneas bidding him seek Italy. Has the poet then failed here? If he has, to be fair to him, it is partly his own truthfulness that has let us see it.

It looks at first as if the gods set the foundation of Rome before everything, and cared no jot for Dido's pain. So the poet seems to assure us; but he knows quite well that it is not so. He is too just a thinker and too great a poet not to know it. He knows, too, how little such things as names and places, in spite of all their appeal, really are, as opposed to the virtues and the character which are the foundation of all society. And yet Dido's anguish seems to suggest that the gods think more of seven hills beside a river than of human woe or of right and wrong. What are we to say?

Once more it seems we have slipped back into the consideration of Dido, and once more we have to brace ourselves to look beyond. This is not to ignore Dido. New thoughts upon character and righteousness gleam from Virgil's work, and by the light they shed we must read it. Dido's story, with everything involved and implied in it, comes from the poet's heart, and it is not to be brushed aside. The quest of Aeneas has indeed suggestions of the arbitrary about it—why the town must be on the Tiber is not explained; that is a sore gap which it is hard to fill, and until it is filled, the ways of the gods will not be justified to the thoughtful reader. Yet a man's task, however realized, when once it is realized, leaves him no choice. That Aeneas must go, we see. The sense of the inevitable task to be fulfilled, whatever the cost,— that also comes from Virgil's heart. The collision of the two lives and the wreckage are of the essence of tragedy; and that Dido's story is tragedy, we saw from the beginning. In every tragedy there is an incompre-

hensible element—but in this one the part played by
the gods is less intelligible than we feel we have a right
to expect, for their purpose—the planting of a city in
a certain place—seems but little connected with moral issues.
Yet for Aeneas there is a moral issue, and it is clear—
whether it is intelligible or not duty must be done. *Italiam
non sponte sequor*—but he follows.

CHAPTER IX

THE INTERPRETATION OF LIFE.—2. AENEAS

Ducimus autem
hos quoque felices, qui ferre incommoda vitae
nec iactare iugum vita didicere magistra.—JUVENAL, xiii. 20.

CHARLES JAMES FOX, writing to his friend Trotter, speaks of the *Aeneid* thus: "Though the detached parts of the *Aeneid* appear to me to be equal to anything, the story and characters appear more faulty every time I read it. My chief objection (I mean that to the character of Aeneas) is of course not so much felt in the three first books; but afterwards he is always either insipid or odious; sometimes excites interest against him, and never for him." The student of Virgil may turn to Dr Henry's tremendous vindication of the phrase *Sum pius Aeneas* (i. 381), to which Fox takes especial exception, and if Dr Henry does not satisfy him, he can read Marlowe's *Dido Queen of Carthage*; and from the Elizabethan Aeneas let him go back to Virgil's hero, and consider whether after all he is not at once more natural, more manly, and more attractive.[1]

But Fox's criticism is one to which it is probable that a large number of Virgil's readers will subscribe, and we are forced to ask ourselves whether it is just; whether it is possible that Virgil's highest conception of manhood is really so worthless? Or even if we suppose Fox to use the words "insipid" and "odious" with something of the exaggeration of Jane Austen's beaux, must we confess that Aeneas is still fundamentally a failure? By lightly accepting such a judgement we should probably lose something which the poet felt intensely to be vital to

[1] Henry, *Aeneidea*, i. 647 ff.

himself and to everybody. Virgil has a right to require us to make some attempt to discover this.

I

Probably no one has ever read Homer and Virgil without remarking the broad gulf between their two heroes. Every one recognizes at once the intense and true humanity of Achilles. There is no doubt that he is a real man, and, as is usual with the creations of a great poet, we like our kind better because Homer has shown us Achilles. We are reconciled to life and death, and have something of Ben Ezra's feeling—"Thanks that I was a man." Aeneas is not the natural man. He represents a stage at once beyond and behind that of Achilles. He has seen a great deal more of life, he has felt the lifting of a great purpose, he is part of a larger world. He is at once an older man than Achilles and the child of a later age of mankind. In the interval between the fall of Troy and his arrival in Italy he has seen many more cities than Odysseus saw and learnt the minds of many more men, and these many minds have confused him. He is a dreamer, and where Achilles looked straight before him, Aeneas "thinks of many things,"[1] and amongst them there are some which remain for him unresolved mysteries. He has a mission ; he is a pilgrim ; he knows that heaven has a purpose for him. *Ego poscor Olympo*[2] is deeply imprinted in his consciousness, but the inner meaning of the call of Olympus he has not reached. Achilles, like the rest of us, has to face the problems of life, but for him there are no such riddles as this which confuses Aeneas.

For though Aeneas can explain to others where he is going and that it is the will of the gods, he does not seem able to make it clear to himself. He knows that he is to seek Italy, but in spite of his abundance of revelations he is outside the counsel of the gods. He needs from time to time the hand of heaven to push him forward. His quest is not a spiritual or inward necessity to him. Crete, Epirus,

---

[1] *A.* vi. 332 ; cf. iv. 390. [2] *A.* viii. 533.

Sicily, or even Carthage would have satisfied himself. That he was not to rest till he reached Italy was no part of his conviction. The Pilgrim Fathers knew why the *Mayflower* crossed the Atlantic, and they knew what they meant to find at or near Plymouth Rock—or some other rock; the place was immaterial, but the impulse which drove them westward they felt, no doubt, to come from heaven, and they understood it. They might not see all that would follow, but they had that priceless gift which their descendants have never lost for long—a conviction of a future, which would be the necessary spiritual outcome of their principles. This Aeneas had not consciously, and though Virgil clearly means that the Roman Empire is the outcome of character of the type of his hero's, this want of clearness and conviction tends to mar a fine conception. Would he, for instance, so soon have yielded to Dido if Italy had been a spiritual necessity? But this, of course, it could not be, for there was nothing as yet that it could suggest to him. Italy was a region, it was not an idea.[1]

Then again, we do not see the whole of Aeneas. It was not the Roman character to show feeling, nor would it perhaps have been natural for a man, schooled by so long a course of affliction, to lay bare his heart. In any case Aeneas does not often do it. We see him in despair for a moment in the storm, but never again does he betray such weakness. He feels other people's sorrows keenly enough, but they do not throw him off his balance. Once, in the parting with Dido, feeling seems to surge up and demand expression, but it is instantly repressed—

Desine meque tuis incendere teque querellis [2] (*A.* iv. 360).

The word *incendere* shows his thought. Dido's words must rouse passion; and passion, he feels, helps nothing forward, and he dreads it. This to the modern reader is one of the weaknesses in the character of Aeneas—there seems to be no passion there. It has been stamped out, or so nearly

---

[1] The faint tales that his remote ancestors came from Italy are of little consequence. They are in *A.* iii. 94-6; 163-8.
[2] " Cease thou to set me on fire, to set thyself on fire with these regrets."

stamped out as to rob him of almost all that play of mood
and feeling which is one of the essentially human things.
Half his humanity is lost by his self-suppression, for it is so
effectually done that we do not realize that there was any
struggle within him.   And a great part of the value of a
man to us is our realizing, without his telling us, that he is
victor in such a struggle.[1]

The result of Aeneas' subjection to heaven, and his consequent suppression of feeling (so far as his experience left
any capacity for feeling which might need to be suppressed),
is that he has lost the air of life.   He has not enough
freedom of will.   There are indeed such people to be met
with in the world, but they rarely interest us.[2]

To sum up, Achilles satisfies us, because at every point
we feel that he is a man; he thinks, he feels, he suffers as
a man ; and his experience, deep and intense as it is, is the
common lot of humanity, felt and interpreted by a poet.
Aeneas does not so readily satisfy us, for his experience,
though not improbable, indeed though highly probable and
often enough actually true, is not entirely interpreted to us.
There remains something unintelligible about him.

The character of Aeneas then is so far a failure,[3] for want
of completeness and conviction, but a failure which threw
into the shade every poetic success between Euripides and
Dante ; a failure which opened for poetry for all time a door
into a new world, which brought under poetry's survey
great conceptions, unthought and almost unfelt before, of
man the agent of heaven, attempting and achieving acts
small in themselves but of incredible consequence for mankind ; of a divine purpose and providence, in the least as in
the largest things, working through individual suffering the
general good ; and of something like a mutual intelligibility

---

[1]   Nay, when the fight begins within himself
                  A man 's worth something,
says Browning's Blougram.

[2] And yet after ten years more of life—I will not attempt autobiography, but
Aeneas seems a more intelligible and sympathetic character. Years ago, I
remember Mr R. A. Neil, of Pembroke College, suggesting that Virgil was no
author for a healthy boy.

[3] I do not like to say this ; I hope the reader will not press the word.

of man and God, a community of purpose, perhaps even a spiritual unity. These things are not indeed worked out adequately in the *Aeneid*, but they are suggested or implied. The poet has caught sight of them and is quickened by the sight, but at times it comes over him that he may be deceived. Hence there is a wavering and an uncertainty about the whole poem, a feeling of pain and suspense—

aut videt aut vidisse putat per nubila [1] (*A.* vi. 454).

Aeneas is not at all a hero of the type of Achilles, and if we come to the *Aeneid* with preconceived opinions of what the hero of an epic should be, we run the risk of disappointment and also of losing Virgil's judgement upon human life. Virgil obviously did not intend to make a copy of Homer's Achilles or of any of Homer's heroes. That was a feat to be left to Quintus of Smyrna. If, as it is, there is an air of anachronism about Virgil's Aeneas, there would have been a far profounder anachronism about him if in the age of Augustus he had been a real Homeric hero. The world, as we have seen, had moved far since Homer's day. Plato's repudiation of Homer meant that a new outlook and new principles were needed in view of new conditions of life and the new thoughts which they waked. In its turn the impulse, with which we connect the literature of Athens, and such names as Euripides, Plato, and Aristotle, was itself spent, though not before it had made an imperishable contribution to the growth of mankind. The world was awaiting another fresh impulse, and, till this should come, it was occupied in analysing, co-ordinating, and developing its existing stock of ideas, not without some consciousness that they were already inadequate.

It was at this moment that Virgil wrote, and as he was a poet rather than a mere scholar or antiquary, he sought to bring his Aeneas into connexion with his own age, while, if possible, still keeping him a Homeric hero. It was hardly to be done. If Aeneas as the ideal hero was to be "heir of all the ages," it would be difficult to keep the simplicity of Homer's outlook and philosophy. Aeneas could not stand

---

[1] " He sees—or else he thinks he saw—through the mist."

in Achilles' relation to men. He must have new virtues which had been discovered since Homer's day, if he was to be a hero near the hearts of Virgil's contemporaries—the new private virtues which Menander and Cleanthes and many more were finding out, and the new political virtues which Alexander and the Ptolemies, Julius and Augustus, were revealing to the world. Aeneas, again, could not stand in Achilles' relation to heaven. The gods no longer came among men in bodily form, they were far away; and yet perhaps they were not so very far away after all—

deum namque ire per omnes.[1]

This is another reason why Aeneas does not appeal to us as Achilles does. The fusion of the Homeric and the modern types is not complete. Virgil's Aeneas is two heroes in one, perhaps more, for beside the Homeric hero and the modern hero one feels sometimes that we have another creature, which is not a hero at all, but an idea,[2] an allegory of a virtue, and a political virtue at that, partially incarnated.

It is true, of course, that Virgil did not put the last touches to his poem; but it is not clear that, even if he had, the character of Aeneas could have been given the final and convincing unity.

To understand the character and the poem of which it is the centre, it will be helpful to analyse the various elements in Aeneas. In this process we shall necessarily lose our consciousness of what we have felt to be the great defect of the hero, his want of unity, and we shall probably gain a clearer notion of what the poet intended.

II

First of all, there is Aeneas conceived as a Homeric hero. Aeneas has of course the heroic manner, in measure, but not quite the manner of Homeric heroes, a more magnificent,

---

[1] *G.* iv. 221, "for God pervades all."

[2] Goethe's word. He told Eckermann (Oct. 29, 1823) "You must do some degree of violence to yourself to get out of the idea."

a more courtly manner. He has the wealth of the Homeric hero, and his habit of giving splendid presents and receiving them. At times, Virgil would have us think, he feels the same wild delight in battle which we find in Homer's heroes. " Lie there now, terrible one! No mother's love shall lay thee in the sod, or place thy limbs beneath thine heavy ancestral tomb. To birds of prey shalt thou be left, or borne down in the eddying water, where hungry fish shall suck thy wounds." [1] This is what Virgil remembers to have read in the *Iliad*; he blends what Odysseus says to Socus with the words of Achilles to Lycaon.[2] But the club has not been wrested from Hercules;[3] the words are still Homer's ; they do not belong to Aeneas. Again, the reservation of eight captured youths to be sacrificed to the Manes of Pallas [4] can be defended by the Homeric parallel of Achilles slaying Trojans over the pyre of Patroclus [5] and by more awful contemporary parallels, but still it is not convincing. Augustus may have ordered or performed a human sacrifice ;[6] but when Virgil transfers this to Aeneas, the reader feels the justice of Aristotle's paradox : " there is no reason why *some* events that have actually happened should not conform to the law of the probable and possible." [7] This may have been an actual event, but it is not " probable " here.

But perhaps the most incongruous Homeric touch in Virgil's story of Aeneas is the beautifying of the hero by his mother to enable him unconsciously to win Dido. That Aeneas is " like a god in face and shoulders " we can well believe; but the addition of the " purple light of youth " [8] to a man of years, " long tossed on land and sea," worn to grandeur by war and travel, is surely a triumph of imitation over imagination.

---

[1] *A.* x. 557 (Mackail). [2] *Il.* xi. 452, and xxi. 122.

[3] Cf. the saying of Virgil in the *Life* by Suetonius, c. 46 ; and Macrobius, *Saturnalia*, v. 3, 16. Cf. p. 59.

[4] xi. 81 *vinxerat et post terga manus, quos mitteret umbris | inferias, caeso sparsurus sanguine flammas* ; cf. x. 517-20.

[5] *Il.* xxiii. 22-3. In ll. 175-6 Dr Leaf finds a "moral condemnation of the act" by the poet possible, though not inevitable, in the Greek—κακὰ δὲ φρεσὶ μήδετο ἔργα.

[6] Suet. *Aug.* 15. [7] *Poetics*, ix. 9. [8] *A.* i. 588.

This perhaps will be best realized if we consider for a moment the passage, or passages, in the *Odyssey* which Virgil had in mind. Twice Athene changes the aspect of Odysseus. First, at his meeting with Nausicaa, the goddess, after his bath, "made him greater and more mighty to behold, and from his head caused deep curling locks to flow, like the hyacinth flower ... Then to the shore of the sea went Odysseus apart, and sat down, glowing in beauty and grace, and the princess marvelled at him." [1] And very naturally, for she was a young girl, and the goddess knew it, and made her appeal to the imagination in a true and natural way.

Again, when Odysseus makes himself known to his wife, the poet uses the very words, and the simile that follows them, once again. Penelope "sat down over against Odysseus in the light of the fire. Now he was standing by the tall pillar, looking down and waiting to know if perchance his noble wife would speak to him when her eyes beheld him. But she sat long in silence, and amazement came upon her soul, and now she would look upon him steadfastly with her eyes, and now again she knew him not." Odysseus withdraws, and bathes, and comes back, and "Athene shed great beauty from his head downwards, and [made him] greater and more mighty to behold, and from his head caused deep curling locks to flow, like the hyacinth flower." [2] Once more it is an appeal to the imagination. Penelope has still a final test to make before she will be sure, but in her mind she sees her husband as he was twenty years before, young, strong and tall, as she had always pictured him during the long years of his absence. Homer is justified.

But is Virgil justified? People tell us that youth and beauty are not without their appeal to women in middle life or toward it, but the reader can hardly think of Dido as Venus would seem to have done. She was not Nausicaa. Nor can the poet claim Homer's plea in the second case, for Aeneas and Dido had never met before. [3] In fact, it is a

---

[1] *Odyssey* vi. 229 f. [2] *Odyssey*, xxiii. 156.

[3] It may be objected that Teucer had told Dido of Aeneas long before (*A.* i. 619, a point made by Heinze, *Vergils epische Technik*, p. 119), and that there was a picture of Aeneas in Dido's temple (*A.* i. 488). It will hardly be maintained that it can have been a photographic likeness.

piece of imitation, dull and unconvincing, as nearly all the purely Homeric touches are in the character and the story of Aeneas.[1]

III

Virgil's Aeneas implies a new relation to heaven. While the whole question of Olympus and the gods will have to be reserved for separate treatment at more length, it will be convenient to anticipate a few points of importance.

Greek thinkers had moved, and brought mankind with them, beyond the Olympus of Homer. Men no longer might expect to

> Have sight of Proteus rising from the sea,
> Or hear old Triton blow his wreathed horn.

There was a gain, however, in their loss, for it was a deepening consciousness of the real character of the Divine nature that carried men away from Olympus to look for divinity in a higher region. The divine was more remote, but it was more divine. It had less contact with humanity, but it was freer from the weaknesses and the vices of humanity. It was perhaps less interested in the individual, but it might exercise a wider and a firmer power over the universe.

The Homeric gods, in accordance with epic usage, had to watch over Aeneas, but they were gods in whom no one really believed. Hence Virgil handles them with a caution that excludes warmth. Though Aeneas is favoured with one theophany after another, and is for the while re-assured by them, he is not on such easy terms with the gods as was Achilles. He sees them less frequently, and his relations are more formal. In fact, the complete rejection of the Homeric pantheon by educated people in favour of eastern religion or Greek philosophy was too strong for the poet.[2]

Yet Virgil is far from refusing the idea of some divine

---

[1] Sainte-Beauve has some excellent criticism on this episode of the beautification. *Étude sur Virgile*, 274-6.

[2] Cf. Sainte-Beauve, *Étude sur Virgile*, p. 276 : "Avec lui (Virgil) on est déjà dans la mythologie ; avec Homère on était dans la religion."

government of the world. Some of the philosophers had rejected the Homeric theology, just because it did not sufficiently relate the world to the gods. They traced the world's origin back to divine intelligence; they recognized the diviner element in man's nature, his power of remembering and re-discovering the divine "ideas"; and they leant to a belief in the moral government of the universe. With the gradual direction of philosophy to individual life, men came to believe in a personal concern of heaven with the individual man. If Fate is hard and unrelenting, it has recognized the individual, and on the whole the individual may accept it without resentment. Hence Cleanthes bade Fate lead him in the destined way and he would be fearless, though, as he reminded himself meanwhile, there was no question about his following.[1] Man is thus entirely dependent upon the divine, and of this Aeneas is always conscious. It was, however, a consciousness never before presented in poetry, and Virgil, in loyalty to the traditions of the epic, endeavoured to present it by the means of the old, incredible Homeric gods. This was indeed to pour new wine into old bottles, with the inevitable result.

This idea of Destiny, perhaps of Providence, is the dominant one in Virgil, and it is one of the things in which he is furthest from Homer.

Destiny, as M. Boissier remarks, has its place in Homer. His heroes often know well that they are doomed to fall, but as a rule they forget it and act as if they had not the knowledge. The action is only now and again darkened by the shadow of Fate, but in general we have the free development of the individual's story, as he carelessly abandons himself to the fever of life, and forgets the menaces of the future in the interests of the present.[2] The same idea is well developed by M. Girard in his

<hr />

[1]   Αγου δέ μ' ὦ Ζεῦ καὶ σύ γ' ἡ Πεπρωμένη
ὅποι ποθ' ὑμῖν εἰμὶ διατεταγμένος·
ὡς ἕψομαι γ' ἄοκνος· ἢν δὲ μὴ θέλω
κακὸς γενόμενος οὐδὲν ἧσσον ἕψομαι.
Cleanthes *ap.* Epictetus, *Manual*, 52, end of book.
[2] *La Religion romaine*, i. p. 244.

chapter on "Man in Homer and Hesiod." In particular
he instances Hector leaving child and wife for a death
he foresaw, but the prevailing tone of the poem he finds,
with Arnold, in the words of Sarpedon to Glaucus—

νῦν δ᾽ ἔμπης γὰρ κῆρες ἐφεστᾶσιν θανάτοιο
μυρίαι, ἃς οὐκ ἔστι φυγεῖν βροτὸν οὐδ᾽ ὑπαλύξαι,
ἴομεν, ἠέ τῳ εὖχος ὀρέξομεν ἠέ τις ἡμῖν.[1]

The Greek and the Trojan heroes in the *Iliad* recognize
Destiny well enough, but they make up their own minds,
and are ready to accept the consequences. They survey
the world for themselves, look facts well in the face, and
then shape their own courses. If the gods intervene, these
calculations may be upset, it is true, but this is accident
after all.

Aeneas, on the contrary, is entirely in the hands of
heaven, and for guidance keeps his eyes fixed on superior
powers. He resigns himself to Providence as a willing,
if not entirely intelligent, agent. Wherever his great quest
is concerned, he is a man of prayer, anxiously waiting for
a sign from heaven, which never fails him. It is the
attitude of the Roman general taking the auspices.

Haud equidem sine mente, reor, sine numine divom
adsumus et portus *delati* intramus amicos [2] (*A.* v. 56).

So says Aeneas, when wind and storm drive him out of
his course, and land him at his father's grave in Sicily.
Delati is the whole story of his voyage in one word—an
involuntary quest, perpetually over-ruled by a somewhat
unintelligible divine will, but with a happy result. The
hero, like a Christian saint, has surrendered his own will,
though not with the same restfulness of mind.[3]

---

[1] Girard, *Le Sentiment religieux en Grèce*, pp. 70-5 ; Arnold, *On Translating Homer*, p. 18 ; *Iliad* xii. 310-28. "But now a thousand fates of death stand over us, which mortal man may not flee from nor avoid ; then let us on, and give a glory, or obtain it ourselves" (Purves).

[2] "Not in truth, I deem, without the thought or the will of the gods are we here, driven as we are into a friendly haven." Years add beauty to such a couplet.

[3] ποιοῦντες γὰρ τὸ θέλημα τοῦ Χριστοῦ εὑρήσομεν ἀνάπαυσιν is a Christian saying of the second century. It is in the homily known as Second Clement, 6, 7.

Aeneas then is the chosen vessel of Destiny from first to last—*fato profugus*;[1] he is guided by fate throughout all his wanderings—

Nate dea, quo fata trahunt retrahuntque sequamur;
quidquid erit, superanda omnis fortuna ferendo est (*A.* v. 709),

says one of his captains.[2] He so entirely subordinates himself to Fate, and, in spite of Virgil's showing him to us "this way and that dividing the swift mind," he so frequently looks to divine intervention rather than to reflection and resolution, that the reader feels that life is after all made plain to him even if it is not easy, and that his pilgrimage is tedious rather than dark or perplexing.

It was a Roman conviction that Rome was under the special care of heaven—a belief which great Roman generals extended to cover their own personal fortunes. " It was not by numbers," says Cicero, "that we overcame the Spaniards, nor by our strength the Gauls, the Carthaginians by our cunning, or the Greeks by our arts, nor lastly was it by that sense, which is the peculiar and natural gift of this race and land, that we overcame the Italians themselves and the Latins; but by piety (*pietas*) and by regard for the divine (*religio*), and by this sole wisdom—our recognition that all things are ruled and directed by the will of the immortal gods—by these things we have overcome all races and peoples."[3]

As this utterance is from a speech, we may take it to represent the belief rather of Cicero's audience than of himself, and this assumption is confirmed by similar language addressed to the Romans by Horace.[4] Probably Virgil shared this popular feeling more than either Cicero or Horace could, and consistently with his habit of showing the future in the past, the spiritual sequence of events from

---

[1] *A.* i. 2, "an exile of destiny."

[2] " Goddess-born whither Fate draws us, onward or backward, let us follow; come what may, every chance must be overcome by bearing it."

[3] Cicero, *de Harusp. Resp.* 9. 19. Cf. Warde Fowler, *Religious Experience of the Roman people*, pp. 249 ff., with notes.

[4] *Dis te minorem quod geris imperas*, and other utterances of the kind.

principles, he endows Aeneas with this thoroughly Rom
attitude towards the gods. Aeneas, the founder of the ra
like all his most eminent descendants, holds the belief th
his country—for he calls Italy his *patria*—is beloved a
chosen of heaven; like them, he subordinates himself
heaven's purpose for his country, and, on every occasion,
seeks to learn at once, and in the directest possible way,
what is the will of the gods; and, once more like them, he
finds that heaven never fails Rome.

One or two questions naturally rise at this point. We
may ask whether this Roman view, that Rome is the
supreme thing for which Providence should care, is a true
one; but there is another inquiry which bears more closely
upon Aeneas. Has he any real conviction that the gods
care for him? They care for Rome—that is evident enough
—and for Aeneas as the destined founder of Rome. But
do they care for the man as apart from the agent?[1] Does
he feel that they care for him?

On the whole, the answer is fairly clear. No one could
well be more loyal than Aeneas to the bidding of heaven,
but his loyalty gives him little joy. He is a man who has
known affliction, who has seen the gods in person destroying
what he had loved above all things—his native city;[2] who
has been driven, and expects to be driven, over land and
sea by these same gods to a goal foreign to his hopes and
affections. He realizes that in the end some advantage
will accrue to his people, or their descendants, from all that
he undergoes, and he is willing to work for them. Sorrow,
it will be seen, has not cramped him, but rather has
broadened and deepened his nature. He lives for others;
and because he is told that the planting of Rome will be
a blessing to his people, he makes Rome "his love and his
country"—

hic amor, haec patria est (*A*. iv. 346).

If his comrades grow weary, and despair, he has words of
hope and cheerfulness for them. But for himself? For

[1] Cicero's Stoic said they did. Cf. *de natura deorum* ii. 65, 164.
[2] *A*. ii. 608 f., 622.

himself, he only expects the repetition of the past. There is little comfort, little hope for himself. Even his goddess-mother seems to think as much of the ultimate Augustus as of her son. Does any one, God or man, think about Aeneas and his happiness? His thoughts are ever of wars behind him and wars before him; and he hates war. He has nothing to which to look forward, and only too much to which to look back.

> Et nimium meminisse necesse est [1] (*A.* vi. 514).
> Infandum, regina, iubes renovare dolorem [2] (*A.* ii. 3).

And with these thoughts he is perhaps the most solitary figure in literature.

Virgil is true here to human experience, for with his story of pain, and with a doubt at his heart, Aeneas could hardly be other than he is. He can never forget the story he tells to Dido.[3] The poet has seized the meaning of the fall of Troy, and interpreted it in this quiet, wounded, self-obliter-ating man. If Virgil's hand shakes here and there, his picture, as he saw it in his mind, is true. Underneath the trappings of the Homeric hero is the warrior-sage, who has sounded human sorrow, and who, though he cannot solve the riddle, will not believe that all is vanity and a striving after wind.

Virgil is anticipating a later age, and Aeneas resembles more closely the character of Marcus Aurelius than any other in classical history. "Such was his calm that neither sorrow nor joy changed his expression, devoted as he was to the Stoic philosophy."[4] This face of impassive calm

---

[1] "But too good cause is there to remember."

[2] "Too cruel to be told, O queen, is the sorrow you bid me revive."

[3] Aeneas' words to Dido, *Aen.* iv. 340, give the keynote of his character.

> *me si fata meis paterentur ducere vitam*
> *auspiciis et sponte mea componere curas,*
> *urbem Troianam primum dulcisque meorum*
> *reliquias colerem, Priami tecta alta manerent*
> *et recidiva manu posuissem Pergama victis.*
> *sed nunc Italiam, etc.*

[4] *Erat enim ipse*, says his biographer of Marcus, *tantae tranquillitatis ut vultum nunquam mutaverit maerore vel gaudio, philosophiae deditus Stoicae. Hist. Aug. M. Anton.* 16. Cf. *ille Iovis monitis immota tenebat lumina* (*A.* iv. 331). It should be borne in mind that Aeneas' eyes were naturally *faciles* (*A.* viii. 310).

was the index of the mind within, unsatisfied in its deepest longings for an explanation of life, yet resolved to endure without satisfaction and with the slightest of hope to work on toward an impossible goal.[1] It implied a consciousness of the inadequacy of all conceptions of the divine yet achieved. Virgil, Suetonius says, meant on finishing the *Aeneid* to give himself to philosophy. Of himself, as of his hero, the words are true—

per mare magnum
Italiam sequimur fugientem et volvimur undis[2] (*A.* v. 628).

IV

We have now to consider Aeneas as influenced by the long study of man which marks the centuries between Pisistratus and Augustus. We must begin by setting aside the elements in his character which are mere external imitations of Homer, and also the episode of Dido, which has not perhaps in the *Aeneid* its proper psychological effect on the mind of Aeneas.[3]

Few epithets have been more misconstrued than the untranslatable *pius*, which Virgil has associated with the

[1] Cf. Lecky, *European Morals* i. 249-255 on Marcus Aurelius and his solitude. "Seldom," he says, "has such active and unrelaxing virtue been united with so little enthusiasm and been cheered by so little illusion of success."

[2] "Over a vast sea we follow a flying Italy and are tossed with the waves." Cf. *nos ad beatos vela mittimus portus* (*Catalepton* 5, 8) and note the contrast of tone.

[3] I quote with pleasure the suggestion of the reviewer in the *Athenaeum* (4 March 1905): "Unconsciously, perhaps, but with profound truth, Virgil draws Aeneas, after the Carthaginian episode, as always *careworn*, brave in action, but pensive in reflection ; there stands between him and his past the shadow of a crime, a shadow which glares but will not speak (*A.* vi. 467-474) and turns away, as one who 'does her true love know from another one,' to rejoin Sychaeus who has forgiven her. That is the most Virgilian thing in all Virgil." It might be urged that the first book shows Aeneas careworn already, but the suggestion deserves study. Mr Warde Fowler, *Religious Experience of the Roman People* (1911), pp. 410, 411 suggests that "the *development* of the character of Aeneas under stress of perils, moral and material, was much more obvious to the Roman than it is to us, and much more keenly appreciated." See the whole chapter. "The character of Aeneas," he holds, "is pivoted on religion." Also cf. his remarks on book v. pp. 417, 418, which seem to me to come nearer the heart of the thing than any comment I recall on that book.

name of Aeneas; yet to understand it thoroughly is necessary, if we are to have a clear comprehension of the whole
poem. What is *pietas*? It is not merely "piety," for that
is only a part of its connotation, nor is it enough to add
"pity" to "piety," in accordance with the happy suggestion
of a French critic, unless one give both the words a large
and generous rendering. Let us take a few illustrations of
the spirit indicated by the word.

First, the death of Lausus, who in rescuing his father was
killed by Aeneas in battle—

> At vero ut voltum vidit morientis et ora,
> ora modis Anchisiades pallentia miris,
> ingemuit miserans graviter dextramque tetendit
> et mentem patriae subiit pietatis imago.
> "quid tibi nunc, miserande puer, pro laudibus istis,
> quid pius Aeneas tanta dabit indole dignum?
> arma quibus laetatus habe tua ; teque parentum
> manibus et cineri, si qua est ea cura, remitto.
> hoc tamen infelix miseram solabere mortem :
> Aeneae magni dextra cadis (x. 821-30).[1]

This is how Aeneas makes war. Stern necessity compels
him to strike down Lausus: but in a moment the dying
face, the boyhood, and the filial love of his victim turn
Aeneas from foe to friend. Lausus is but a boy—*puer*—
but he has done what Aeneas did himself years before, he

---

[1] But when Anchises' son surveyed
The fair, fair face so ghastly made,
He groaned, by tenderness unmanned,
And stretched the sympathizing hand,
As reproduced he sees once more
The love that to his sire he bore.
" Alas ! what honour, hapless youth,
To those great deeds, that soul of truth,
    Can good Aeneas show ?
Keep the frail arms you loved to wear ;
The lifeless corpse I yield to share
(If thought like this still claim your care)
    Your fathers' tomb below.
Yet take this solace to the grave ;
'Twas great Aeneas' hand that gave
    The inevitable blow " (Conington).

has saved his father—the patronymic *Anchisiades* is not
without purpose—and now all the honour that a hero can
pay to a hero Aeneas will render to Lausus. *Pietas* covers
his feeling for Lausus as well as his feeling for Anchises.

We pass naturally to the scene that rose in the mind of
Aeneas—the fall of Troy and the rescue of Anchises and the
little Iulus. Enough has been said of Anchises, but mark
the picture of the child—

> dextrae se parvus Iulus
> implicuit, sequiturque patrem non passibus aequis[1] (ii. 723).

The instinctive act of the child—slipping his hand into his
father's—is his comment on Aeneas' *pietas*, and it is surely
significant that at such an hour and in such a place the
little footsteps of the child are one of the signal memories
of the night.[2]

Now another picture of Iulus. During the siege of the
camp (Book ix) he is galled by the taunts which Remulus
Numanus levels at the Trojans, and, with a prayer to
Jupiter for success, he shoots an arrow at him and brings
him down. The boy is delighted with his shot, and the
Trojans cheer him. His father is not there, but his place
is for the moment taken by Apollo, and though the action
and the words are Apollo's, they are in the spirit of Aeneas,
and may illustrate the quality which we are considering—
pietas. The god applauds the boy in an aside, and then in
clearer tone adds a word for gentleness—

> atque his ardentem dictis adfatur Iulum :
> "sit satis, Aenide, telis impune Numanum
> oppetiisse tuis ; primam hanc tibi magnus Apollo
> concedit laudem et paribus non invidet armis ;
> cetera parce puer bello "[3] (ix. 652).

---

[1] " My little Iulus has fastened his hand in mine and follows his father with
ill-matched steps " (Conington).

[2] J. R. Green, *Stray Studies*, p. 267, brings this out well.

[3]   Enough, Aeneas' son, to know
         Your hand, unharmed, with shaft and bow
         Numanus' life has ta'en ;

"C'est à la fois," says Sainte-Beuve, "ménagement et respect pour le fils de leur roi et pour l'espérance de la tige ; et puis Ascagne est trop jeune pour la guerre ; *si jeune, on devient trop aisément cruel.* J'entrevois ce dernier sentiment sous-entendu. "[1]

That we are right to suppose that this is the real sentiment of Aeneas as well as of Apollo we can see from Aeneas' words of farewell at the bier of Pallas—

> Nos alias hinc ad lacrimas eadem horrida belli
> fata vocant ; salve aeternum mihi, maxime Palla,
> aeternumque vale [2] (xi. 96).

It is the revolt of *pietas*, in its broadest and finest quality, against a destiny which drags the hero against his will into war.

Let our last illustration of *pietas* be the familiar utterance of Aeneas when he saw the pictures of the Trojan warriors, including himself, on the walls of Dido's temple—

Sunt lacrimae rerum et mentem mortalia tangunt (*A.* i. 462).

Professor Tyrrell holds that *rerum* and *mortalia* mean "things inanimate" and "the works of men's hands." In this case Virgil would mean to suggest the appeal of art to the sympathetic temper. Wordsworth and Sainte-Beuve think rather of the appeal of man's lot to man.

> Tears to human sufferings are due ;
> And mortal hopes defeated and o'erthrown
> Are mourned by man.[3]

Such glory to your first of fields
Your patron god ungrudging yields,
Nor robs of praise the arms he wields :
From further fight refrain.

Conington has here omitted the significant *puer*, which Sainte-Beuve seizes so well.

[1] Sainte-Beuve, *Étude sur Virgile*, p. 178.

[2] "Once again war's dreadful destiny calls us hence to other tears: hail thou for evermore, O princely Pallas, and for evermore farewell." The modern reader will think here of the farewell of Catullus (ci.) to his brother, at the grave at Rhoeteum, and Tennyson's comment on *in perpetuum*, and he may wonder how, if it were in Virgil's mind also, it squares with book vi.

[3] *Laodamia.* Attention may be called to Henry's note, *Aeneidea, ad loc.*

15

The former rendering is not at all impossible or un-Virgilian, but the latter gives a broader and deeper sense. Aeneas recognizes that at Carthage too, human creatures have human hearts, and he takes courage, knowing what appeal human sorrow makes to the human heart in himself.

If to Terence's *humani nihil a me alienum puto* we might add *nihil divini*, the enlarged expression (if rather cumbrous) would very fairly represent that new attitude of the quickened man, with which Virgil endows his hero, giving it the name *pietas*, by which he links a modern and rather Greek habit of mind to an old Roman virtue, enlarging the one, and naturalizing the other.

V

We have not yet considered Aeneas as prince. Achilles and Agamemnon are called kings by Homer, but the royalty of Virgil's Aeneas dwarfs them at once into Highland chieftains. Mycene may have been rich in gold, and yet had, like Ithaca, a midden at the palace doors; but Virgil was writing under a monarch who could boast that he had found Rome brick and left her marble.[1] It was a boast that implied imperial resources, imperial power, and an imperial outlook, and all these come between the Homeric chiefs and Aeneas, and make him a prince in manner, in attitude, and in ideal.

To take a telling example of the princely manner of Aeneas, we may turn to the episode of his killing the stags in the first book, which is of course modelled in Virgil's way after Odysseus' story of his stag-killing. It has been well handled by Sainte-Beuve, whose account of it may be paraphrased. "The difference between the two pictures," he says, "one feels instinctively. Aeneas and Odysseus are voyaging at the same time, but there is a distance of some centuries between their manners and methods. Odysseus, the hero of the simple ages, whose only aspiration is toward his poor Ithaca, withdraws alone from his companions and

---

[1] Suet. *Aug.* 28 *marmoream se relinquere quam latericiam accepisset.*

goes to spy out the island ; he sees a big stag, one only, and
it is quite enough ; he kills it without needing to ask his
arms of his squire (he has no squire or confidant), and, as it
is necessary to bring back the beast at once and this involves
difficulty, he tells us in detail how he did it, how he made
a cord, and how he lifted the animal on to his neck, and
made his way, leaning on his spear ; he forgets nothing.
All is naïve and frank, quite in the style of Robinson
Crusoe, a style which Virgil is careful not to apply to the
founder of the future Roman Empire. How could these two
men, Aeneas and Achates, have carried their seven big
beasts to the ships? It is a question not even asked in so
dignified a tale. Imagine the figure of Aeneas drawn with
a stag upon his shoulders and his head appearing among
the four feet of the animal! Virgil could not for a moment
entertain the idea of such a picture. Between his Aeneas
and Odysseus had come *cette production sociale fine, délicate,
dédaigneuse ; l'urbanité était née."* [1]

Yes, *urbanitas* had been born, and Aristotle had written
of the Magnificent Man. It was the mark of a vulgar
mind, according to a Greek comic poet, to walk " unrhythmic-
ally " in the street. Court etiquette had grown up round
Alexander, and probably still more round his less great
successors. Some part of this would inevitably find its
way to Rome, where it would fit in well with the national
affectation of *gravitas*. The world was still a long way
from Abraham Lincoln. Let us, however, call the thing
dignity in Aeneas, and recognize it as a mark of the great
prince.

But, if Aeneas has the outward bearing of the prince,
he has the higher qualities too, for he is Virgil's picture
of an ideal ruler. Morality for princes was probably

---

[1] Sante-Beuve, *Étude sur Virgile*, p. 243. The passages of Homer and
Virgil are *Odyssey* x. 144-71, and *Aeneid* i. 180-93. The German critic Rohde
has also called the *Odyssey* " die älteste Robinsonade." Another French critic,
however, shared the Roman feeling. La Motte, according to M. Patin (*Euripide*,
i. p. 52), " regrettait qu'Homère eût dégradé son Achille en lui faisant de ses
propres mains apprêter son repas, et ne lui eût pas donné, pour soutenir son rang
de héros, un maître d'hôtel, ou, tout au moins, un cuisinier." See also on Homer's
method, the letter of Cowper to Samuel Rose, 4 October 1789.

already becoming a branch of ethics; certainly a little time after Virgil's day it is well developed. Seneca's tract on Clemency, written for Nero, and Dio Chrysostom's treatises addressed to Trajan are early examples of this sort of literature; while by the fourth century A.D. Julian, Claudian, and Synesius had a plentiful supply of honourable and ancient maxims for Emperors. But it is unlikely that Virgil troubled the minor philosophers for their commonplaces. With a poet's feeling he read the story of Alexander, and watched the work of Augustus, and rising, in his way, from the particular to the universal, he developed in his own mind the idea of a great prince and drew him in Aeneas.

Aeneas has the statesman's temper. A man of broad outlook and of quick intelligence, he thinks for a nation, and as their ruler subordinates himself to the good of his people. Apart from the affair of Dido, nowhere does he fail to put his people, his people present and future, before himself. Not that he submits to their will or inclination, for he is every inch a King and not a President; he gives orders and they are carried out, he does not take mandates except from the gods. Yet he is not unwilling to listen to advice— from Anchises or Nautes, from the old and the trusted. He will humour the weak, who judge themselves unworthy of his quest, and like an Alexander he dots the world with his foundations. The Homeric chief had destroyed towns; Aeneas builds them.

He makes war and peace as a prince with full apprehension of what they mean for his people. If as a man, worn with war and travel, he desires peace, he also desires it as a prince for his people and his neighbours. To the Latins, who come to beg the bodies of the slain, he speaks thus—

Pacem me exanimis et Martis sorte peremptis,
    oratis? equidem et vivis concedere vellem [1] (xi. 110).

This is always his attitude, but, if war is forced upon him,

[1] " Is it peace for the dead you ask of me, for them on whom the War-God's lot has fallen? Nay, to the living also would I grant it."

he makes war like a prince. He carries his allies into action with him, and no cost of death or suffering will tempt him to falter. War, and real war, his enemies shall have, if they choose it ; but he had rather they chose peace.[1] Aeneas is here a thorough Roman, and he hardly needed his father's words to supplement his own instinct—

> Tu regere imperio populos, Romane, memento,
> hae tibi erunt artes, pacisque imponere morem
> parcere subiectis et debellare superbos [2] (vi. 851).

Latinus and Turnus are his foils ; the one unable or unwilling to make up his mind and act on it, and by this weakness bringing defeat and death on his people ;[3] the other heedless of national well-being or divine decree, if, at any cost to anybody and everybody, he can gratify his own wishes. If the reader wearies at times of Aeneas in the pageantry of the prince, still, as prince in council and prince in action Aeneas is well and strongly drawn. The weariness, which the reader feels, may be his own fault as much as the poet's, for it takes more mental effort to picture and to realize to oneself the hero as king than in some other characters.

Aeneas represents, here as elsewhere, a later age than Homer. No doubt, in Homer the chief leads, and the people follow the chief as "shepherd of his people." But the Homeric chief is nearer Remulus Numanus ; he has the weakness, too persistent in Greece, for petty war and the pillaging of his neighbours—

> semperque recentes
> comportare iuvat praedas et vivere rapto [4] (ix. 612).

Aeneas' mind is other, and he belongs to a later and more developed society. Witness his admiration of the rising

---

[1] One might compare Caesar's ejaculation when he saw the dead of the enemy upon the field of Pharsalia—*hoc voluerunt*—quoted from Pollio by Suet. *Iul.* 30. Plutarch *Caesar*, 46, τοῦτο ἐβουλήθησαν, εἰς τοῦτό με ἀνάγκης ὑπηγάγοντο.

[2] Translation on p 143.

[3] The querulous weakness of Latinus (*A.* vii. 598) *nam mihi parta quies*, etc.

[4] "Ever it is our delight to gather fresh booty and to live by plunder."

Carthage, its walls, its senate-house, its port, its theatre—
even its streets and their noise—

> miratur molem Aeneas, magalia quondam,[1]
> miratur portas, strepitumque et strata viarum (i. 421).

But it is as a prince that he looks at the great city, with
the spirit of an Alexander rather than of a Pericles.
Democracy and its factions flourish among the Italian
tribes; Drances and Turnus have each his party; but there
are no parties among the Trojans. They have no politics
but loyalty to their prince. This means a certain lack of interest. The Trojans generally, as we have seen, " want
physiognomy." Like the Romans under the later Emperors,
they lack initiative; they are apt to be rather helpless,
almost spiritless, when without their prince; and the life
of the nation is summed up in the prince. Virgil's political
philosophy is not Cicero's. On the whole perhaps the poets
are not generally very whole-hearted republicans. " For
myself," Goethe said to Eckermann, " I have always been
royalist." [2] Aeneas is Virgil's ideal of a princely character, as
he is his ideal of manhood.

VI

In conclusion, when we have weighed the character of
Aeneas, and allowed for the incompleteness of presentation
which we have remarked, we may sum up the matter
perhaps most truly by saying that Aeneas is Virgil's
picture of the " Happy Warrior." [3] The traditions of
epic poetry, involving the Olympian gods, make Aeneas
less reliant upon the " inward light " than Wordsworth's

---

[1] " Aeneas admires the mighty structure, once mere huts; he admires the
gates, and the noise and the paved streets." The *magalia quondam* has a trans-
Atlantic tone. The thought behind it lies, as a rule, outside the experience of
Englishmen, who misjudge the utterance in consequence.

[2] 25 February 1824.

[3] It should be remembered that the delineation of the perfect man was much in
vogue. The Epicureans had their ideal sage in Epicurus. Lucretius' attack on
Hercules points to a similar glorification of that hero. A later example is
Apollonius of Tyana. We may add the adoption by the Stoics of the reference
to the personal example—*e.g.* Socrates and Zeno.

warrior, even if Virgil had been as clear as Wordsworth
on the possibility or sufficiency of such a guide in life.
Aeneas,

> if he be called upon to face
> Some awful moment, to which Heaven has joined
> Great issues, good or bad, for human kind,

is certainly not "happy as a lover," nor "attired with
sudden brightness like a Man inspired." A genuine Roman,
he is not supremely concerned with the labour "good on
good to fix," nor, perhaps, to "make his moral being his
prime care." Yet much of Wordsworth's poem is true of
Virgil's Aeneas—

> Who, doomed to go in company with Pain,
> And Fear and Bloodshed, miserable train !
> Turns his necessity to glorious gain :
> In face of these doth exercise a power
> Which is our human nature's highest dower ;
> Controls them and subdues, transmutes, bereaves
> Of their bad influence, and their good receives ;
> By objects, which might force the soul to abate
> Her feeling, rendered more compassionate . . .
> Who comprehends his trust, and to the same
> Keeps faithful with a singleness of aim ; . . .
> Is yet a Soul whose master-bias leans
> To homefelt pleasures and to gentle scenes . . .
> More brave for this, that he hath much to love.

The differences between the two characters are not so
much contradictions as the result of a progression in the
ideals of humanity. If Aeneas has sight of virtues unknown to Achilles, the "Happy Warrior" has in like
manner advanced beyond Aeneas. The greatness of
Achilles is not lost in Aenas, but developed by the ripening
and enlarging of human experience. Aeneas is morally
on a higher plane, in spite of the occasional vagueness in
Virgil's drawing of him, and in spite of some uncertainty
about the supreme things, which passes from the poet into his
creation. The "Happy Warrior," in turn, has lost nothing
of Aeneas' greatness, but he has regained the clear look

of Achilles; he is not distracted by unreconciled views of the universe; he "finds comfort in himself and in his cause," and is "happy as a lover," because he has, what Aeneas at heart lacked, "confidence of Heaven's applause." Aeneas falls short of the "Happy Warrior," but he is of the same family.[1]

[1] I may be allowed to quote Sainte-Beuve once more, *Étude*, p. 112: "Ce personnage si distinct, si accompli, le *pius Aeneas*, pieux envers les hommes autant qu'envers les dieux, et que (sauf son moment d'erreur et d'oubli à Carthage), considérant toutes ses vertus, ses dévotions et religions, ses preuves d'humanité, de prud'homie, de courage, je suis tenté de nommer le Godefroy de Bouillon, ou mieux (je l'ai dit déjà) le saint Louis d'antiquité ;—le plus parfait idéal de héros que puisse présenter cette religion des Numa, des Xénophon, dont Plutarque est pour nous le dernier prêtre."

CHAPTER X

INTERPRETATION OF LIFE.—3. HADES

Thou soul of God's best earthly mould !
Thou happy soul ! and can it be
That these two words of glittering gold
Are all that must remain of thee ?—WORDSWORTH, *Matthew.*

Hoc habet argumentum divinitatis suae [*sc.* animus] quod illum divina delectant nec ut alienis sed ut suis interest. SENECA *Naturales Quaestiones* i., *Prol.* § 12.

"ALL Virgil is full of learning," says Servius, in opening his commentary on the sixth book of the *Aeneid*, "but for learning this book takes the chief place. The greater part of it is from Homer. Some of it is simple narrative, much turns on history, much implies deep knowledge of philosophers, theologians, and Egyptians, to so great an extent indeed that many have written complete treatises on points of detail in this book." So much said, Servius turns at once to the text. Our purpose, however, is rather to obtain a general view of Virgil's ideas about the other world, and to see, if possible, the various parts played by Homer and the philosophers in forming those ideas.[1] Once more we shall find traces of the progress of human thought, and once more a strong Roman feeling running through the whole. " He knew,"

[1] In a poet with so many literary affinities as Virgil, a larger amount of space must be taken up with the study of his literary antecedents than in the case of a more original speculator. Hence in this and the following chapter more attention is given to the history of speculation upon Hades and Olympus than may at first seem necessary, while for the specialist the chapters will not be interesting. I have a feeling that the specialist in primitive religion knows a great deal more about it than Virgil did and that this special knowledge of his therefore lies outside our present sphere. I am also quite clear that what Virgil did know meant incomparably more to him—if some friendly scholars will let me say so.

says Servius, "that various opinions are held on the sway of the gods, so very wisely he gave it a general treatment (*tenuit generalitatem*). In the main he follows Siro, his Epicurean teacher. The men of this school, as we know, deal with the surface of things, and never penetrate very deep."[1] Servius here speaks, as the Neo-Platonists of his day spoke, of Epicurus, but the hint he gives must not be disregarded. Whatever Virgil learnt from Homer and the philosophers, he was not a Neo-Platonist, and the early influence of Siro, and still more of Lucretius, could never be wholly eradicated from his mind. No doubt he was never so thorough an Epicurean as Lucretius; his adherence depended more on training than on conviction; but still his Epicureanism was enough to keep him from ever holding such a point of view as that of Plutarch. Again, we must remember that Virgil is pre-eminently a poet rather than a philosopher or a *theologus*, and we must expect him to treat this subject, like others, with the full freedom of a poet. In a word, while we look for dependence upon others who have treated the subject before him, we must also look for detachment.

I

When we begin to examine the sources of Virgil's Hades, we are apt to think first of literature, of descriptions of Hades which we find in extant books, particularly in great books; but the archæologists would turn our attention elsewhere. By dint of careful reading of books, which are *not* literature, some, ancient manuals of antiquities, some, polemical treatises; by elaborate study of ancient ritual with the constant aid of the excavator, they have brought to light another and very different side of ancient life. We have been accustomed in our study of the classics to hold to a traditional account of mythology, accepted eventually by Greeks and Romans as the traditional account of Old Testament history was by the Jews, and amongst other

[1] Servius, *ad Aen.* vi. 264 *superficiem rerum tractare, nunquam altiora disquirere.*

matter a fairly consistent picture of Hades has reached us. Literature and art organized the mythology, and we have habitually accepted this organization.

But nowadays the comparative study of religion has given us new principles and taught us to look for much that was before unnoticed, and the archaeologists have given us abundant material from the Greek world itself to which to apply our new methods. We find then in only too bewildering profusion ideas of things divine, demonic, or devilish, which we had not suspected; now and then we find them glimmering perplexingly behind passages and phrases of our poets long familiar; often it is the excavation of a grave or the discovery of an inscription which tells us how little we really knew of what the common people were thinking while the great minds were

Voyaging through strange seas of Thought, alone.

One or two important points should be noted. First of all, one feels more and more the imperative need of caution until our acquisitions are better known. We do not yet know from whom came the conceptions of the other world current in classical Greece, or indeed where, and still less when, they began. We may use such words as Pelasgic, chthonic, Orphic, and so forth, but it is difficult to use them with much definition, partly because our knowledge is only partial; partly because, as M. Boissier says,[1] where there is no monotheism there are no false gods, and it was even easier for one set of ideas to be merged in another, especially where neither dealt with anything definitely known, than for Catholicism to absorb and adapt the ideas and practices of its pagan environment. In the next place, as we gain insight into the confused and superstitious thinking of the common people, we realize more forcibly the grandeur and the value of what we call the Greek genius. The significance of that transcendence of current notions and of that clear strong grip of reality, which are its constant marks, becomes intensified.

[1] *La Religion romaine*, i. p. 335: "Pour des gens qui ne croyaient pas à l'existence d'un Dieu unique, il n'y avait pas de faux dieux."

Let us turn at once to Homer's world of the dead. Homer has been scanned through and through by eager eyes anxious to find traces of what is called primitive religion, and singularly little has been found.[1] Aeschylus is a richer field for such investigation. For the great mind, which it is hardly possible not to feel behind the *Iliad* and *Odyssey* as we have them (whatever their ultimate origin in whole or in part), divination, magic, the cult of the dead, ritual generally, are outside the circle of supreme interests; they are dead, unreal, to be disregarded. That great mind, seems as unconscious of such things as Shakespeare habitually is of the religious controversies that raged around him.

To take the first example, discussion has risen about the libations which Odysseus pours at Circe's bidding, and the blood which the ghosts drink. Is there here some trace of the cult of the dead? If there is, the German critic Kammer would cut the passage out as an insertion; or, if the passage is not so easily to be detached, the whole Nekyia, the visit to the dead, must be set down as of late date; so alien to Homer is the suggestion of such a cult. On the other hand, Rohde maintains that, while the cult of the dead is long anterior to Homer's age and lasted long after it, it was not practised at the actual time—it was remembered, however, and the poet used it. But at all events, whatever the origin of the rites performed by Odysseus, the poet has his own explanation—the "strengthless heads of the dead" drink of the blood to gain vision and speech. Anticleia, the hero's mother, is not suffered to approach the blood till Teiresias has spoken, and then Odysseus says, "I see here the spirit of my mother dead; lo, she sits in silence near the blood, nor deigns to look her son in the face nor speak to him! Tell me, prince, how may she know me again that I am he?" Teiresias says that she must drink the blood. So Anticleia "drank the dark blood, and at once she knew me."[2] The sacrifice is lost in the contrivance. Thus, in general, Homer's is the

---

[1] The reader may consult Professor Gilbert Murray's *Rise of the Greek Epic*; and Mr Andrew Lang's *World of Homer* (1910) pp. 126, 127, 133.

[2] *Odyssey*, xi. 141 f. (Butcher and Lang).

poetry of live men, and he "lets the dead bury their dead."[1]

But why does Odysseus go to visit the dead at all? Especially, it is asked, why should he go to learn of Teiresias what Circe can and does tell him in more fullness? In reply, another question is raised. Did he go at all in the oldest form of the story? Now, when we begin to speak of the oldest form of the story, it is time to pause. What *is* the oldest form of the story? We take the *Odyssey* as we find it; and, analysing it, we recognize stories here and there which we meet elsewhere. Failing another name, we call them "folk-tales"—stories told from of old everywhere: to whom do they belong or what is their oldest form? More than three hundred variants of *Cinderella* have been collected. When we have recognized our folk-tales in the *Odyssey*, we can make our conjectures as to how the poem *may* have grown. Whatever the original germ, it now includes so many elements of immemorial antiquity—who shall say how, or when, or where it came by them? Some of them fit into their places only loosely, some have interpolations within themselves.[2]

Odysseus really visits the dead in virtue of the old instinct, which in other lands and among other peoples sent some one to explore the undiscovered country and return, and the very looseness of connexion between book xi and the rest of the *Odyssey* betrays the original character of the tale. In the *Kalevala*, Waïnamoïnen, "like all epic heroes,

---

[1] See H. Weil, *Études sur l'antiquité grecque*, p. 12, on Homer's attitude to the abode and the religion of the dead generally. "Dans ses poèmes il fait grand jour." See also the fine chapter on "The House of Death" in Miss F. Melian Stawell's *Homer and the Iliad*—on the question of the blood and the ghosts, p. 157.

[2] Rohde *Psyche*[3], pp. 49 ff., on the descent of Odysseus, holds it is "one of the few certain results of critical analysis" that this was not originally a part of the *Odyssey*. Miss Stawell, *Homer and the Iliad*, p. 165, has another view: "The loss of weight to the Odyssey if this Book were removed can hardly be overestimated." I am less and less in a hurry to discuss the Homeric question; I feel that so far more learning than real feeling for literature has been in most cases brought to bear on it. It is for that reason that with a warm welcome for the books of Mr Murray, Miss Stawell, Mr Lang and others, I do not want to make up my own mind. The study of poety grows more fascinating and more perplexing as one reads the poets.

visits the place of the dead," [1] and from his story we can glean a hint or two for future use. " The maidens who play the part of Charon are with difficulty induced to ferry over a man bearing no mark of death by fire or sword or water " —this was what Aeneas found. Again, on his return, Waïnamoïnen warns mankind to "beware of perverting innocence, of leading astray the pure heart; they that do these things shall be punished eternally in the depths of Tuoni. There is a place prepared for evil-doers, a bed of stones burning, rocks of fire, worms and serpents." The "somewhat lax and wholesale conversion" of the Finns to Christianity left them much where they were, but we can feel here, with Mr Lang, that this revelation is coloured by ideas which were not those of the primitive Finns. In the same way we are not surprised to be told that scholars question the age of that passage in the Nekyia where Odysseus sees Minos judging and Tityos, Tantalus, and Sisyphus in torment (568-600).[2] Whoever added them to the story was so absent-minded as not to notice that they could not well come to Odysseus like the other shades. They are there, it is clear, to point a moral. Similarly to safeguard tradition, a late hand added the explanation, not a very lucid one, of how it is that Herakles can be at once a god in Olympus and be seen by Odysseus, a shade in hell.

Odysseus visits the other world, and while it is better for us not to question too closely as to the reason for his going, we may ask what he finds there. We have put on one side the moral tales of Sisyphus and the others, and it is generally agreed that we must also set aside the charming but rather irrelevant heroines, who seem to have been sent to see him to please another and a less poetic age.[3]

[1] Andrew Lang, *Custom and Myth*, p. 171.

[2] Weil, *Études*, p. 22, points out that ancient and modern criticism agrees here. Miss Stawell, *op. cit.* p. 154, would omit Minos, Sisyphus, and Herakles.

[3] Miss Stawell, *op. cit.* 159, defends the heroines, against the view of Wilamowitz that the choice of figures is accidental. In view of recent research in the folklore of the Dioscuri, it is perhaps worth while to note in passing that every heroine who is mentioned in the passage as having a god for her lover bore twins. The mother of Herakles is not an exception. But this is a little remote from Virgil.

Odysseus, then, sets his sails, and "a breeze of the North wind" (x. 507), sent by Circe (xi. 6), bore the ship "to the limits of the world, to the deep-flowing Oceanus. There is the land and the city of the Cimmerians, shrouded in mist and cloud, and never does the shining sun look down on them with his rays, neither when he climbs up the starry heavens, nor when again he turns earthward from the firmament, but baleful night is outspread over miserable mortals. Thither we came and beached the ship." He disembarks and goes on foot to "the place which Circe had declared." Circe's geography is still a little vague. She had told him to beach his ship by deep-eddying Oceanus, "but go thyself to the dank house of Hades." "Thereby, she continues, "into Acheron flow Pyriphlegethon and Cocytus, a branch of the water of the Styx, and there is a rock and the meeting of the two roaring waters." One may wonder whether Circe actually named these streams, which Odysseus does not again mention, or whether they came into the story with Sisyphus and the heroines.

However, on reaching the place, wherever it was, Odysseus drew his sword, dug his pit, a cubit in length and breadth, and "poured a pouring" to all the dead, of mead and wine and water. Then he sprinkled white meal, prayed and promised other offerings—a black heifer for them all, and a black ram for Teiresias—to be given on his return. So much said, he bled the sheep over the trench, "and lo! the spirits of the dead that be departed gathered them from out of Erebus. Brides and youths unwed, and old men of many and evil days, and tender maidens with grief yet fresh at heart; and many there were, wounded with bronze-shod spears, men slain in fight with their bloody mail about them. And these many ghosts flocked together from every side about the trench with a wondrous cry, and pale fear got hold on me."[1] The sheep are burnt and prayer made to mighty Hades and to dread Persephone.

When at last the dead begin to speak with Odysseus, we get from them the clearest picture of their state. "Wherefore," asks Teiresias, "hast thou, poor man, left the sunlight

[1] *Od.* xi. 36-43.

and come hither to behold the dead and a joyless land?"[1] Odysseus tries to embrace his mother, but thrice she flits from his hands "like a shadow or a dream," and he asks if she is but a phantom. "Ah! me! my child, Persephone, daughter of Zeus, doth in no wise deceive thee, but even thus is it with mortals when a man dies. For the sinews no more bind together the flesh and the bones, but the great force of burning fire abolishes these, so soon as the life has left the white bones, and the spirit like a dream flies away and is gone. But to the light haste with all thy heart" (216-23).

The shade of Agamemnon wept and shed tears, but could not embrace Odysseus. "It might not be, for he had now no steadfast strength nor power at all, such as was aforetime in his supple limbs" (393). "How," asks Achilles, "durst thou come down to the house of Hades, where dwell the senseless dead, the phantoms of men outworn?" (475). "Nay, speak not comfortably to me of death," he cries. "Rather would I live on ground, as the hireling of another, with a landless man, who had no great livelihood, than bear sway among all the dead that be departed" (488-91).

"Persephone doth in no wise deceive thee!" The dead are as shadows or dreams, dwelling in a joyless land without light or sun. Their lot is duller than the dullest and weariest the living can know—"a nerveless, noiseless existence." So judged the poet of the *Odyssey*.[2] Later hands confused his tale with moral instances, and the long development of hell began.[3] But even so, apart from the three great sinners of legend, it is startling to realize how empty

---

[1] Note the force of omitting line 92, which is absent from the MSS. Teiresias does not recognize the visitor, until he has drunk the blood. "Anticleia," says Mr Nairn, "seems to have had a vague knowledge of her son *before* she had drunk the blood : hence she lingers . . . *full* consciousness she only attains with the draught."

[2] The second Nekyia does not belong to the picture. The ghosts are, perhaps a little livelier—they have at least something to talk about ; they are not the ghosts of the first Nekyia, they are an imitation and not a good one. The local colour of the "White Rock" and Hermes and his rod are all of a later age. See Ettig, *Acheruntica*, p. 276.

[3] Dieterich, *Nekyia* (Teubner, 1893), p. 77, holds that these insertions were made by men who were far above the ideas criticized by Plato (see p. 249), but who yet were Orphics.

after all is the eventual hell of the *Odyssey*. Whatever may
be the function of the Homeric Erinnyes,[1] it is not exercised
in this Hades. There is no Tartarus, no Elysium, so no
Minos is needed to send the dead to the one or the other.[2]
Proteus, it is true, prophesies to Menelaus that he will not
die in Argos, "but the deathless gods will convey thee to
the Elysian plain and the world's end, where is Rhadamanthys
of the fair hair, where life is easiest for men. No snow is
there, nor yet great storm, nor any rain ; but always Oceanus
sendeth forth the breeze of the shrill West to blow cool on
men ; yea, for thou hast Helen to wife, and thereby they
deem thee (σφιν) to be son-in-law of Zeus" (iv. 561-70).
Of all this Odysseus sees nothing whatever, and, even on
Proteus' showing, it seems to be reserved for the sons-in-law
of Zeus. The history of the Greek ideas of the other world
is the story of the conquest of Elysium for common people,
the introduction of merit and eventually of morals into life
beyond the grave and the consequent necessity for Tartarus.

Perhaps the first order introduced into the world of the
dead is due to "the clear but clumsy intellect"[3] of Hesiod,
but even he does not take us very far. The dead of the
golden age are "good demons, above ground, guardians of
mortal men"; those of the silver age are underground,
but blessed, conspicuously coming second, yet in honour;
those of the bronze age are in "the dank house of chill
Hades, nameless"; the heroes, the fourth race, are no longer
where Homer left them, but, "with hearts free from care,
are in the islands of the blessed, by the eddies of Oceanus"
(*Works and Days*, 109-73). As for the men of his own
day, Hesiod shows us that things are bad enough on earth,
but their eventual lot he omits to mention. The Titans are
in murky darkness, with no escape, girt by a wall and gates
of brass (*Theog.* 720-45).

---

[1] See *Iliad*, xix. 259 Ἐρινύες, αἳ θ' ὑπὸ γαῖαν ἀνθρώπους τίνυνται, ὅτις κ' ἐπίορκον
ὀμόσσῃ. In *Il.* iii. 278 the Erinnyes yield place to a vaguer οἵ.

[2] Minos θεμιστεύει for the dead (l. 268), who ask him for pronouncements
(δίκας). In other words, just as Orion hunted in life and goes on hunting below,
so Minos goes on judging. Even so, both Orion and Minos are insertions.
Plato's view of Minos is not Homer's, even though he quotes the passage, *Gorgias*,
526 D. [3] Gomperz, *Greek Thinkers*, i. p. 38.

16

II

The chief sources of teaching on the other world were the various mysteries, especially those of Eleusis. It is difficult to distinguish the confluent streams of thought, but three stages in the history of Eleusis and its rites are recognized—the first, that represented in the Homeric hymn to Demeter; the second, marked by the gradual introduction of orgiastic and Dionysiac rites and associated with the mystic name of Iacchus; and the third, connected more closely with the name Dionysus Zagreus, with Orphic religion and Oriental rite, and dating from about the time of Alexander the Great.[1]

The Homeric hymn speaks of Demeter teaching Triptolemus and other kings, whose names grew more mystic in later days, "the doing of sacred things, and awful rites (ὄργια σεμνά), that none may transgress nor ask of, nor tell —great awe of the gods checks speech. Happy is he among men on earth who has seen them; and he that is not initiate, and he that has part therein, have never the same lot, when dead, and in dank darkness below" (474-82). Does happiness imply immortality?

Many strange ideas have been current about what was done in the mysteries and what there was to conceal. Excavation of the site of the Hall of Mysteries has revealed that it was not a temple, had no statue of a deity, knew no sacrifices within doors. The arrangements for exit, seating, and so forth are so free from any suggestion of mystery as to cause "a shade of disillusion"[2]—in fact, as Pompey found at Jerusalem, we find at Eleusis *nulla intus deum effigie*

[1] Percy Gardner, *New Chapters in Greek History*, ch. xvii. p. 385 f. ; Lenormant, *Contemporary Review*, May, 1880 (vol. i. p. 859). Here again, as in the previous section on Homer, I may be allowed to apply to myself the remark of Servius quoted at the beginning of the chapter—"he knew there were various opinions, but *tenuit generalitatem*"—or, like Poins, tried to keep to the middle of the road. The real aim of the chapter is lightly to sketch such views as Virgil probably knew about—not to discuss archaeological problems, *non nostrum inter vos tantas componere lites.*

[2] P. Gardner, *op. cit.*, p. 391 ; Lenormant, *C. R.*, Sept., 1880, p. 419.

vacuam sedem et inania arcana.[1] It would seem that miracle plays, as we should call them, and these of no very intricate or elaborate machinery, were performed—plays turning on the stories of Demeter, and, later on, of Zagreus. That representations of the tortures of Tartarus or the delights of Elysium were given is apparently very doubtful. Confronted with Aristophanes' *Frogs*, Lenormant holds that "the boldness of the poet appears to demonstrate just the opposite of that which it is sought to infer from it. If the sight of the infernal regions had been placed before the eyes of the initiated in the mysteries, an allusion so direct would have been considered as a violation of the secret."

Nor does it seem that the priests taught any theological or mystical doctrine, or had indeed any ideas, very different from those current without the precincts. Synesius of Cyrene (not yet a bishop), in criticizing the ecstatic virtues of the Christian monks and priests, complains that there is no reason or reflection about them; the monks remind him of what Aristotle said of men being initiated in the mysteries—"they learnt nothing, but had feelings, were put into a frame of mind—supposing, of course, they were in a fit state beforehand," and this fit state (is this Aristotle or Synesius speaking?) was ἄλογος, had nothing to do with reason.[2] No wonder that Pindar, hinting at the mysteries, says φωνάεντα συνετοῖσιν.[3] Professor Gardner suggests a comparison with Christian sacraments, which may be only too apposite.[4]

More important than the original contribution of Eleusis to the doctrine of another life are those of two schools of thought, differing in their initial aims and ideas but uniting at last in one great tradition—the Pythagoreans and the Orphics. Into their origin we cannot here inquire. It will be enough to say that direct or indirect indebtedness to the

---

[1] Tacitus, *Hist.* v. 9. "No image within of a god, the shrine vacant, the mysteries empty."

[2] Synesius, *Dio*, p. 48, Migne col. 1133. Ar. *Frag.*, ed. Heitz, p. 40; Οὐ μαθεῖν τι δεῖ (γρ. τι δεῖν) is Migne's text.

[3] *Ol.* ii. 93, "with a voice for such as understand."

[4] *Op. cit.*, p. 402. Cf. Dr Hatch's *Hibbert Lectures*, x. pp. 295 ff., on the historical connexion between Greek and Christian "mysteries."

far East has been asserted of Pythagoras, and that side by side with the Thracian connexion of Orphism there has been recognized considerable affinity with Egyptian thought.[1] To be brief, Pythagoras was led to emphasize the doctrine of the transmigration of souls.[2] The Orphic teaching found its centre in the myth of Dionysus Zagreus, the child-god mutilated and devoured by the Titans, whose heart, however, was rescued by Athene and swallowed by Zeus to reappear as the new Dionysus.[3] The Titans were struck by the thunderbolt, and from their ashes rose mankind, creatures of a two-fold nature, Titanic and divine, ever to be torn this way and that by these conflicting elements of evil and good linked in uneasy union. Traces are here of very different lines of thought—in the rending of the child-god asunder we are near the strange rites that cluster round the sacramental animal, the camel of the Arabs, the calf of the Maenads, rites surviving in a purified form in the Hebrew Passover.[4] In the war of Titans and gods, and the resulting double nature of man, we are not far from doctrines most familiar to the western world in Manichaeanism.[5] With

[1] See Gomperz, *Greek Thinkers*, bk. i. ch. 5; Dieterich, *Nekyia*, pp. 72-107. Jevons, *Intr. to Hist. of Religion*, pp. 352 f., 376. Miss Jane Harrison, *Prolegomena to the Study of Greek Religion, passim.*

[2] "Leave off beating the dog; for I recognize in his tones the voice of the soul of a friend." So Xenophanes reports him to have said; *ap.* Diogenes Laertius, viii. 36:

κal ποτέ μιν στυφελιζομένου σκύλακος παριόντα
φασὶν ἐποικτεῖραι καὶ τόδε φάσθαι ἔπος,
παύσαι μηδὲ ῥάπιζ'· ἐπειὴ φίλου ἀνέρος ἐστὶ
ψυχή, τὴν ἔγνων φθεγξαμένης ἀίων.

Holm (*Gk. Hist.* i. 369) takes the story to be parody. Gomperz, even so, finds it true to character. See also Rhys David's *Hibbert Lectures*, iii. "The Buddhist Doctrine of Karma." He distinguishes between the Platonic and Buddhist theories, and doubts if transmigration was ever held by an Aryan race uninfluenced from outside.

[3] Clement of Alexandria, *Protrepticus*, 15 P. citing "Orpheus the poet."

[4] See Robertson Smith, *Religion of the Semites*, lecture ix. p. 338. In January 1897 there was some little trouble with the Indians of British Columbia, owing to the government's objection to a rite, in which a live dog was torn up by the participants with their teeth and eaten raw.

[5] See Gustav Flügel, *Mani, seine Lehre u. seine Schriften aus dem Fihrist*, Leipzig, 1862 (pp. 89-105, a translation of the fragments of Mani's original teaching).

both Orphics and Manichaeans the problem was the universal one, to explain the strange contradiction in human nature, and then to disentangle the divine element.

The common doctrine of Pythagorean and Orphic "may be epitomized in a single significant phrase as the 'fall of the soul by sin.' The soul was of divine origin, and its earthly existence was unworthy of it. Its body was a fetter, a prison, a grave. . . . Its sin involved it in penitential punishment, for through atonement and purification alone would it be able to return to the divine home whence it came. This process of purification and atonement was accomplished in two ways—by the penalties of Hades and by the cycle of births. We may conjecture that the penalties of Hades were a later accretion to the Pythagorean doctrine of metempsychosis, derived from the Orphics and fused with it through their influence." [1] After a long series of re-incarnations, interrupted by epochs of punishment in the pool of mire (a great feature in Orphic schemes of the other world), the soul, pure once more, escaped to re-enter its home and be with the gods. The wheel which we know in Buddhism,[2] or one very like it, reappears in Orphism. An actual wheel was used in Orphic ceremonies ; a pictured wheel appears in their presentments of the other world.[3] It will be seen that here we have the origin of much in Virgil's Hades. The wheel itself reappears in his story,

ubi mille rotam volvere per annos [4] (*A*. vi. 748).

"The best witness to the faith of the Orphic as to the future life," says Miss Harrison, " are his own confessions, buried with him in his tomb, inscribed, happily for us, on imperishable gold." Eight tablets of very thin gold have been found in graves, most of them in southern Italy, and they date apparently from the third and fourth centuries B.C.

---

[1] Gomperz, *Greek Thinkers*, p. 128. See also Dieterich, *Nekyia*, ch. iii.

[2] See W. Simpson, *The Buddhist Praying Wheel*, Notes, p. 272, for a picture of a Tibetan Buddhist Wheel of Life, taken from *Journal of Royal Asiatic Society*.

[3] See Miss Harrison, *Prolegomena*, pp. 589-94, and figures 163, 164. Simpson, *Buddhist Praying Wheel*, figures on pp. 41, 266, 267.

[4] "When they have rolled the wheel for a thousand years."

Two will suffice us for the present. First, the Campagno tablet, found near Naples, close to the hand of a skeleton—

> Out of the pure I come, Pure Queen of Them Below,
> Eukles and Eubuleus and the other Gods immortal.
> For I also avow me that I am of your blessed race,
> But Fate laid me low and the other Gods immortal
> . . . . starflung thunderbolt.
> I have flown out of the sorrowful weary Wheel.
> I have passed with eager feet to the Circle desired.
> I have sunk beneath the bosom of Despoina, Queen of the Underworld.
> I have passed with eager feet from the Circle desired.
> Happy and Blessed One, thou shalt be God instead of mortal.
>   A kid I have fallen into milk.[1]

The second tablet is from Petelia, and it runs—

> Thou shalt find on the left of the House of Hades a Well-spring,
> And by the side thereof standing a white cypress.
> To this Well-spring approach not near.
> But thou shalt find another by the Lake of Memory,
> Cold water flowing forth, and there are guardians before it.
> Say : " I am a child of Earth and of Starry Heaven ;
> But my race is of Heaven (alone).   This ye know yourselves.
> And lo ! I am parched with thirst and I perish.   Give me quickly
> The cold water flowing forth from the Lake of Memory."
> And of themselves they will give thee to drink from the holy Well-spring,
> And thereafter among the other heroes thou shalt have lordship . . .

Three lines follow, of which only scattered words remain.[2]

---

[1] Miss Harrison, *Prolegomena to Greek Religion*, ch. xi. p. 586. There is no lacuna or illegibility on the tablet itself answering to the dots; but metre and sense show there is an omission. The tablet is in the National Museum at Naples. H. Weil, *Études*, pp. 37 ff.

[2] Miss Harrison, *op. cit.*, p. 574. This is in the British Museum.

Before we pass on, it bears upon our present purpose to notice that both Orpheus and Pythagoras were said to have descended into hell. Orpheus' descent is of course famous—how much of its fame comes from the fourth *Georgic?*—but it seems highly probable that the romantic motive, on which it turns in the common story, is not the original one. Either he did not descend to regain the lost Eurydice but to learn about things below with a view to teaching them above ground; or, if he did go to recover Eurydice, it seems highly probable that the story is a variant of the descent of Dionysus to recover Semele.[1] Pythagoras, according to one story, saw the soul of Hesiod bound with brass to a pillar, and squeaking (τρίζουσαν), while Homer's was hanging to a tree with serpents round it— punishments for their stories of the gods. An interesting fragment of the *Pythagorean* of the comic poet Aristophon brings us back into touch with the actual world : " He said that he went down to the régime below and saw the various groups ; and that the Pythagoreans were by far the best off among the dead ; for they were the only people with whom Pluto dined—on account of their piety.——Well, he's an easy-going god, if he enjoys the company of such unwashed fellows." [2]

Whatever the date of Aristophon, who is supposed to be a poet of the New Comedy, Orphic and Pythagorean teaching about the other world seems to have been widely known, and traces of it are found freely in the great literature of the fifth century B.C. In one of Pindar's *Threnoi*,

---

[1] Miss Harrison, *Prolegomena*, pp. 603 ff. : Dieterich, *Nekyia*, p. 128. It may be noted that the end of Orpheus also suggests one story of Dionysus. Orpheus was torn in pieces by women, *G.* iv. 520. Plutarch *de sera numinum vindicta* 565 F on the recovery of Semele and the place of Lethe.

[2] Diogenes Laertius, viii. 21 and 36 :

    A. ἔφη τε καταβὰς ἐς δίαιταν τὴν κάτω,
    ἰδεῖν ἑκάστους· διαφέρειν δὲ πάμπολυ
    τοὺς Πυθαγοριστὰς τῶν νεκρῶν. μόνοισι γὰρ
    τούτοισι τὸν Πλούτωνα συσσιτεῖν ἔφη
    δι' εὐσέβειαν.
    B.   εὐχερῆ θεὸν λέγεις
    εἰ τοῖς ῥύπου μεστοῖσιν ἥδεται ξυνών.

See also Dieterich, *Nekyia*, pp. 78, 129 ; Ettig, *Acheruntica*, p. 288.

for instance, we read: "The body of all men is subject to all-powerful death, but alive there yet remains an image of the living man; for that alone is from the gods. It sleeps when the limbs are active, but to them that sleep in many a dream it revealeth an award of joy or sorrow drawing near."[1]

The ideas of reward and punishment after death stamped themselves upon the common mind. Cephalus, in the *Republic*, tells how in advancing age he is haunted by them.[2] The forms which reward and punishment would take were also well known—as is shown by the dialogue in the *Frogs* between Dionysus and the slave newly landed in Hades—

Dionysus. Well, and what have we here?
Slave.   Darkness—and mud.
Dionysus. Did you see any of the perjurers here,
             And father-beaters, as he said we should?
Slave. Why, didn't you?
Dionysus.   I? Lots.[3]

Public opinion was just as clear about the rewards: "the blessings which Musaeus and his son give from the gods are gayer still (νεανικώτερα); for in their story they take them down to Hades and make them sit down, and then they get up a banquet of the 'holy' and display them, crowned, with nothing to do henceforth and for ever but to get drunk. For the finest possible prize for virtue, they seem to think, is eternal drunkenness."[4]

---

[1]   καὶ σῶμα μὲν πάντων ἔπεται θανάτῳ περισθενεῖ,
  ζωὸν δ' ἔτι λείπεται αἰῶνος εἴδωλον· τὸ γάρ ἐστι μόνον
  ἐκ θεῶν· εὕδει δὲ πρασσόντων μελέων, ἀτὰρ εὑδόντεσσιν ἐν πολλοῖς ὀνείροις
  δείκνυσι τερπνῶν ἐφέρποισαν χαλεπῶν τε κρίσιν.
                                        Pindar, *Threni* fr. 96.
See Dr James Adam, "Doctrine of the Celestial Origin of the Soul from Pindar to Plato," in his *Vitality of Platonism*, 1911.

[2] *Rep*. i. 330, D καταγελώμενοι τέως τότε δὴ στρέφουσι τὴν ψυχὴν μὴ ἀληθεῖς ὦσιν.

[3] Aristophanes, *Frogs*, 273 (Murray). Dionysus looks at the audience as he speaks these last words.

[4] Plato, *Rep*. ii. 363 c. See Dr Adam's notes. Weil, *Études*, p. 41; "c'est nn idéal quelque peu thrace."

The interesting word here is "the holy," which is almost
a technical term for the initiated.[1] It shows us at once the
weak spot in the Mysteries. They are not in any decisive
way connected with morality. The language of the gold
plates, already quoted, is beautiful, but what is meant by
"pure"? Is it actually and spiritually "pure," or only
ceremonially and technically? We may be fairly sure that,
with the majority of people, there was a general consensus
of opinion that to secure the joys of "eternal drunkenness"
it was only necessary to be initiated, that a sacrament, in
fact, could veto the operation of moral law. Virtue, says
Plato, is hard ; wickedness pleasant and profitable ; and
then "quacks and prophets go to rich men's doors and
persuade them that they have power from the gods, by
means of sacrifices and chants, to cure any wrong deed of
their own or their ancestors in a course of pleasures and
feasts" ; they quote Homer to the effect that even the gods
themselves can be won by prayer, that men turn them
aside by sacrifices and winning supplications, by drink
offering and the smoke of the victim ; they produce piles
of books by Musaeus and Orpheus, sacrificial liturgies in
fact, and "persuade men and cities that there are absolu-
tions and atonements by means of sacrifices and pleasures
for them while they live, and, when we are dead, the mysteries (τελεταί), as they call them, rid us of trouble, over
there; but if we have not sacrificed, terrible things await us."[2]

Yet Plato did not reject Orphism.[3] His apocalypses (if
one may use the word) are full of Orphic and Pythagorean
ideas. The accounts of the other world given by him in the
Phaedrus, the *Gorgias*, the *Phaedo*, and the *Republic* have
been woven by Döring into a complete and harmonious
whole.[4] The whole story of the soul is given in the
Phaedrus—its condition before incarnation, the fall due to

---

[1] The reader will remember the use of the term "saints" in the New Testament.

[2] Plato, *Rep.* ii. 364 A-365 A. Homer, *Iliad*, ix. 497-501. See Robertson
Smith, *Religion of the Semites*, lect. vii. p. 261, on the gaiety of sacrifices.

[3] See article by Mr F. M. Cornford, in the *Classical Review*, Dec. 1903, " Plato
and Orpheus."

[4] A. Döring, *Die eschatologischen Mythen Platos*, in *Archiv für Gesch. der
Philosophie*, vol. vi. 1893. Weil, *Études*, pp. 65 f., 82.

the inability of reason to control desire, the first incarnation and its meaning (σῶμα=σῆμα),[1] the judgement with punishment or reward, and lastly the new choice of life. It is in the *Gorgias* that the most vivid account is given of the judgement after death. "The judge must be naked, dead, with very soul contemplating the very soul of each immediately on death (αὐτῇ τῇ ψυχῇ αὐτὴν τὴν ψυχὴν θεωροῦντα ἐξαίφνης ἀποθανόντος ἑκάστου), alone without a kinsman beside him, all the trappings of his life left behind on earth, that the judgement may be just (523 E)." "Everything is visible in the soul when it is stripped of the body. Everything that belongs to it by nature, and the results in a man's soul of every pursuit" (524 D.) The judge does not know whose soul it is—it may be a king's soul, which he finds unsound through and through, "full of scars of deceit and injustice, which each man's deeds have left printed (ἐξωμόρξατο) upon the soul, all crooked with lying and trickery, nothing straight" (524 E). Such were Tantalus, Sisyphus, and Tityos in Homer, "most dynasts being bad" (526 B). The main concern of life is to go to the judge with the healthiest possible soul, so made by the search for truth (τὴν ἀλήθειαν σκοπῶν 526 D). "For you will suffer nothing terrible, if you will really be honourable and good, and practise virtue" (527 D). It should be noticed that nothing is said here about service of the state, which plays a large part in the judgement as described by Cicero and Virgil.

In the *Phaedo* we have the topography of the other world, its underground rivers of fire and mud, and its abysses. The souls judged are divided into five classes. "Average" people are sent by way of Acheron to the Acherusian lake for shorter or longer terms, to be rewarded and purified as they deserve, and thence they pass to be born again as animals (113 D, A). Incurable sinners go at once to Tartarus for ever (113 E). Those guilty of great sins, but not too great for punishment, go to Tartarus for a year, when, if those they have wronged are willing, they may pass to the Acherusian lake (114 A, B). The fourth class, who have been pre-eminent for holiness, "ascend to their

---

[1] The doctrine may be compared with the Hindu Karma.

pure habitation and dwell on the earth's surface. And those of them who have sufficiently purified themselves with philosophy live thenceforth without bodies and proceed to dwellings fairer than these, which are not easily described " (114 B, C). "A man of sense," concludes Plato, "will not insist that these things are exactly as I have described them. But I think he will believe that something of the kind is true of the soul and her habitations." In the last book of the *Republic* Plato adds more on choice in reincarnation, but as Virgil passes over this we need not now discuss it.

The Orphism of Plato is thus quite distinct from the confused thinking of the mass of Orphics, and quite distinct too from the miracle-plays which Clement of Alexandria so pitilessly describes. Which of these forms was dominant at any given time is a question perhaps hard to answer ; which influenced most the development of Greek thought it is easier to say.

Before we leave Greece for Rome, one point already mentioned may be recalled. A short study of popular Orphism and a little acquaintance with Orphic mysteries will help to explain the real greatness of Epicurus. Neo-Pythagoreans, Neo-Platonists, religious men, and men who made their living by religion, united in giving him a low place in the hell he denied. But his bold application of the science of Democritus to religious questions, his reference of all existence to law, in spite of all inconsistencies and failures, was, as Lucretius says, a great victory.

> Quare religio pedibus subiecta vicissim
> opteritur, nos exaequat victoria caelo [1] (i. 78).

To-day we are able to sympathize with both sides in the quarrel, and to avail ourselves of all they had of permanent value. It is part of the greatness of Virgil that after an Epicurean training he was able to grasp and use the real contribution of the other side, without surrendering the freedom which Lucretius had taught him to prize.

[1] "Therefore religion is put under foot and trampled upon in turn ; us his victory brings level with heaven" (Munro).

III

The Italians seem to have developed no very definite or well organized scheme of things divine, though it is clear that they had some notions of an after-world, not less dreadful for being dim. There are in Etruscan tombs pictures of demons of frightful aspect. One, called Tuchulcha, is drawn brandishing a snake, and yelling. Another, who occurs very frequently, is called Charun—a perversion of Charon. He has a large mouth and teeth, wings on his back, and a hooked nose; he carries a hammer, and, to crown all, he is painted green. In one picture he stands by Achilles, who is sacrificing his prisoners in honour of Patroclus.[1]

In the age of Virgil two great men of letters dealt deliberately with the other world in works which are of interest and importance to the student of the sixth *Aeneid.* In his attack upon the gods Lucretius could not overlook the popular dread of punishment after death, and he discussed it at some length. Cicero likewise, imitating Plato, concluded his *Republic* with a myth of his own, which turns upon the future life.

A thorough-going materialist, Lucretius energetically argues for the mortality of the soul. It is like the body material, and Nature has a claim upon all matter for her own purposes, and only lends it to us—

vitaqua mancipio nulli datur, omnibus usu [2] (Lucr. iii. 791).

Even if time gather again our matter after our decease, rearrange it in the same way, and again give it the light of life, that has nothing to do with us when once our consciousness of identity has been broken—

interrupta semel cum sit repetentia nostri (iii. 851).

---

[1] Boissier, *Horace et Virgile*, pp. 94-7 (tr. 87-90).
[2] Cf. a slightly different turn of the same thought in Euripides, *Phoenissae*, 555 οὗτοι τὰ χρήματ᾽ ἴδια κέκτηνται βροτοί, | τὰ τῶν θεῶν δ᾽ ἔχοντες ἐπιμελούμεθα·— ὅταν δὲ χρῄζωσ᾽, αὔτ᾽ ἀφαιροῦνται πάλιν.

No, the great truth is that mortal life ends for us in immortal death—

mortalem vitam mors cum immortalis ademit (iii. 869).

Philosophy thus effects the emancipation of man's mind by driving headlong out of doors "the dread of something after death," which disturbs and paralyses all within.[1] Nature cannot afford to dismiss any matter to Tartarus; her economy is our salvation (iii. 964-6). But what of Avernus? Is it not the mouth of Hell, as people said?[2] No, the fact is that Avernus near Cumae is only one of several such places, where birds and other creatures cannot breathe because of sulphur fumes, an entirely natural phenomenon easily explained by natural law.[3] The stories which poets, and Ennius in particular, tell of hell are really true of this life—Tityos is merely the lustful man, while Sisyphus is the politician with ambitions, defeated again and again at the poll.[4] In short, the only real hell is the hell fools make of their lives on earth—

hic Acherusia fit stultorum denique vita (iii. 1023).

Lastly, as if Lucretius had divined what the sixth *Aeneid* would be, he applied to one of its central doctrines the most splendid *reductio ad absurdum*, and finally disposed of the ideas of immortality and transmigration. He pictures the transmigrant souls jostling to get places in new bodies. Is it at birth, or perhaps at conception, he asks, that the immortal beings elbow one another in their headlong eagerness for mortal members? Or do they arrange to go on the plan of "first come, first served?"[5]

In the first book of the *Tusculan Disputations* Cicero discusses the immortality of the soul as a philosophical question, and in the epilogue to his *Republic* he gives a vivid

---

[1]   *Et metus ille foras praeceps Acheruntis agendus,*
        funditus humanam qui vitam turbat ab imo
        omnia suffundens mortis nigrore (iii. 37-9).

[2] Strabo, c. 244, tells us that this idea is as old as Ephorus. He seems to imply that the story about the birds was fiction, or had at least ceased to be true.

[3] Lucr. vi. 738-68, *omnia quae naturali ratione geruntur* (760).

[4] Lucr. iii. 978-1023.   [5] Lucr. iii. 776-83.

and startling presentation of the after-life. It is in the form of a dream, which came to Scipio Africanus the younger outside the walls of Carthage. He finds himself with the elder Africanus and his own father, Aemilius Paullus, in a place high and bright and full of stars, which proves to be the Milky Way. From it he beholds the world, and the sense of infinite space and infinite time is brought home to him.[1] The soul, he learns, is but a prisoner in the body; the life men know on earth being more really death. It comes from the eternal fires called stars, for the stars are animated with a divine intelligence. All on earth is transitory except the soul, the gift of the gods, while beyond the moon all is eternal. The mind is the man (*mens cuiusque is est quisque*), and it is divine. Man's work is the service of the community of which he is a member. " For all who have saved, helped, or increased their country (*patriam*), there is a sure and definite place in the sky (*certum esse in caelo definitum locum*), where in happiness they may enjoy eternal life. For to that supreme God, who rules the universe, nothing that is on earth is more grateful than those gatherings and ordered societies of men which are called states. The rulers and saviours of these proceed hence and return again hither "—to the Milky Way. The universe consists of nine related spheres, of which the outermost, which guards and contains the rest, is the supreme God himself. It is he who has given man his soul, and without his order (*iniussu eius*) man must not leave life, lest he "seem to have abandoned the human task assigned by God."

The myth is a medley of borrowed matter. It is chiefly valuable for our present purpose because it shows so clearly the ideas of a Roman of culture and sensibility. Infinite time and infinite space—the centre of them for the Roman in Rome. The gods have set him there, and without their leave he must not quit his post. No one will quarrel with such a view, however fantastic the setting, and we shall find that Virgil holds it fully as strongly as Cicero.

As for the tales which the poets in the old days had told

[1] Cf. Seneca, *Nat. Quaest.*, i. Prologue § 7 ; and Carlyle's *Reminiscences*, vol. i. p. 44 (of James Carlyle).

about Hades, Cicero several times lets us know that they are freely ridiculed—should not a philosopher be ashamed to boast that he is not afraid of such things?[1] For people— and even Epicureans—did fear them. On the other hand, there were those who marked with anxiety the passing of belief in Hades. Long before Polybius had said that the scrupulous fear of the gods kept the Roman commonwealth together—that it was not idly that the ancients had instilled into the vulgar the belief in punishments in Hell; there was risk to the state in the rejection of these beliefs.[2] So, in Virgil's own day, the historian Diodorus remarked that the old tales—"the mythology," fictitious as it might be— did contribute to piety and righteousness in the many.[3] The restoration of religion, attempted by Augustus, was no doubt in part a police measure to counteract the spirit of the times, though that it was not merely this is proved by the clear traces of superstition and romanticism in that hard and shrewd character.

The poet's view of the matter will probably not be that of the pure philosopher. Still less will he take up the position of the practical moralist or of the Emperor, the arch-policeman of the state. Yet it is quite possible that, however unphilosophic and unpractical, he may come nearer to the truth of things, and that is what we have now to see.

In the first *Georgic* Virgil gently laughed at "the Elysian fields which Greece admires";[4] he could never deride or attack in the style of Lucretius. In the second book he spoke with admiration of the philosopher victorious over "all fears" and "the noise of greedy Acheron,"[5] but he did so with some consciousness of detachment from him—his own happiness lying elsewhere.

In his story of Orpheus in the fourth *Georgic* he has given a sketch of Hades himself, but, as the dominant motive is the recovery of Eurydice, it will not surprise us that the treatment leans more to literature than to religion.

---

[1] *Tusculans*, i. 21, 48.   [2] Polybius, vi. 56.

[3] Diod. Sic. i. 2 ἡ τῶν ἐν ᾅδου μυθολογία, τὴν ὑπόθεσιν πεπλασμένην ἔχουσα, πολλὰ συμβάλλεται τοῖς ἀνθρώποις πρὸς εὐσέβειαν καὶ δικαιοσύνην.

[4] *G.* i. 38 *quamvis Elysios miretur Graecia campos.*

[5] *G.* ii. 490-3 *felix qui potuit*, etc.

It is, in fact, the Hades of literary convention.[1] The
passage which most concerns us at present, though not that
which most permanently moves us, runs as follows in Lord
Burghclere's rendering [2]—

> Then through the jaws of Taenarus he passed,
> The cavernous gates of Dis; the grove of gloom.
> Wherein the horror of the darkness broods,
> And stood before the powers of nether Hell
> With their dread king; and wrestled with the hearts
> That know not pity for the prayers of men.
> There, startled by his song, wan spectres flocked
> Forth from the utmost deeps of Erebus,
> Dim phantoms that had lost the light of day,
> Swarming around like flights of myriad birds,
> Who seek the sheltered wood when winter storm
> Or chilly evening drives them from the hills:
> Matrons and husbands, and the forms long dead
> Of high-souled heroes, boys and spouseless girls,
> And well-loved youths who in their parents' sight
> Were laid to rest upon untimely pyres.
> All these were they whom black Cocytus binds
> With darkling ooze, with fringe of loathly reeds,
> With sleepy waves that lap the loveless shore;
> They whom abhorrent Styx for ever chains,
> Girt with the ninefold fetters of its flood.
> The very denizens of deepest Hell
> Listened, astonied, to the strains he sang:
> The Furies with their locks of livid snakes,
> Grim Cerberus with triple mouth agape,
> While the hushed whirlwind stayed Ixion's wheel.

The description, one might guess, may date from Virgil's
Alexandrine days. If the story is true that the fall of
Gallus involved a new conclusion to the book,[3] as seems
generally agreed, it is quite possible that in the episode of

---

[1] Similar descriptions are in Horace, *Odes*, ii. 13 and 14; iii. 11.

[2] *G.* iv. 467 f.

[3] Servius *ad Ecl.* x. *fuit autem amicus Vergilii, adeo ut quartus Georgicorum
a medio usque ad finem eius laudes teneret; quas postea iubente Augusto in
Aristaei fabulam commutavit.*

Aristaeus, of which this is a not specially relevant part, Virgil used old material. The student of philosophy or religion might ask the poet how he reconciled this literary hell with the Pythagoreanism of the earlier part of the book (l. 221), where he speaks of God pervading all things, and of their life, drawn from His, ascending after death to the stars. Whatever reconciliations readers may make, probably the poet would be content to make none.

When he began to draw Hades in earnest, Virgil remembered this passage. The lines, "Matrons and husbands" to "untimely pyres," he took over as they stood, but the simile he altered. The alteration was slight, but it is significant of the poet's own change of mind and mood. The birds in the *Georgic* are driven by storm from hill to wood. In the *Aeneid* it is "the chill of the year" that "chases them oversea and sends them to sunny lands," and the poet adds the old simile of the fallen leaves—

οἵη περ φύλλων γενεή, τοίη δὲ καὶ ἀνδρῶν (*Iliad*, vi. 146).

In place of a pretty simile we have two deeply moving analogies of man's life. Autumn comes, and the leaves fall—"surely," said, the Hebrew poet, "surely the people is grass." The birds seek another home, "and man goeth to his long home." The shades, which Aeneas sees, have no longer any heart for music ; they think only of crossing Acheron—

tendebantque manus ripae ulterioris amore.

The picturesque figures which listened to Orpheus in the *Georgic* have all the air of being borrowed from Greek painters ; they were borrowed by Horace more than once, and not without a touch of humour.[1] If Ixion reappears in the *Aeneid*, it is in more seriousness. There no casual visitant, not even an Orpheus, can interfere with eternal law. We are nearer Thomas of Celano and his great hymn—

> Mors stupebit et Natura
> cum resurget creatura
> iudicanti responsura.

[1] *Odes*, ii. 13 ; iii. 11.

He at least is doing with the apocalypses of the early Church what Virgil did with the Orphic and Pythagorean apocalypses, from which those are in part descended.

IV

We now come to Virgil's sixth book. We have seen something of the long development of men's ideas upon the other world, and we find here as elsewhere that Virgil tries to sum up all that is of value in the traditions, the philosophies, and the fancies of the past.[1] The phrase may be vague, but a poet has his own scheme of values, which is not the philosopher's nor the historian's. Much that to them is idle is to the poet significant, and he will not let it go. The result is one that might have been foreseen. Full of beauty, of suggestion, of moral worth and religious feeling, the book is not rigidly consistent with itself. Attempts have been made, notably one by Norden, to bring everything into harmony, but it must be owned that they have not been very happy. The question first to be answered is, whether it is conceivably possible to give a presentment of a world which none of us have seen, and to give it with the very considerable precision which marks Virgil's treatment as contrasted with the loose and vague descriptions of others, and not in doing it to involve oneself in contradictions.

Aeneas prepared for his journey by sacrificing in the most legitimate way, but if we are to form any strictly spiritual conception of that other world and its powers, what can we suppose to be the efficacy of sacrifice? If the world below (or beyond) is governed through and through by moral law, as Plato taught and as Virgil implies, what relevancy have black cattle? Would not some more moral preparation of heart be preferable? Of course it would seem so to a modern mind, but Virgil had not to part company with the religion of his fathers, bound up with which was, or seemed to be, what hope remained of the triumph of

[1] Cf. Servius *ad Aen.* vi. 719, *Miscet philosophiae figmenta poetica, et ostendit tam quod est vulgare, quam quod continet veritas et ratio naturalis.*

moral ideas in the Roman world. Similarly, what are we to make of the golden bough, which Aeneas must take to Proserpine? It is not, so far as we know, borrowed from any Greek apocalypse or other Greek source. It is not the golden tablet of the Orphic grave. However it may be connected with tree worship, as Dr Frazer's famous book suggests, Virgil is moving in a different order of ideas altogether from those primitive fancies and usages connected with woods and cornfields. It is quite possible that the thing is originally a symbol of something connected with Nature-worship; but in Virgil it is a borrowed symbol, and its precise significance it is hard, if not impossible, to guess. But we must not press the poet.

It will perhaps be enough to say that, just as to-day the ritual and symbolism of a rejected faith may appeal to the mind in which aesthetic considerations outweigh philosophy, —yes, and also in certain moods to the mind in which philosophy still rules, which refuses to accept any dogmata, whatever their aesthetic company, unless justified by reason, —so, side by side with all the teaching of Epicurus, Plato, Pythagoras, and the Stoics, a crowd of usages and fancies, dreams and hopes, from out of the past, appealed to the poet with all the charms of beauty and association. This appeal, not valid against the findings of reason, but surely valid so far as to claim the attention of philosophy, had at all events a claim to be heard in the highest court to which Virgil had access, that of poetic truth. We may not be able to reconcile by logic, still less perhaps by philosophy, all that Virgil tells us in this book, but it is all full of beauty, and beauty has a logic and philosophy of its own; its symbols are not to be treated as algebraic letters representing so many logical or philosophic ideas, into which they can be converted without trouble, but as combining to open avenues of thought and emotion by following which the mind will find itself at last not far from truth.

When the required sacrifices have been duly made, Aeneas and the Sibyl start their journey; and the poet addresses to the gods who rule over souls, to the shades and Chaos and Phlegethon, the prayer that he may be allowed to tell of what he has heard, of things in the depths of earth and night. Through darkness, solitude, night, and shadow, hero and Sibyl go through the vacuous land of Dis, the empty realms, as men feel their way through a wood on a night when the clouds about the moon give just enough light to make darkness visible.[1] About the very jaws of Hades hang Sorrow, Care, Disease, Age, Fear, Hunger, Toil, the common ills of man, and pre-eminent among the Furies (as one would expect of Virgil) death-dealing War and mad Discord. Here is the elm where nest vain dreams, and here the substanceless forms of Chimaeras, Scyllas, Gorgons, and Centaurs, separated by the river Acheron from the actual dwellings of the dead.

Acheron is reached, and Charon is seen. The poet draws him in a few lines with extraordinary life and power; no one would take him for a ghost or spirit, so lifelike he is with his rough garb and his crazy boat, his eyes of flame and his clear brain—

cruda deo viridisque senectus.

On the river banks are the throngs of the dead, many as the leaves of autumn, the fallen leaves. The simile is doubly effective, at once for its suggestion of mortality and the added awfulness of numbers. We never realize how many are the leaves till they fall, and here are the dead gathered from how many homes, here one and there one, swept together like the fallen leaves to one spot, impressive for their mere numbers, only here to be understood. To the simile of the leaves is added, as we saw, that of the birds. A blind instinct within drives the dead to Acheron, and teaches them they must cross it. The contrast with the simile in the *Georgics* has been already remarked, but a further point calls for attention here. As we saw, the picture in the *Georgics* was drawn with something of Virgil's early playfulness. Here the comparison with the birds is in keeping with the whole Virgilian Hades—life survives in some degree even in death, and the other world, void and

[1] See note on p. 16.

empty though it be in contrast with the Nature we know, is yet throbbing with earnestness and purpose. Right through the story, through the mythological, the religious, and the philosophic contributions, runs meaning, intention, effort. Every human personality we meet is touched with the sense of the seriousness of being. Life is not extinct at all; the soul is quit of its encumbrances and more in earnest than ever. It is the very antithesis of the Hades of the *Odyssey*. The Orphic and Platonic doctrine that the body is a tomb of the soul (σῶμα and σῆμα) we shall meet explicitly later on, but surely we have it here already implicitly.

Through the darkness comes a dim and sad figure—barely recognizable as the ghost of Palinurus, the unburied steersman.[1] This is clearly suggested by the similar episode in the *Odyssey*,[2] where Odysseus sees among the dead Elpenor, whom he had supposed to be alive. The ancient world at large had gloomy thoughts about the unburied and their lot in the other world, in spite of the assurance philosophers felt. We cannot imagine the appearance of such a story as this in the *Gorgias*, but the popular idea was long-lived. Four centuries later Synesius tells us that he and his fellow passengers on a ship in distress fastened gold or jewels to themselves in order to tempt any, who might find their dead bodies on the beach, to bury them in return for the gift they brought.[3] Elpenor was in no more distress than any other ghost. His desire for a grave was a natural one ; and his suggestion that he might become "a curse from the gods " (θεῶν μήνιμα) to Odysseus, if he were left unburied, is very far from the passionate sense of need which is marked in Palinurus. Virgil is here in close touch with popular sentiment, and though we may reconcile it somehow with the rest of his picture, we feel that philosophy has here waived its rights to poetry—and

---

[1] See the curious note of Servius *ad Aen.* vi. 340, who explains the dimness on the ground that Palinurus had not reached the *loca purgationis* ; the wiser, he says, say of souls in the world beyond, that *purgatae incipiunt esse clariores.*

[2] *Od.* xi. 51-80. See Miss F. Melian Stawell, *Homer and the Iliad*, p. 157.

[3] *Ep.* 4. Cf. Horace, *Odes*, i. 28, on the unburied Archytas.

perhaps to patriotism, for Cape Palinurus is our parting thought.

> Aeternumque locus Palinuri nomen habebit [1] (vi. 381).

Italy haunts the poet's mind even in Hades.

Once across Acheron Aeneas passes through five regions of Hades, about which there has been a great deal of controversy.[2] They are occupied respectively by children who died in infancy, by those unjustly condemned to death, by innocent people who have committed suicide, by unhappy lovers, and by those who have fallen in war. Norden wishes to group these five regions as one intermediate state, finding the common likeness among these five rather different classes of people in the fact that they all have been cut off prematurely. He produces a certain amount of evidence to show that views were current upon the ἄωροι or βιαιοθάνατοι, as such people were called, to the effect that they had to reach the period originally assigned to their lives before they could be properly ranked with the dead.[3] In this he is not generally followed. Fallen heroes, for example, do not belong to this class in any case, and if they did, it is hard to see why some should be in Elysium already (649) and others not. If Virgil had meant to represent all his five classes as βιαιοθάνατοι, he could, as Norden admits, have explained this in a line or two. He did not explain it, and Norden says it is not worth while to ask why he did not.[4] It is simpler and sounder not to attempt reconcilia-

---

[1] "For ever the place shall bear the name of Palinurus."

[2] See E. Norden, *Vergilstudien* in *Hermes*, 1893. See also Weil, *Études*, p. 88, and Dieterich *Nekyia*, 152, n., for criticisms of weight and significance upon Norden's views.

[3] e.g. Servius on *Aen.* iv. 386 *dicunt physici biothanatorum animas non recipi in originem suam nisi vagantes legitimum tempus fati compleverint.* Plato, *Rep.* x. 615 C, alludes, without explanation, to the condition below of those who die at birth.

[4] Norden's own words may be quoted. *Hermes*, 1893, p. 388: "Hätte Vergil nur mit *einem* Worte darauf hingedeutet, dass alle diese in der Zwischenregion sich aufhaltenden Seelen, wenn ihre Zeit erfüllt sei, aus diesem Ausnahmezustand erlöst werden, so wäre die missverständliche Auffassung dieser Stelle ausgeschlossen gewesen. Warum er es nicht gethan hat, ist überflüssig zu fragen : dass er keineswegs die Kenntniss dieser abstrusen Lehre bei seinen Lesern voraussetzen durfte, wird dadurch bewiesen, dass in den ausserordentlich

tions which the poet has not troubled to make. Norden's
thesis is that the book is a finished and consistent whole,
and to support this he feels that discrepancies must be
reconciled. But the almost casual allusion to Minos (431-3)
suggests incomplete revision; or, if it does not mean this,
it is surely significant that so vital and important a figure
is introduced in connexion with one small and insignificant
group of people.

But, whatever logical consistency we may introduce into
this passage by bringing all five classes under one description, it is important to remember that, even if Virgil meant
this, there still remains a moral inconsistency. We can
understand Plato putting infant children in a class by
themselves (*Rep*. x. 615 C); they at least have some claim
to a limbo of their own, as they are neither moral nor
immoral. The intermediate position in Hades held by the
spirits of adult persons of no very distinct moral character,
which Plato describes in the *Phaedo*, is also thoroughly
intelligible. But here some heroes are in Elysium, others
are not—why should mere lapse of time make such a difference? Among the lovers, too, Pasiphae, Phaedra, and
Dido seem widely different in character. Why should
Sychacus be here? It is clear that this grouping of the
lovers by themselves is an idea borrowed from the *Odyssey*.[1]
There is no philosophy about it. Take again the wounds
of Deiphobus—his ghostly form bears, like some of the
ghosts Odysseus saw,[2] the wounds his physical body
received at his death. That is, we think of Deiphobus
for ever as we saw him last. How wide the interval
between these wounds and the scars which the souls of
tyrants lay bare to Rhadamanthus in the *Gorgias!* In
fact, Virgil has sacrificed "consistency" to his endeavour
to use every thought, popular or philosophical, of the other

zahlreichen Nekyien der nachvergilischen Dichter trotz ihrer offenbaren, zum
Theil sehr starken Nachahmung des 6. Buches der Aeneis keine Spur deiser
Scheidung mehr vorhanden ist."

[1] The Elysium of good lovers is described by Tibullus (I. iii. 57 f.), and
contrasted with a Tartarus, which has a Tisiphone and the three great classic
sinners, &c. In fact, it is a literary tradition—and a charming one.

[2] *Od*. xi. 40.

world which could lend itself to poetic treatment and had beauty within it.

One point should be noticed, however, before we pass on. We have seen that those who killed themselves had been innocent, and that their unhappy position below is the result of their casting away their lives (*proiecere animas*). This condemnation of suicide was Pythagorean, and was afterwards a prominent feature in Neo-Platonism. One must not, said the Neo-Platonists, leave life so long as there is possibility of self-development.[1] "How gladly would they choose now," says Virgil, "in the air above to bear to the end poverty and hard toil" (438). Once more the tendency of his Hades is all against surrender, all for the earnest and strenuous life.

Inde datum molitur iter [2]

is said of Aeneas at the end of this passage (477), and his is pre-eminently a life in earnest.

Aeneas now reaches the parting of the ways.[3] On his left is Tartarus, which he does not visit, but which the Sibyl describes to him. In its awful abysses (the depth is twice that of Homer's old phrase)[4] there are of course the classical sinners of antiquity—Titans, Tityos, Ixion—but there are others of a more everyday order, sinners who have never indeed tried to overthrow Jove from his throne in heaven, but who in their own way have struck at those laws on which human society rests, who have betrayed their country for gold, who have sold justice, who have cheated their clients, committed adultery, and hated their brothers. The poet's language approaches, as near as it may, the phrase of the Twelve Tables,[5] that code which, down to Cicero's day at least, every schoolboy learnt by heart,[6] and

---

[1] Plotinus, *Enn.* i. 9 ; Porphyry, *vita Plotini*, 11 ; Macrobius, *Comm. Somn. Scip.* i. 13. 15-16.

[2] " Thence he presses on the path given."

[3] Plato, *Gorgias*, 524 A ; *Rep.* 614 C.

[4] *Il.* 8. 16 τόσσον ἔνερθ' Ἀΐδεω ὅσον οὐρανός ἐστ' ἀπὸ γαίης.

[5] Norden, *op. cit.*, p. 390 ; and Servius on *A.* vi. 609.

[6] Cicero, *de Legibus*, ii. 23, 59 *nostis quae sequuntur. Discebamus enim pueri xii. ut carmen necessarium, quas iam nemo discit.*

the very words of which must have risen to the minds of many of his readers. Once more Virgil has linked ancient and modern thought. His Tartarus may be an Orphic Tartarus, it may have elements from Homer and Hesiod, but the quiet power with which the poet subjects it all to the simple old code, to the fundamental laws of home and state, takes it out of the region of folklore and brings it home to men with a new force and a new seriousness. Plato had already established moral law beyond the grave, as we have seen, and had consigned most "dynasts" to Tartarus, but it was a new thing when Virgil so triumphantly asserted the divine right of the state. As Tartarus seems to have lain outside the circle of re-birth, the Sibyl could not well give instances of Roman sinners there, but the gap is made good on the shield of Aeneas, where Vulcan set in his picture of Tartarus no Tityos or Ixion, but Catiline,[1] while on the throne of Minos he set Cato.[2] A long period of individualism, and a much longer one of identification of duty to the state with duty to the privileged, have made it hard for us to-day to grasp Virgil's thought, but signs are not wanting that in our own re-mapping of Tartarus and Elysium, wherever we may place them, the claims of the state and of its ideals will not go unconsidered. Here at least we can hail *Maro vates gentilium*. But for the present we must return to Aeneas.

The Sibyl has now brought Aeneas to Elysium, "the glad region, the fair bowers of the glades of happiness, the home of the blest."[3] Here is the larger air, the bright light, of those old islands of the blest where the sons-in-law of the gods went in Homer's days; but another teacher has told mankind more about it all, and his is the first figure we recognize. "The Thracian priest in the long robe" is Orpheus, not the sad lover of the *Georgics*, but the teacher and purifier of mankind, clad as he is drawn in Orphic pictures. With him is Musaeus. Here (as in Pindar's *Dirge*) are the heroes of ancient days, still happy as of old

---

[1] Plutarch, later on, does the same with Nero ; *de sera numinum vindicta* 567 F.   [2] viii. 666-670.
[3] *A.* vi. 638. These *amoena virecta* are borrowed by Prudentius for the garden of Eden, *Cathemerinon*, iii. 101.

in song and dance and chariot. If one did not know how hard others have found it to give any picture of a Christian heaven, one might confess to a certain reminiscence of Alcinous and his Phaeacians here—

αἰεὶ δ᾽ ἡμῖν δαίς τε φίλη κίθαρίς τε χοροί τε.[1]

But we shall do better to notice who the company are. They are men who have bled for their country, holy priests, true poets, men who have enriched human life with the arts they have discovered, men who have made themselves names by doing service. Mark here again how Virgil borrows but remains independent. The whole atmosphere is Orphic, but that popular Orphism, which Plato denounced, is not here. No mention is made of mysteries or initiation, hardly any of the gods. As Hector in the *Iliad* dismissed divination, so Virgil dismisses initiation—

εἷς οἰωνὸς ἄριστος, ἀμύνεσθαι περὶ πάτρης.[2]

He looks at the state and at mankind in assessing the worth of a man's life. In his five doubtful regions we saw him fail a little in using canons of justice and righteousness, and here again, while we recognize the grandeur and worth of his teaching, we feel that Plato is on a higher level when he makes the final judgement turn on what a man *is*, rather than on what he has done. But, as we have seen, it was not the Roman's way to

Make his moral being his prime care.

At last Aeneas is face to face with his father's shade ; the avowed object of his descent into Hades is attained. In the dream in Sicily Anchises had bidden him come—" then shalt thou learn of all thy race and of the city to be given thee " (v. 737). So now, after a vain attempt at an embrace (like that of Odysseus in the *Odyssey*), Aeneas sees in a secluded valley of woods, by the side of a quiet stream,

---

[1] *Od.* viii. 248. " Ever to us is the banquet dear, the lyre and the dance."
[2] *Iliad* xii. 243. Polydamas wishes to draw an omen from a bird ; Hector rejoins : " The one best bird (omen)—is to fight for our country."

innumerable souls, many as the bees in summer.[1] Who are
they, he asks, and what is the river? It is Lethe, the river
of forgetfulness, the waters of which are drunk by souls
destined again to enter the body.[2] Here we touch once
more the teaching of the Orphics and Plato. Souls which
are to be free from the wheel of Birth drink of the spring
of Memory, according to the Orphics; and Plato tells
how souls returning to earthly life cross the plain of
Forgetfulness, and, reaching the river of Negligence (or
Forgetfulness, as he calls it later on), they are "all obliged
to drink a certain quantity, and those who are not saved
by wisdom drink more than is necessary and forget all
things."[3] Virgil avails himself of this Pythagorean and
Orphic teaching to enable Aeneas to see the souls of the
great Romans of the future. These great men we may
pass by, and consider instead the philosophy of life which
Anchises unfolds to his son.

> Know first, the heaven, the earth, the main,
> The moon's pale orb, the starry train,
>   Are nourished by a soul,
> A spirit whose celestial flame
> Glows in each member of the frame
>   And stirs the mighty whole.[4]
> Thence souls of men and cattle spring,
> And the gay people of the wing,
> And those strange shapes that ocean hides
> Beneath the smoothness of his tides.
> A fiery strength inspires their lives,
> An essence that from heaven derives,[5]

[1] The simile goes back surely to early days at Andes or Mantua, cf.
p. 14, n. 2.

[2] *A.* vi. 713 *animae quibus altera fato corpora debentur.* The comment of
Servius on this passage is most interesting, with its Neo-Platonic tinge.

[3] *Rep.* x. 621 A; Dieterich, *Nekyia*, p. 90; Miss Harrison, *Prolegomena*,
cited already.

[4] Cf. E. Caird, *Greek Philosophy* ii. 87-89; and the "Something far more
deeply interfused" of Wordsworth's *Tintern Abbey.*

[5] *Igneus est ollis vigor et caelestis origo* (730). Cf. the πνεῦμα διάπυρον of the
Stoics and their *divinae particula aurae*, Hor. *Sat.* ii. 2. 79, with Epictetus *D.*
ii. 8 σὺ ἀπόσπασμα εἶ τοῦ θεοῦ.

Though clogged in part by limbs of clay
And the dull " vesture of decay."
Hence wild desires and grovelling fears,
And human laughter, human tears : [1]
Immured in dungeon-seeming night,
They look abroad, yet see no light.
Nay, when at last the life has fled,
And left the body cold and dead,
E'en then there passes not away
The painful heritage of clay ;
Full many a long-contracted stain
Perforce must linger deep in grain.
So penal sufferings they endure
For ancient crime, to make them pure :
Some hang aloft in open view
For winds to pierce them through and through ·
While others purge their guilt deep-dyed
In burning fire or whelming tide.

743 Each for himself, we all sustain
The durance of our ghostly pain ;
Then to Elysium we repair,
The few, and breathe this blissful air :

745 Till, many a length of ages past,
The inherent taint is cleansed at last,
And nought remains but ether bright,
The quintessence of heavenly light.

748 All these, when centuries ten times told
The wheel of destiny have rolled,
The voice divine from far and wide
Calls up to Lethe's river-side,
That earthward they may pass once more
Remembering not the things before,
And with a blind propension yearn

751 To fleshly bodies to return.[3]

   The terminology of this passage is Stoic ; the matter shows indebtedness to Plato and the Neo-Pythagoreans. As in the

[1] Virgil is nearer the philosophers here, *dolent gaudentque.*
[2] Cf. the account given by Pythagoras of Homer's soul in Hades.
[3] *A.* vi. 724-51 (Conington).

famous passage in the *Georgics* (iv. 219-27), Virgil leans to the belief that all nature is alive with one divine life, permeating through race and individual. This life has a fiery origin and nature, which continues in the creature of flesh, except in so far as the body dulls and blunts its faculties by hope and fear, pain and pleasure, blinding it with the darkness of the prison-house—σῶμα, as we saw, being identical with σῆμα. The influence of the body survives death, and, as Plato taught us, the soul appears before its judge (though he is not mentioned in this passage) bearing all its scars and wounds and sickness. These have to be treated, as Plato and the Orphics said, till they are healed, and the treatment is punishment. And now we have reached the difficult part of the passage.

" We suffer, each a several ghost," [1] says Virgil, "and then we are sent through broad Elysium and a few of us abide (*tenemus*) in the happy fields." So far Plato and the others go with him, but our text continues amazingly—" until long days, a full orb of time, have taken away the ingrown stain and left untainted the aetherial sense and the pure spiritual flame (*aurai simplicis ignem*). All these, when the wheel has revolved for them a thousand years, the god calls in vast array to Lethe's stream, that in forgetfulness they may see once more the dome of sky above, and begin again to wish to return to the body." The confusion is obvious. Do the elect who *hold* the happy fields go through purification and then drink of Lethe? are all involved in the "wheel"? Are there two purgations—one before Elysium is reached, one within it?

The general teaching of the school which Virgil is here following is clear, and various attempts have been made to reconcile his text with his teachers. Should we transpose ll. 743, 744 with ll. 745-7? " This and that soul are purged with wind, water, and fire, till long time has taken away the stain and left the fiery nature pure. Each suffers in his

---

[1] *Quisque suos patimur manes* (*A.* vi. 743). This famous phrase Servius explains by reference to the doctrine of the *genius*. *Nam cum nascimur, duos genios sortimur: unus qui hortatur ad bona, alter qui depravat ad mala.* The doctrine is important in the history of religion, but its introduction illustrates the commentator rather than the poet.

spirit; a few hold (for ever) the happy fields. All these (with a wave of the hand to the souls on Lethe's brink), as distinguished from the few, drink of Lethe and are reborn." To this it is objected the Anchises has not had to wait "a full orb of time." His purgation has been at the very longest a year. It may be replied that our Orphic gold tablets suppose the buried Orphic to become a god at once; and also—a sounder argument—that Virgil is inconsistent and does not mind being inconsistent. The second remedy is to put ll. 745-7 last of all, i.e. "these, the ordinary run of men, continue to be born over and over again, they drink Lethe, revisit the light, till after a full orb of time the ingrown taint is at last removed." This, like the other transposition, gives us good Orphism, but in neither case is it explained how the order of the passage came to be upset. The third remedy is that of Dieterich. He puts a pause in the speech at the mention of the few who reach and keep Elysium (l. 744). Then Anchises begins (a little rhetorically) by an immense inversion—" Until long time has purged them, &c., *these* (with great emphasis and a most marked wave of the spectral hand) the god keeps calling to Lethe and sending to fresh bodies." It is hard to credit the shade of Anchises with so much rhetoric. Fourthly, Norden cuts the knot by saying that we have here two recensions, quite distinct, but both by Virgil, one of which the poet meant to reject; and that Varius, finding both in the manuscript, and, not clear which to choose himself, left every reader the same freedom and perplexity.[1] If Varius did this, it may be permissible for us to come to no decision.

We have now seen Virgil's Hades, and we have dealt, in a summary way enough, with its relations to the various descriptions which the poet knew of the abode and the life of the dead. What does it all mean? We shall probably not try to make one consistent scheme of elements taken from sources so wide apart in time and thought. The traditional and the philosophical, the new and the old,

---

[1] See, on the whole passage, Dieterich, *Nekyia*, pp. 154-60 (full of interest); Norden, *Vergilstudien* (*Hermes*, 1893), pp. 395-402; Ettig, *Acheruntica* (*Leipziger Studien*, 1891), pp. 349 ff. ; Rohde, *Psyche*³, ii. 165 Anm.

nave all their charm and their suggestion for us, but if we attempt to apply a rigid logic to them, we shall lose much and gain very little. But we have none the less to ask our poet what truth he is embodying for us here; what truth he had consciously in mind when he wrote. Had he, apart from inconsistencies superficial or fundamental, any clear idea to convey; or does he mean by the ivory gate, through which Aeneas leaves Hades, a hint to us that the best in this kind are but shadows, that we have been dreaming dreams with no interpretation?[1] Let us go back to Plato for a moment.

"I do not mean to affirm that the description which I have given of the soul and her mansions is exactly true— a man of sense ought hardly to say that. But I do say that, inasmuch as the soul is shown to be immortal, he may venture to think, not improperly or unworthily, that something of the kind is true. The venture is a glorious one, and he ought to comfort himself with words like these, which is the reason why I lengthen out my tale. Wherefore, I say, let a man be of good cheer about his soul, who has cast away the pleasures and ornaments of the body as alien to him, and rather hurtful in their effects, and has followed after the pleasures of knowledge in this life; who has adorned the soul in her own proper jewels, which are temperance, and justice, and courage, and nobility, and truth—in these arrayed she is ready to go on her journey to the world below, when her time comes."[2]

Is this Virgil's meaning? Would he go so far? Possibly not quite so far. He would tell us perhaps: "This and that is what men have said about the other life. Epicurus and Lucretius utterly denied it all, but, as Cephalus said,[3] it comes back upon one, and one does not altogether know what to think. Yet one or two things seem probable —if there is another life, it must be like this life in the main; it must be bound up with love and under the sway of moral law. One thing is certain—that of

---

[1] *Et poetice apertus est sensus: vult autem intellegi falsa esse omnia quae dixit,* says Servius.

[2] *Phaedo,* 114, Jowett's translation. [3] Plato's *Republic* i. 330, D.

all that men do, service of the state or humanity is the best worth doing. If there are rewards for anything, they must be for this—Cicero, you will remember, says the same in his myth. As to your personal immortality or mine being assured, we shall know better by and by—and, after all, what does it matter, if he is not to see his Tullia, and I—? Did you notice what Anchises said?

> Venisti tandem, tuaque expectata parenti
> vicit iter durum pietas?[1]

Meanwhile there is our earth here."

[1] " Art thou come at last ; and has that love thy father looked to conquered the hardness of the way?" (*A.* vi. 687).

CHAPTER XI

INTERPRETATION OF LIFE.—4. OLYMPUS

The souls of now two thousand years
Have laid up here their toils and fears,
And all the earnings of their pain,—
Ah ! yet consider it again.

We ! what do we see? each a space
Of some few yards before his face ;
Does that the whole wide plan explain ?
Ah ! yet consider it again !—   CLOUGH.

LUCAN'S *Pharsalia*, as Voltaire remarked, is distinguished from all other ancient epics by the bold omission of the whole mythological apparatus, which tradition, resting upon Homer, had exacted of the poets.[1] Lucan was a young man, and he had that intolerance of old ways and old ideas which is often, though not always, a sign of promise.   Antiquity—

famosa vetustas
miratrixque sui [2]—

had for centuries encumbered its poetry with gods in whom men had ceased to believe, and it is one of the merits of the *Pharsalia* that its author resolved to be independent of artifice so outworn and so insincere, and to give to his readers a poem resting on the actual and the real.   If he was not successful, if his poem fails of poetic truth, he was at least so far honest.

The noble lines spoken by Cato, though marked by Lucan's inevitable haste and rhetoric, still take us nearer to the truth of things than any epic machinery—

Haeremus cuncti superis, temploque tacente
nil facimus non sponte dei . . .

---

[1] Voltaire, *Essai sur la poésie épique*, ch. iv. (vol. x. p. 437).
[2] *Phars.* iv. 654, "antiquity with its tales and its admiration of itself."

18   273

estque dei sedes nisi terra et pontus et aer
et caelum et virtus? superos quid quaerimus ultra?
Iuppiter est, quodcunque vides, quodcunque moveris.[1]

The poet is in touch with the same thought which Virgil
expresses in the *Georgics*—

esse apibus partem divinae mentis et haustus
aetherios dixere : deum namque ire per omnes
terrasque tractusque maris caelumque profundum [2]

(*G.* iv. 220).

Yet a critic of Lucan's day, a man not without discernment or literary skill, was moved to write two or three
hundred lines of a *Pharsalia* of his own, to show how it
ought to be done. The main defect of Lucan would appear
to be that he had left out the gods.[3] That Statius had the
gods in his *Thebaid* was natural enough; it was the right
place for them. But Silius Italicus could not let Hannibal
fight at Cannae without the co-operation of Juno and Aeolus
and Anna Perenna. Three hundred years later Claudian could
find no better explanation of the power of a prime minister,
whom he disliked, than the direct intervention of the
fury Megaera on the motion of a conference of infernal
authorities [4]—a view which may appeal to us as politicians
more than it will to serious lovers of poetry.

Every one of these writers would probably shield himself
with the great name of Virgil—and Virgil was, or had been,
an Epicurean. It is a question which the student of Virgil
has to face—How comes an Epicurean poet to introduce
so much of Olympus into his last and crowning work,
and what does he mean by it? It is, of course, easy to say

---

[1] *Phars.* ix. 573-80. "We are all of us bound up with the gods, and though
the shrine be silent, there is nothing we do without God's will. . . . Nay! is
there an abode of God, save earth and sea and air and sky and virtue? Why
seek we gods outside ? Jupiter is all you see and all that lives within you!"

[2] " Some have said that bees have received a share of the divine intelligence,
a draught from aether ; God, they tell us, pervades all, earth and the expanse of
sea, and the deep vault of heaven."

[3] Petronius puts the poem into the mouth of Eumolpus. Boissier,
L'Opposition, ch. v. p. 244, holds that Eumolpus expresses his creator's view;
E. Thomas, in his *Pétrone*, without going so far as to deny this, questions it.

[4] See the opening of *In Rufinum*.

that he is following Homer, but a little study of the *Aeneid* reveals the influence of other leaders. For example, Euripides is an author whom Virgil studied closely; Plato and Pythagoras, the Stoics and Epicurus, have contributed to the growth of his mind, directly or indirectly. If we admit that literary convention required the introduction of the Homeric gods, are the gods of the *Aeneid* Homeric? How do they accommodate themselves in the poet's mind to the company of the philosophers? When we have analysed the various elements from various sources which are combined in Virgil's pantheon, we have still to explain Virgil's attitude towards the divine. The study is not merely a literary one, but it is a chapter in the history of religion, and an important one, for in Virgil we have a forerunner of the great religious revival of the Roman Empire.

I

Whatever unity there may be in a man's conceptions of God and of the universe, it is almost impossible that there should not be among them survivals from systems which he has inherited and outgrown. Just as the "life-history" of the individual man is a sort of epitome of the history of the race, the analysis of his opinions will tend to show in measure a similar history of the thinking of mankind, and if he will take the trouble to trace the origins and affinities of his ideas, he may very well find points where he is in contact with almost every stage of religious thought. A great part of the religious life is the habit of constantly re-thinking the old in the terms of the new —it is a long and confusing process for the individual and for the race, but any one who is pursuing it and who will study the record of his own mind will bring a new insight and sympathy to the study of the thinkers of the past.

When, in this temper, we try to understand the presentment of the divine which we find in Homer,[1] we are

---

[1] For the moment it is not very material whether "Homer" is one man or several.

impressed first by the confusion of the ideas,[1] and then by the fact that there is an order in this confusion. For as soon as we realize that we are looking at things in perspective, and are following the processes of thought still moving onward, it becomes easier to grasp the relations of the parts of the picture left upon our minds.

Far away upon the horizon we see dimly the awful and disgusting figures of the old gods, dethroned by Zeus, and the monsters, children of earth, Titans, and so forth, of whose struggles with Zeus and his dynasty broken fragments of narrative tell us a little, but enough.[2] In Hesiod these ancient powers are still in the foreground, and they re-emerge from time to time in various forms in the history of Greek religion. They, and not the true household of Homer's Zeus, lie behind the mysteries which Clement of Alexandria attacked. They emerge again for the last time in the epic of Nonnus, monstrous as themselves, though here Neo-Platonism is doing its best to keep them rational and clean. In fact, we might almost say that in religious thought action and re-action are equal as well as opposite, for wherever a great step in advance has to be taken, those who refuse it seem to take as great a step, but backwards.

However, in Homer, these gods, whom we may call (though he does not) rude embodiments of forces of Nature, observed but not yet brought into subjection to law, are already towards or upon the horizon, and the divine beings in the foreground are made in the likeness of man. How great an achievement this was is hinted in the legends of the wars of Zeus. It was a triumph, hard-won, but a triumph indeed. " The soul," says M. Girard, " a prey to darkness and uncertainty, oppressed and timorous, the slave of matter and external nature, had re-acted against the forces that crushed it, and set to work to conceive them in accord with laws which its instinct divined. Its first act was to clothe them in human form. In whatever century it happened, it

---

[1] It is one of the dangers of the anthropologist to project his own confusion upon the primitive man, who sees only one order of ideas, while the inquirer is conscious of several. Homer, however, is very little more " primitive " than Shakespeare.

[2] See Gomperz, *Greek Thinkers*, pp. 28-30 ; also pp. 38, 39 for Hesiod.

was the awakening of the Greek spirit, the barriers were removed from the activity of the intelligence. It was the outcome of an effort, great in itself, greater still in its consequences." [1]

The process had been begun, which philosophy was to continue—intelligence rather than brute strength becomes the characteristic of a god. Passion may influence the divine being, but it is human passion and intelligent, it is no longer blind fury. Poseidon hates Odysseus, but for clear reasons which any rational being can understand. Poseidon is in fact a personality. Yet he is more. If the Titans and their kind were forces of nature, we may call the new gods powers of nature—and the difference is great. This is clear, for instance, in Homer's Poseidon. " There came he and yoked beneath his car his bronzen-footed horses, swift to fly, with long manes of gold ; and he arrayed himself in gold, and grasped a golden well-wrought whip, and stepped upon the car, and drove across the waves ; and the sea-beasts came from their chambers everywhere, and gambolled beneath him, knowing well their king ; and the rejoicing sea parted before him ; swiftly the horses flew, and the bronzen axle was not wet beneath." [2] Here we have the ruler of the sea, whose rule, like all ideal rule, means harmony, and at the same time we have the intensely human god. The two are combined in one. The "ancient feud of philosophy and poetry " [3] has hardly begun, or at least it is not yet acute.

There is also progress to be seen within the Homeric poems. In the *Iliad* Athene plucks Achilles by the hair to check him. In the *Odyssey* she speaks to the mind of Odysseus, suggesting a thought rather than uttering a command. [4] To say that the conception of the goddess has

---

[1] Girard, *Le Sentiment religieux en Grèce*, bk. i. ch. ii. on "the Gods of Homer and Hesiod," p. 42. I have omitted phrases and sentences in the passage quoted. See also Professor John Watson, *Christianity and Idealism*, ch. ii.

[2] *Iliad*, xiii. 23-30, Purves.

[3] Plato, *Rep.* x. p. 607 B παλαιὰ μέν τις διαφορὰ φιλοσοφίᾳ τε καὶ ποιητικῇ.

[4] Cf. also *Iliad*, xv. 80, " As when the mind of a man runs up and down, a traveller over much of earth, and he thinks in his deep heart, ' Would I were here or there,' in his keen desire ; as swift as that did lady Hera fly."

become more "spiritual" might be ambiguous in view of
Christian terminology. Yet the gods are beginning to
connect themselves with moral as well as with physical law.
Zeus is "protector of those rights on which depend all the
relations of men with one another." He is god of the oath,
of the family, of the suppliant, the herald and the beggar.
There are signs, dim and intermittent, that he will yet be
the sole and supreme god.[1]

In a famous passage Homer gives a premonition of this
future faith, though in a strangely anthropomorphic garb.
"Make trial," says Zeus, "if ye will, that all may know; let
down a golden chain from heaven to earth, and all ye gods
and goddesses take hold; but ye will not draw down Zeus,
the most high counsellor, from heaven to the ground,
no, not with much endeavour. But were I to draw, and put
to my strength, I could updraw you all and earth and sea to
boot, and bind the chain about a horn of Olympus, and
leave all hanging."[2]

But after all, it is neither as powers of nature nor as
guardians of moral law that the Homeric gods make their
strongest impression upon the reader : it is rather as a society
of very human persons. One is tempted at first to think
that their individual characters as presented in the poems
are survivals of an earlier age, for it is clear that human
morality is far in advance of divine. No one in heaven, in
the best circle of heaven, has at all the moral grandeur
of Achilles, Hector or Sarpedon. Yet while this suggestion
may be partly true, it is also to be remembered that the
god closely resembles the Greek tyrant of a later day.
"Absolute power," says Herodotus, "would set even the best

---

[1] Cf. Girard, *Le Sentiment religieux*, p. 59, "C'était un monothéisme incomplet
et grossier." Cf. also Watson, *Christianity and Idealism*, p. 29, "Even in Homer
there are elements which show that the Greek religion must ultimately accomplish
its own euthanasia. There was in it from the first a latent contradiction which
could not fail to manifest itself openly at a later time."

[2] *Iliad*, viii. 18-26, Purves. This chain is turned by Plato into the sun,
Theaetetus, 153 c. Macrobius and the Neo-Platonists made it into the
descent in being from the Supreme One through all nature. *Comm. Somn.
Scip.* i. 14, 15. The English reader will remember how Spenser, speaking of
"this worlds faire workmanship," thinks of "that great golden chaine," "with
which it blessed Concord hath together tide."

of men outside the customary thoughts."[1] The Homeric
god has not the safeguard that lies for us in consciousness
of limitations. The gods are stronger than men, but they
have no moral or spiritual superiority whatever.[2]

The gods then are a community of immortals living on
Olympus, and Zeus is their king. When they meet in
council, they can remonstrate with Zeus, but they dare not
oppose him. They have their own functions and their
relative dignities, though there is occasional vagueness in
these. On the other hand, their characters are clearly and
strongly marked. Homer's gods are as individual as his
heroes, and their histories are as well known. The sensu-
ality and favouritism of Zeus are not cloaked. He likes
sacrifices, he enjoys the strife of the Olympians;[3] he is cut
to the heart by the death of Sarpedon; and he indulges
in furious outbreaks of anger against other gods. Hera out-
wits and cajoles him easily and successfully, though she
too has suffered from his anger.[4] She is of all the immortals
the most unpleasant; she is very powerful, quite unscrupulous, and frankly savage. Zeus twits her with the will to
eat Priam and Priam's sons alive. Poseidon is similarly
arbitrary and unrestrained in his animosities. Athene and
Apollo are of all the gods the most rational and honourable.
Athene is the cleverest and most effective of all the
Olympian deities, though " she will never be forgiven for the
last betrayal of Hector."[5] Apollo is a genial god, prophet,
giver of oracles, and lord of the bow, but hardly as yet the
sun-god, for Êelios (Helios) is a distinct personality, nor yet
god of healing, for that place is taken by Paieon. As
god of the Lycians and lord of Chrysa he befriends the
Trojans. Aphrodite is a goddess of great power, but yet
contemptible. Athene urges Diomedes not to fear her on
the field of battle, and thus encouraged he wounds Aphrodite
on the wrist without incurring any special censure from

---

[1] Hdt. iii. 80 ἐκτὸς τῶν ἐωθότων νοημάτων.

[2] Mr Andrew Lang, in *The World of Homer* (1910) p. 120, draws a distinction,
well worth noting, between the religion of Homer, "a good faith to live and
die in," and his mythology.

[3] *Iliad*, xx. 22.   [4] *Iliad*, i. 586-94.

[5] Gilbert Murray, *Ancient Greek Literature*, p. 36.

higher powers.[1] She is harsh and cruel, as, for instance, with Helen; and in the lay of Demodocus in the *Odyssey* the most explicit tale is told of her humiliation in the net of Hephaestus.

II

Had oxen or had lions but had hands
Wherewith to draw and work such work as men,
They too had painted pictures of the gods,
And given them bodies like unto their own;
The horse's god were horse, the cow's a cow.[2]

So wrote Xenophanes of Colophon in the sixth century B.C., and in this vigorous fashion called the attention of the Greeks to the fact that anthropomorphism was outworn. Asiatic Greece had fallen before the Persians, and in long wandering and observation the philosopher had pondered the matter and had found the explanation in the low moral standards of his people, and these he connected with their religion. Homer and Hesiod, whom the Greeks regarded as the founders of their religion, he attacked in epic, elegy, and iambic, for what they said of the gods.

Homer and Hesiod cast against the gods
All that is shame and blame among mankind.
The gods, they said, work all unrighteousness,
They steal, deceive, commit adultery.[3]

Himself perhaps the first geologist, impressed by Nature and her power, and by the vast variety of human opinion, he made no gods in human or other form; yet he allowed gods to be, but thought of One Supreme, "a uniform and all-pervading power, governing the universe as the soul governs the body, endowing it with motion and animation, but inseparably bound up with it." He was, says Aristotle, "the

---

[1] Dione, in consoling Aphrodite, threatens Diomedes very gently, *Il.* v. 381-415. Contrast *Aen.* xi. 269-77, where Diomedes speaks of his act. The change of tone is noticeable.

[2] Ritter and Preller (sixth ed.) § 83. Clem. Alex. *Strom.* v. § 109, p. 715 P. Cf. the ironical passage in Heine *Atta Troll*, viii. on bear-theology.

[3] Ritter and Preller, § 82. Sextus Empiricus *Adv. Math.* i. 289; ix. 193.

first partisan of the One." The attack upon the gods springs from a higher conception of the divine nature, and it is made by one "god-intoxicated"—a phenomenon which will recur.[1]

Within a century these views of the gods had found a more enduring position in literature. A poet, the most popular after Homer of all Greek poets, steeped in the teaching of the philosophers, and above all things impressed by man's capacity for wretchedness, set the legends of Olympus side by side with human misery, and left the world to draw its inferences. Dissatisfaction had long been felt with the moral content of the popular religion, but so far the great poets, Pindar, Aeschylus,[2] and, in measure, Sophocles had accepted the religion and endeavoured to inspire it with higher conceptions of God and more serious ideals of duty.[3] It was not to be done. The new thoughts refused to blend with the old legends. Euripides realized this, and instead of trying to blend them he contrasted them.[4]

A striking example of this contrast is to be found in the *Troades*. The play begins with a dialogue between Poseidon and Athena. The goddess complains that the Greeks have treated her and her temple with disrespect—Ajax has violated its technical sanctity without comment or rebuke. She proposes to destroy the fleet, and Poseidon agrees. God and goddess bury their old quarrel in their desire for revenge, for it is nothing else. And all the while in the dirt at their feet Hecuba is lying unpitied. The gods are coolly discussing their own trivial wrongs, and they never betray the slightest feeling for the great queen's

---

[1] For Xenophanes see Gomperz, *Greek Thinkers*, bk. ii. ch. i. Burnet, *Early Greek Philosophy* (2nd ed., 1908) §§ 55-62 ; Adam, *Religious Teachers of Greece*, pp. 198 ff. The question of the monotheism of Xenophanes is remote from our present purpose. The quotation in the text is from Gomperz (on whom, however, see Burnet's criticism) ; it is he too who borrows for Xenophanes the phrase "god-intoxicated" from Novalis, who used it of Spinoza. The geology is proved from Hippolytus, *Ref. Haer.* i. 14, who tells of his speculations about fossil shells found near Syracuse : ταῦτα δέ φησι γενέσθαι ὅτε πάντα ἐπηλώθησαν πάλαι, τὸν δὲ τύπον ἐν τῷ πηλῷ ξηρανθῆναι. Aristotle, *Met.* A. 5. 986 b 21, cited by Burnet.

[2] Cf. Butcher, *Aspects of Greek Genius*, p. 108.   [3] Butcher, *op. cit.*, p. 44.

[4] Cf. Dr Verrall's *Euripides the Rationalist*, and his introduction to *Ion*.

misery and widowhood, for the fallen city, the captive women, or the fatherless children. With a tenderness and sympathy, hardly to be equalled in literature, Euripides paints the incredible anguish of Hecuba, deepening with every scene in the play, yet not crushing her capacity for helping others to bear their sorrows. In the *Hecuba* the horror of the triumph touches even the conqueror. "All is well done," says Agamemnon, "if in such things aught is well"[1]—but here god and goddess are utterly indifferent to it all. The spectator and the reader of the play are left to draw their own inferences.

It is the same in the *Ion*, where we have the story of the rape of a girl by Apollo.[2] Years afterwards she herself tells with the clear and precise detail, which belongs to painful memories, how she exposed the child of shame, and how the little thing's helpless hands have been before her eyes ever since.

The Servant: τίς γάρ νιν ἐξέθηκεν ; οὐ γὰρ δὴ σύ γε.
Creusa: ἡμεῖς, ἐν ὄρφνῃ σπαργανώσαντες πέπλοις . . .
The Servant: τλήμων σὺ τόλμης· ὁ δὲ θεὸς μᾶλλον σέθεν.
Creusa: εἰ παῖδα γ᾽ εἶδες χεῖρας ἐκτείνοντά μοι.[3]

Homer has many allusions to such legends, but no one had thought them out before Euripides.

When Aristophanes attacked Euripides and said that the drift of his tragedies was atheism,[4] it is clear that, if we understand atheism in the sense intended, the charge was just. At the same time it would be difficult to see how belief in the traditional gods was fostered by the author of the *Frogs* and the *Birds*, if the orthodox were not

---

[1] *Hec.* 731 τἀκεῖθεν γὰρ εὖ πεπραγμέν᾽ ἐστίν, εἴ τι τῶνδ᾽ ἐστὶν καλῶς.

[2] The choric ode in which Creusa tells the tale is indescribably powerful, Euripidean *in excelsis*, ll. 881-906. The reader may compare the tale of Iamos in Pindar, *Olympian* vi. 47-63.

[3] *Serv.* "Who was it that exposed him? Surely not thou."
  Cre. "I did it in the darkness, wrapped in swaddling bands " . . .
  Serv. "Stern must thou have been to dare it ; and the god more."
  Cre. "If thou hadst *seen* the child, reaching his hands to me."

[4] Ar. *Thesm.* 450:
  νῦν δ᾽ οὗτος ἐν ταῖσιν τραγῳδίαις ποιῶν
  τοὺς ἄνδρας ἀναπέπεικεν οὐκ εἶναι θεούς.

always entitled to more freedom of speech than their critics.
Yet the indignation of Euripides against the gods is not
atheism at all ; it is revolt against inadequate views of God.
The only enemy that a religion or a theology need fear is
one in closer touch with truth and morality ; and, however
vague in a general way the theology of Euripides may have
been, it at least set truth and morality in the forefront of
everything. To associate God and immorality was to lie;
it was better to say God meant morality, even if nothing
more was said. "God," said Plato, "should always be
represented as he really is."[1]

In discussing education, Plato, it would appear, went out
of his way to make a slashing attack on Homer, but on
further study it becomes clear that Homer stood directly in
his path, and with him Hesiod. These two poets, Herodotus says,[2] had made the Greek theogony ; the Greeks had
learnt from them "whence the several gods had their origin,
and whether they were all from the beginning and of what
form they were" ; they gave their titles to the gods, and
distributed to them honours and arts and set forth their
forms. These poets formed the basis of Greek education.
"I will quote the poem," says Aeschines, "for I suppose we
learn the thoughts of the poets when we are boys that we
may use them when we are men."[3]

Plato, however, held that education began with religion,
and when he looked at the religious teaching of these two
poets he peremptorily banished them from his ideal state.
"If we would have our guardians grow up to be as godlike
and godfearing as it is possible for man to be,"[4] such teaching would be intolerable. The object of life was assimila-
tion to God—εἰς ὅσον δυνατὸν ἀνθρώπῳ ὁμοιοῦσθαι θεῷ.[5] "We
must not," then, "tell a youthful listener that he will be
doing nothing extraordinary if he commit the foulest
crimes, nor yet if he chastise the crimes of a father in the
most unscrupulous manner, but will simply be doing what
the first and greatest of the gods did.[6] . . . Nor yet is it

---

[1] *Rep.* 379 A οἷος τυγχάνει ὁ θεὸς ὤν, ἀεὶ δήπου ἀποδοτέον.   [2] Hdt. ii. 55.
[3] Aeschines, *in Ctesiph.* 135, quoting Hesiod.   [4] *Rep.* ii. 383 C.
[5] Ibid. x. 613 A.   [6] A reference to Hesiod's *Theogony, e.g.* l. 490.

proper to say in any case—what is indeed untrue—that gods wage war against gods, and intrigue and fight among themselves ; . . . Stories like the chaining of Hera by her son, and the flinging of Hephaestus out of heaven for trying to take his mother's part when his father was beating her,[1] and all those battles of the gods which are to be found in Homer, must be refused admittance to our state, whether they are allegorical or not." [2] But what, asks Adeimantus in the dialogue, is to be the type of our stories about the gods ? [3] Plato lays down two canons—first, that God is good and the cause of good alone ; the second, that God is true and incapable of change or deceit. It was to be some time, however, before the poets would definitely accept these canons, yet they made themselves felt in poetry none the less.

A turning-point had been reached in the war between philosophy and polytheism. The Olympians had borne the brunt of the first campaign, and had been hopelessly defeated. The decline of the Greek city state completed their rout. Their cults were bound up with the existence of the city state, and passed away with it.[4] Their names remained, but the real issue was fought elsewhere. The second campaign was one, we may say, of guerilla warfare. The gods no longer "come forth into the light of things," they keep to the bush. Apollo and Athene had been destroyed by being seen. The new gods were not seen except by the initiated. Secret rituals and mysteries kept them out of sight and in safety. They had no legends like those of the Olympians, but they had myths. When attacked, they entrenched themselves behind symbol and allegory, and passed themselves off as philosophic conceptions. Their cults may be dignified by the name of Nature-worship, but

---

[1] *Il.* i. 586-94.

[2] Ibid. ii. 377 to end ; iii. 392 ; echoed by Cicero, *N. D.* i. 16. 42.

[3] Ibid. 379 A οἱ τύποι περὶ θεολογίας.

[4] Cf. Watson, *Christianity and Idealism*, p. 20, on polytheism, "as the vehicle for the religious ideal of peoples who cannot conceive of a wider bond than that of the nation, or of the nation, as other than a political unity based upon the natural tie of blood " ; and p. 22, " The Greeks only reached this stage (Monotheism) when their narrow civic state had already revealed its inadequacy."

their practice was a mixture of ritual and obscenity—a religion of harlots.[1]

Religion offered a choice between Cleanthes and (let us say) Diana of the Ephesians, and literature for the moment did not care greatly for either. It shifted its quarters from Athens to Alexandria, and in the splendid isolation of the Museum, "the birdcage of the Muses,"[2] devoted itself to pedantry and prettiness, and paid the penalty of apostasy from reality in the loss of every human interest.

The learned poets of Alexandria were Virgil's early models, and it is so far of importance to realize their attitude toward the gods. They are catholic enough in their taste, for any and every divine legend or myth is acceptable to them, but they write with neither the good faith of Hesiod, the moral sense of Aeschylus, nor Plato's indignation. The type of story they prefer to tell about the gods is exactly that which Plato would censure, though the poets might have defended themselves by the plea that nothing which they wrote was likely to have any wide effect in the corruption of morals. They wrote for the learned, for an audience which was far past believing at all in any Olympus except as literary material. When they used the mythology it was almost a sign that they were not serious.

Yet when Apollonius set about writing his *Argonautica*, his intention was to create a serious epic, in which skill might supply the place of faith. But, as Boissier puts it, it is vain to cherish the firm resolve to be antique ; a man always belongs to his own age in spite of himself.[3] Apollonius is writing of a pre-Homeric age, for his heroes belong to an earlier generation than Homer's, yet his Zeus is a much later Zeus than the Zeus of the *Iliad*.[4] The other gods also bear upon them marks of a later date. The steady tendency of thought away from polytheism made daily broader the gulf between Zeus and the gods, for while he

[1] Cf. Catullus, 10. 26 ; the *Attis* ; Ovid, *Am.* iii. 10. Plutarch's tract *de Iside et Osiride* is a defence, with admissions.

[2] Μουσέων ἐν ταλάρῳ, a phrase of Timon of Phlius, quoted by Athenaeus, 22 D.

[3] *La Religion romaine*, i. 193.

[4] So de la Ville de Mirmont, *Apollonius de Rhodes et Virgile*, p. 217. I have drawn a good deal here and elsewhere from this most ample of all treatises.

gained by it, as bearing the only available name for a god who could be conceived of as supreme, the rest proportionately lost ground.[1] He became a philosophic conception; they became literary toys. Consequently in the *Argonautica* Zeus is a remote and invisible power, ruling the moral and physical universe alone,—well on the way, one might say, to the eventual god of the philosophers, of whom nothing whatever, not even being, could be predicated.[2]

The other gods would recognize themselves in Ovid's pantheon. Goddesses who have private rooms, who use dainty golden combs, who pay one another surprise visits, who are threatened by their little sons, are mere ornaments, mere literary prettiness, as little divine in literature as in art. As a result, de la Ville de Mirmont remarks the real want of relation between gods and men. There are no prayers but official ones. Zeus is above and beyond prayer; the rest of the gods are hardly likely to awake it. Yet the Argonauts were by no means impious—(they were initiated into the rites of Samothrace)—it is only that prayer is not a thing that would occur to the mind.

The Argonauts are so far, to all intents and purposes, Epicureans. Such gods as there are do not come into a practical man's calculations; they are a negligible quantity.[3] It will be more convenient to deal with Epicureanism in the form in which it made its main appeal to Virgil—the *de Rerum Natura.*

III

So far we have been considering the literary influences of Greece upon the conceptions of the gods embodied in

[1] See Gardner, *Manual*, p. 124. Boissier, *La Religion romaine*, i. 254, speaking of Jupiter by Virgil's day, sums up the same tendency thus : " Il est devenu tout à fait le dieu des dieux, celui en qui les autres doivent finir par s'absorber, et qui profite tous les jours des progrès que fait le monothéisme." Cf. Plutarch, *de defectu oraculorum*, 426 D, the contrast between ὁ μὲν Ὁμηρικὸς Ζεύς and ὁ δ' ἀληθινός.

[2] See Hatch, *Hibbert Lectures*, lect. ix. pp. 254, 255, on the Gnostic οὐκ ὢν θεός who is ἀνεννόητος καὶ ἀνούσιος. "God, who was not, without thought, without perception, without will, without purpose, without passion, without desire, willed to make a world," said a Gnostic (quoted by Hippolytus 7, 21), who then proceeded to explain away the words "willed" and "world."

[3] Cf. Tertullian, *ad Nationes*, ii. 2 *Epicurei [deum esse volunt] otiosum et in-exercitatum et, ut ita dixerim, neminem.*

the *Aeneid.* We have now to look at the Roman world, and to note the attitude to things divine which prevailed in Virgil's Italy. The treatment must be in bare outline.

The Italian pantheon is at once remarkable for the number of its gods and for their obscurity. To paraphrase a few words of St Augustine, it is as if "all human goods were set out with minute particularity," and they tried "to provide a minute and particular god for every one of them." [1] For every contingency in life a god or goddess was provided, and the whole of life was pervaded by this crowd of little gods (*turba minutorum deorum*),[2] though some of them must have had an activity of only a few minutes or seconds. Thus Cunina watched over the child in its cradle, Rumina presided over its nutrition, Vaticanus over its crying, and Numeria taught it to count.[3] As might have been expected, these gods and goddesses were colourless, they had neither character nor legend; they were little more, in many cases, than verbal nouns. Yet there were some, who had to do with agriculture and country life, who in time under Greek influence became more than names—Liber, Saturnus, Proserpina, Faunus. Some were for centuries after the Christian era objects of dread to the country people. Probably we should understand their nature better if we called them fairies or goblins—"little people." [4]

Many of them can have had little or no worship, but others had definite rituals, but generally of an unemotional type. Numa, according to Dionysius of Halicarnassus, was to be praised on account of the cheapness of the sacrifices he ordained.[5] The prayers had the hard, dry character of legal formulae, and altogether it was a "layman's

---

[1] *Cf.* St Augustine *de Civitate Dei*, iv. 21, and also iv. 8.

[2] Ibid., iv. 9.

[3] Ibid., iv. 11. On this section see Warde Fowler, *The Religious Experience of the Roman People* (1911) Lecture vii.

[4] It is hard sometimes for those who love Hans Andersen to understand that the fairies were pre-eminently malign beings—a terror and an incubus tending to the paralysis of the human mind. The early Christians ranked it among the greatest benefits of the Gospel that it "set them free from ten thousand tyrants"—the small gods and the demons.

[5] Dion. H. *Antt.* ii. 23 τῆς εὐτελείας τῶν θυσιῶν.

religion,"[1] cautious rather than imaginative or reflective. The ancients, says Gellius,[2] were in their religion *castissimi cautissimique*—if a god sent an earthquake, and some ceremony were decreed, they took care not to mention the god's name for fear of mistake; the right god (or goddess) would know. No god or temple could receive gift or legacy of land even from a private person without a decree of the people.[3]

Different views have been taken of this religion. The Romans themselves attributed to it the superior honesty and patriotism which marked the old days, and this was the view of Polybius. "The most important difference for the better," he says, "which the Roman commonwealth appears to me to display is in their religious beliefs. For I conceive that what in other nations is looked upon as a reproach, I mean a scrupulous fear of the gods (λέγω δὲ τὴν δεισιδαιμονίαν), is the very thing which keeps the Roman commonwealth together. To such an extraordinary extent is this carried among them (ἐκτετραγῴδηται), both in private and public business, that nothing could exceed it. Many people might think this unaccountable; but in my opinion their object is to use it as a check upon the common people. If it were possible to form a state wholly of philosophers, such a custom would perhaps be unnecessary. . . . To my mind, the ancients were not acting without purpose or at random when they brought in among the vulgar those opinions about the gods, and the belief in punishments in Hades: much rather do I think that men nowadays are acting rashly and foolishly in rejecting them."[4] In fact, as Varro put it, it was to the state's advantage that people should be deceived in religion.[5]

But there was another side to the religion. The very vagueness of the powers and characters of these gods made them more awful, just as under the early empire the in-

---

[1] The phrase is Boissier's. [2] Gellius, *N. A.* ii. 28.
[3] Cic., *de Leg.* ii. 9. 22 *nequis agrum consecrato.* Cf. Cic. *de domo sua*, 49, 127
[4] Polybius, vi. 56. 6-12, tr. Shuckburgh.
[5] Varro *ap.* Aug. *C. D.* iv. 27. *Expedit homines falli in religione.* Cf. the *very* remarkable verses of Critias on the invention of the gods; cited by Sextus Empir. *adv. Math.* ix. 54.

determinate nature of the relations of emperor and senate
made both miserable and nervous in their dealings with
one another.[1] No one knew where or how he might meet
and offend a god. "To tell the truth," says Cicero,[2] "superstition has spread everywhere, and has crushed the minds
of wellnigh all men, and made itself mistress of human
weakness. . . . It follows you up; it is hard upon you;
wherever you turn it pursues you. If you hear a prophet,
or an omen; if you sacrifice; if you catch sight of a bird;
if you see a Chaldaean or a *haruspex*; if it lightens, if it
thunders, if anything is struck by lightning; if anything
like a portent is born, or occurs in any way—something or
other of the kind is bound to happen, so that you can never
be at ease and have a quiet mind. The refuge from all our
toils and anxieties would seem to be sleep. Yet from sleep
itself the most of our cares and terrors come."[3] So too said
Plutarch of superstition—"Alone it makes no truce with
sleep."[4] Plutarch's *Lives* are full of dreams. In the reign
of Marcus Aurelius a work in five books was written on the
interpretation of dreams by Artemidorus Daldianus, which
is still extant.[5]

All this superstition Lucretius attacked with an energy
and an anger that testify plainly to its power over men's
minds, and perhaps over his own. Over and over he insists
that such gods as there are live lapped in eternal peace,
unconcerned with us and our doings; that nothing happens
that cannot be explained by natural causes, or by pure
chance; that therefore neither in this life need we fear the
gods, who take no interest in us in any way, nor in any other
life, because there is no other life. Epicurus has brought us
salvation; he is the real god of mankind; he has given us
peace of mind and happiness. And yet—

"When we look up to the great expanses of heaven, the

---

[1] On this aspect of the Empire see Boissier, *Cicero and his Friends* (tr.)
p. 386 f. [2] Cicero, *de Div*. ii. 72. 148-50.

[3] See Martha, *Lucrèce*, ch. iv. La religion de Lucrèce. It should be noted
that the Stoics accepted divination.

[4] Plutarch, *de Superstitione* 165 E (§ 3) μόνη γὰρ οὐ σπένδεται πρὸς τὸν ὕπνον.

[5] Similar works, of some size too, are current in modern Greek, and there is
a steady sale for small "books of dreams" in English.

aether set on high above the glittering stars, and the thought comes into our mind of the sun and the moon and their goings; then indeed in hearts laden with other woes that doubt too begins to wake and raise its head—Can it be perchance, after all, that we have to do with some vast divine power that wheels those bright stars each in its course?" [1]

What the great poet felt and expressed in this moving way we need not doubt that smaller minds experienced, who had less grasp of Epicurean principles, and fluctuated wretchedly between unbelief and superstition.

There is yet a third aspect of the old religion. To some minds it was full of quiet charm and beauty. A tendency akin to romanticism meets us in the age of Virgil, and perhaps it is to this that we should refer the affection felt by some for the old gods of the countryside rather than to conviction of their divinity. " Lares of my fathers! " says Tibullus, " keep ye me safe ; for ye were my guardians when a tiny child I ran about at your feet. No shame it is that you are of ancient wood ; even thus it was ye dwelt in the house of my grandsire of old. In those days they kept faith better, when in the little shrine a god of wood was content with humble offerings." [2]

But neither tradition, nor Epicureanism, nor romanticism will suffice for the religious temper, and for it there was nothing so strong and helpful as the practical Roman Stoicism. Whatever the origin of its various doctrines, a summary of them is given by Cicero in his second book *De Natura Deorum*.[3] Surveying the gods, the Roman Stoic

---

[1] Lucretius, v. 1204-10 :

> *Nam cum suspicimus magni caelestia mundi*
> *templa super stellisque micantibus aethera fixum,*
> *et venit in mentem solis lunaeque viarum,*
> *tunc aliis oppressa malis in pectora cura*
> *illa quoque expergefactum caput erigere infit,*
> *nequae forte deum nobis immensa potestas*
> *sit, vario motu quae candida sidera verset.*

[2] Tibullus, i. 10. 15-20 *aluistis et idem cursarem vestros cum tener ante pedes.*

[3] Cicero owns frankly that he used Greek originals in composing his philosophic works—ad Atticum xii. 52, 3, ἀπόγραφα *sunt, minore labore fiunt; verba tantum adfero quibus abundo.*

found some to be deified men—Hercules, Castor, and Romulus (24, 62)—some deifications of divine gifts (23, 60), and some personified forces of nature; "but when we look up at the sky and contemplate the celestial bodies, what is so clear as that there is a divine power of excelling intelligence, whereby they are guided?" (2, 4). The universe is a vast organism permeated and controlled by an intelligent and sentient nature; "and when we say the universe consists and is directed by nature, we do not speak of it as a clod, or a chip of stone, or something of the kind with no natural cohesion, but as a tree or an animal" (32, 82). The gods, the Stoic holds, are not distinct and opposed beings, but the varied activity of the one God under various names; and their proper worship is veneration with pure, honest, and incorrupt mind and voice (28, 71). Divine Providence thus rules the universe (30, 75), and not only do the gods think for mankind, but for men (65, 164).[1]

IV

Our preliminary survey has been long, but it may have enabled us to get a clearer view of the elements which went to form Virgil's conceptions of the divine. He was an Italian, brought up in his native village, no doubt, to hold the old traditional views of his people. His first great teacher, however, in early youth was Lucretius. As his experience of life enlarged, he began to feel the weak points of Epicureanism, and simultaneously he was reading very widely in Greek literature. That he studied Euripides carefully is clear, and it is hardly conceivable that he read none of Plato's works. A matured man, he wrote his epic on the model of Homer; and he had, in accordance with tradition, to produce gods of a conventional Homeric type.

[1] I quote the last clause, as of special import : *Nec vero universo generi hominum solum sed etiam singulis a dis immortalibus consuli et provideri solet.* I have borrowed a phrase or two from Dr J. B. Mayor. Since this book was written, three volumes have appeared, dealing with Stoicism—Prof. W. L. Davidson, *The Stoic Creed* (1907); Mr R. D. Hicks, *Stoic and Epicurean* (1910); Prof. E. V. Arnold, *Roman Stoicism.* There is also a chapter on it in *The Conflict of Religions in the Early Roman Empire* (1909).

But to do this exactly was impossible for one of so independent a character and such wide sympathies. The gods in consequence have a tendency to fall away from the standard of Homer, and to betray other influences.

In the *Eclogues* and in the second conclusion to the fourth *Georgic* the gods are frankly literary and Alexandrine. But in the rest of the *Georgics* we come nearer to the poet's mind. The clear and picturesque outlines of the literary gods fade away, and we find sometimes a half-romantic leaning toward the old country gods of Italy, sometimes a gleam of a vaster and still more moving conception.

He tells us of the fascination for him of the scientific outlook on life.[1] The Muses, dear above all things to him, would teach him, if they would hear his prayer, the laws of heaven and earth and sea, the great principles that underlie all Nature. But if this is beyond him—the reflection shows a certain consciousness that his true sphere is elsewhere—be it his to love the country with its gentle streams and woods, and to let glory go. Happy indeed is he who has mastered Nature's secrets and by their aid has triumphed over the terrors of superstition (*metus omnes*) and of death; but there is another blessedness in the knowledge of the country gods, Pan, Silvanus, and the nymphs. These names are not to be taken literally, as the rustics might have taken them, but as embodying a point of view which is on the whole new to literature. He means that he will turn to Nature herself in her smiling rather than in her scientific mood; he will "view the outward shows of sky and earth, of hill and valley," and, while the man of science is busy and bustling on the track of laws, he will wait for "impulses of deeper birth," feeding his mind "in a wise passiveness." And this he did, and after deciding in his first *Georgic* that the weather-wisdom of the crows is not a divine gift,[2] he came at last to a view, which may be called technically Stoic or Pythagorean, but which is no mere dogma of the schools but an acquisi-

---

[1] *G.* ii. 475.

[2] Contrast Epictetus (*D.* i. 17) οὐδὲ τὸν κόρακα θαυμάζομεν ἢ τὴν κορώνην ἀλλὰ τὸν θεὸν τὸν σημαίνοντα διὰ τούτων.

tion of his own, suggested no doubt by the philosophers, but, like Wordsworth's philosophy, learnt from Nature herself—God pervades earth and air and sea, and He is the life that moves in all living things, bird and insect, farmer and flower, all dear to the poet.[1] It must not be supposed that Virgil grasped this at all with the clearness of Wordsworth, or drew Wordsworth's inferences from it, but it was still his theory when he wrote the famous speech of Anchises in the underworld. Round it is a vast fringe of uncertainties, and the greatest of them is the doubt as to Providence caring for the individual—the final difficulty of every religious mind, on the solution of which everything depends.

In the *Aeneid* the presentment of Virgil's own views is complicated by the convention of epic poetry, which in its turn is modified by the poet's endeavour to draw it as far as may be into touch with the higher conception of divinity which mankind had learnt from philosophers. He has also to bring the Olympian gods into friendly relations with the native gods of Italy—a process helped by the common Roman habit of recognizing their gods in other forms in foreign pantheons ; and he also finds a place for Cybele, who was probably the most living of them all. It must be said that he manages his task well. *Sciens de deorum imperio varias esse opiniones*, says Servius, *prudentissime tenuit generalitatem*.[2] There is a uniform tone about them all, and peculiarities are not emphasized. Even the Italian stories, quaint and primitive as they are, do not seem out of keeping. It should also be remarked how free the poem is from divination and magic—the lamentable side-tracks of popular and even of literary religion.

Beginning with the Homeric aspect of Virgil's gods, we find a close adherence to the *Iliad* and the *Odyssey*, and sometimes even too faithful an imitation. The gods act as they did in Homer's poems, they do the same things, but they do them rather stiffly. Venus appears from time to time to help Aeneas, as Athene does to help Odysseus, and Juno never for very long forgets to put difficulties in the way, as

---

[1] *G.* iv. 221. [2] On *Aen.* vi. 264. See p. 233.

Poseidon does in the *Odyssey*. There is also divine intervention in battle in the old style. Juno, for example, borrows a
hint from Apollo. In the *Iliad* Apollo, to safeguard Aeneas,
snatched him from the battle and left a phantom of him,
over which Greeks and Trojans went on fighting. Juno, to
save Turnus, applies the device in another way. The rescue
of Aeneas had hardly been heroic enough, so Juno frames
an image, not of Turnus, but of Aeneas, which Turnus in
fury pursues from the field and on to a ship which is standing in the river. Juno at once cuts the moorings, and
Turnus is safely but most honourably kidnapped. This is
sufficiently mechanical.[1]

Then there is the nymph Juturna, the sister of Turnus.
She took her name from a medicinal spring near the
fountain of Numicus, from which water was brought to
Rome for sacrificial purposes.[2] She is, therefore, entirely
Italian, but in Virgil's hands her story becomes Homeric.
She owes her divinity and her sovereignty over pools and
streams to the love of Jupiter, though Juno has graciously
made an exception in her case and does not hate her.[3]
Informed by Juno of her brother's peril, Juturna begins
to take an active part in the story. She emulates Athene in
upsetting the arrangements which Trojans and Rutulians
are making to end the war by a single conflict between
Aeneas and Turnus. But Athene was more expert, for she
disguised herself as a Trojan, and induced the Trojans
to break the truce, thus saving the honour of the Greeks,
while Juturna employs her arts with the Latins and so
involves her own friends in disgrace.[4] Later on, she again
imitates Athene by ousting her brother's charioteer and
taking the reins herself, just as Athene turned out Sthenelus
and drove the chariot of Diomedes.[5]

But of all the cases in which the Virgilian gods imitate
the Homeric, the episode of the arms of Aeneas is the most
conspicuous. In the *Iliad* Thetis goes to the house of

---

[1] *Iliad*, v. 449 ; *A.* x. 636-88.
[2] Teuffel suggests that her association with Turnus is due to the last two
syllables of her name.
[3] *A.* xii. 137-45.   [4] *Iliad*, iv. 86 ff. ; *A.* xii. 222 f.
[5] *A.* xii. 469 ; *Iliad*, v. 835.

Hephaestus to ask arms for Achilles; but, before she has made known her request at all, Hephaestus himself recalls how she and Eurynome, daughters of Ocean, had saved him when Hera flung him from heaven, "and now is Thetis come to our house: surely I am bound to pay the price of life to sweet-haired Thetis."[1] Then in a direct and pathetic speech the goddess tells him why she has come, and he at once goes off to make the arms. Virgil, however, had another and very different divine mother to deal with, whose relations with Vulcan were much more difficult. Venus has to intercede with her husband on behalf of her son who is not his, and Virgil has taken as his model the deceiving of Zeus by Hera.[2] The passage is not a very successful one; it was severely criticized in antiquity,[3] and it is hardly likely to find defenders now.

Side by side with the Homeric are the Italian gods. Saturn, Janus, Picus, Pilumnus, and Faunus do not indeed take an active part in the story, but they are recognized, and they are given Olympian rank. More it was hardly possible to do, for, like Italian gods generally, they are very dim figures. Most of them had one solitary charm to weigh against the various activity of the true Olympians; they are inert and colourless, but they are *veteres*,[4] the "old gods"—a name which would seem to imply more affection than faith.

They are apt to be adorned with traits borrowed from the Greek gods. Picus, for example, the woodpecker-god, is married to Circe, and owes his bird-form to her enchantments.[5] Tiber himself appears garbed as a Greek divinity —"thin lawn veiled him with its grey covering, and shadowy reeds hid his hair"[6]—but he has a genuine Italian oak hung with spoils of conquered foes.[7] We read of the god of Soracte "for whom the blaze of the pinewood heap is fed,

---

[1] *Iliad*, xviii. 406, 407.   [2] *A.* viii. 370 ff.; *Iliad* xiv. 153-353.
[3] Gellius, *N. A.* ix. 10. See also Servius *ad loc.* Statius is still less happily inspired. He makes Venus remind Mars of *Lemniacae catenae*, *Theb.* iii. 272.
[4] Cf. *A.* vii. 254 *veteris Fauni*; viii. 187, and ix. 786 *veterumque deorum*.
[5] *A.* vii. 189.   [6] *A.* viii. 32.   [7] *A.* x. 423.

where we thy worshippers in pious faith print our steps amid the deep embers of the fire " [1]—he is called Apollo, but we may be sure it was not his original name. In close connexion with Apollo are the Penates, who, according to the story, came from Troy,[2] but are certainly Italian. Ancient antiquaries indeed debated whether Apollo were not one of the Penates himself, which would be quite un-Homeric.[3] Jupiter has both Greek and Italian traits. To Evander he is (by a beautiful inspiration) the Arcadian Jupiter ;[4] in another place he is Jupiter Anxurus ;[5] he is at the same time Jove of the Capitol, as a famous passage attests ;[6] and to Iarbas he seems to have been Ammon.[7] In a word, he is the Jove of the Roman Empire, a god of many names and characters, a symbol of Rome's policy in dealing with religions. Juno likewise is Hera of Samos,[8] Juno Lacinia,[9] Juno of Gabii,[10] and Juno Caelestis of Carthage. The rites which are paid to these gods are generally Roman, without distinction between those of Greek and those of Italian origin.

Virgil is endeavouring to bring all the gods into real contact with Rome, and to dó this he has to make them serious beings, possessed of Roman dignity and gravity.

---

[1] *A.* xi. 785-8 (Mackail). Pliny (*N. H.* vii. 2. 19) alludes to the fact, but says nothing. Servius' comment may be quoted. " So says Virgil ; but Varro, everywhere an opponent of religion (*ubique expugnator religionis*), in describing a certain drug, says, ' as the Hirpini do, who, when they have to walk through fire, touch their soles with a drug.' " Fire-walking may still be seen in Japan ; a friend of mine has described to me how one of his own students in Economics pulled off his patent leather boots and did it before his eyes. Mr Saville, of the London Missionary Society, saw it done on Huahine, near Tahiti. It is also done on Kandaru, in the Fiji group, by the inhabitants of a particular village, with whom it is hereditary. See Andrew Lang, *Modern Mythology*, ch. xii.

[2] *A.* ii. 296 ; iii. 12, &c.

[3] Macrobius, *Sat.* iii. 4. 6. Nigidius and Cornelius Labeo thought the Penates must be Apollo and Neptune. Warde Fowler, *Religious Experience of the Roman People*, Lecture iv. (on the religion of the family).

[4] *A.* viii. 573 :

> At vos, o superi et divum tu maxime rector
> Iuppiter, Arcadii, quaeso, miserescite regis.

De la Ville de Mirmont, *Ap. et Virg.* p. 230 on this conflate Jupiter.

[5] *A.* vii. 799.   [6] *A.* viii. 351 f.   [7] *A.* iv. 198.

[8] *A.* i. 12-16, Carthage is preferred by her to Samos.   [9] *A.* iii. 552

[10] *A.* vii. 682.

Consequently he no longer plays with them as the Alexandrine poets did, and as he did himself with the delightful
old Silenus in the sixth *Eclogue*, whose bad ways we forgive
for his good temper and the song he steals from Lucretius—
and for his brow and temples stained with the mulberry
juice. Everything is more serious. For instance, the interview between Venus and Cupid, with reference to Dido,
was suggested by a similar episode in the *Argonautica*, but
it is graver, more dignified, and less pretty. Cupid is not
a Ptolemy baby like Eros in the poem of Apollonius, but "a
puer bullatus of the good old days." [1]

Virgil's gods are thoroughly Roman, in whatever epics
they have adventured themselves in the past. There is
a fine Roman propriety about them, which is a little stiff
perhaps, but very proper to reclaimed characters who are
trying to forget they were ever at Alexandria. Venus,
a cruel and rather contemptible character in the *Iliad*,
is in the *Aeneid* pre-eminently a divine mother—*alma
Venus*. Sainte-Beuve calls her " invariably charming, tender,
loving, and yet sober and serious." In an interesting study
he contrasts the meeting of Aphrodite and Anchises in the
Homeric *Hymn to Aphrodite* with that of Venus and Aeneas
in the first *Aeneid*. [2] Virgil had read the Hymn, but his
treatment is very different. That Venus is Aeneas' mother
accounts for much of the change, but the whole interview
is conceived in a different tone. Venus appears in the
garb and guise of Diana, as a huntress maiden. There is
grace, dignity, and charm about her, but nothing voluptuous,
as in the Hymn.

Jupiter, however, is in many ways the most interesting
of Virgil's gods. [3] He has Homeric traits, but he is mainly
Roman. He has come nearer to mankind than Apollonius
allowed him ; from a Ptolemy, we might say, he has become
an Augustus. He is a grave and wise god, free from the
tyrannical and sensual characteristics of the Homeric Zeus.
As with Aeneas, so in Jupiter's case, Virgil lapses at times

[1] De la Ville de Mirmont, *Ap. de Rh. et Virgile*, p. 647. See p. 57.
[2] *Étude sur Virgile*, pp. 250-8.
[3] Boissier, *La Religion romaine*, i. 254.

into weak imitations of Homer, and we hear of Juturna and of Ganymede in connexion with him; but as a rule he conforms more to what Plato thinks the divine nature should be. "If the poets will not so far respect all the gods," says Plato, "at least we shall entreat them not to presume to draw so unlike a picture of the highest of the gods as to make him say, 'Ah me, now is it fated that Sarpedon, my beloved, shall fall beneath the hand of Patroclus, Menoetius' son.'"[1] Accordingly in the *Aeneid* it is Hercules who sheds unavailing tears for Pallas, while Jupiter consoles him. "'Each has his own appointed day, short and unrecoverable is the span of life for all; but to spread renown by deeds is the task of valour. Under high Troy town many and many a god's son fell; nay, mine own child Sarpedon likewise perished. Turnus too his own fate summons, and his allotted period has reached the goal.' So speaks he, and turns his eyes away from the Rutulian fields."[2] Jupiter feels the sorrow of men here, but he does not propose, as he did in the *Iliad*, to overturn the order of things by rescuing the doomed hero. His attitude at the Council of the Gods has been compared to the undecided conduct of Latinus, and his general position with reference to Destiny is on the whole vague. But in the main he sustains the character of a great and wise god very successfully.

Hercules too is a god who owes something to the philosophers. The Herakles of the Attic stage, braggart, bully, and glutton, has given way to the Herakles of Prodicus' fable, a god vowed to the service of Virtue,[3] not undeserving of his canonization by the Stoics.[4] Virgil

---

[1] Plato, *Rep.* iii. 388. *Iliad*, xvi. 433.   [2] *A.* x. 467-74, Mackail.

[3] Xenophon, *Mem.* ii. 1. 21 ff., "The choice of Herakles." Cf. Diod. *Sic.* i. 2.

[4] Seneca, *Dial.* ii. 2. 1, counts Hercules among the sages; Epictetus *D.* iii. 24, on his trust in Zeus his father, and *D.* iii. 26, on Herakles as εἰσαγωγεὺς δικαιοσύνης καὶ ὁσιότητος; Apuleius, *Florida*, iv. 22, calls him a philosopher; and Julian, *Or.* vi. p. 187 c, says that, besides conferring other benefits on mankind, he was the founder of the Cynic philosophy. Horace himself recognizes the god's new dignity: *hac arte Pollux et vagus Hercules* (*C.* iii. 3. 9). See Nettleship, *Essays*, i. p. 135. Compare also the question of Cotta in Cicero, *N. D.* iii. 20. 42 *quem potissimum Herculem colamus, scire velim; plures enim tradunt nobis.*

puts into the mouth of Evander, the most serious and venerable figure in Italy, the story of Hercules' connexion with Rome, and the justification of his cult, as that of a saviour and deliverer.

> Non haec sollemnia nobis,
> has ex more dapes, hanc tanti numinis aram
> vana superstitio veterumque ignara deorum
> imposuit [1] (*A*. viii. 185).

Conington remarks that one might almost suppose Virgil here to be defending religion against Lucretius, who had taken pains to depreciate Hercules in comparison with Epicurus.[2]

In the same spirit Virgil tones down or apologizes for legends which he has to tell. For instance, Misenus challenged Triton to a contest in trumpeting, and the god slew him for jealousy (*aemulus*). So said the legend; but envy, according to Plato, "stands outside the divine chorus,"[3] so the poet adds a *caveat* of his own—

> si credere dignum est.[4]

Si credere dignum est! The exclamation raises a deeper issue and one of wider import than the character of Triton; for is not all Olympus involved? So at least the poet hints, or half hints, at the very beginning of his poem.

> Tantaene animis caelestibus irae?[5]

He knew the answer that all the philosophers, from Plato to Lucretius, would make. It was his own answer. At the

---

[1] "No idle superstition that knows not the gods of old has ordered these our solemn rites, this customary feast, this altar of august sanctity" (Mackail).

[2] Lucretius, v, *exordium*.

[3] Plato, *Phaedrus*, 247 A : φθόνος γὰρ ἔξω θείου χόρου ἵσταται.

[4] *A*. vi. 173. "If belief is due." Cf. the same expression (*G*. iii. 391) in the case of another legend, borrowed by Virgil from Nicander (Macr. *Sat*. v. 22. 10), and from Virgil by Browning, *Pan and Luna*.

[5] "Can heavenly natures hate so fiercely and so long?" (Conington).

end he addresses the question directly to Jove himself, and in a more searching form—

> Tanton' placuit concurrere motu,
> Iuppiter, aeterna gentes in pace futuras?[1] (*A.* xii. 503).

The question goes beyond Jupiter, for even he admits that things lie on the knees—not of gods, but of still higher powers. At a critical moment in the war between Aeneas and Turnus, Jupiter declares that he will do nothing; he will be impartial—

> rex Iuppiter omnibus idem.

Venus elsewhere hints that Fate, which she loosely connects with Jupiter, is the supreme power in the world;[2] and Juno at the last admits, on the suggestion of her husband, that Fate is too powerful for her and yields to it.[3] But Jupiter is more frank. He will take no part in the war, he says, cloaking his inaction with the fine phrase quoted, and continuing "the Fates will find a way."

> Fata viam invenient.

"The poet seems," writes an ancient commentator, "to have shown here that the Fates are one thing and Jupiter another."[4] But Jupiter says more than this, for, though we must give him leave to speak as loosely as we do ourselves in common talk, it is remarkable that he recognizes another factor in human affairs—

> Sua cuique exorsa laborem
> fortunamque ferent.

"As each has begun, so shall his toil and his fortune be."

Jupiter is raising the same question which Tacitus debated a century after Virgil's day. "As for myself,"

---

[1] "Was it thy will, O God, that nations destined to everlasting peace should clash in so vast a shock?" (Mackail).

[2] *A.* iv. 110.   [3] *A.* xii. 794, 795; 810-20.

[4] Interpolation in Servius, *ad A.* x. 111 (the passage in question) *videtur hic ostendisse aliud esse fata, aliud Iovem.*

wrote the historian, "my mind remains in doubt whether
human affairs are ordered by fate and unchangeable
necessity or proceed by chance. For you will find the
wisest of ancient philosophers and their followers at
variance on this point. Many firmly believe that the gods
take no care for our beginning or our end, or for man's
life at all . . . Others again hold that there is a corre-
spondence between fate and the course of events ; only
that this does not depend upon the movements of the
stars, but on certain elemental principles, and on the
sequence of natural causes. Yet even so they would leave
to us our choice of life ; which once made, what comes
after is fixed immutably."[1] Does Jupiter mean by his
sua exorsa at all what Tacitus means by his *ubi elegeris*?
—that in some way men are the authors of their own
destiny, and must go through with what they begin ?
Is this Jupiter's idea? He does not explain it, and the
gods do not ask.[2]

Whatever interpretation we put on Jupiter's speech, it is
quite clear that the gods are not the supreme rulers of the
universe. Nor are they, it also follows from the study
of the *Aeneid*, even those manifestations of the supreme
divinity, which the Neo-Platonists later on held them to be.
Virgil, filled with the thought of the divine life pervading
all things, hardly seems to conceive of the Olympian gods as
sharing that life. He has done everything possible for
them ; he has toned down the dark elements in their
stories ; he has emphasized the grave and moral ; he has
Platonized them as far as he could ; but he has not made
them live. Set in the *Aeneid*, as in the plays of Euripides,
side by side with human life and all it means of love and
sorrow, but drawn with more kindliness of feeling, the

---

[1] Tacitus, *Annals*, vi. 22 (Ramsay's translation) *Fatum quidem congruere rebus putant, sed non e vagis stellis, verum apud principia et nexus naturalium causarum ; ac tamen electionem vitae nobis relinquunt, quam ubi elegeris, certum imminentium ordinem.*

[2] Evander, *A.* viii. 333-6, attributes his coming to Italy at once to fate, fortune, and divine oracles. Servius tries to explain the statement by reference to the Stoics and to the ingenuity of Virgil. See Gellius, *N. A.* vii. (vi.) 2, for an interesting discussion by Chrysippus of fate and freewill.

Olympian gods are found to be dead beyond disguise—the truth cannot be hid. They are mere epic machinery. Nor is it otherwise with the gods of Italy ; they perhaps had never lived in any personal way. Is the throne of heaven vacant, or is there no throne at all, or has it another occupant ?

It is quite clear from the sixth book that Virgil is no longer an Epicurean. The traditional gods of heaven are conspicuously absent from man's existence before birth and after death, but all his life is permeated by divine law and is indeed itself divine, and this is Stoic doctrine. Throughout the whole *Aeneid* we are taught to think that Destiny, if not divine, at least greater than the traditional gods, has plans and aims, which it achieves; in other words, that Providence rules the affairs of men, whatever Providence may be and in whatever way it works. This again is Stoic doctrine. But this is not the whole matter.

"'Dear city of Cecrops,' says he of old ; and will not you say, 'Dear city of Zeus'?" So wrote Marcus Aurelius in his diary,[1] and the form of utterance is significant. The exclamation may seem a natural deduction from the Stoic view of the world, but the Stoic does not easily say, "Dear city of Zeus," because it remains after all only a deduction for him. But to the poet of the *Georgics* it is no mere deduction, it is a living truth. The world is a "dear city" to Virgil—

The beauty and the wonder and the power,
The shapes of things, their colours, lights [2] and shades,
Changes, surprises.

To him, as to Goethe, the world is the living garment of Deity.[3] The Stoic finds little value in the particular beauties

---

[1] Marcus Aurelius, iv. 23 Ἐκεῖνος μέν φησι· Πόλι φίλη Κέκροπος· σὺ δὲ οὐκ ἐρεῖς· Ὦ πόλι φίλη Διός ; "He" is Aristophanes in a lost play.

[2] Cf. *Georgics* i. 46 [*incipiat*] *sulco attritus* splendescere *vomer*.

[3] *Faust*, Part I. Sc. 1.   The Geist speaks :
In Lebensfluthen, im Thatensturm
Wall' ich auf und ab . . .
So schaff' ich am sausenden Webstuhl der Zeit,
Und wirke der Gottheit lebendiges Kleid.

of Nature, which mean so much to Virgil. "Decay is in the material substance of all things; they are but water, dust, bones, stench."[1] The "dear city of Zeus" is after all a depressing place of abode, or at least the visible part of it, the suburb of our habitation. Pan and Silvanus and the nymphs are very unphilosophic creatures, but they at least represent a feeling that all Nature is *not* "water, dust, bones, stench," and they are so far real—a poetic protest against one side of Stoicism.

Again, the "dear city of Cecrops" is the expression of a poet's love for Athens, a feeling which the Stoic would only doubtfully approve. "The Stoics," writes Dr Caird, "are driven back upon the isolated inner life of the individual, and have to confine the absolute good to the bare state and direction of the will. Now the mistake of this negative attitude may easily escape notice, so long as it shows itself merely in treating wealth, or fame, or pleasure, as indifferent; but when it leads the Stoics to deal in the same way with the ties of kindred and friendship, of family or nation, and to place virtue in obedience to an abstract law which is independent of all these, we begin to suspect some mistake or over-statement. . . . They do not realize that the consciousness of self as a moral being, and the consciousness of other selves as members of one society, are two factors that cannot be separated."[2] Dr Caird writes from a point of view which will hardly be attributed to Virgil, and yet Virgil in his own way felt the same weakness in the Stoic position.

Tantae molis erat Romanam condere gentem.[3]

Was there not a danger that in turning away from Juppiter Capitolinus, from Vesta and the Penates, the philosopher might lose something real, of which these had been a symbol?

---

[1] Marcus Aurelius, ix. 36. This is not the only mood of Marcus, it may be noted.

[2] Dr Edward Caird, *Evolution of Theology in the Greek Philosophers*, vol. ii. p. 153.

[3] "So mighty a task it was to found the Roman race."

There lies the essence of Virgil's uncertainty. On one side is the teaching of the philosophers with an imperious call which he was glad to obey; but on the other side there was the poet's instinct, as imperious and as true. The delight he took in Nature, the deep love he felt for his country, seemed to be bound up with the old gods of farm and city. Figments they might be, or slight embodiments of the divine, but so long as men had held by them the great cardinal virtues had lived and flourished in Italy, and men had set the state before themselves. Who was to guarantee as much of Stoicism? Marcus Aurelius had not yet lived, and even he did not keep all that Virgil wanted.

But we may go further still. Individualistic as Stoic teaching was, it did not provide enough for the individual. The Stoic sage is a solitary in the world around him, however much he is at home in "the city of Zeus" of his thoughts—and perhaps even Zeus leaves him a little too much alone. He has to be for ever assuring himself and adjuring himself; it is all his own mind's doing, and no assurance, none at least of a distinct kind, comes to him from heaven. The diary of Marcus is a melancholy record. Now the old religion had been cheerful. The sage might smile at the gods of clay and ancient wood, and at their poor little offerings of meal and salt; yet in the old days and in the old religion man and god had come very near together, they had known one another, the god was interested in the individual—and this was a happiness which the Stoic would have as a rule to forgo, which he might despise. But if ever a man's being was an expression of a need of the divine, the character of Aeneas is just such an expression. His melancholy anticipates that of Marcus, and has the same root. The poet craves for recognition by God, and if he does not express this craving in the articulate speech of philosopher or devotee, in the no less real voice of poetry it is clearly to be heard.

Stoicism draws him and holds him, but the poet in Virgil cries out against a world with no content and no meaning, where the only reality is the individual, and even he is incomplete. The old religion had in its crude and poor way provided against these evils, and so far the poet felt it to be true and clung to it. His mind and his reason go with the philosophers; his heart turns to the faith of the past. He realizes the truth in both, but how to reconcile them was his problem, as it is ours.

CHAPTER XII

INTERPRETATION OF LIFE.—5. RESULTS

'Tis not the calm and peaceful breast
That sees or reads the problem true ;
They only know on whom 't has prest
Too hard to hope to solve it too.—CLOUGH.

'Αρμονίη ἀφανὴς φανερῆς κρείττων.—HERACLITUS, *fr.* 47.

ONE day in conversation with Eckermann the aged Goethe began to talk of certain poets of the time. "They write," he said, "as if they were ill and the whole world were a lazaretto. They all speak of the woe and misery of this earth. . . . All are discontented, and one draws the other into a state of still greater discontent. This is a real abuse of poetry, which was given to us to hide the little discords of life and to make man contented with the world and his condition. . . . I have hit on a good word to tease these gentlemen. I will call their poetry 'Lazaretto-poetry,' and I will give the name of Tyrtaean-poetry to that which not only sings war-songs, but also arms men with courage to undergo the conflicts of life." [1]

The "ancient quarrel between poetry and philosophy" is still kept alive by their camp-followers, and an *obiter dictum*, such as Goethe has here let fall upon the function of poetry, will scarcely escape challenge from the adherents of certain poetic schools. He implies, they will say, too much purpose in poetry ; for, if a poet turn moralist or philosopher, all is over with his art. Goethe knew this as well as any one, and so far was he from betraying poetry to the philosophers that he has not escaped their censure for some of his utterances upon philosophy. "Man," he said, "is born not to

---

[1] Eckermann, *Conversations with Goethe*, Sept. 24, 1827 (Tr. John Oxenford, 1850).

solve the problems of the universe, but to find out where the problem begins, and then to restrain himself within the limits of the comprehensible." [1] But perhaps even this will not satisfy his critics in the camp of poetry. Poetry, they say, has nothing to do with problems of the universe, or with problems at all; its business is with man and what he does, what he suffers, and what he enjoys. To this the great poets would probably make no objection. But somehow when they handle these subjects they have a tendency to come very near philosophy —everything means so much more to the great mind; the universe and its problem are involved in even the smallest things. Carlyle, in discussing Schiller's shortcomings, has indicated that they are due to nothing so much as his failure to feel the values and implications of the small and the ordinary. "The common doings and interests of Men," he says, "mean as they seem, are boundless in significance; for even the poorest aspect of Nature, especially of living Nature, is a type and manifestation of the invisible spirit that works in Nature. There is properly no object trivial or insignificant: but every finite thing, could we look well, is as a window, through which solemn vistas are opened into Infinitude itself." Aristotle and Wordsworth [2] have said very much the same, each in his own way.

If we attach any serious value to Virgil's poetry, we are almost bound to ask how it will stand criticism upon these lines; to inquire how far he realizes the problem of the universe; whether the individual case is to him a type and manifestation of some invisible spirit at work in Nature; how far he takes in the whole experience of man, what value he attaches to it, and finally what inference he draws from it all; and whether he belongs to the Lazaretto school or to the Tyrtaeans. It will be of interest and indeed important to determine, if we can, to which school he belongs; it will be of far more interest and import to learn how he stands toward the problem of the universe.

A favourite way of criticizing the universe is the method recommended by Robinson Crusoe. "I began," he said, "to

---

[1] Ibid., Oct. 15, 1825.
[2] In the preface he wrote for the 1800 edition of *Lyrical Ballads*.

comfort myself as well as I could and to set the Good against the Evil, that I might have something to distinguish my Case from worse; and I stated it very impartially, like Debtor and Creditor, the Comforts I enjoy'd against the Miseries I suffer'd." The balance in his account, it will be remembered, was in favour of good "upon the whole"; and he proceeds to the generalization "that we may always find something to comfort ourselves from and to set, in the Description of Good and Evil, on the Credit side of the Account." The something may indeed be "negative," he admits, as:—"I see no wild Beasts to hurt me." Now, all this was very philosophic of the "Solitaire," but we shall want more of our poet when he deals with life in general. If his view is merely that, on subtracting the evil from the good, there is a balance of ten per cent. in favour of the good, we shall feel that nine-tenths of life is without meaning for him, and we shall find little satisfaction in his ten per cent. optimism. Still less shall we be content if, adopting the debtor and creditor plan, he forgets to make his subtraction. But we shall prefer some other method that will give back the lost nine-tenths—some method of addition rather than subtraction—by which we may find meaning in the whole of life. It will be harder to manage, but we have a feeling that we cannot be content with less, and that "the problem of the universe" is after all to make this addition.

It is not easy to add up happiness and misery, but the poet must do it—and know what he is doing, He must, for example, stand with Lear upon the heath, and share his mood.

> In such a night as this! O Regan, Goneril!
> Your old kind father, whose frank heart gave all,—
> O! that way madness lies: let me shun that.

But the poet must not shun it, he must suffer and understand it, as he enjoys and understands the happiness of Perdita among her flowers. Brutus, and Sir Toby Belch, and Timon—he must sympathize with them all.

> Humani nihil a me alienum puto.

When he has surveyed all, suffered all, and enjoyed all ; when he has been through "the whole tragedy and comedy of life,"[1] he will be able to make his addition, for he will know what he has to add to what. And then perhaps he will not be in so great a hurry as people of less experience to say what is good and what is bad, and to make subtractions and strike balances. He will have a feeling that heaven does not make quite the same distinctions as we do, and that the universe means more when we look at it from that point of view.

I

Seneca, moralizing to Lucilius, quotes three words of Virgil in a way which shows at once how the poet's phrase had passed into common speech, and how his thought answered to the experience of his readers. "You will feel," he says, "and you will acknowledge it, that of all these dear and desirable things none is of use, unless you fortify yourself against chance and all it involves ; unless often and without complaint, as one thing after another is lost, you quote to yourself the poet's *dis aliter visum*."[2]

Dis aliter visum breaks from Aeneas' lips when he tells of the death of Rhipeus, "most just, most careful of right of all men in Troy "—

> Cadit et Rhipeus, iustissimus unus
> qui fuit in Teucris et servantissimus aequi—
> dis aliter visum (*A.* ii. 426-8).

It is not a suggestion of any divergence of view as to the merits of Rhipeus. It is rather an ejaculation on the difficulty of understanding Heaven's ways—"Heaven's will be done !" is Conington's rendering.[3] Mortal gratitude would have made the man some return, but the gods are not grateful to men for their piety. Goodness constitutes no claim to be exempt from the common lot, and, if the gods give any rewards for spiritual excellence, they are not

---

[1] Plato, *Philebus*, 50 B τῇ τοῦ βίου ξυμπάσῃ τραγῳδίᾳ καὶ κωμῳδίᾳ.

[2] Seneca, *Epp.* 98. 4. He goes on to say that *Di melius* would be *carmen fortius ac iustius*.

[3] Mr Mackail renders it : " The gods' ways are not ours."

paid in material currency. Aeneas is stating in a vivid way the criticism which Adeimantus in the *Republic* brings upon the teaching of Hesiod and Homer.[1]

No one, again, has lived a better or more useful life than Evander. He sends his son off to the war, with a moving prayer to the god of his fathers that they may meet again.

> At vos o superi et divom tu maxime rector
> Iuppiter Arcadii, quaeso, miserescite regis,
> et patrias audite preces [2] (*A*. viii. 572-4).

The gallant Pallas encounters Turnus in single conflict, and addresses a prayer to Hercules, the god whose cult Evander had been celebrating with such ceremony a day or two before. But it is in vain. Hercules, we are told, wept, but they were idle tears, and when Jupiter himself sought to console him his words only emphasized the hapless lot of men. " Each hath his own appointed day ; short and irrecoverable is the span of life for all ; but to spread renown by deeds is the task of valour. Under high Troy town many and many a god's son fell ; nay, mine own child Sarpedon likewise perished." [3] Saying so much, Jupiter turned his eyes from the battlefield. If he felt for men, his pity was ineffectual. Pallas had won glory, but it did not keep Evander's heart from breaking—the gods had not heard his prayers,

> nulli exaudita deorum
> vota precesque meae [4] (*A*. xi. 157).

But not all who thus fall reach glory. Mimas, the friend of Paris, is a man who gains none. His story is that of many a common man—pain, exile, death, and obscurity.

---

[1] *Rep.* ii. 363. Cf. A. C. Bradley, *Shakespearean Tragedy*, p. 326, discussion on the death of Cordelia in *King Lear*.

[2] " But you, great powers above, and thou, Jupiter, mightiest ruler of the gods, pity, I beseech you, an Arcadian king, and hear a father's prayers."

[3] *A*. x. 467 :
> *Stat sua cuique dies : breve et irreparabile tempus*
> *omnibus est vitae : sed famam extendere factis,*
> *hoc virtutis opus.*

[4] " Alas for those my vows and prayers, that found no audience with any of the gods " (Conington).

" His mother Theano bare him to Amycus on the same night that queen Hecuba bare Paris, the torch she had carried in her womb. Paris lies in the city of his father ; Mimas on the shore of Laurentum, a stranger in a strange land."

Ignarum Laurens habet ora Mimanta [1] (*A*. x. 702-6).

Born on one night in one town, Paris has ruined his people and lies with his ancestors in his own land; Mimas falls hundreds of miles away on a foreign shore. But there is more than this, for the *Laurens ora* is the land of promise, sought for seven years in weary travel over land and sea, and found at last; and now the journey is over, the goal is reached, and all the land of promise has to give is a grave.[2]

There is perhaps a certain consciousness of glory, or at least of right-doing, in a life of quest for him who chooses it—but for those who do not choose it? In the fifth book, while the men celebrate Anchises with game and race, Virgil shows us the women sitting apart and weeping for him.

Amissum Anchisen flebant,

says the poet; but the reader thinks of the captive women who wailed for " Patroclus in seeming, but every one in her heart for her own calamity."[3] And Virgil tells us that we are right.

Cunctaeque profundum
pontum aspectabant flentes.

They weep as they look at the sea; and yet, as Sainte-Beuve says,[4] it is the same Sicilian sea, with its blue horizon, which the little shepherd in Theocritus only asks to see for ever, for ever to have before his eyes, as he sits on the rock with his shepherdess in his arms, while his flock and hers

---

[1] Dr Henry holds with Servius that *ignarum* means that he is killed by an unexpected blow, before he knows it.

[2] Compare the death of Aeolus : *domus alta sub Ida, Lyrnesi domus alta, solo Laurente sepulcrum* (*A*. xii. 546); and the Latins killed in their city gates, *sed limine in ipso moenibus in patriis atque inter tuta domorum confixi expirant animas* (*A*. xi. 881).

[3] *A*. v. 614. Cf. *Il*. xix. 301 ἐπὶ δὲ στενάχοντο γυναῖκες, Πάτροκλον πρόφασιν, σφῶν δ' αὐτῶν κήδε' ἑκάστη.   [4] *Étude sur Virgile*, p. 166.

graze round them.[1] "But exile changes the colours." So
many seas they have crossed, and still one more, is the
women's thought.

Per mare magnum
Italiam sequimur fugientem et volvimur undis [2] (*A.* v. 628).

It is a picture of human life in general—ever some unknown Italy before us, but the nearer we come to it the
further it flies from us, and meanwhile wave and storm-
wind have us at their mercy. Once more for what?

That we find in the eleventh book. We seek a flying
Italy to bury the dead there. The episode is a moving one.
First we see the hewing of timber for the pyres, a vigorous
picture of activity. Then the day breaks which is appointed
for the burial. Dawn, as ever, displays her genial light, but
to the eyes of these Trojans it is not welcome; it brings back
pain and trouble. Yet they must be up and doing. All
along the winding shore stand the pyres, and on them they
lay their dead. The fires are lit, and the thick smoke of
the kindling wood rolls in clouds to the sky. They wait till
the pyres blaze, and then in old Roman fashion, with
shout and trumpet, they ride thrice round them. Some
throw into the flames the spoils the dead had taken; but
some of the fallen had taken no spoils and receive only their
own shields, their own luckless arms,

ipsorum clipeos et non felicia tela.

Victims are slain over the pyres, and then the ceremonies are
over that kept the mind occupied. Now comes the waiting,
and the mind is released to prey upon itself. "Then all
along the shore they sit and gaze while their friends
are burning, and watch the slow-consuming pyres, nor can
tear themselves away, till dewy night wheels round the
sky, set with its burning stars." [3]

The picture is drawn with the same realism which has
given their charm to the *Georgics*, but which here with
every touch deepens the impression of pain. The poet

---

[1] Theocritus, 8, 53-6.
[2] "Over a vast sea we follow a flying Italy and are tossed by the waves."
[3] *A.* xi. 134-8; 182-202.

makes no reflection, except perhaps in the *miseris mortalibus*, and that is traditional and from the past.[1] It is doubtless, also, not without purpose that he uses at the end the familiar phrase of his great predecessor Ennius—

> caelum stellis ardentibus aptum.[2]

The contrast gains from the old words. Here is human sorrow—

> Infinite passion, and the pain
> Of finite hearts that yearn—

set before us in these silent watchers, brooding beside the dying flames, and the background is the night and the eternal and passionless stars. It is Pindar's old thought again—

> ἐπάμεροι· τί δέ τις; τί δ' οὔ τις; σκιᾶς ὄναρ
> ἄνθρωπος.[3]

It is not only what we have to bear that gives life its pain. Doing is sometimes worse than suffering. Aeneas has to make war and how reluctantly! He bids Lausus withdraw, but Lausus still presses on, till Aeneas must kill him. One blow drives the sword through the poor gear of the brave lad, through the tunic his mother's love had woven. In that instant the look of death passes over the boyish face, and the older man groans to see what he has done. It is with meaning that Virgil here calls him *Anchisiades*.[4]

With the picture of burning Troy ever in his mind and memories of the brutal flames (*flammae furentes*) that leapt

---

[1] Servius says, from Homer ; δειλοῖσι βροτοῖσι.

[2] A combination of two forms, for Macrobius tells us (*Sat.* vi. 1. 9) that Ennius twice used *caelum stellis fulgentibus aptum*, and once *nox stellis ardentibus apta*. Virgil had already varied it in *A.* iv. 482 *axem . . . stellis ardentibus aptum*. The *Iliad*, 23, 217-25, may be compared, but the starry night is not there.

[3] Pindar, *Pythians*, 8. 95, "Creatures of a day ! what are we, or what not ? A dream of a shadow is man."

[4] *A.* x. 821—
> At vero ut voltum vidit morientis et ora,
> ora modis Anchisiades pallentia miris,
> ingemuit miserans graviter, dextramque tetendit,
> et mentem patriae subiit pietatis imago.

Contrast the satisfaction of the young Ascanius in killing a man for the first time—*A.* ix. 652—and *cetera parce puer bello.* See p. 224.

and exulted amid scenes which meant everything to his heart, Aeneas is hounded by fate from land to land, and when he reaches Italy it is the tale of Troy again. He has to fight, to kill men—and boys even—to make women childless and children fatherless. Is it strange that, when among the shades his father showed him souls hastening to reincarnation, the words sprang from his lips—

O pater, anne aliquas ad caelum hinc ire putandum est
sublimes animas iterumque ad tarda reverti
corpora? quae lucis miseris tam dira cupido?[1]   (*A.* vi. 719).

He has had enough, too much, of life:[2] they must be pitiable who could wish a second life. This is not Achilles' thought—βουλοίμην κ᾽ ἐπάρουρος ἐών. For Achilles life in the sun is good, and the shadowy existence beyond the grave is not to be compared with it. But the mood which inspired *Ecclesiastes* was by now familiar to the western world—" I praised the dead which are already dead more than the living which are yet alive "—and it sprang from the same source—from " all the oppressions that are done under the sun, and the tears of such as were oppressed."

" The gods in Jove's house marvel at the rage, the empty rage of both," Trojan and Italian, " and all the agonizing of mortals."[3]   In the *Iliad* the gods had enjoyed the sight; they would even take part in the fray. But Virgil's gods, like philosophers, look at it sadly. The troubles and labours of man are an amazement to the gods themselves, and they are after all " a striving after wind." The gods pity man, but their pity is idle as his pain—fruitless and ineffectual.[4]

---

[1]   " O my father ! and are there, and must we believe it," he said,
        " Spirits that fly once more to the sunlight back from the dead ?
        Souls that anew to the body return and the fetters of clay ?
        Can there be any who long for the light as blindly as they ? "
                                                                (Bowen).
[2] Cf. *King Lear* v. 3, 304, " And my poor fool is hanged ! No, no, no life ! "
[3] *A.* x. 758.
[4] Cf. Hugo von Trimberg (cited by Carlyle, Essay on Early German Literature). " God might well laugh, could it be, to see his mannikins live so wondrously on this earth ; two of them will take to fighting, and nowise let it alone ; nothing serves but with two long spears they must ride and stick at one

The problem, it will be agreed, is fairly adequately presented by Virgil. Has he a solution for it?

II

When Virgil wrote his description of the watchers by the dying flames of the funeral pyres, he was raising once more a question which his master Lucretius had settled. One of the most striking passages of the *De Rerum Natura* deals with death and bereavement. "Now no more," say the mourners, "shall thy house give thee glad welcome, nor a most virtuous wife and sweet children run to be the first to snatch kisses and touch thy heart with a silent joy. No more mayst thou be prosperous in thy doings, a safeguard to thine own. One disastrous day has taken from thee, luckless man, in luckless wise all the many prizes of life." "We, with a sorrow that would not be sated, have wept for thee as on the hateful pyre thou didst turn to ash, and no length of days shall pluck everlasting sorrow from our heart."[1] That is a fair presentment of the question of human sorrow.

The answer of Lucretius is that such feelings are largely irrational. Reflect, he says, that if the dead shall see no more his wife or child, it is as true that "now no longer does any desire for them remain to him"; sunk in the deep sleep of death, so shall he continue for all time, free from all pain and grief. "What," he asks, "is there so passing bitter, if it come in the end to sleep and rest?"—particularly when, as he states, in that sleep of death no dreams will come.

Finally, he pictures Nature suddenly uttering a voice and herself rallying us. "What hast thou, O mortal, so much at heart to yield to this excess of sorrow? Why moan and bewail death? For say thy life past and gone has been welcome to thee, and thy blessings have not all, as if

another: greatly to their hurt; for when one is by the other skewered through the bowels or through the weasand, he hath small profit thereby. But who forced them to such straits?" Carlyle's own rendering of this in *Sartor Resartus* will be remembered.

[1] Lucr. iii. 894-9; 906-9.

poured into a leaky vessel, run through and been lost without avail; why not then take thy departure as a guest who has had his fill of life (*ut plenus vitae conviva*)? . . . There is nothing more that I can contrive and discover for thee to give thee pleasure." Life, he says, is not given us in fee-simple, we have it only in usufruct—

Vitaque mancipio nulli datur, omnibus usu (Lucr. iii. 971).

Our substance is needed for other beings.[1] Why not accept the fact quietly? "Is there aught that looks appalling in death, aught that wears an aspect of gloom? is it not more untroubled than any sleep?"

So sounds the voice of Nature to Lucretius, but eager spirits are not always the best listeners. Much as Lucretius heard of what Nature had to say, there was a word which he did not notice, but which caught his pupil's ear—

Insatiabiliter deflevimus, aeternumque
nulla dies nobis maerorem e pectore demet [2] (Lucr. iii. 907).

The master had indeed heard the sentence and triumphantly brushed it aside; it was merely the voice of man, irrational man. The pupil was not so sure; he could not rid himself of the feeling that Nature speaks in man as well as elsewhere—that a broken heart is as distinctly a voice of Nature as any syllogism. To him Nature does not argue so quickly and so logically—

> gives birth
> To no impatient or fallacious hopes,
> No heat of passion or excessive zeal,
> No vain conceits; provokes to no quick turns
> Of self-applauding intellect.[3]

For Virgil, as for the modern poet,

> the lonely roads
> Were open schools in which I daily read

---

[1] For a Stoic view of the resolution of man εἰς τὰ φίλα καὶ συγγενῆ, εἰς τὰ στοιχεῖα, see Epictetus (*D.* iii. 13), though he adds rather curiously πάντα θεῶν μεστὰ καὶ δαιμόνων.

[2] "Insatiably we wept; and that everlasting sorrow no time shall take from our heart." [3] See the *Prelude*, bk. xiii.

With most delight the passions of mankind,
Whether by words, looks, sighs, or tears, revealed;
There saw into the depths of human souls,
Souls that appear to have no depth at all
To careless eyes.[1]

His chosen theme being

No other than the very heart of man,[1]

from long study of it he holds that

From Nature doth emotion come.[1]

Thus it came about that the very utterance, which
Lucretius invoked this dramatic interference of Nature
to refute, became for Virgil, above all other voices, Nature's
own. For when he "saw into the depth of human souls"
he realized that the deepest and most permanent thing
there is love, and listening to this, as to the voice of Nature,
he heard again in clearer and clearer tone, with deepening
intensity and passion, the question, which for Lucretius
was hardly a question at all—what is the meaning of human
sorrow?

The same voice of Nature invalidated for him much of
the teaching of the other great philosophic school, to which
he obviously leaned in later life. The Stoic[2] admitted that
it was natural to long for the lost friend, but in moderation.
He pointed out to the weeping mother the short and quiet
grief of the cow;[3] he suggested that such grief as hers
was "rather feminine"; that the barbarian felt it more
keenly than the man of culture; that time would mend it:
"What harm does it do to whisper to yourself, as you kiss
your child, 'To-morrow you will die'?"[4] "I knew," said

See the *Prelude*, bk. xiii.
[2] Seneca, *de Consolatione*, 7, 1-3. *At enim naturale desiderium suorum est.
Quis negat, quamdiu modicum est?* . . . There is, of course, a certain value in
all this.
[3] *Vaccarum uno die alterove mugitus auditur.* But contrast Lucr. ii. 352.
[4] Epictetus *D*. iii. 24. Cf. *D*. iii. 18, and *Manual* 14, 16. "If you weep
with a friend, let it be μέχρι λόγου, look to it μὴ καὶ ἔσωθεν στενάξῃς."

Anaxagoras,[1] "that I had not begotton an immortal."[2] In fact Stoic and Epicurean are at one in their practical advice, for if the pleasure of life is to be unruffled, or if the soul is to live in the universal and eternal, it is better without the temporary connexions of state and family; on the whole, insensibility is best. But Nature has refused us this gift—Nature, as to whom, according to Pliny,[3] we can never quite decide whether she is mother or step-mother.

Starting from the obvious, our moral philosophers have led us on amiably and logically, till they ask us to affirm that the ideal of humanity is virtually inhumanity.[4] It is here that the poets intervene. They may theorize too, but they have an instinct to keep " in company with flesh and blood." They have divined

The value and significance of flesh,

and they come to the aid of the philosophers, when they grow abstract. The deep indebtedness of poetry to philosophy, despite the ancient quarrel, must not obscure for us the fact that the obligations are not all on one side. Long ago Euripides had put into the mouth of one of the very unhappiest of mothers words true to human experience, truer far than Stoic or Epicurean taught in theory.

πᾶσι δ' ἀνθρώποις ἄρ' ἦν
ψυχὴ τέκν'· ὅστις δ' αὔτ' ἄπειρος ὢν ψέγει,
ἧσσον μὲν ἀλγεῖ, δυστυχῶν δ' εὐδαιμονεῖ.[5]

Though Virgil does not make an aphorism of it, his poetry

[1] The ascription is doubtful, as the story is also told of Solon and Xenophon. See Epictetus D. iii. 24 (near end) ; Seneca Cons. ad Pol. 30 ; Cic. Tusc. iii. 13 ; Plutarch, Cons. ad Apoll. 118 D.
[2] The magnificent treatment of this in Tristram Shandy is only too just.
[3] Pliny, N. H. vii. 1 parens melior homini an tristior noverca.
[4] Cf. the revolt of Plutarch (Cons. ad Apoll. 102 B) against τὴν ἄγριον καὶ σκληρὰν ἀπάθειαν, citing (102 D) Crantor τὸ γὰρ ἀνώδυνον τοῦτ' οὐκ ἄνευ μεγάλων ἐγγίνεται τῷ ἀνθρώπῳ· τεθηριῶσθαι γὰρ εἰκὸς ἐκεῖ μὲν σῶμα τοιοῦτον ἐνταῦθα δε ψυχήν.
[5] Andromache, 418. " Children after all are the soul of life ; and as for those who know them not and doubt of them, their troubles may be less, but their very happiness is misfortune."

reaffirms this utterance of experience. We may wonder about his philosophy at times—he owns himself in the *Georgics* that he is not great or original as a thinker—but he does the proper work of a poet in calling us back from the barren ways of abstract dogma to "the universal heart."

It was thus that Wordsworth, shocked at the excesses into which abstract political speculation led the men of the French Revolution, turned back to Nature, and, looking into "the depth of human souls," did not despair of the greater Republic—the "dear city of Zeus." Theories are very fascinating, we all know, but the poet "rejoices more in the spirit of life that is in him."[1] Hence it comes that Virgil sees more truly than Stoic or Epicurean, and he has done genuine service in bringing home to us the fact that their solutions of the question of human sorrow were not solutions at all. Whatever answer he may himself offer, he has at least advanced matters by making it clear that the question is no accidental or easy one, no side issue, but that it goes to the very depth of man's being and is an integral element of the problem of the universe.[2]

III

In the *Georgics*, as we have seen, Virgil faced the question of man's dealings with Nature, and he found that the underlying purpose of Jove had justified itself. The name Jove was perhaps traditional, and must not be pressed, but the main drift of the poem is that the universe, so far as it concerns the farmer, is intelligible, and the mind behind it not unfriendly. The life of the farm is hard, but man's life has always been hard since the beginning, and it is to this hardness that we owe everything. The arts of life spring from it, and the sciences too—all our knowledge of earth and its creatures and their ways, and our knowledge of the sky and the stars. Need has brought us into touch with all our

[1] Preface to *Lyrical Ballads*, 1800.
[2] Dr Henry translates *sunt lacrimae rerum* in this sense—"Tears belong to the constitution of Nature."

environment and established the greatness and the worth of man.

Labor omnia vincit
improbus et duris urgens in rebus egestas [1] (*G.* i. 145).

Mankind, like the Happy Warrior, has "turned necessity to glorious gain." [2]

Man has emerged from his long contest with necessity stronger and better. In the *Aeneid* we have a further stage of his history. He is applying the faculties which he has acquired in a higher and harder warfare. He has now to battle not with hunger, or blight and weeds, but with other men and with himself in his attempt to lift the race higher yet. Far in the future he divines a happiness for coming generations which depends in measure upon his own moral quality. It is represented that the gods assure him of this, but as a rule Aeneas seems to act, as we all act, more upon the instinctive feeling for right than upon external divine command. The enemy is nominally Juno; more really it is inward weakness. Juno, Aeolus, Turnus, and others throw difficulties in the way, but the real fight is within. It is the stuggle to keep facing in the right direction, to think first of kin and country, and to overcome every chance by endurance.

Quidquid erit superanda omnis fortuna ferendo est [3]
(*A.* v. 710).

Aeneas has seen Troy burning; he has been "much battered to and fro on land and sea"; but he never ceases to look toward his goal—

tendimus in Latium (*A.* i. 205).

---

[1] "So toil conquered the world, relentless toil, and Want that grinds in adversity" (Conington).

[2] The same idea is revived by Claudian in his *Rape of Proserpine* as the key-note to his story. See the speech of Jove, iii. 18-65, modelled after Virgil—

Quod dissuasor honesti
luxus et humanas oblimat copia mentes,
provocet ut segnes animos rerumque remotas
ingeniosa vias paulatim exploret egestas,
utque artes pariat sollertia, nutriat usus.

[3] "Whatever it be, every chance must be overcome by bearing it."

With all his reverses and despondencies, he may fairly be said to triumph over life; he never surrenders. There is wavering in Virgil's portrait of him, due, as we have seen, to sensitiveness to the claims of the Homeric tradition, but it is clear enough that Virgil conceived his character as of the true "Tyrtaean" strain. His story should "arm men with courage to undergo the conflicts of life," and it does.

It is not here a fair objection to urge that the connexion between Aeneas and Rome is a mechanical one. There are certainly traces of the mechanical in the story, but it is far nearer the truth to say that Virgil is making an honest attempt to present the type of manhood that made Rome. Legend—one legend—said that Aeneas founded Rome; then what sort of man was he? What sort of people did he leave behind him? He is cast in their mould. The necessities of poetic treatment require that he shall be individualized, and this is done. Troy comes into the story of Aeneas, and this, for one thing, differentiates him from other Romans. The man who had been through the siege and the fall of Troy would not be as other men. If he were not hardened by it, he must have been ripened, and it is so with Aeneas. He has far more sensibility than the average Roman; the truth is, that there is a good deal of Virgil in him. Now while all a man does will show, in some way or other, all that he is, and the whole man is apt to be revealed, more or less, in every act, we can separate out in the character of Aeneas certain features which he has in common with all the great men of Rome whose names are mentioned in the poem as representative of the Roman people. And if we are too cautious or too prosaic to say that Aeneas made Rome, and prefer to say that certain other heroes and a great many "common people" made her, we shall still find on examination that, whoever it was who did the work, it was done in exactly the spirit of Virgil's Aeneas—by men who have essentially the same character, though they may lack the *differentiae* which make him Aeneas and have others of their own.

The outcome of the poem, then, is that character of this type does not fail of effect and achievement. "They little

suspect," said Goethe of some people, "what an inaccessible
stronghold that man possesses who is always in earnest with
himself and the things around him." The implication of
the *Aeneid* is the same. The Romans are *rerum domini*
in virtue of this character. The farmer in the *Georgics*
had got his reward from *iustissima tellus* by no other magic.
How many heroes and worthies of Roman history are named
in the *Aeneid*, and did any of them ever attain greatness—
let us be careful to give the word Virgil's meaning—by any
other arts? Modern readers complain of the part played
by Augustus in the poem, really judging him from the
standpoint of Tacitus; but for Virgil, who died a whole
generation before Augustus, the main thing in the Emperor's career is the fact that he had represented the old
Roman character in the world, and once more conquered
the world in virtue of it. Augustus had taken thought
for his country and the empire, and had been in earnest,
as conspicuously as Antony had trifled about everything
but personal pleasure; and history's verdict, given at
Actium, was profoundly just.

It has, however, been suggested that Virgil does not
make in the *Aeneid* such prophecies of the Golden Age
as he made in the fourth *Eclogue*. It might be a sound
reply to say that the poet who wrote the hymn (is it anything else?) to *Labor improbus* in the *Georgics* will hardly
conceive of so great a reversal of human history as a millen-
nium resplendent with purple and saffron rams.[1] The
Eclogue is, in spite of the early Church, much more a poetic
exercise than a prophecy of the Messiah. It must, however,
be owned that as men grow older they become less and less
ready to predict speedy returns of either golden ages or
millenniums, and Virgil will prophesy no more than the
reign of Peace. That is the only golden age he can now
conceive.[2]

Aspera tum positis mitescent secula bellis [3] (*A.* i. 291).

[1] *E.* iv. 43— *Ipse sed in pratis aries iam suave rubenti
murice, iam croceo mutabit vellera luto,* &c.
[2] Cf. *A.* vi. 792.
[3] "War shall cease and harsh times grow gentle."

The ancients knew much less than we know of anthropology and history, and they did not realize in full the grandeur and promise of mankind's long progress. All our speculation, moreover, on man and his destiny is illumined by some idea of evolution,[1] and our prevailing feeling is that the race has far more triumphs before it than we can imagine. Hence Wordsworth can bid "the most unhappiest man of men" take comfort in "man's unconquerable mind." Virgil naturally cannot go nearly so far, but he has gone further, I think, than any poet before him in this direction, when he emphasizes, as he does, the steady progress of the past. He is more silent as to the future, as men are apt to be who know life deeply. Yet, whatever we may take to be the poet's personal inference from his facts, if we fairly grasp those facts, we at least shall suck no melancholy from the *Georgics* and the *Aeneid*. We shall find in them true pictures of man's history, and if the mood, to which the poet brings us, is one of pensive and chastened thought, it will yet be one of hope for the race.

IV

But what has Virgil to say of the individual? It is, comparatively, easy to be hopeful for mankind in a general way. The Stoic, it has been said, lived in the best of all possible worlds, in which, however, everything was a necessary evil.[2] The poet has to avoid such a conclusion, if his poetry is to be reconciling. For him, if for no one else, universal truths must prove true in particular cases; he cannot accept a general statement which he finds false in every individual application of it. If a certain temper or attitude of mind is satisfactory for the race at large, as

---

[1] There is a danger of careless thinking when we speak of evolution—those of us who are not men of science, so the reader, I hope, will not press the word too hard.

[2] The epigram is borrowed by Professor Caird from Mr F. H. Bradley for the Stoics. Plutarch (*de repugnantiis Stoicorum* 1048 F) anticipated the criticism: "all men are mad, bad and sad, the Stoics say ; εἶτα προνοίᾳ θεῶν διοικεῖσθαι τὰ καθ' ἡμᾶς οὕτως ἀθλίως πράττοντας; could it be worse if the gods hated us? could we not quote (Eur. *H. F.* 1245) γέμω κακῶν δὴ κοὐκέτ' ἐσθ' ὅπου τεθῇ?"

Virgil sees, it should be so for the individual man. The question for the poet, in short, is the question of Plato's *Republic*,[1] whether righteousness in itself and by itself is (in popular phrase), "worth while."

There will always be strong support (at least, strong numerical support) for the view advanced by some of Plato's friends that righteousness "pays" better than unrighteousness,—frequently, they will say, even in this world, and most certainly in the next. It may be said that Virgil represents this view in his picture of Elysium, and that he holds out to the righteous the hope of happy groves, with larger air and purer light, the gymnasium and the dance and the songs of Orpheus. This is true, but these things are no more to be taken literally in the *Aeneid* than, in the *Rhythm* of St Bernard, the milk and honey of the golden Jerusalem,

> The song of them that triumph,
> The shout of them that feast.

The whole of Virgil's Hades is animated by the strenuous mind, "always in earnest with itself and the things around it." While he avails himself, as usage perhaps required, of the traditional symbols of damnation, and extends their application from Titanic sinners against Jupiter to commonplace sinners against humanity, there is one place where his thought is unveiled without symbol. He speaks of those who have made their own quietus; innocent people— he gives them credit for that—but people who quailed, who shirked their task, and for them the only punishment is the sense of failure—

> quam vellent aethere in alto
> nunc et pauperiem et duros perferre labores [2] (*A.* vi. 436).

---

[1] *Rep.* 363 A, Criticism of people οὐκ αὐτὸ δικαιοσύνην ἐπαινοῦντες ἀλλὰ τὰς ἀπ' αὐτῆς εὐδοκιμήσεις.

[2] "How gladly would they choose now in the air above to bear to the end poverty and hard toil." Cf. Browning, *Statue and the Bust*—

> Let a man contend to the uttermost
> For his life's set prize, be it what it will !
> The counter our lovers staked was lost
> As surely as if it were lawful coin :
> And the sin I impute to each frustrate ghost
> Was—the unlit lamp and the ungirt loin.

This is a hint of Virgil's mind. He leaves it to moralists
and minor poets to tell us that virtue is its own reward—

ipsa quidem virtus pretium sibi [1]—

the most discouraging platitude which ever disguised the
feeling that virtue has no reward at all. For, as a rule, he
prefers to let his thoughts "slide into the mind of the reader
while he is imagining no such matter," [2] and it is from the
Aeneid as a whole that we shall best learn what he means.
Whatever his view of them may be, it will not be in Hades
only that virtue and vice reveal their essential nature, for
a great poet will not falsify our experience and our standards
by dividing life in two in so arbitrary a way.

Let us, however, begin with two more or less definite
statements. The old Aletes, in thanking Nisus and Euryalus
for their valour, uses these words :

> quae vobis, quae digna, viri, pro laudibus istis
> praemia posse rear solvi? pulcherrima primum
> di moresque dabunt vestri [3] (*A.* ix. 252).

Aeneas, in a similar strain, says to Dido—

> Di tibi (siqua pios respectant numina, siquid
> usquam iustitia est et mens sibi conscia recti)
> praemia digna ferant [4] (*A.* i. 607).

Each of these utterances has the spontaneity which the
dramatic situation requires. As in popular speech, there
is a slight and very natural confusion—do the gods give
rewards to the good, or is the real worth of goodness to be

---

[1] Claudian, *Paneg. Manl. Theod.* 1. It was not his own invention—*Virtutum omnium pretium in ipsis est*, wrote Seneca, *Ep.* 81. 19.

[2] Lamb's phrase in a letter to Wordsworth, Jan. 1801, criticizing *The Old Cumberland Beggar*.

[3] "What guerdons, gallant men, what can I fancy of worth enough to pay you for glories like these? first and richest will be the praise of heaven and your own hearts" (Conington).

[4] "May the gods—if there are powers that regard the pious, if justice and conscious rectitude count for aught anywhere on earth—may they give you the reward you merit!" (Conington). Editors dispute whether to read *iustitia* or *iustitiae*. Heyne, Henry, Conington, Forbiger, and Ribbeck are for the former. The latter seems prosaic, and indeed on a lower moral plane.

found in character and conscience? The course of the story offers some comment upon this. In the first case, Nisus and Euryalus are killed within twelve hours; in the other, the gods, so far from rewarding Dido, entangle her in an affection which brings upon her untold misery and death. It is plain that the first theory, that of rewards of goodness, has failed, and if we trust popular standards we shall be at a loss.

But if the poet habitually shows us men and women living strenuous lives, doing brave deeds, giving themselves up for love of child and father and people, and content to get no visible or tangible rewards, preferring to do the service, whatever comes of it—has he not indicated to us where we should look for our explanation of things? Why does Lausus rescue his father at the cost of what must be certain death for himself? What reward is in his mind? What takes Aeneas over land and sea? Is it really hope of ease—or praise? Are high deeds ever done for such motives? Is not the poet tacitly revealing his own thought that rewards and punishments are hardly pertinent in this case; that the good man, hero in battle or ploughman in the field, does right because it is right and because he " cannot help it"? It is " in him" to do it, and do it he will—"though it rains duke Georges"—though, like Lausus, he knows he will be killed upon the spot—though Juno's unrelenting hate move earth and heaven and hell against him. Of course, Virgil has not said all this explicitly; but is it not the implicit meaning of his story of life on farm and on the sea and in war, that righteousness in itself and by itself is worth everything else?

Character, then, in Virgil's view, means achievement in the long run for the race and for the individual, but, quite apart from results, character is achievement in itself, and the righteous man does not look for rewards for righteousness. But we must come back to what is perhaps the hardest case of all. What has Virgil to say to the mourners beside the funeral pyre?

We have seen how Seneca advised moderation in grief— a wise enough counsel, if it did not mean the cramping and narrowing of affection, the most obvious way in which to be independent of accident. Lucretius, on the other hand, urged that the dead really need no commiseration; why mourn for those who are not to be pitied?

To Lucretius, the mourner (if he cared to answer) might reply by asking whether, even assuming the Epicurean doctrine of extinction at death, the childless father is so much better off? Is a blank and empty life here better because there is no other?

> Aeternumque
> nulla dies nobis maerorem e pectore demet.

Lucretius may have shown that all is well for the dead, but has he helped the living? Will the "eternal sorrow in his heart" really yield to such arguments? Is it quite certain, too, that the dead have no longer any love or longing for the living? The philosopher may argue as he likes, but the lover will never believe it. Virgil's Anchises is a figure of legend, but is there no meaning for real people in his words beyond the grave?

> Venisti tandem, tuaque expectata parenti
> vicit iter durum pietas? datur ora tueri
> nate tua et notas audire et reddere voces [1] (*A*. vi. 687).

To the Stoic Virgil's mourner might reply with Euripides' Andromache that the happiness of the days when he had no son was poor compared with what he has since known; he has enlarged his experience; love has made him another and a larger man, and he cannot unlearn or go back—would not even if he could. The poet is all on the side of largeness of sympathy, not merely in theory, like the Stoics, but in fact and life. He does not wish to escape the risks of sorrow to which love exposes him. The price is too high for one thing. But he looks more earnestly at the matter, and he finds that the evils which the Stoic sought to avoid are at once far more painful than the man of deadened sensibility supposes, and far too valuable to be

---

[1] "Here thou comest at last, and the love I counted upon
    Over the rugged path has prevailed. Once more, O my son,
    I may behold thee, and answer with mine thy voice as of yore."
                                                    (Bowen).

called evil. For the very uncertainties of life, and the perils to which love is subjected, make love more intense and more conscious. To share a danger deepens friendship—

O socii, neque enim ignari sumus ante malorum [1]
(*A.* i. 198).

Does it mean less to love? We have an illustration in the description of Allecto blowing the trumpet (*A.* vii. 511).

Standing on a watch-tower, the Fury sounds the war-note, putting into it the full capacity of her voice of hell—

Tartaream intendit vocem.

It is a picture of mere irrational and devilish malevolence—pure evil, if it is to be found anywhere. The forests trembled at the sound, it flew by lake and stream,

et trepidae matres pressere ad pectora natos (*A.* vii. 518).

Allecto does her worst, and the effect is to make the mother *press* her child to her breast—the Fury has quickened maternal love into new consciousness. She is a symbol of evil opening our eyes to good; the evil vanishes, but the good, once seen, remains ours.

Virgil shows us the effect of pain and sorrow upon character in the deepening and broadening of love. As toil and want gave mankind the joy of action, the knowledge of earth and sea and sky, and the great sense of achievement, so pain and sorrow open the eyes of men to the human world around them, and bring men into sympathy with one another. In short, they teach men "humanity," and if we give the word all the fine suggestion of its etymology, we shall feel with the poet that the lesson is too great and too valuable to allow us to call our teachers evil.

If proof is needed that Virgil has some such thought,

---

[1] "Comrades, for we are not unacquainted with misfortune ere this."

Dido's utterance may be cited as its most succinct expression—

Non ignara mali miseris succurrere disco [1] (*A.* i. 630).

But great poets seldom entrust their deepest mind to solitary lines. If this is Virgil's mind, we shall find it pervading his whole poem ; and we do find, in fact, that it is his way to draw characters who have been "humanized" by "deep distress" [2]—Dido, Evander, Andromache, and the kindly Tityrus, for instance, and, most of all, the central figure of the poem. If we have been right in our study of Aeneas, the key-note to his character, as conceived by Virgil, is the full and strong humanity that results from long but victorious knowledge of pain and sorrow—" our human nature's highest dower." It had been Virgil's own experience from the days of the plantation of the veterans.

To the mourner by the pyre, then, if Virgil had said anything at all—poets have their own times and ways of speaking—he might have said—or, more probably, he would himself have felt—that capacity for sorrow is a measure of love, that love is often best learnt in sorrow, and that there is nothing for man better worth learning at whatever cost. And he would have felt the gap in what he said.

But life is not all battle and bereavement, and one of Virgil's great achievements is to open up for us many avenues to delight. What pleasure he has found in books, in "the strong-winged music of Homer"—and also in the studied rhythms of Alexandria! Who can have an utterly miserable life who has a beehive to study, or can watch earth and sky and sea, all filled with delightful living things, manifestations, each and all, of divinity?

> A poet could not but be gay
> In such a jocund company.

---

[1] "Myself no stranger to sorrow, I am learning to succour the unhappy" (Conington).
[2] Wordsworth, *Elegiac Stanzas* (1805) "A deep distress hath humanized my Soul."

Even the wicked old Cilician pirate settles down to a sober and happy life in a garden of his own contriving on a strip of waste Italian land.[1] If Virgil is melancholy, it is with constant gleams of happiness. Few poets of antiquity have found so much to enjoy in man's life and environment, and perhaps it was the melancholy that opened his eyes to see it all—once more the soul of goodness in things evil.

V

It comes out clearly in the study of his poetry that Virgil has felt, with the rest of mankind,

> The heavy and the weary weight
> Of all this unintelligible world,

and also that he has known the mood in which it is lightened. He does not leave the reader long in doubt as to the burden of thought that comes upon us when we look on man with sympathy, nor as to the reflections which tend to make it tolerable. He has not done as Robinson Crusoe suggests, because he has found that good and evil, as men call them, will not be separated in thought any more than in experience. He has not refused to recognize the existence of evil ; but he tries to bereave it of its bad influence, holding that this can be done by looking it well in the face.

To say that he gives us a full presentment of every aspect of the problem of mankind would of course be absurd. Does he, for example, realize the power of evil passion? The *animae candidiores* seldom understand it, and it was reserved perhaps for a later age to feel with Augustine the force of sin. It is clear, too, that Virgil is himself conscious of having something still to gain, for the melancholy which haunts him is not wholly vanquished by his philosophy and his pleasure in the world. Where lies its strength?

When we consider the age in which he lived, it is not hard to account for the depression of a man so human and so tender as Virgil.

For a century, or near it, right and wrong had been confounded, the world full of war and every kind of crime ;

[1] *G.* iv. 125-46.

the ploughman had been marched away to become a
soldier ; East and West it had been the same, everywhere
the fury of murder and destruction, and the paralysis of
man's better faculties.[1] The wonder is that with such a
consciousness of human misery Virgil could write a poem of
such enduring happiness as the *Georgics*.

The mischief resulting to the world from a century of
civil war was not to be mended in a decade, nor was the
grim experience of forty years to be obliterated from such a
mind as the poet's. But there is no pessimism about him.
Like his hero, he never surrenders, though it is with a
terrible sense of effort that hero and poet keep facing for
Latium, particularly when with time it seems to come no
nearer.

> It is but to keep the nerves at strain,
> To dry one's eyes and laugh at a fall,
> And baffled, get up and begin again,[2]

but eventually the "getting up and beginning again " becomes
acutely painful, for the new hopes needed are slow to frame
themselves, and the doubt recurs more and more often
whether the struggle is really leading to anything. The world
offered Virgil nothing by which this doubt might be finally
killed. Apart from the Jews, there was no nation in the
Mediterranean world which consciously hoped. Amid all
this depression who will wonder that Virgil knew melancholy?
And yet his is the great voice of hope, reality and gladness
in the Roman world.

Virgil, again, as we have seen, felt the mystery of death.
Ancient religion did not look much beyond the grave. As
for contemporary philosophy, we know what Lucretius said,
and the best the Stoics could say was " Disembark ; if for
another life, nothing is without the gods, even there."[3]
Neither could satisfy one to whom love meant so much.
Love being the one thing in the world that refuses to accept

---

[1] *G.* i. 505.

[2] Cf. Marcus Aurelius, 5. 9 μηδὲ ἀπαυδᾶν . . . ἀλλὰ ἐκκρουσθέντα πάλιν
ἐπανιέναι.

[3] Marcus Aurelius, 3. 3 τί ταῦτα; ἐνέβης, ἔπλευσας, κατήχθης· ἔκβηθι. Εἰ μὲν
ἐφ' ἕτερον βίον, οὐδὲν θεῶν κενόν, οὐδὲ ἐκεῖ.

the fact of death, the poet in Virgil cannot accept it, but the philosopher in him cannot yet see how to escape it. Meanwhile, as we have seen, whatever the outcome, Virgil stands with the lovers for the larger life.[1]

Most of us will probably allow that if Virgil has not solved the problem of the universe he has felt it with some fulness.

"La venue même du Christ n'a rien qui étonne quand on a lu Virgile," says Sainte-Beuve.[2] The early history of the Church illustrates the truth of this conclusion. To minds touched with the same sense of life's problems which pervades the poetry of Virgil, the Gospel brought the rest and peace which they could not find elsewhere. The early Church was quick to recognize a friend and a forerunner in Virgil. If to-day we discard the interpretations which the early Christians put upon the fourth *Eclogue*, we can share their deeper feeling for *Maro vates Gentilium*.[3]

An unknown student of the poet has embodied in a stanza of a Mass of St Paul a fine appreciation of the worth and significance of Virgil's poetry and of the one thing which the new view of life could have added to it. He pictures St Paul pausing on his journey to Rome to visit the mausoleum of Virgil at Naples.

> Ad Maronis mausoleum
> Ductus fudit super eum
> Piae rorem lacrimae;

---

[1] A very remarkable letter of Mazzini to Mrs Carlyle on this subject (date of 15 July 1846) will be found in Froude's *Carlyle's Life in London* i. p. 413.

[2] *Étude sur Virgile*, p. 68. This phrase was criticized in *The Spectator* as "a silly and audacious epigram, which . . . will hardly be accepted by real students of Virgil and of the Gospels." After an interval of years I still deliberately accept it. The critic, I may mention, gave his own point of view by adding: "To study the philosophical or religious views of some great poet is an amusement which is now very fashionable." I am glad to find that Mr Warde Fowler (*Religious Experience of the Roman People*, p. 404) compares the phrase of Sainte-Beuve with the more cautiously worded judgement of Sellar, *Virgil*, p. 371, and gives his verdict that "the feeling that underlies both utterances is a true one." I think that any one who has tried in earnest to grapple with a great poet of antiquity will not call it an amusement, but a discipline, and will be glad to have submitted his mind to such a teacher in such an intimacy.

[3] Ἐπαιδαγώγει γὰρ καὶ ἡ φιλοσοφία τὸ Ἑλληνικὸν ὡς ὁ νόμος τοὺς Ἑβραίους εἰς Χριστόν, wrote Clement of Alexandria (*Strom.* i. 28). If Greeks had read Latin poetry, so catholic a mind could have said as much for Virgil.

Quem te, inquit, reddidissem,
Si te vivum invenissem,
Poetarum maxime.[1]

[1]
"Virgil's tomb the saint stood viewing,
And his agèd cheek bedewing,
Fell the sympathetic tear;
' Ah ! had I but found thee living,
What new music wert thou giving,
Best of poets and most dear !'"

Cited by Comparetti, *Vergil in the Middle Ages*, pt. i. ch. 7, p. 98. The use of Virgil's peculiar adjective should be noted.

INDEX

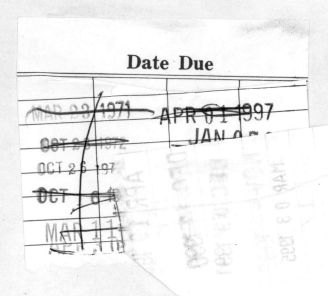